Kentucky
Colonels

OF THE
AMERICAN BASKETBALL ASSOCIATION

Kentucky Colonels

OF THE
AMERICAN BASKETBALL ASSOCIATION

The Real Story of a Team Left Behind

GARY P. WEST

LLOYD "PINK" GARDNER

Acclaim Press
MORLEY, MISSOURI

AP
TM
Acclaim Press
— Your Next Great Book —

P.O. Box 238
Morley, MO 63767
(573) 472-9800
www.acclaimpress.com

Designer: Tiffany Glastetter
Cover Design: Tiffany Glastetter
Cover Photo: Courtesy of Nathan Gardner.

Library of Congress Cataloging-in-Publication Data

West, Gary.
  The Kentucky Colonels of the American Basketball Association / by Gary West.
      p. cm.
  ISBN-13: 978-1-935001-82-9 (alk. paper)
  ISBN-10: 1-935001-82-5 (alk. paper)
  1. Kentucky Colonels (Basketball team)--History. 2. Basketball teams--Kentucky--Louisville--History. 3. American Basketball Association--History. I. Title.
  GV885.52.K46W47 2011
  796.323'640976944--dc23
                                    2011025016

First Printing: 2011
Printed in the United States of America
10 9 8 7 6 5 4 3 2

CONTENTS

DEDICATION

This book is dedicated to everyone who was ever involved with a team in the American Basketball Association. It was certainly a risk for that first group of owners who came forth to compete with the established National Basketball Association. There were many players who were given a second chance to play a game they would have played for nothing. They plowed through the adversity that made it much easier for those who followed.

It is these owners, management, players and fans who have made professional basketball what it is today.

FOREWORD

I am looking forward to reading this book as much as you are. Pink Gardner and Gary West are recalling a slice of professional basketball history in Louisville, Kentucky, that many people may have forgotten or are even unaware.

The Kentucky Colonels of the American Basketball Association is that piece of history.

You might be wondering why a baseball announcer like me would be writing a foreword to a basketball book.

Good question.

I haven't always been just a baseball guy. Prior to my arrival in Cincinnati as a broadcaster with the Reds in 1974, I was the radio voice of the Virginia Squires of the ABA.

The Squires and Colonels were divisional rivals, so I had the opportunity to be in Louisville, and Freedom Hall in particular, for three and a half seasons.

With all due respect to the other ABA teams, there were only a handful of cities that I, as a radio guy, looked forward to visiting: Indianapolis, Salt Lake City and New York were three, and then there was Louisville and the Kentucky Colonels.

The city of Louisville, and Kentucky as a whole, go hand and hand with great basketball at any level, and Freedom Hall was really special when all its boisterous fans were packed in there.

But, boy, did the Colonels have good players! Dampier, Carrier, Ligon, Powell, Ladner, and the great twosome of Dan Issel and Artis Gilmore were just some of the talent list that goes on and on.

Just as important was the way the organization went about its business. It was a major league franchise, if you will pardon the baseball lingo, in every sense of the word, and the Colonels over the years won more regular season games than any team in ABA history.

There was a certain increased level of excitement when the Squires played the Colonels. I saw some great matchups that included future hall-of-famers … Dan Issel and our Charlie Scott, Gilmore and our Julius Erving and George Gervin.

The personalities of those ABA games were truly memorable, and I have to believe that every team in the league recognized just how outstanding the Colonels franchise was. I did then, and still do today.

I am still shocked, after all these years, that when the NBA-ABA merger came about, Kentucky was not included.

I hope that what I have written conjures up great memories of those magical times of the ABA. If you weren't around then, you are going to enjoy this riveting history of the Kentucky Colonels.

Marty Brennaman

PREFACE

I've known who Lloyd Gardner was for a long time, years before he became Pinky. Both Lloyd and I attended Western Kentucky University back in the early to mid-60s, and while he was a part of the Hilltopper basketball team as a manager, I was writing sports for the *College Heights Herald*. Still, we did not really know each other.

If I had known then what I know now, I would have quickly befriended Lloyd. Team managers and trainers are the best sources for sports stories, because they know what's going on.

It was years later that I got to know Lloyd more than just saying hello in passing. I was the Director of the Hilltopper Athletic Foundation at Western and doing the color commentary on the Hilltopper Basketball Network with my friend, Wes Strader. In the meantime, Lloyd had become somewhat of an authority on the ABA, and the Kentucky Colonels in particular, and had moved on to be a state championship coach at Fairdale High School.

It took the book I wrote on King Kelly Coleman several years ago to bring Lloyd "Pinky" Gardner and I closer. I ran into Pinky at the high school state tournament in Rupp Arena, where King Kelly and I were doing a book signing. "You ought to do a book on me," Lloyd laughed. "I've got some good stories to tell, and I've already got the title for it." Lloyd couldn't wait for me to ask what it was, so he immediately proclaimed, "If They Only Knew."

If they only knew what? I remember asking him. "If they only knew all of the stories I have from my Western and Colonels days and then at Fairdale and everything else I've done," he continued.

Pinky didn't need to say any more. He had me hooked. Over the next six years, the "If They Only Knew" thing stayed with me. But so did some of Lloyd's stories. He is a great storyteller. He can keep you entertained for days, it seems. And it was one of those Colonels tales that really got me thinking.

It is said there is a defining moment in every person's life, and at that moment everything that person is shines its brightest. Many of those moments involved the ABA Kentucky Colonels.

For whatever reason a book had yet to be written about the Colonels. I was surprised. Newspaper articles across the state, long after the team was gone, at least indicated there was still an interest in the old team.

I'm not sure how to describe this book. It's much more than just about basketball, and for sure it takes a few detours along the way. Pink and I have written, not only about the Colonels, but also about the association they and their families had throughout their lives.

It was time.

It was time for Pinky to start talking, telling about his times with the Colonels. And the door he has opened, with not only his stories, but also his connections, has culminated in an entertaining, intriguing and historical story.

Gary P. West

INTRODUCTION

Where did they go?

It seemed like one day they were here, a professional basketball team called the Kentucky Colonels, actually playing for championships and even winning one. Then suddenly, almost as quickly as they had appeared, they were gone.

In the beginning when the American Basketball Association appeared on the scene, skeptics were often more plentiful than the fans who came to watch. But why shouldn't they be? These perceived NBA rejects played with a three-colored basketball, and the referees wore red, white and blue outfits with their names boldly displayed on their backs. A non-traditional 3-point shot only added another gimmick in an effort to separate itself from the well-established National Basketball Association. To say the NBA had a monopoly on the best basketball players in the world would be an understatement. The reality of it all is that anyone playing in the ABA was deemed not quite good enough to play in the NBA. At least that's the way it was in the beginning.

Lyndon Johnson was president, it cost thirteen cents to mail a letter, a new home averaged $13,000, and a loaf of bread cost about twenty-five cents, when the American Basketball Association bounced its first red, white and blue basketball in 1967.

The odds of this very odd organization surviving were slim to none, and you know the rest, slim just left town. But, survive they did. For nine wonderful years they became a part of Kentucky, especially Louisville. When the air finally went out of that beautiful basketball, it took with it a piece of every man, woman and child who ever saw the Kentucky Colonels play.

Forget the fact that even in the early years there were a handful of ABA players who could not only have played in the NBA, but could have been stars. Ultimately it took money, and lots of it, to bring some of the ABA's best teams to the level of the NBA's best. Even so, although NBA hierarchy, team owners and players were slow to admit it, the ABA was ultimately good, good enough that later on ABA players and coaches appeared front and center on NBA rosters. Before long, the NBA was even playing the same game the ABA had been playing for years.

This is a story about those Kentucky Colonels. Lloyd "Pinky" Gardner lived it, and I wrote about it.

Pinky's, "I was there" accounts, are inside stories, many of which have never been told. Even though his team title might have been Trainer, he was much more than that. He was often seen sitting to the right or the left of Colonels coaches, as much into the game as they were, except he had a zillion other responsibilities, too. There were also times when he sat at the far end of the bench as well, because, for whatever reason, that's where he needed to be.

Gardner was a man for all seasons, as you will see in this book. His role in the organization allowed him unparalleled access to not only the Colonels players, but also to the coaches, owners, management, and even the fans. There was also something else unique about his position — it gave him access into the opposing ABA teams.

Gardner and I have conducted hours upon hours of interviews with Kentucky Colonels owners, players, coaches, management, and fans in an attempt to humanize their lives in order to reveal much more than a snippet in a game program or a sound bite on radio or television.

I thought it was important to weave personal aspects of their lives into the book in an effort to keep alive the Colonels story. He wanted to tell more than how much money was lost or made, or how many points and rebounds were collected, or why this or that player was traded. His are the untold stories, the forgotten ones, and the behind-the-scene ones that can only be told by those who lived them.

Gardner and I readily admit that Wendell Ladner could probably have had an entire chapter devoted to him, and it might be surprising to learn that he was a Colonel less than two full seasons. So instead, they let all of those involved with the Colonels, players, coaches, management, and broadcasters individually tell their Wennie stories.

It's been more than thirty-five years since the Colonels played their last game, and as the team's history slips further and further away, these are stories that not only have been told, but have also persevered.

Perhaps this book should have been written years ago, but then again, maybe it couldn't have been. There always seemed to be plenty of time. But then one day, a generation or two removed, someone asked, "Whatever happened to that pro basketball team back in the '60s and '70s that played in Louisville?"

BAM! Right in the middle of the face, it hits you. To some, it was only yesterday or last night, that they saw the Colonels play, but in reality, it has been almost four decades, and gone with these passing years are some of those stories that can never be told again.

Here, Gardner and I are sharing their passion in resurrecting the Kentucky Colonels, and telling some of the greatest stories never told.

Kentucky Colonels

OF THE
AMERICAN BASKETBALL ASSOCIATION

The Real Story
of a Team Left Behind

CHAPTER ONE
A LEAGUE IS BORN

The birth of the American Basketball Association came with little celebration, few announcements, and absolutely no expectation that it would survive ... at least on its own.

The mayor of Buena Park, California, Dennis Murphy had come up with the hairbrain idea of starting a professional basketball league, not to rival the NBA, but to be absorbed by it.

Murphy's blueprint was the old American Football League, and the success it had in forcing a merger with the NFL. That was Murphy's goal, to force a merger between his upstart ABA league and the aristocratic NBA.

Perhaps Murphy had seen the 1959 Cold War satirical Peter Sellers movie, "The Mouse That Roared." An imaginary country in Europe declared war on the U.S. over a wine dispute, expecting a quick and total defeat, since its army was equipped only with bows and arrows. What the country anticipated was immediate financial aid, like the U.S. had a reputation for. Instead, the little nation in the Alps defeats the U.S. by accident, landing by boat in New York City during a citywide disaster drill.

This was Murphy's plan: declare war on the NBA and let them take the ABA in.

Initially it might have seemed like the ABA was a bow and arrow league. An occasional mortar round would be fired from a league that was heavy on guards, but then when the big artillery started to arrive, the NBA finally took notice. For some of the teams, however, it was too late.

Often perception is reality. The perception among basketball purists was that the ABA was a circus, and George Mikan was its ringmaster, starting with the red, white and blue basketball. The reality of it all was that there were actually some very talented basketball players in the ABA. Many of the sideshows took place in the front offices rather than on the court.

More times than not, owners were not basketball people, and that hasn't changed over the years. They were usually very successful business people who wanted a diversion from their day-to-day lives, and owning a professional sports team was one way of accomplishing this. The problem was, not only did they want to own the team, but to manage, and even sometimes coach it as well.

Before the ABA, the NBA had a monopoly, plain and simple, on any players wanting to play after college. If a player was drafted by a team, he played for that team. End of discussion. If he didn't sign a contract, his playing days were over, and at the time, playing overseas was not an option.

The ABA gave players a chance to play who had all but given up the game. The new league was an opportunity, a chance to revive a career. However, as teams began to fold and finally when the merger, or expansion, as the NBA preferred to call it, came about, a few more players were literally dumped out of basketball. Also gone was all of that leverage players from both leagues used against the owners when it came to salaries.

From the beginning, there was nothing traditional about the American Basketball Association's efforts to challenge the establishment, which in this case was the National Basketball Association. Often it resembled episodes from the "Three Stooges," starting with the multi-colored ball, to the seemingly clown outfits worn by the referees, to an assortment of gimmicks that did almost anything to draw fans. The new league did little to strike fear in the owners of NBA teams.

Lee Meade was the ABA's first publicity director, and he had his own idea about doing some things the NBA wasn't doing. His changes involved league and team statistics, and it was different than anything the NBA was doing at the time. If nothing else, the 3-point goal would make it different, but Meade wanted more. He wanted a complete box score so that, when reviewed, it would reveal what teams, as well as individuals, had done during the game.

The NBA kept stats on total rebounds, but not a breakdown of offensive and defensive. Early on, turnovers were referred to as errors by the ABA. The NBA didn't keep this. They didn't chart steals either, nor blocked shots or team rebounds. After all, if the big-time NBA didn't do it, why would the upstart ABA even consider it?

But Meade's way of thinking was that's exactly why the ABA should implement it. It was cutting edge back then. Some ABA teams didn't want to go to the extra trouble. For sure it would take more time and possibly even other employees, two things most league teams didn't have available.

Today, the rebound breakdown, turnovers, blocked shots and steals have become a standardized part of every box score at every level of basketball.

Anything that would show that the new league was different was the intent. For the most part, the good ole boys were smug. No need to worry. No sweat. All of the real basketball players were already in the fold.

Who would want to see teams play with NBA castoffs or players they had little or no interest in? No competition here. At least it was that way until the money began to show up in the form of several new owners with deep pockets and even bigger bank accounts. They were ready for action and the prospects of spending whatever it took to sign good players, players good enough to attract fans, but most of all, good enough to win championships.

Attract the fans and win. Simple enough. Accomplish these two initiatives and surely the NBA would come calling, begging for a merger.

THE BALL

The ABA had a red, white and blue ball because newly named Commissioner George Mikan said it would. It was that simple.

The game was basketball, and Mikan wanted his ball to be different from anyone else's. He wanted everyone to know which league played with it.

It was well documented that the red, white and blue colored ball was implemented as a connection to the name of the new league. The thinking was that when you hear the word America, you automatically think patriotic, and that means red, white and blue. Soon the ball and its color scheme were synonymous with the ABA.

Probably not another man alive could have demanded the use of such a basketball, other than George Mikan. He was a modern-day Clark Kent, even down to the hairstyle and glasses. And everyone knew, except those who lived in Metropolis, who Clark Kent really was.

So there he was, Superman, telling the new league owners there would be no boring brown balls in his league. The ABA ball would look different, and even comical to some, but guess what? Every kid in America would want one.

Mikan spoke with authority. He had been an All-American under Ray Meyer at DePaul, and in the pros he put the Minneapolis Lakers on the map. He was considered basketball's first great big man. One poll even named him the greatest basketball player in the first half of the 20th century.

So, with those credentials, and looking like a Philadelphia lawyer, the 6'10" Mikan could suck the air out of a room full of owners when he walked into it.

On the surface, the ABA knew its credibility and any chance of getting through that first year rested almost entirely on George Mikan and his name. And, by the way, he really was a lawyer, so that only added to his clout.

Decades later Mike Storen, who was general manager of the Pacers in the early years, says he was openly against the red, white and blue ball.

"But then I realized what we had here," Storen laughed. "We had a ball that everyone wanted, and it wasn't just kids either. We put it to a vote and I supported continuing the ball. It was a great marketing tool."

Among the owners, coaches and players, some liked it, some didn't. Others said the seams were too narrow, some said too wide, too heavy said some, and too light said others. "Slippery, real slippery," were some of the complaints.

But then there were those who loved the new ball. "It was a shooter's ball," offered Kentucky Colonels guard Darel Carrier, looking back on it years later. "I could follow the rotation of my shot with all of those different colors."

Over the years there have been estimates that some 40 million of the red, white and blue balls in various sizes have been given away or sold. And because of the popularity of the ball, even today, it would seem that a missed marketing opportunity has gone by the wayside.

OFFICIATING

Officiating was a big issue in most of the early day ABA games. The two-man crews were subject to verbal abuse from fans as well as players and coaches. Even though the league had a rule that could assess a player or coach up to $500 in fines for criticism of an official, it really had to be extreme abuse to be called.

Sid Borgia, the working supervisor of officials for the ABA, took his share of the wrath.

An angry Indiana Pacer who wanted to remain nameless because of the stiff fines called Borgia "A senile old man who shouldn't be out there. And you can print that."

It was common for referees to ask for security following a game, particularly if the home team lost, and a game at the Convention Center in Louisville was no exception.

Game security seemed to occupy much of the post-game comments not only from the players and coach's viewpoint, but from team owners and general managers as well. Paper cups, often filled with ice, were common projectiles hitting ABA floors across the league.

3-Point Shot

From the very beginning when the owners first got together, the 3-point shot was going to be the key element that separated the ABA from the NBA. It was going to make guard play, especially the shooters, an important part of the game. What little man wouldn't like this?

Actually, the 3-pointer had been used in pro basketball before. Abe Saperstein, of Globetrotter fame, had initiated the play in his old American Basketball League, and ABA officials were quick to make it the cornerstone of their efforts to make the new league both different and more exciting.

The league promoted the shot as being from 25-feet, with a corner shot being from 22-feet, but in actuality, from top of the key area it measured 23-feet, 9-inches behind the strip. The NBA uses this exact measurement today.

Of course for the Colonels the 3-point shot was a Godsend, especially when they had what many say even today was the greatest shooting guard duo in the history of professional basketball.

Louie Dampier and Darel Carrier were the best long-range bombers in the business. Sure other teams boasted they had great shooters, too, but no other team had anything close to what the Colonels had in Dampier and Carrier. They could have moved the 3-point line back to 40-feet and it would still have been a decent percentage shot for these two. They made it mighty tough on the defense, and a zone was not even considered.

Dampier even scored 3-points off of designed fast break plays when he would pull up beyond the line and BAM! He was that good. And so was Carrier. Frank Ramsey, who coached both Carrier and Dampier during the 1970-71 season, recalled that in close games he had no problem in giving the ball to Carrier.

"We'd be in the huddle setting up a shot to win the game," says Ramsey the former UK All-American and Boston Celtic great. "Darel would say, 'just get it to me and I'll take care of it.' So I said, 'Just get it to Darel.'" He was a great pressure shooter."

For their careers, Carrier shot 42 percent from the field and 38 percent from 3-point. Dampier shot 44 percent from the field and 36 percent from 3-point. They were both very good at the free throw line, with Carrier in at 85 percent, and Dampier 83 percent.

Carrier played five seasons with the Colonels after a year with the AAU Phillips Oilers. Dampier is one of only three players to play every season the ABA operated. He and Denver's Byron Beck were the only players to play their entire ABA careers with the same team.

Tough Guys

Reputations for being tough guys were plenty. Heck, in the ABA guys who weren't even tough got into fights. It was imperative that teams have at least one so-called enforcer. Two would be nice in this league, but one was essential. It was common for a team to go out and trade for a tough guy; whether he could play or not seemed to matter little.

The ABA's image was clouded with lots of action even when play had stopped on the court. Hockey and all of its extracurricular activity had nothing on the ABA. Some said that even if the game was bad you could always count on a couple of good fistfights.

Anyone around in the ABA days is quick to point out that not only did the tough guys fight opposing players, but often teammates as well. Intimidation had a lot to do with it, and it started with their own team.

It didn't take long for word to spread that certain guys liked to fight, and even relished it. Also, there were players who not necessarily went looking for a skirmish, but wouldn't back down from one either. This combination sometimes proved exciting and more entertaining than the game.

At the head of the tough guy list were John Brisker and Warren Jabali. The two were considered players you didn't want to mess with on or off the court. Lots of players played, well, not necessarily dirty, but perhaps on the edge. Once the game was over, their personality reverted back to one of the good ole boys. However, when it came to Brisker and Jabali, little changed in their personalities on or off the floor.

There were times when coaches even put out bounties on certain opposing players. One time involved Brisker, who was playing for Pittsburgh. Tom Nissalke, who was coaching Dallas at the time, said in Terry Pluto's book "Loose Balls," that he offered $500 to "first guy who decks Brisker." Lenny Chappell, a substitute Dallas forward, asked Nissalke to start him in this game. Nissalke figured Chappell would nail Brisker on a lay-up or rebound. Not many were watching Chappell as the referee tossed the ball in the air to start the game. Everyone was watching the ball. That's when Chappell punched Brisker out. "He was flat on the floor," Nissalke said.

Following the game Chappell was $500 richer, and from then on there was a standing $500 bounty on Brisker whenever he got out of line.

Jabali, when playing an exhibition game for Oakland, got his against another pretty tough guy, Neil Johnson of the Virginia Squires. Jabali kept roughhousing Johnson, even knocking him to the floor. It may have only been an exhibition game, but Johnson got up, walked over to Jabali and KO'd him with one punch, then stood over him screaming for him to get up. At the time, even Jabali's teammates were glad someone had stood up to him.

Several players were known more than others. The best of the best were Brisker, Jabali, Wendell Ladner, Cincy Powell and Johnson, who were all known as enforcers.

Play was so rough and tumble in the ABA that national sportswriter, Jim Murray, said that play isn't so much a game as a Pier 6 brawl in short pants. "They recruit their teams in Central Park after dark. If they did on a street corner what they do under the basket, someone would call the cops," he wrote. Murray noted that they needed helmets more than kneepads. In the rival NBA, the refs have a rule, "no harm, no foul." In the ABA, it should be "no death, no foul."

Fights were more frequent in games, not just among players, but against fans. One such incident came the first year of the ABA when Babe McCarthy brought his New Orleans team to Louisville. One of his former players at Mississippi State, Leland Mitchell, was apparently attacked by a Colonels fan while sitting on the Buc bench. They fought it out, with Mitchell getting the upper hand.

"This stuff cannot go on, people coming out of the stands and attacking the players," McCarthy said. "Suppose Louie Dampier came to New Orleans and some of our fans came out of the stands and beat the hell out of him because there were no policemen."

McCarthy, of course, reported the Louisville incident to Commissioner George Mikan and said that there was inadequate police protection. McCarthy emphasized there was not even one uniformed policeman to stop the fight.

It seemed like the Colonels were always getting into fights with the Virginia Squires. With Dan Issel and Charlie Scott being Co-Rookies of the Year, and both teams battling it out for the Eastern Division title, the rivalry really got heated. But when Dr. J and George "Iceman" Gervin were traded, the Squires' fight for survival in the league grew, and the rivalry faded away.

CHARACTERS

The ABA was full of characters. They were characters in the sense that they were colorful, even controversial, and always unpredictable.

One of those characters was Art Heyman. He had been an All-American at Duke, playing for Coach Vic Bubas, and a teammate for a year of Jeff Mullins.

Heyman was considered a flake, by many. His temper tantrums and sudden outbursts on the court made even his teammates wonder what was next.

Those who have known Heyman recall his days at Duke, and the fighting and taunting that were a part of his on-court personality. As a sophomore when Duke was playing archrival North Carolina, Heyman and the Tarheel's Larry Brown and Donnie Walsh (future NBA executive) were suspended for the remainder of the basketball season following a February fight.

As quirky as Heyman was, he was a fantastic player. At 6'5" he could both score and rebound. Following his senior season he was National Player of the Year as well as the NCAA Tournament Most Outstanding Player, even though he didn't play in the finals. To further point out just how good he was, he is only one of three players in history to be named three times to the All-ACC Basketball Team. The other two were David Thompson and Tyler Hansborough.

Heyman was the number one draft choice in 1963, taken by the New York Knicks. His 15-point average placed him on the NBA all-Rookie team.

But soon his on-court antics caught up with him, and after stints with Cincinnati and Philadelphia, he joined Pittsburgh in the ABA, where he averaged 20 points in helping his team win an ABA title in 1968.

He retired in 1970, but, for sure, left his mark. The mere mention of his name over the PA often brought a chorus of boos, and Heyman seemed to relish it all. When things would calm down, his gyrations, facial expressions and body language, wherever he played, kept the crowd in the game.

Heyman could get Colonels fans so worked up that one even came to the Pittsburgh bench and delivered a punch to his face. It took police, ushers and other players to keep Heyman out of the Convention Center seats. Piper coach Vince Cazzetta was drenched with a cup of beer.

Pittsburgh's Connie Hawkins himself was down on the floor under his team's basket following a punch under his left eye. "I didn't see it coming," Hawkins later said.

Cazzetta was so upset over it all that he threatened to pull his team from the floor. But instead, not wanting to risk a forfeit, his team hung around for a 107-98 win. It was the Piper's 15th consecutive win.

Here's what Heyman told the *Courier-Journal* back in 1968:

"Give my warmest regards to the Colonel fans in Kentucky. Their throat-cutting remarks only make me play harder … but we will be back one more time, and I'm going to bring some of my New York friends."

Heyman went on to identify those friends as Joe Don Looney, the former Oklahoma football star, baseball players Dean Chance and Jimmy Piersall, and his closest friend, Joe Namath of the New York Jets.

"But then I'll be back for the Kentucky Derby, too," he concluded.

CHAPTER TWO
DEEP POCKETS AND PATIENCE

For almost a decade, from 1967 to 1976, Louisville and the state of Kentucky flirted with a big time professional sports team.

The American Basketball Association's Kentucky Colonels seemed to have arrived out of nowhere, crawling at first under the ownership of a most-unlikely couple, known primarily for their show dogs.

A group of Louisville young-guns then purchased the team and soon it was walking. Later, just as the team began to run under the guidance of another couple, whose reputation and fortune had come from the fried chicken business, the Colonels were gone.

Much was said about the Gregorys, Joe and Mamie, in the early days of the Colonels. Their charisma and lifestyle were talked and written about almost as much as the team itself.

The Gregorys took Louisville by storm. Well, Mamie did, anyway. At the age of 22, and the heiress of several family fortunes, Mamie Spears Reynolds Gregory was said to be worth at least $40 million when she eloped with a Cloverport, Kentucky dog-handler named Joe.

She bragged that she and Joe had a deal that he handled all of the money because, by her own account, she would go through it all if he didn't. She even told friends that her allotment was $10 a week. It mattered little that the Gregorys' lived in a $100,000 Civil War-era, 850-acre plantation home in Simpsonville, with its polar bear rug, gold plated bathroom fixtures, huge paintings and antique chandeliers, nor did it matter that they owned almost thirty pedigreed show dogs, two yachts, homes in Asheville, North Carolina and Fort Lauderdale, Florida, and now a professional basketball team. Still Mamie, like most women through the ages, liked to talk about one dollar shoes, two dollar jeans, twelve dollar sweaters and dime store earrings. She said little about her mink wrap-around that seemed to make it all work. She didn't need to. "Just because I wear a ten dollar Timex watch doesn't mean I don't have jewelry," she offered. The real stuff, the watches, rings and necklaces were stowed away in a New York vault.

The Kentucky Colonels were born.

In late March of 1967, Joe and Mamie Gregory were in Nassau soaking up the sun, like they had a right to do. Joe picked up a newspaper and learned that a new professional basketball league, the American Basketball Association, was trying to locate a team in his hometown of Louisville, but was struggling in finding someone with enough money and the willingness to make it happen.

He made a phone call, and he quickly got one in return from Joe Hullett. "We were on a 100-foot yacht having a party for the Governor of Nassau when we got the call," says Mamie.

Hullett was Louisville's best-known sportsman and had been the first local man contacted about an ABA franchise. He had gained a reputation for his involvement in the annual Kentucky-Indiana High School All-Star basketball game that had received national recognition.

Hullett knew that it would take someone with deep pockets and patience. To see a new basketball league, and especially a team in Louisville, go up against the NBA would take far more than just having an interest in basketball.

When Joe and Mamie came forward and put down nearly $65,000 for the franchise, the Kentucky Colonels quickly became a big part of the Louisville sports landscape.

"Joe wanted a basketball team," Mamie recalls over 40 years later. "He was Mr. Basketball in our family. And I'll tell you straight up, I bought the team for him."

According to the Gregorys years later, they paid 80% of the initial $65,000 and attorney Bill Boone and pro-golfer Bobby Nichols shared the remaining 20%.

Who the actual stockholders in the beginning were has long made for interesting conversation. Bill Boone says he was never a stockholder, and early media guides of the Colonels seem to verify it. While stating that Burr Long, Bill Motsch, and Nichols are stockholders, it doesn't include Boone.

Without the Gregorys it might not have happened.

There may have never been a Louie, Darel, Goose, Dan or Artis playing at the same time for a pro team in Louisville. A professional basketball championship? Forget it.

The saga of the American Basketball Association Kentucky Colonels involved owners who were the least likely couple to become involved in owning a professional sports team. Joe, a basketball fan from his childhood days growing up in Cloverport following Coach Diddle's teams at Western, always enjoyed an occasional pick-up game. And though he no longer plays basketball, well into his '80s he still plays softball.

"I can still run fast," he offers with a big smile, "But not for long."

Their "yes, we'll do it" attitude might be compared to diving head first into the shallow-end of a black-bottomed swimming pool. It was risky business for sure, but they lived to talk about it.

Other than enjoying watching basketball, the Gregorys, in somewhat of an understatement, were completely naïve when it came to owning a team. And like other owners of professional franchises, they wanted to do more than just pay the bills. Their financial commitment, they felt, gave them the right to be front and center when it came to their Kentucky Colonels.

Joe and Mamie did more than just show up and sit quietly in their seats near the Colonels bench. They yelled to the coaches and players on both teams; they did likewise with the referees and anyone else who would listen, all while the game was going on.

Whereas before, the Gregorys' life had revolved around breeding and showing their world-class dogs, albeit in some quite famous arenas like Madison Square Garden, their ownership in the Colonels had become a lifestyle, one that squarely placed Mamie and her dog Ziggy in the Louisville limelight.

Mamie thrived on it, enjoying the stir she created at Colonels home games, relishing the attention and all of the photo ops she and Ziggy presented.

Mamie dressed somewhat casually according to fans whose seats were near hers and Joe's. Some even said when it came to dress, Ziggy often upstaged Mamie in one of his thirty-nine different outfits, while sitting in his own seat.

In fact, Ziggy was a Colonel before any of the coaches or players. It was written that Colonels promotional material contained 138 words about Ziggy, while only 79 words were used to describe Dampier.

The first team logo showed a little dog chasing a Kentucky Colonel dribbling a basketball. It might have been more appropriate if the Colonel had been chasing the dog, because in the beginning, Ziggy was the star, the most visible symbol of the franchise.

Ziggy was not just any mutt. It was the Gregory's prize champion Brussels Griffon named Gaystock LeMonsignor, who answered to Ziggy.

Ziggy was at games, office meetings, league meetings, and there was the Ziggy package, a promotional season ticket deal, and the Ziggy Room where VIP's and season ticket holders could schmooze.

In 1966 Ziggy won best of breed at the Madison Square Garden world championships. He matched that effort at the Chicago International Show and for his career won more than 150 best of breed titles.

One of the good Ziggy stories, and there were many, happened on a road game to New York. As Joe, Mamie and Ziggy entered the arena, security informed the Gregorys they couldn't bring a dog inside. Mamie, being Mamie, informed the doorman that "this dog owns the team." It didn't take long before the Gregorys had their three mid-court seats. There sat Ziggy in the middle with Joe on one side and Mamie on the other.

The Gregorys made sure Ziggy was in attendance at all of the Colonels home games and any road games they traveled to. It was reported that he even had a tuxedo he often wore to dinner when at home.

Bob Bass, who coached several teams in the ABA before becoming general manager of the San Antonio Spurs, reported in Tony Pluto's "Loose Balls" that at one of the league's first meetings, he met Joe Gregory with his dog. "A $10,000 dog," Bass said. "That dog was worth more than a lot of the players. But can you imagine sitting at a league meeting and looking right across from you and seeing a damn dog?" Bass went on to say that league meetings were more fun than some of the games.

Ziggy died in 1974 at the age of 12 and is buried at one of the Gregorys' homes in Fort Lauderdale, Florida.

Anything that Joe lacked in aggressiveness, Mamie more than made up for. It was common for her to have run-ins with Colonels coaches during their nearly three years of ownership.

They pulled the plug quickly on Johnny Givens, their first coach, after a 5-12 start. Gene Rhodes, his successor, had his own way of doing things, and it didn't always agree with the Gregorys, particularly Mamie.

Givens was Joe's choice, he said, because he was from nearby New Albany, Indiana, and would give the new team a local connection. But ultimately, and quickly the Gregorys, with the advice of

Bill Boone, Bill Motsch and others, decided they could get Gene Rhodes, who at the time was an assistant coach at Western Kentucky. Reportedly, Rhodes had been their first choice all along, but he wanted some financial guarantees that at the time the Colonels were unwilling to make.

"We made the coaching change because we weren't winning," said Gregory. "We had to do something to turn it around."

The 40-year-old Rhodes' first day as a coach was Thanksgiving Day, and the team started the day with a 9 a.m. practice in preparation for the following night's game against New Orleans. The team had learned of the coaching change only the day before, just after returning from a two-game Texas trip. Givens told David Adams of the *Courier-Journal*, "It was as if I'd been slapped in the face with a baseball bat."

In a footnote to it all, Givens, Rhodes, and assistant coach Buddy Cate had all played on Ed Diddle's 1949-50 team at Western.

Givens went on to say that, "I may be thinking differently about things tomorrow, but regardless, I'm still the Colonels number one fan. If it means that I've got to be behind the scenes to make the Colonels succeed in this town, I'll do it."

Although acknowledging his loyalty to the Colonels, Givens pointed out that it was no secret his team needed some new personnel.

"You know when you win the players get the credit. When you lose, the coach gets the blame," he offered.

The fired coach revealed that he had been blocked in making three player deals with New Jersey and Oakland the week before. It was apparent that his coaching future with the Colonels was over.

Mamie may not have been royalty, but she often acted as if she thought she was. By her own admission, after selling the Colonels, she missed the spotlight.

"I was a star, on center stage," she remembers about her Colonels days. "I liked all of the attention and being able to tell coaches off, not only our coach, but visiting ones as well."

It surprised no one when Rhodes and Mamie clashed, and Mamie recalled an exhibition game at Shelbyville High School in the beginning. "He sassed me," she said. "I thought he was going to throw a chair at me."

Some three years later they decided to sell the team to a group of five Louisville businessmen.

Admittingly, the Gregorys had fun with the team. Their financial stability allowed them to withstand those ground-floor years and, like most ABA owners, lose money along the way. Joe was not ashamed to admit that if he and Mamie had not jumped in and bought the franchise, professional basketball would not have come to Louisville. Sure there were others who could have afforded to do what the Gregorys did, but none came forward.

After the franchise had become successful, it was time to sell. I always had the idea that we could take the team only so far," Gregory said back then. "Then we'd have to put it in the hands of solid businessmen, men like those we are selling to." Gregory continued, "Just recently, I had a chance to sell to some out-of-town people; I didn't want that, this is a Kentucky team."

There'll be the dog shows, of course, for Joe and Mamie, perhaps 50 shows a year all over the nation. Joe even said something about jumping in as a racecar owner and hanging out in Daytona.

He talked about the possibility of selling Marlbank, their farm near Simpsonville. But make no mistake, he told anyone who would listen that he would always be a part of the Colonels, but now as a fan.

"I did a lot of hollering at the referees the first year," reflected Gregory, shortly after selling the team. "I cut down some last year, because I didn't think it looked too good for the owner to be jumping up and down all the time. Now I can get back to hollering."

According to Louisville Attorney J. Bruce Miller, when the Gregorys sold their team to the Wendell Cherry Group, they retained 3% of the ownership, but when the team transferred hands from that group to the Cincinnati group and then to John Y. and Ellie Brown, their ownership interest increased to 7½%.

Miller goes on to say that Cincinnati Sports, Inc. retained a 40% limited partnership interest, the Browns' controlling interest of 52½%, and Joe and Mamie owning the remaining 7½%.

The question here is that through all of these high stake transactions that only CPA's and financial lawyers could make heads or tails of, whatever happened to the Gregorys' ownership interest?

When John Y. folded up the Colonels, and he collected his ABA dollars and bought the Buffalo Braves NBA team, did the Gregorys have money coming?

"We kept 10% of ownership all the way to the end." Joe said years later. "When Brown got his $3 million, we didn't get anything."

Could Joe have been mistaken about his and Mamie's ownership? After all, Miller had detailed out who owned what and when, and his figures added up to 100%. Still what happened to that 7½%?

The Gregorys were jet setters for sure, and could have easily been material for "Lifestyles of the Rich and Famous." Over a 45-year period they owned 27 different houses, some in pricey locations like Beverly Hills, Santa Barbara, Los Angeles and the Mississippi coast.

But the home that drew the most attention, at least in Louisville, was their 800-acre spread called Marlbank, a name that came with the property when they purchased it in 1967 from the family that supposedly owned the Bunny Bread Company. "We liked the name enough not to change it," said Joe years later.

In 1969, Marlbank was sold to a group of bank investors in Louisville. Joe and Mamie moved directly to a home they had purchased in Fort Lauderdale. There they bought and sold homes over the next few years, one of which was a penthouse condo just off well-known Las Olas Boulevard.

Mamie enjoyed talking about Darel Carrier, always has, always will.

"We made him captain of the team," she says, further pointing out the active influence they had as owners. On lots of teams, the players elect the team's captain. But not with the Colonels.

Carrier frequently worked at Marlbank, and other than on the basketball court, he felt at home working in a field, doing farm chores. "Darel and Goose (Ligon) would be out on the farm doing some work," Mamie recalled laughingly, and Goose would watch Darel do all of the work."

The Colonels were more than a business with the Gregorys. The players and their personal lives became intertwined with Joe and Mamie. They genuinely cared about them, and it showed.

"We loved our team," Mamie says. "We had them to our house all of the time. After we sold the team, we heard the players couldn't stand John Y. All he cared about was the money. If a player got hurt, John Y. just thought about the money. We cared about the players."

For sure, Joe and Mamie Gregory had a flamboyant two-year run as owners of the team. Without them, who knows? Perhaps someone else might have stepped up with a positive response to Joe Hullett's phone call at the eleventh hour, but probably not.

Along the way, Joe and Mamie had two children, Joseph, born in 1967, and Evalyn in 1969. Joseph graduated from Belmont College in Nashville, the city where he has lived for over 20 years. He is a music business image consultant as well as a writer of books and songs. Evalyn works closely with her parents in the dog breeding, training and showing business. She lives in Louisville.

To understand why the Gregorys had the wherewithal to come forward at a time that seemed like no one else was willing, it might make it a little easier to understand where they've come from, both figurative and literally. On the surface they would appear very unlikely to be ground floor pioneers of a professional basketball team, but when you put them together, they become a force that proved to be quite effective.

A look back on their lives makes the end result much easier to understand.

First, there's Joe. His parents, John and Cecil Gregory, knew what hard work meant in order to provide for their seven children, of which Joe was the middle child. An older brother, William Ernest, was killed in World War II in 1943, leaving Joe to grow up with five sisters in the small town of Cloverport, Kentucky, some 10 miles west of Hardinsburg, in Breckinridge County.

Like many youngsters growing up in a small town in the 1940s, he worked where he could to pick up spending money. But his first love was basketball. He shot baskets and played with friends wherever there was a goal, and by the time he was a senior he was good enough to make the all-regional team while playing for Cloverport High School.

Gregory thought he was a pretty good player, perhaps even good enough to play for coach Peck Hickman and the Louisville Cardinals. "I went out for the team," he says. "But then I started getting some interests other than basketball. Plus, I knew I wasn't going to make the team."

One of those interests was in dogs. Not just any dogs, but the Boxer breed. And how it came to be Boxers is about as unusual as lots of other things that happened in his life.

But it was only the beginning.

"I was looking in the *Courier-Journal* one day and saw a picture of a Boxer," he recalled. "I really liked the look of the dog and decided then I wanted to know more about them. I had had a good day at the track on Derby Day, I believe it was 1947, and bought the dog."

True to his word, and only in his early '20s, Gregory got involved in training the breed, and then with the knowledge and experience he gained, he became a professional show dog handler. One of those championship dog shows took him to Asheville, North Carolina, in 1963. Joe Gregory's life was about to change. But so were a lot of other things.

"I was showing a famous Boxer named Painted Lady," Joe said. "Mamie saw me and the Boxer and liked us both. She wanted to buy Painted Lady for $25,000, but the owner wouldn't sell. I told him if he sold the dog, I went with it."

Mamie was living in Asheville, the home of her father, U.S. Senator Robert Reynolds, and Joe says Mamie had come to the show because her family always donated trophies and awards for the event.

At the time Joe and Mamie met, Joe was 36 and Mamie was 21, but the fifteen year age difference seemed to matter little to either one. What did matter was that Mamie was married.

In August 1963, at the age of 20, she had married Italian racecar driver Luigi Chinetti, Jr., also 20, whose father owned the first Ferrari dealership in America and the rights to Ferrari dealerships in more than half of the United States. Chinetti Sr. was a world-class driver, even winning the 24-hour LeMans.

This helps to explain a missing link in a Kentucky Colonels media guide distributed before the team's first-ever game back in 1967. In profiling Mamie's background, the guide states that, "Mrs. Gregory's other sporting interest includes stock car racing. She was the first person to run a stock car on a sports car track at Nassau. She holds national and international records. She has raced at Daytona, LeMans, Spa Montremont, and other world famous courses."

At such a young age, Mamie had done a lot, so why would buying a professional basketball team be out of the ordinary for her?

On September 4, 1965, Mamie divorced Chinetti and married Joe in Juarez, Mexico, on the same day.

While Joe's early life had consisted of long hours of studying, learning and trial and error lessons in the world of show dogs, Mamie's, on the other hand was a bit silver spoonish, beginning several generations before her birth.

When Joe and Mamie suddenly appeared on the Louisville scene as high profile, wealthy owners of the newly formed Kentucky Colonels, almost every newspaper article talked about the 20-something young woman as heiress to a gold mining and newspaper fortune, and even alluding to the fact that Mamie's grandmother once owned the famed Hope Diamond.

But, what about those goldmines, newspapers, and diamonds? Mamie's life, and that of her family, could easily be a book unto itself. Mamie's grandmother, Evalyn, was the only daughter of Irish immigrants Thomas and Carrie Walsh, who had indeed been involved in goldmines, first discovering and mining them in Colorado and the Dakotas, and then selling them off for millions of dollars in the late 1800s.

When Evalyn Walsh married Edward Beale McLean in 1908, it brought another piece of the financial puzzle into the picture. Edward's parents, John and Emily McLean, owned two major newspapers, *The Washington Post* and *The Cincinnati Enquirer*. It was even reported that their parents gave them $100,000 each for an outlandish honeymoon around the world where they were said to have run out of money in Paris.

Nevertheless, the McLeans, in 1911, purchased the Hope Diamond from Pierre Cartier Jewelers in New York City for an astronomical $180,000. Mamie's grandmother was 25-years-old.

As a toddler, Mamie remembers the 45-karat blue diamond necklace. "Before my mother and grandmother died, I had a chance to wear it, play with it, and supposedly teethed on it," she recalled. "It wasn't a necklace until my grandmother designed it to be, with the help of Pierre Cartier," Mamie said. "It was originally set in platinum as a stone with diamonds surrounding it."

Evalyn Walsh McLean was for sure one of the true socialites of her time. She loved showing off the Hope Diamond, often bringing it out for friends to try on, including President Warren G. Harding and his wife, Florence. She would even strap the Hope to her pet's dog collar. There were also stories that Evalyn would frequently misplace it at parties, and then make a children's game out of finding it.

The Hope Diamond dates back to the 1600s from India, and was said to have been cursed, bringing trouble to all who had owned it. Even though Evalyn and her husband Edward, by all accounts, pretty much had anything money could buy, the curse of the Hope Diamond took its toll on the family.

Their son Vinson, at the age of nine, died in an automobile related accident, and Edward, Evalyn's husband, was declared insane and committed to a mental institution until his death in 1941. Then in 1946, Mamie's mother, Emily Washington McLean Reynolds, at the age of 25, died of an apparent overdose of sleeping pills while living in Washington, D.C. Mamie was five-years-old.

Years later, Mamie and Joe's daughter, Evalyn, recounts that her grandmother, Emily, actually changed her name to Evalyn when she was very young, long before she married her grandfather Reynolds.

Mamie's grandmother had endured a lot, good and bad. Perhaps one of the most bizarre events in her life occurred when on March 1, 1932, the baby boy of aviator Charles Lindbergh and wife Anne was kidnapped.

To this day it is safe to say the Lindbergh kidnapping is the most notorious kidnapping in history. Evalyn McLean, because of her social status and wealth, felt like she could help recover the 20-month-old child.

Evalyn put the word out, and soon a former FBI agent named Gaston Means contacted her saying he had connected with the kidnappers, and with $100,000 from her he could get the baby back. Means, it turned out, was a con man and scam artist rolled into one. He had even been suspected of murder a few years before. Means took the money and disappeared, only to return weeks later saying he needed more money to secure the baby. This time Evalyn called police. Means was found guilty and eventually died in Leavenworth Prison in 1938 while serving a 15-year sentence.

The Lindbergh baby was found dead on May 12, 1932.

As the family's run of bad luck continued, in 1947 Evalyn McLean was not able to overcome pneumonia and died at the age of 60, just one year after the death of Mamie's mother.

Although the Hope Diamond had been willed to the grandchildren, a court ordered the famous diamond to be sold in 1949 to settle some outstanding family debt.

A New York diamond merchant bought the diamond and several years later it was donated to the Smithsonian, where it became one of the more popular exhibits.

Today Mamie says the Hope is priceless, but that rumors have swirled that it could now be worth over $400 million.

Mamie's father, Senator Reynolds, had served North Carolina in the U.S. Senate from 1932-1945. In 1941 he was Chairman of the Senate Committee on Military Affairs. It was in October of that same year that the 57-year-old Senator married 19-year-old Emily McLean, Mamie's mother. It was his fifth marriage, and a year later Mamie was born.

Mamie was named after an aunt, Mamie Spears Reynolds, who had actually been married to two of Mamie's dad's brothers. First Mamie Spears married Senator Reynolds' older brother, William. He died in 1892 at the age of 42, and ten years later she married younger brother Natt Reynolds.

Not long after the deaths of Mamie's mother and grandmother, her dad took her to his hometown of Asheville.

Mamie's education included some schooling in Madrid, Spain, and along the way she learned to speak Spanish and French. It was in 1963, the same year she met Joe, that her father died at the age of 79.

As the Gregorys' interesting and sometime controversial era with the Colonels came to a close in 1970, there may not have been an appreciation from the city of Louisville for what they did at the time. They had shown a horse race and college basketball town that there was room for a major league professional sports team. If Joe and Mamie are remembered for nothing else, they did that. Years later, as fiery and contentious as Gene Rhodes had been when coaching the Colonels, he says that even though he didn't get along with them, the Gregorys at least gave him a chance to coach.

That same thing can be said about Joe and Mamie's relationship with Louisville. At least they gave the city a chance, too.

When Joe and Mamie sold their beloved Colonels, for all practical purposes they were through with basketball other than being fans. By April 1972, they were getting a bit restless, missing the game, so when it became known that the financially troubled Memphis Pros might be for sale, they were interested, very interested. However, it was not to be, as the ABA board of trustees turned down their offer and decided, instead, to give the current Memphis management one more chance.

The Gregorys had also made an attempt to purchase the Floridian franchise at one time.

CHAPTER THREE
ATTORNEYS, ACCOUNTANTS, JOCKEYS AND COACHES

WILLIAM BOONE

William Boone was a 33-year-old Louisville attorney when he received a phone call from Bill Motsch, a CPA in the city, inquiring about an interest to be involved in a brand new professional basketball team, the Kentucky Colonels, in a brand new basketball league, the American Basketball Association.

At the time Boone was doing some work as a sports agent, representing Louisville professional golfers Frank Beard and Bobby Nichols, as well as Dick Stockton.

Boone was a Louisville guy. After graduating from Atherton High School, he went to Baylor University where he received his undergraduate and law degrees, and then returned to his hometown.

From the beginning Boone seemed like a natural to be involved with the Colonels. His local reputation as a sports attorney would fit in well with the new team, as would his experience with contracts and dealings with pro athletes. "I loved sports," said Boone. "But I didn't know a thing about pro basketball." With that said, neither did anyone else in the Colonels organization. The Colonels organizational chart listed Boone as its secretary.

Boone recalls what it was like during those first couple of years: "We were the blind leading the blind," he laughed. "We had signed Louie (Dampier) for $15,000, and then made a trip out to Oakland for the first ABA draft. That was really something. Joe Gregory, Bill Motsch and I made the trip. If you can believe it, all we had to go on in identifying players were a couple of sports magazines."

Boone is not sure how it happened, and didn't realize it at the time, but one of the Colonels draftees turned out to be one of the all-time great stories in pro-basketball.

"After the draft I sent a telegram to this guy at Kansas State and asked him to call me because we had drafted him. He called and said, "I don't know why you drafted me, I'm 5'6" and 55-years-old. In all of the confusion we drafted a 5' 6" professor from Kansas State," laughs Boone. "The guy was a teacher, not a basketball player and we somehow, someway ended up with him on our draft list. We didn't know it until he called and told us there must have been a mistake."

It definitely was, and Boone says there were others, but perhaps not of that magnitude.

They also followed up on a phone call from Knoxville, Tennessee. A little nearby college supposedly had a 7-footer averaging 40 points and 28 rebounds. Charlie Mastin, Director of Publicity, reported that they checked out the school and actually found it, but they didn't find the player.

Mastin told the story about how he was involved in trying to win over former Kentucky Mr. Basketball, and Duke star Jeff Mullins, from the NBA San Francisco Warriors.

Mastin said that Mullins was then making $15,000 a year, and the Colonels were trying to put together a four-year, $200,000 deal. It all went for naught when the restaurant band they were eating in struck up, "I Left My Heart in San Francisco."

There were other stories, some with just enough facts and details to be believable.

UK All-American Pat Riley had been a prime target of Gregory and the Colonels. A $200,000 deal was mentioned, which was huge money then. He dropped a hint of playing pro football, maybe with the Dallas Cowboys. After all, he had been a top flight grid player in high school in Schenectady, New York, before coming to Kentucky to play hoops. Riley's bad back and all made it even more difficult to imagine him taking a hit on a pass route over the middle. Surely he was bluffing. He soon signed to play basketball with San Diego in the NBA.

Boone then told the story about how Cotton Nash, a big deal signee with the Colonels, decided to give up basketball for good after playing only half a season. Reported to have received all of his $20,000 yearly salary up front, Nash, according to Boone, with tears in his eyes said he was a super athlete and didn't want to go on the way he was playing. Boone then went on to say that the next summer while in Hawaii he went to see Nash play baseball. His batting average was .201, and as Boone tells it, he wanted to call him to see how the super athlete was doing.

Without question, Boone says, Dan Issel was the best Colonel he ever saw play. And he also remembers what Issel told the Colonels when they were in negotiations to sign the UK All-American:

"Issel said if you want me, you also take Pratt," referring to Mike Pratt, his teammate at Kentucky.

As for Wendell Ladner, Boone offered that he was "the toughest SOB I've ever seen ... a rebounding fool and hatchet man."

Boone talked about what all the Colonels went through in signing 7'2" Artis Gilmore, the Jacksonville All-American. "His season was over, but he was still in school," recalled Boone. "He came to Louisville and we hid him out at the Executive Inn. Now how do you hide a 7'2" black man with a five inch afro? But we did it. We had him under an assumed name and he went in and out of the hotel's back door."

Boone remembers the game bonuses the Colonels used to entice a couple of the players. "We told Darel Carrier he would get a $20 bonus for every 3-pointer he made, but then when he quit passing the ball, we had to revoke that one," Boone chuckled.

There was also a bonus for Goose Ligon, not for scoring, but for rebounding. "Motsch told Goose he would get $20 for every rebound, to be paid in cash right after the game," Boone said. "But, he would have to pay us $20 for every rebound under 10 for the game."

Ligon was a real character and had become one of the more popular players on the team. "I went out one night to an after-hours joint with Goose," Boone said. "I was the only white guy there, but Goose told everyone that I was with him, so that made it okay. We had a few drinks, nothing illegal going on, just a joint with drinks and lots of women."

Then there was also the effort to sign Wes Unseld, the Louisville native and U of L All-American. "It was interesting," Boone said. "We busted our balls trying to sign him. We even took out two full pages in the *Courier-Journal*. I think it cost $5,000 back then. Motsch about died over the cost, but we had to do it to save face in Louisville, to let people know we tried.

COLONELS OFFER UNSELD

$500,000

The following are the facts with regard to the Westley Unseld negotiations, from start to date:

In December of 1967, the Kentucky Colonels contacted Coach John Dromo of the University of Louisville to consult with him about meeting and talking contract terms with Westley Unseld. Coach Dromo advised the Colonels that since Westley was still playing college basketball, he did not want them to talk directly to Westley, and that all negotiations should be conducted through him. The Colonels complied with this request. Several sessions then took place between Mr. Dromo and Colonels' officials, and, in February of 1968, the Colonels handed to Mr. Dromo the outline of a written proposal under the terms of which the Colonels agreed to pay Westley Unseld $210,000.00 for a four-year contract. Mr. Dromo was advised at that time that this was a negotiable figure, but the Colonels had previously been asked by Mr. Dromo to make a proposal in writing, so this was done.

Several days later Mr. Dromo reported back to the Colonels' officials that the Unseld family was "not too happy with that offer". The Colonels then asked that Westley submit a counter-proposal. None was forthcoming and Mr. Dromo still insisted that he was Westley's representative and that the Colonels not negotiate directly with Westley. Mr. Dromo stated, during these sessions, that he knew that Westley wanted to stay in Louisville and play for the Colonels but that it would "all depend on the money".

Mr. Dromo advised the Colonels during the first week of March that Westley had now retained a Louisville law firm to represent him in his negotiations.

On Saturday, March 9, 1968, Colonels' officials met with the attorney, Westley Unseld, Mr. & Mrs. Charles Unseld and John Dromo. The Colonels asked for this meeting at that time because the American Basketball Association "secret draft" was to be held in Louisville that afternoon. At this meeting, the Colonels told the group that the draft would be held that afternoon and said they wanted to know for sure that Westley would like to play in Louisville before they used their first round draft choice on Westley. The attorney then said that Westley did want to play in Louisville "if the money is right". He further stated that he felt that the Colonels' original offer of $210,000.00 was "about half what it should be".

The meeting adjourned and the attorney promised that he would prepare a formal written offer specifying exactly how much Westley wanted and how he wanted it to be paid.

Shortly after this morning meeting, one of Westley's representatives called the Colonels' officials and stated that they should certainly proceed to draft Westley because he felt certain Westley wanted to stay in Louisville.

The Colonels did make Westley Unseld their number one draft choice in the ABA meeting on the afternoon of March 9.

Early the following week the Colonels gave the attorney blank copies of the standard form American Basketball Association Player Contract for him to study. At that time, the Colonels were assured that he would call them the next day and submit a written proposal. Nothing was heard from the attorney for approximately ten days from that time and finally, upon being contacted by the Colonels on March 19 or March 20, the attorney advised that Westley wanted $400,000.00, which included a $20,000.00 attorney fee, for four years to play for the Kentucky Colonels. He also said that he would advise the Colonels within the next day or two how Westley wanted the money paid, from a tax standpoint. Approximately two days later, the attorney advised the Colonels how the money should be spread. At that time, the Colonels asked the attorney to reduce this to writing, have it signed by Westley, and call a meeting of all of the principals involved at which time the Colonels would either accept or reject the offer. Several days again elapsed and still the attorney did not present the written offer. Finally, the attorney agreed to have a meeting between all of the principals in his office on Monday, April 1, 1968, at 4:00 o'clock p.m., at which time he assured the Colonels that he would have the written offer prepared and signed by Westley and ready for signing by the Colonels.

Throughout the negotiations, Westley Unseld's representatives made it clear to the Colonels that they wanted the contract terms to be personally guaranteed by Mr. & Mrs. Joseph Gregory or secured by an escrow account or a surety bond. Mr. & Mrs. Gregory agreed to this.

On Monday, April 1, Mr. & Mrs. Joseph Gregory and other Colonels' officials went to the attorney's office at 4:00 o'clock p.m., the appointed time, and met with Westley Unseld, John Dromo, and the attorneys. The attorney had prepared, in longhand, a written proposal, substantially identical to the one he had previously verbally given the Colonels. This was read aloud to the Colonels, in the presence of Westley and his coach, from the handwritten sheet which the attorney had prepared. This was an offer in the amount of $400,000.00 for a four-year contract, and again included a $20,000.00 attorney fee. After it was read aloud by the attorney, the Colonels asked him to put it in proper contract form, and have Westley sign it so that it could be accepted.

At this point Westley Unseld and the attorneys left the room and conferred for approximately 15 minutes. When they returned to the conference room, the attorney announced that he was "embarrassed", that Westley was not prepared to sign that proposal on that date, but wanted to "go home and talk with his mother and father about it."

At this time, Mr. Dromo stated that he wanted the Colonels to agree, in writing, that they would not play a game

in Louisville for ten years that would conflict with a University of Louisville home basketball game. This matter was discussed and it was pointed out that the Colonels do not set the league schedule but that they would do everything within their power not to compete with the University of Louisville. Mr. Dromo also stated that he thought the Colonels should give Westley Unseld a $6,000 or $7,000 automobile, in addition to the $400,000.00.

The meeting was adjourned with the understanding that the parties would meet the next day, Tuesday, April 2, at 4:00 p.m. in the attorney's office, at which time the signed contract would be put on the table.

At approximately 2:00 p.m. on Tuesday, April 2, the attorney called the Colonels and said "all negotiations were off and that they would not meet further with the Colonels."

After this statement, Mr. Joe Gregory contacted Westley Unseld at Seneca High School and asked him if he had made an irrevocable decision. Westley said that he had not signed with the NBA, and Westley further said "I have always said it is the money that counts".

The Colonels talked with the attorney again on the morning of Wednesday, April 3, at which time the attorney stated that "Westley has made his decision to play in the NBA and he did not make this decision alone. However, he has not signed a contract with the NBA yet." The attorney did not advise how much Baltimore might have offered Westley. The Colonels asked him if he would permit them to immediately come to his office and make Westley another offer. He refused to permit this.

The Colonels have been willing to meet Westley's verbal offer since it was first announced, were ready to sign a contract for $400,000.00 at the April 1 meeting and are still ready to do so. Since Westley and his representatives have stated this day that he has not yet signed with the NBA, the Colonels want to publicly announce that they hereby offer Westley Unseld $500,000.00 for a four-year contract, payable in the manner previously suggested by Westley's attorney. This is $60,000.00 more than Elvin Hayes reportedly received from San Diego for the same length contract.

Westley's representatives have repeatedly said that the Colonels would have the final opportunity to match or better the best NBA offer. The Colonels ask now for this opportunity to make this statement in order to advise the basketball fans of Kentucky and the nation of the exact situation as it has developed and what they are willing to do.

The Colonels urge all basketball fans in Kentucky to tell Westley, by wire or phone, that they want him to play in Kentucky, before he signs with the NBA.

THE KENTUCKY COLONELS ATHLETIC ENTERPRISES, INC.

JOSEPH E. GREGORY, President

"I remember Motsch saying he hoped Unseld didn't take the $500,000 we offered him, because he didn't know where we'd come up with the money."

There was also a single full-page advertisement that ran in the *Courier-Journal* on Friday, April 5, 1968. In bold letters it read: "Colonels Offer Unseld $500,000. The following are the facts with regard to the Westley Unseld negotiations, from start to date."

The ad detailed what had gone on from the time the Colonels first contacted Unseld's coach at U of L, John Dromo, in December 1967. The coach had informed the Colonels organization that he did not want them talking directly to Unseld since he was still "playing college basketball," and that all negotiations should be conducted through him.

With Joe and Mamie Gregory actively involved in trying to land Unseld, the communication between the Colonels, Dromo, and Unseld's attorney, and Unseld and his family continued from February 1968, into March, and then into early April.

The copy in the ad stated that at every step the Colonels had met the requirements requested to close the deal for Unseld. Dromo had even requested in writing that the Colonels would not play a game in Louisville for ten years that would conflict with a University of Louisville home basketball games. It was pointed out that the Colonels do not set the league schedule. Dromo also requested a $6,000 or $7,000 automobile in addition to the $400,000 that the Unseld group indicated would be needed to finalize a contract. Unseld's attorney even included $20,000 for his fee.

The Colonels ad stated they were under the impression a final contract was to be signed at 4 p.m. in the attorney's office. However, a 2 p.m. phone call advised them that "all negotiations were off, and that they would not meet further with the Colonels."

Joe Gregory proceeded to personally contact Unseld at Seneca High School, where he had played before U of L, and asked him if he had made an irrevocable decision. Unseld told Gregory that he had not signed with the NBA, and according to the advertisement copy he further said, "I have always said it is the money that counts."

According to the Colonels, they had met every one of Unseld's requests, but that with this full page ad they were publicly announcing they hereby offer Westley Unseld $500,000 for a four year contract. The ad also pointed out that "this is $60,000 more than Elvin Hayes reportedly received from San Diego for the same length contract."

At the bottom of the page it was "signed" The Kentucky Colonels Athletic Enterprises, Inc., Joseph E. Gregory, President.

Even though the money might have been as good or better, Unseld decided to cast his lot with the NBA.

Boone also likes to tell about his early days of sitting with Joe, Mamie, and, of course, Ziggy, at the Colonels games.

"There was something going on all the time," he says. "One of the things Mamie wanted me to do was get Ziggy ice cream during the game, and I did. That dog, you know, had his own seat at all of the games."

Bill Boone was in on the ground floor with the Kentucky Colonels, and even after the Gregorys sold out to the Wendell Cherry group, he remained a part of it, representing John Y. Brown and his Kentucky Fried Chicken corporation.

BILL MOTSCH

In 1966 Bill Motsch had been a CPA for several years and had just opened a new CPA firm in downtown Louisville, settling into what he hoped would be a successful accounting career. As fortune would have it, in late summer of 1967, he met Burr Long.

Long, it just so happened, was a lifelong friend of Joe Gregory. The two of them had grown up together in Cloverport and had been business partners over the years. Long, like Gregory, was a renowned dog handler who also participated in the world-class shows.

When Joe and Mamie decided to get into the professional basketball business, it was a given that Long would be a part of their efforts.

So, with Long having met Motsch and knowing the new venture would need someone with Motsch's ability, he quickly suggested that Joe give the accountant a call.

He did, and soon Motsch had agreed to become part of the Kentucky Colonels staff with the title of executive director.

"At our first organizational meeting," Motsch says. "There was Bill Boone, Burr Long, Joe, Mamie and Ziggy. We talked about various aspects of the business and decided we needed to quickly form a corporation." Athletic Enterprises, Inc. was the name of the new corporation, and soon Motsch was overloaded with titles for the upstart Colonels.

Alice Miller's name never appeared on a Colonels roster, but her value to the organization was never underestimated. "She was the first person Bill Motsch hired in the office and she was the last to leave when the team folded," Pink Gardner fondly recalled. Miller did it all. She kept detailed seating charts before computers. "We put it in pencil," she laughed.

She took care of paychecks, even to the point of telling the players they wouldn't get one. There was a time Maurice Lucas came by to get his check, and Miller had to inform him that coach Hubie Brown told her not to give it to him. It seemed that Brown felt like the Colonels forward hadn't done enough lately to earn it. He eventually got it.

Miller also remembers when Artis Gilmore came by the office and asked them to come out to the parking lot. "He wanted us to see his news Rolls Royce," she said. "He told us it cost him $34,000."

One of Miller's duties in the early days at the Colonels games in the Convention Center was to deliver statistics to the radio crews. They weren't at courtside, but seated above the floor. In order to reach them Miller had to walk across a narrow catwalk.

She remembers one year when John Y. and Ellie bought red, white and blue TVs for everyone in the organization. "There were about 35 of them and we had to gift wrap every one of them," Miller said.

By then, not only had the 37-year-old Motsch become a stockholder, along with Long, but his executive director title also included the duties of a professional basketball team's general manager.

"One thing led to another, and before I knew it I found myself doing more and more," he said.

"We were the last team to get in the league," he added. "And it was already June or July, and the opening game was in October. Joe Hullett's name came up, so I went to Freedom Hall to meet him. I knew he'd be there."

Hullett, if you recall, was the first Louisvillian to be contacted about putting an ABA team in Louisville, and many considered him the city's foremost authority when it came to putting on a sporting event.

"Joe knew about putting on a game, and I didn't," laughed Motsch. "He knew about scorekeepers, timekeepers, tickets, refs and all of the promotions that went with it.

"We had all of this going on and didn't even have a coach," Motsch said. "Joe and I drove to Lexington to talk to Ralph Carlisle."

Carlisle had been a successful high school coach at Lexington Lafayette, winning two state championships (1950 and 1957), and had been runner-up in another (1949), and he turned out two Mr. Basketballs, Billy Ray Lickert in 1957, and Jeff Mullins in 1960. Lickert had a nice career at Kentucky, and Mullins went on to make All-American at Duke and had an all-NBA career.

By 1967 Carlisle had left the game and was selling insurance in Lexington. That Colonels contact with the coach went no further.

"Someone even talked to Peck Hickman about it," Motsch said in referring to the former U of L coach.

Soon, after several names had been tossed around, including Gene Rhodes, Johnny Givens was named as the coach of the Kentucky Colonels.

"We had tryouts for several days at Bellarmine," says Motsch. "And Givens really wanted Goose Ligon on the team." Ligon, who's given first name was Jim, had picked up the Goose nickname because of his resemblance to Goose Tatum, the former Globetrotter funny man.

Ligon had already been cut by the Indiana Pacers, but it had more to do with his history than his basketball ability. Following an all-state career at Kokomo High School, Ligon had run afoul of the law and spent some time in the Indiana State Penitentiary. The Pacers organization wasn't quite sure how this would play out with their fans in light of them being a new team looking to project a certain image.

For sure Ligon could play, even if he had been away from the game for almost five years. He made the team, and over the years became one of the better players in the ABA.

Colonels games for the most part were played in the downtown Convention Center, with a few exceptions when they hooked up against the Pacers, and those games were moved to Freedom Hall.

The very first Colonels game was played in Freedom Hall.

Motsch remembers the night the Colonels signed Louie Dampier to a Colonel contract. It was a very big deal.

"Bill Boone and I met with Louie and Lawson King (attorney) at the Pendenis Club over dinner. Everything went great, and we signed him that night. I called Dave Adams at the *Courier-Journal* to give him an exclusive on the Dampier signing," says Motsch. "They came over to the Convention

Center where our offices were located. The next day they had a little on Louie's signing, and the rest of the story was about how barebones the Colonels offices were."

The thing you have to remember, Motsch added, was that when Joe called me and said he'd bought a pro team, what he actually bought was a piece of paper saying he had bought the rights to start a team here.

"My recollection was that Joe and Mamie paid less than $30,000," he went on to say. "If they paid any more than that it was probably contingent on other things happening."

Motsch remembers the time he and Joe Gregory drove to Indianapolis to talk to a future player, who at the time was playing minor league baseball for the Indianapolis Indians.

"Joe Hullett really wanted Cotton Nash," says Motsch. "So, Joe and I headed up there to talk to him. We knew his commitment was to baseball, but he was such a great name in Kentucky."

Indeed he was. Nash had been a three-time All-American at Kentucky, and when he graduated in 1964, he had become the school's all-time leading scorer with 1,770 points during his three years of varsity play. He would eventually move up to the majors for a short period with the Chicago White Sox, and even before that he had played briefly with the NBA Los Angeles Lakers before being released.

Nash had become a Kentucky legend while at UK. The fans loved him. Make no mistake about it, he was a great college basketball player. But his apparent lack of dedication to basketball after UK, combined with a laid-back demeanor, didn't set well with Cotton's new coach, Johnny Givens.

For sure Given's coaching resume was far short of Nash's credentials as a player. Givens was continuously trying to challenge Nash to play the way he had at UK.

It was even reported that Givens was said to have told Cotton that he was a has-been ... just like he was. The coach even challenged the former UK great to a one-on-one-game. Now keep in mind that it was common for Givens to lace-em-up back then and go two-on-two to tryout a Colonels prospect. He still liked to play and must have liked his chances against Nash. Givens told others he played Nash ... and beat him. Nash had been out of basketball for three years, playing baseball, so perhaps he did.

From the outset, a season ticket base was the lifeblood of the team. Everyone remotely associated with the Colonels had a responsibility to sell, sell, sell.

Tommy Finnigan, who had been an all-stater at Flaget in 1960 and played at U of L, sold season tickets on a commission basis. So did Joe Reible, the Bellarmine College coach.

Well into that first year, Motsch says they all knew they had to do some heavy promotions, continuously coming up with fresh ideas. One of those he will never forget was a St. Patrick's Day promotion.

"We wanted everything green" he laughed. "Green nets, green popcorn, green ice cream, and anyone with green hair got in free. But you know what? We never could come up with the green popcorn."

Motsch and Long represented the Colonels at all of the ABA league meetings, and in doing so they became more aware of the financial affairs of the other ABA teams. Each team had made a commitment to make the league successful, and although this was only the ABA's first year, George Mikan, the league's commissioner, wanted to keep a handle on each team's finances.

As the second season rolled around, Motsch, by his own admission, was getting caught up in professional basketball in Louisville.

"I had become quite enthused about it all," he said. "But I had a decision to make as to whether or not to give up my CPA practice and devote my life to sports management."

He finally came up with the answer in an odd sort of way.

"My 10-year-old son and I were talking," he remembers, "And I just asked him what he thought I should do? He said, 'Dad I think you ought to do what you know best.' My son was right."

He kept his accounting business going, but Motsch was still very much a part of the Colonels, and almost every day was an education, especially when it came to signing players. "We had players in and we learned if we didn't sign them right then, that would be the last we'd see of them. The league wanted Lew Alcindor, and each franchise put up $100,000 in order to come up with a million dollars to offer him. Of course that went nowhere."

Motsch recalls when Charlie Mastin, the team's director of public relations, came to him about signing Penny Ann Early, the female jockey, to a pro basketball contract, albeit for only a single game.

"I called Burr Long," says Motsch. "He said it should be fine, but we both agreed we should call George Mikan. Mikan said okay. We paid her one or two thousand dollars. We had a good crowd that night, but there were a few boos."

By the time the Gregorys had decided to sell the team, several in the organization had decided it would be a "tough row to hoe" for any ABA franchise to be successful.

"We decided we had taken the team as far as we could." Motsch offered. "Bill Boone went out and put together the group that eventually bought the Colonels from Joe and Mamie, who stayed involved as minority stockholders."

Early on Motsch had developed a good relationship with Mike Storen while he was general manager of the Indiana Pacers, and later on when Storen became the ABA commissioner, he hired the Louisville CPA to do a little work for the league.

Because of Motsch's previous role as the Colonels league rep, and his learning about the finances of other teams, he had the established contacts with all of the teams, and Storen wanted Motsch to go around the league to make sure how much of their budgets had been committed to players' salaries.

In an odd sort of way Motsch described Burr Long as Joe Gregory's alter ego, saying that 95 percent of his involvement with management during the Colonels years was through him.

However, after the team was sold and Motsch no longer was with the Colonels organization, he did work for the Gregorys until he retired from his CPA practice in 2001.

It was the same CPA firm, which years before, his 10-year-old son had advised him to stick with.

BUDDY CATE

Buddy Cate had played for Mr. Diddle at Western Kentucky, and had been a roommate of Johnny Givens in the coach's house, appropriately called Diddle Dorm. So when Joe and Mamie Gregory decided to hire Givens as their coach for the newly formed ABA Kentucky Colonels, he needed an assistant who could also multi-task, doing things like taping ankles, handling the equipment, coordinating the schedule, and even selling tickets.

With Givens expected to spend much of his time on the road, away from the court promoting the new team and selling tickets, it would fall on his assistant, Buddy Cate, to run the practice sessions in his absence.

"I had been coaching at Tennessee Wesleyan," recalls the Cleveland, Tennessee native. "Givens called and I went with him. My first year contract was $10,000.

"I never will forget meeting Mamie, Joe and Ziggy. If Ziggy liked you, Mamie liked you, and Ziggy really liked Joy, my wife."

Cate also remembers that Mamie called all of the shots with the Colonels. "She always seemed to have something going on with somebody," Cate laughed. "And I remember that when Gene (Rhodes) came on as the coach, he didn't get along with her at all."

Cate talked about those first three days of tryouts the Colonels staged at Bellarmine College, and the more than 50 players who envisioned making the team.

"That first year we had four college All-Americans on the bench that couldn't really play at this level," Cate says. "We had great guards, but our big men inside weren't able to really help us. That's the way the ABA was at first, lots of good guards."

Cate thought a lot of Darel Carrier. "Darel was such a physical player," he said. "It seemed like after every game I was taking him to the hospital to get something sewed up or x-rayed."

He also talked about the relationship Carrier and Kendall Rhine had with the Gregorys, especially Carrier. "Darel and Kendall lived out at the Gregory's house. Darel did lots of farm work for them and they really loved him," Cate said. "He backhoed, did everything they needed. There was some talk that Darel got special treatment from the Gregorys. People definitely talked about it some."

Talking some more about the Gregorys, Cate says that for the most part people really tried to make over them, but that he just tried to treat them like a neighbor. "You didn't call her Mamie until she was ready and told you to," Cate said, referring to Mamie's wishes to be called Mrs. Gregory. "One day she said, 'Damn it, Buddy, call me Mamie."

PENNY ANN EARLY

The 1968-69 season saw the Colonels go to a gimmick of their own, and it took special league approval to pull it off.

Penny Ann Early, a 25-year-old would-be jockey, had recently been notified that three previously assigned mounts had been taken away when the male jockeys at Churchill Downs refused to ride against her.

Because of all the local attention the apparent boycott of Early received, the Colonels public relations director, Charlie Mastin, jumped on the possibility of making her a part of the team, if only for a short time — a very short time. On November 27, 1968, she officially became the first female to play in a men's professional basketball game

Colonels General Manager William Motsch told *Courier-Journal* and *Times* writer Marvin Gay, Jr. that the team had every intention to see that Penny Ann Early became the first woman to appear in a major league basketball game.

"We sympathize with Miss Early in her hopes to be a jockey and we want to help her." Motsch said. "She still intends to be one, so we signed her only to a short-term contract." Years later he recalled that it was $1,000 or $2,000 they paid her.

Motsch, in an effort not to mislead anyone, pointed out that Early's game appearance would be extraordinarily brief. He said she would wear the usual green and white Colonel colors and possibly wear a skirt instead of shorts.

Early had requested the No. 3 on her uniform. This, she said, would represent the three horses she did not get to ride at Churchill Downs.

Of course a separate dressing room was assigned to Early, on the second floor of the Convention Center. As delighted as the Colonels organization was with the promotion, few locals understood how such an event would help her become a jockey.

Miss Early's signing did not set well with Arthur Brown, owner of the New York Nets. He didn't think Commissioner Mikan had the authority to approve such a contract.

Brown offered that this was special, and when something special or unusual came up, it was up to the owners, and not Mikan. "If the league lets her play, there's no reason for having an ABA," Brown said.

Motsch pointed out that the Colonels were one player under the league's player limit, but to further get under the New York Net owner's skin, Early traveled with the team to New York, not to play, but to be introduced to the crowd and eastern media. Although dressed in a sleeveless, above the knee black dress, she attempted two shots at halftime in front of the crowd at Long Island Arena. She missed both.

By all appearances Penny Ann Early would not be a threat when the Colonels returned home to play the Anaheim Amigos.

One New York writer went as far to say that Miss Early's most impressive statistics were her 34-22-35 figure.

Mastin stayed close to Early, as she was overwhelmed by New York writers and photographers. She quickly pointed out that she didn't know anything about basketball, but that when Mastin came to her with the proposal she thought it would be a good way to prove a point.

"I don't want to wear one of those undershirts," she said when asked about her uniform. She proclaimed that she was not publicity hungry, but that the team just offered to help out. Mastin explained that the ploy was more of a sympathy gesture than anything else. "I'm an introvert and I never expected the public to take so much interest in me," she said. "All I really want to be is a jockey."

Louisville Times sports editor Dean Eagle agreed with some of the naysayers, in saying that Early's appearance was stooping to burlesque depths and questioned why the ABA was so desperate.

Eagle even compared it to major league baseball's Bill Veech stunt of sending midget Eddie Gaedel to bat for his St. Louis Browns. But the Colonels stunt, he said, was even more bizarre. At least Gaedel batted only once, and drew a base on balls. "We would advise the Colonels to stick to basketball and Miss Early to stay with racing, where even the Supreme Court will defend her rights," Eagle concluded.

After her few seconds on the hardwood she didn't return to the bench as might be expected, but instead she was presented a basketball by Mastin. Even more booing included one fan who became so obnoxious that Louisville Mayor Kenneth Schmied's personal bodyguard led the out-of-hand fan from the arena.

Although her official stats show she played one minute, everything else was zeros. She never attempted a shot, didn't get a rebound, and in fact, never even bounced the ball. Probably no one could recall that the Colonels were defeated by the Los Angeles Stars 111-107 that night in overtime.

It would be a complete disservice to Penny Ann Early, and the Colonels, too, by not delving into the real reason she is a footnote to professional basketball history.

Make no mistake about it, she was signed to a contract for one reason only, to sell tickets. Coach Gene Rhodes for sure was against it, thinking he didn't need a distraction like this. But behind the scenes, Mamie Gregory was for it, and since she had the checkbook, that's what counted.

Lost in all the hubbub was the plight of female riders who wanted to do more than ride in half-mile races at county fairs. It is ironic that Early found it easier to get into a men's professional basketball game than climb on a saddle and race against them at Churchill Downs. She had become the first officially licensed female jockey in the United States, but couldn't race.

Eventually Early got to ride against the guys, and over the years she had a mediocre racing career, eventually quitting to become a trainer. However, in 1974 she attempted a comeback, only to suffer a terrible fall that broke her arm, ankle, wrist and several ribs.

CHARLIE RUTER

For all nine of the years of the Kentucky Colonels' existence, Charlie Ruter had perhaps the best seat in the house, at least for all of the home games.

As the team's official score keeper, his mid-court position allowed him to see and hear things that others didn't. Sitting alongside PA man John Tong and timekeeper Rosie Rozel, the three of them referred to themselves as "our table."

Ruter was a Louisville boy who played basketball well enough in high school to earn some playing time for coach Diddle at Western Kentucky State Teachers' College back in the '40s.

Even after college, Ruter stayed interested in sports, particularly basketball and track. Pick-up games at the YMCA were a regular occurrence, and as an official at local track and field competitions, he eventually became a world renowned Olympic official in track and field meets.

Charlie Ruter's name as the official scorekeeper of a basketball game most certainly gave it legitimacy.

He worked 50 straight high school Louisville Invitational Tournaments, 41 Boys High School State Tournaments, 12 Girls' State Tournaments, and every Mason-Dixon Track and Field Games since 1961.

"I've seen some pretty unusual things over my career," laughed the 91-year-old Ruter. "There was the time in Freedom Hall when the guy fell out of the ceiling onto the floor while the teams were warming up."

Apparently an individual had made his way to the catwalk area above the playing court, and upon making a misstep on one of the rafters plunged to the floor.

"Some way he grabbed the flag and slid to the floor," Ruter continued. "He almost hit Louie Dampier. I thought the guy was dead."

Ruter says Johnny Givens, whom he had known from his Western days, was just a wild man that first few months of coaching the Colonels. "It was common for Johnny to run up in the stands after someone," he said. "This guy just kept yapping at him, and Johnny finally had heard enough and off he ran after him … the craziest thing you ever saw."

And then there were the coaches.

"Our table got along with them all," he said. "We decided we'd not get involved with personnel things. We just listened. Of course the three of us talked among ourselves."

Ruter remembers Babe McCarthy's take on dealing with professional players. "I always thought Babe enjoyed the college game much more than the pros," he says. "He said the son-of-a-bitches (players) were making more money than he was and they wouldn't listen to anything he had to say."

Ruter called Joe Mullaney "a good Irish lad," and as for Frank Ramsey, he was with the Colonels "only for a short time."

"Gene Rhodes and Hubie Brown were both really good coaches," he continued. "But Brown was without question the best ever."

He was also working the table when jockey Penny Ann Early checked into the Colonels lineup. With flash bulbs popping, he motioned her officially into the game against the Los Angeles Stars.

But that same night Ruter was drawn into a bit of controversy when Stars' coach Bill Sharman protested long and loud that Kentucky's Sam Smith should not get two free throws with 38 seconds left in overtime and the Stars up 108-106.

Sharman screamed that Ruter had misled him into ordering his players to foul Smith, only because he believed the Colonels would shoot only one free throw.

It turned out, however, to be the Stars second foul in the final two minutes, which by the rules allowed Smith the two free throws. He missed the first, made the second, and Los Angeles went on to win 111-107.

There were a couple of exhibition games of which Ruter has good memories, not because of anything that happened on the floor, but to him. "We traveled by bus over to Lexington to play a game at Memorial Coliseum," he said. "I thought I was dressed pretty good. I had on one of those, I think you call it, leisure suits back then. You know, the top kind of went with the bottom. I ran into coach Rupp. He looked at me and said 'my Gawd, Ruter, do you have to wear your pajamas to keep score?'"

There was the other exhibition game at Fort Knox. "John Tong was doing the PA," he said. "Here we were on an Army post with 4 or 5,000 people in the stands, and Tong announces that the official scorer for tonight's game is Charles Melton Ruter, Commander U.S. Navy Retired. I got booed pretty good."

"Dan Issel," he said. "Our table all agreed John Y. had made a big mistake when he sold him. "He was a good businessman," Ruter said of Brown. "But there was no one who thought selling Issel was the thing to do. But of course John Y. got all of his money back by selling off the players individually. He was all about business."

Mike Storen made a good impression on Ruter, and so did David Vance. "I had a lot of confidence in both of those gentlemen," he said. "Storen ran a tight ship, and I remember he wanted Rosie to dress up a little more at the official table. Rosie didn't like it, so he quit."

Of course Ruter had his take on Joe and Mamie Gregory. "I got along with both of them," says Ruter. "But Mamie and her dog were really a pair. She'd get it an ice cream cone and both of them would eat off of it. John Tong told me it made him sick to watch it.

"But you know what? If Mamie had sent Ziggy to the scorer's table, I'd have checked him into the game. After all, she owned the team."

Chapter Four
Pink Lloyd or Pink Floyd?

Lloyd Gardner

Many youngsters dream of making the team, any team. It doesn't always have to be an athletic team, either. It could be pep bands, debate teams, speech teams or, well, you get the picture.

In Lloyd Gardner's case it was all about making his high school basketball team in the late '50s at Fairdale. But, when his coach Forest "Frosty" Able cut him from the team, looking back on it, Lloyd says it was the most defining moment of his life. Give Able credit because he knew what talent he had in the 5'8" freshman, who could neither jump very high nor shoot very well. That's why he told Gardner he'd like for him to be the team's manager and trainer. Lloyd's life was forever changed, and Able's judgment of talent set the youngster on a path that might as well have been pointed toward heaven.

"He told me he'd enroll me in Creamers Trainers' School, and he'd get me a scholarship at Western working for Mr. Diddle," Gardner said of Able.

True to his word, following graduation from Fairdale in 1962, Gardner headed to Bowling Green, and in 1963 moved into Diddle Dorm, Hilltopper Coach Ed Diddle's private home that had been expanded a few years earlier so the coach could keep a close eye on "his boys."

Lloyd had made the team again. Thoroughly enjoying his life at Western, and most of all his association with the players and Mr. Diddle as a student manager and trainer, life couldn't get much better.

But as often happens in life, things change. Mr. Diddle decided to retire, after forty-two years on the Hill. Becoming one of the winningest college coaches in history, his Hilltopper basketball teams literally put Western Kentucky University on the map from coast to coast.

So in the summer of 1964, Johnny Oldham, a former All-American at the school, was lured away from Tennessee Tech to return to his alma mater hoping to resurrect a program that had slipped to back-to-back 5-16 records.

Lloyd was back home in Fairdale for the summer when he heard the news. He immediately put a call into the new coach, only to hear from Oldham that he planned to bring his own managers. Being persistent, Gardner asked Oldham if he could drive to Bowling Green to talk to him. Oldham agreed and almost immediately Gardner was on his way.

"I realized right away I'd made a mistake, and wanted to correct it." Oldham said later about changing his mind about Gardner. "He told me two things that day before I left," Gardner said.

"Don't ever lie to me, and keep yourself out of trouble." Gardner had no problem with either of Oldham's demands.

As Gardner finished his studies and basketball team duties at Western, Joe and Mamie Gregory had just purchased the franchise rights to start a team in Louisville in a brand new professional basketball league called the American Basketball Association.

By their own admission, few involved with the new team knew much about running a pro team, much less coaching one.

It was in the spring of '67 and Gene Rhodes was an assistant coach at Western when he went to Gardner and asked if he would like to be his trainer if he became the head coach of the new Kentucky Colonels.

But Rhodes didn't take the job. At least not then.

"I then met with Johnny Givens who had just been hired as their coach." He said, "'Lloyd, I really need an assistant coach.'" Givens told Gardner that as the new coach he would be traveling around the state making lots of speeches, and needed someone to run the practices when he was away. The person he hired was Buddy Cate, who had played with Givens for Mr. Diddle at Western back in the late '40s.

By this time Rhodes had become the head coach in that initial year after a dismal 5-12 start by Givens, and Gardner was teaching full time at Fern Creek and Valley high schools.

Still, that didn't stop Gardner in his pursuit of becoming part of the Kentucky Colonels. Even though he was denied the job, he still worked the tryout camp and home games for Givens.

"I went to Johnny and asked if I could help," he says. "I was at all of the home games and taped both of the teams, the Colonels and their opponents. I did it for no pay. I became very good friends with Larry Conley, Howard Bayne and several other players, and once in a while they would give me extra tickets and I'd sell them on the street before the game for two bucks. It made pocket change."

The next year Gardner helped Rhodes with organizing the Colonels training camp for the 1968-69 season at the Masonic Home Gym. On the surface everything looked good for Gardner to officially become a Kentucky Colonel, but there were still issues.

Gardner was an Industrial Arts teacher and this was the Vietnam War era. As a teacher his job was deemed critical by the Selective Service, and in plain and simple terms he was told he could continue to teach or get drafted, and the latter usually meant a tour in Vietnam.

The Colonels would have to wait once more.

Rhodes then hired his former St. X High School manager and trainer, Bill Antonini.

Soon after, Gardner was back at Fairdale as a full-time teacher and assistant to his old coach, Frosty Able. Life was good. He was around the game he loved, and not only was he coaching, he was also the trainer for all of the school's athletic teams.

But things had also changed within the Colonels organization. Rhodes had been let go by new general manager Mike Storen and replaced as the Colonels coach by Alex Groza, who had stepped out of the front office for a two-game stint as the coach until Frank Ramsey could be brought in. Not long after, Ramsey had a run-in with trainer Bill Antonini. After returning home on a late Sunday night, February 13, 1971, Antonini got off the plane and headed to the newspapers, blasting Ramsey, and quit the team.

"The very next day Alex called," Gardner said. "He said he needed me to help them get through the season. I was thrilled to death, and told him I'd help until he got somebody.

"When I replaced Antonini midway through the season, I was hired as a part-time trainer. The days that we didn't travel out of town I was in my classroom teaching woodshop at Fairdale High School. About a week after the season was over Storen called me at home and asked me to come to his office. Usually when Mike subpoenaed you, you were very apprehensive. I met him in his office and, it was at that time he asked me if I would be interested in becoming the team's full-time trainer, travel secretary, and equipment manager.

"These were the duties handled by all the other trainers in professional basketball. Mike then added one more assignment. He told me that I would need to join the rest of the office staff and sell season tickets for six-eight weeks. This wasn't something that I really wanted to do, but I had dreamed of this profession since I was in the ninth grade in 1958. I was making about $6,500 teaching and he offered me $7,500. On top of that, the players had just voted me a one-half share of playoff money that was about $900. After talking with my former wife, Sandy, I jumped at the chance of a lifetime. There were only 28 professional basketball teams in the ABA/NBA. Just think, I was one of the 28 trainers!"

Schedule-wise there were nine regular season road games remaining when Gardner wrote to the Jefferson County School Board asking for a leave of absence for those nine games.

"I left them my lesson plans and everything," he said. "It was approved. It might have helped that the Colonels scorekeeper was Charlie Ruter, who just happened to be chairman of the school board."

Those nine games, however, turned into 23.

"We were runner-up in the division to the Virginia Squires, and lost in a seven game final at Utah."

When the season concluded, Storen called and Gardner heard what he had been waiting for a long time, a full-time offer from a professional basketball team.

Finally, Lloyd Gardner, the kid from Fairdale, was a Kentucky Colonel, the professional basketball kind.

And what about his nickname, Pink?

"When I first started, Dan Issel always called me Floyd instead of Lloyd. The Colonels had recently traded Bobby Croft to Denver for Dan Hester. I was taping Dan's ankles when Hester walked in and he looked at me and said, 'Who are you?' Dan replied, 'This is Floyd.' Hester blurted out, 'Oh, Pink Floyd?' From that very moment, the nickname "Pink" was what everyone called me, and in the later years it was more "Pinky." The name has stuck with me and still stands today in the sports community for those that know me.

"It was the end of June, I was working at my desk when Mike motioned me to come into his administrative center. You never knew what he wanted, but it was always one of two things, good or bad. He told me that his trainer with the Indiana Pacers, Bernie Lareau, was in his second year as the head trainer for the Chicago Bears. He wanted me to gain more expertise in the treatment of athletic injuries and he wanted me to go to the Bears' training camp. The pre-season workouts were held on the St. Joseph College campus in Rensselaer, Indiana. I flew to Lafayette, Indiana, and caught a Trailway bus to Reynolds. I sat on the steps of an old country store for three hours and listened and watched old men whittle and tell stories. I had no idea I was only 13 miles away from the campus. By the time my bus came, it was totally dark. I asked the bus driver if he knew where the Chicago Bears training camp was being held. He said he did. He stopped the bus and told me to cross in front of the bus and walk down that road. I got off the bus and crossed the road; there wasn't a light anywhere. It was pitch black! I was scared to death! I walked, suitcase in hand, until I saw a dorm with lights on. I went inside and there they were, players as big as Mt. Rushmore. They guided me to the training room and there I met Bernie Lareau.

"Believe me, I got a lot of experience. As trainers, we started treating injuries at 6 a.m. We got 30-45 minutes for breakfast at 7 a.m., then went back to the training room preparing for 10 a.m. practice. All players were required to get their ankles taped. We were taping 100 players twice a day. We were also taping about 20 knees, as knee braces were not very reliable in those days. We took a short lunch break, then went back to the taping table. Practice would be at 3 p.m. After dinner we would go back to the training room, which was in the basement of the dorm, and perform special treatments on injured players. Gale Sayers and Dick Butkus were both recovering from knee surgeries. One of my tasks was to stay inside with Sayers while he exercised his knee that he was rehabilitating. While he was exercising, he was reviewing the script (which he must approve) for the movie "Brian's Song." This real-life movie was based on the relationship between teammates Brian Piccolo and Sayers, and the bond established when Piccolo discovered that he was dying of cancer. Parts of the film were being taped on the St. Joseph campus.

"The first weekend I was there, the Bears scrimmaged the College All-Stars with Stanford's Jim Plunkett, Ohio State's John Brockington, and Penn State's Jack Ham, to name a few. They were to play the NFL Champion Baltimore Colts the next weekend on Chicago's Soldier Field.

"My second weekend we scrimmaged the St. Louis Cardinals (now the Arizona Cardinals) on the St. Joseph field. On Friday, the day before the scrimmage, Bears' head coach Jim Dooley told the players that everyone that is injured and cannot play tomorrow must stay this weekend and receive treatment. We had a lot of players injured, but after three weeks without seeing wives and girlfriends, everybody wanted to go home for a day and a half. Saturday morning, Doctor Fox, George Halas' friend and the team doctor, came in the training room carrying something that looked like a toolbox. He ran me out, and shut the door ... every player played in that scrimmage.

"My third and final week we boarded buses on Friday evening and headed to Milwaukee for our first pre-season game against the Green Bay

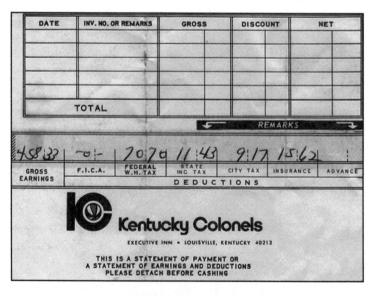

Check stub of Lloyd Gardner

Packers at Milwaukee County Stadium. Friday night several of us went to see the movie 'MASH." Jack Concannon, the Bears' quarterback, was the quarterback in the movie.

"The Packers beat the Bears on Saturday night, and I flew back to Louisville on Sunday morning. Before I left, Bernie Lareau gave me a paycheck for three weeks, and when I got home Mike had also paid me."

Gardner says as a general manager, Storen was tough. He did evaluations on every person in the Colonels organization.

"I got excellent on everything except bench conduct," says Gardner. "Every time I got a technical foul, I'd be in his office the next morning for a butt chewing and an ABA $50 fine."

American Basketball Association

1700 Broadway
New York, N.Y. 10019
(212)765-6880

October 6, 1971

Mr. L. Gardner
Kentucky Colonels
Executive Inn
Louisville, Kentucky 40213

Dear Lloyd,

A sum of $50.00 will be deducted from your next paycheck by your team as payment for the technical foul(s) which you received in the Carolina   @ Kentucky   game of October 2nd. This is pursuant to the playing rules and By-Laws of the American Basketball Association and approved by the Trustees.

Your General Manager has received a copy of this notice and is aware that this fine must be received by the League Office by October 19, 1971   or you will be suspended and not eligible for any participation in the League.

Sincerely,

AMERICAN BASKETBALL ASSOCIATION

Thurlo E. McCrady
Executive Director

TEM/pd
cc: Mike Storen

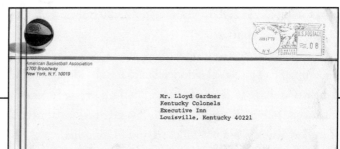

CHAPTER FIVE
A SHOOTER'S SHOOTER

LOUIE DAMPIER

By all rights Louie Dampier never should have been a Kentucky Colonel, or for that matter probably never even a Kentucky Wildcat where he was an All-American.

Dampier had been an All-Stater at Southport High School, just south of Indianapolis, and it was naturally assumed that any Hoosier prep player good enough to make the Indiana All-Stars would go to Indiana University, or at worst Purdue or Notre Dame.

Indiana high school basketball is known for great shooters: Oscar Robertson, Terry Dischinger, Jimmy Rayl, Ron Borham, the Van Arsdale twins, Rick Mount and Larry Bird. For sure Dampier fit the mold.

"I was not heavily recruited," Dampier says years later. "My uncle Louie took me up to Bloomington to see their coach, Branch McCracken. We were having a conversation and my uncle told me to step outside the room. I don't know what was said between him and Coach McCracken, but when I came back in they offered me a scholarship."

For whatever reason the offer didn't seem sincere to Dampier, and his allegiance was to UK assistant Neil Reed who had been staying in contact with him that led to his signing with the Wildcats. It was Adolph Rupp and Kentucky's gain for sure as Dampier became one of the school's all-time greats. Later on Dampier would like to have been an Indiana Pacer, but by fate it was not to be.

Dampier had played on the 1966 NCAA runner-up Kentucky team, and because no starter was over 6'6", the team became known as "Rupp's Runts. "Graduating in 1967, he was drafted by the NBA Cincinnati Royals where he would be required to try out in order to make the team. On the other hand the Kentucky Colonels drafted him with a guaranteed spot on the roster, and a Lexington attorney, Lawson King, helped Dampier negotiate his first professional contract. Dampier recalls that his attorney and Colonels executive Bill Motsch worked out a three year contract that paid $12,000 a year plus a $2,500 bonus. On June 7, 1967, he became the first player to sign a Colonel contract.

However, there was a problem.

Dampier had joined a National Guard unit headquartered in Danville, and he had been notified that he would have to report for basic training in late summer at Fort Campbell, Kentucky.

In what helped Dampier solidify his Kentucky connection following basic training, he was sent to Fort Knox just a few miles south of Louisville.

And wouldn't you know it, he was assigned to play basketball for the post team where another former UK player, Pat Doyle, was the coach.

"They pulled some strings to keep me at Fort Knox because I was supposed to be sent to Fort Sill," remembers Dampier. "So I was playing on a team at Fort Knox, and on the weekends I was playing for the Kentucky Colonels."

Although Dampier was on the initial Colonels roster he didn't join them full time until November 24, when he was released from active duty and began playing in all their games. For the season he managed to play in 72 of the 78 regular season games and all five in the playoffs.

So there he was, Louie Dampier, in the beginning with Indiana written all over him, a former UK All-American, now playing for the Kentucky Colonels, whose arch rival in the ABA was none other than the Indiana Pacers.

"It was the toughest place for me to play on the road," Dampier recalled. "Of course I knew the players and coaches, but the crowd really let me have it."

Traitor was one of the words he would frequently hear from the big crowds in Indianapolis.

"It was probably from my Uncle Louie," laughed Dampier years later in recalling that his uncle had wanted him to play at I.U.

Dampier played for every Colonels coach, beginning with Johnny Givens and ending with Hubie Brown. In between there were Gene Rhodes, Alex Groza, Frank Ramsey, Joe Mullaney, and Babe McCarthy. And even though over his nine-year Colonels career most of the coaches and management felt like they'd be able to bring in a guard who would be good enough to replace No. 10 in the lineup, they never did. He was that good and that consistent for that long a period.

It would be difficult to prove that over the nine-year life of the Kentucky Colonels that Louie Dampier would not be considered the face of the team.

After all, he was there from the beginning to the end with the same team. Denver's Byron Beck was the only other ABA player who could claim such longevity.

With some 81 players, including jockey Penny Ann Early, listed on the Colonels all-time roster, there was only one who crossed paths with them all, and that was Dampier. Any time there is a conversation about the good old days of the Colonels, the names of Issel, Gilmore, Carrier and Ligon are mentioned. But for sure, the name of Louie Dampier is at the top of any list involving the Colonels.

And in more ways than one.

When the dust settled and the Colonels were no more, Little Louie not only led the Colonels, but incredibly is the ABA all-time leader in points and assists. With 13,726 points and 4,044 assists, and a career 19-point scoring average, it shows just how consistent he really was. What was perhaps even more impressive about his numbers was that he played in 728 games and missed only 13.

For sure it was Dampier and Carrier who first elevated the 3-point shot in professional basketball. No guard tandem did it better in any league.

As might be expected, Dampier also shot it well from the foul line, hitting 2,352 out of 2,849 for a solid 83%. At one time he held the ABA and NBA mark when he hit 57 in a row during the 1970-71 season.

While many basketball purists were not particularly fond of the multi-colored basketball being used as a gimmick in the upstart league, Dampier didn't seem to mind what color it was.

"The color of the ball was not a problem," said Dampier. "The texture was slick until it got worn down, but the color showed the rotation of my shot and that was good."

Pinky Gardner, in verifying what Dampier had said about the feel of the ball and its slickness, recalls that as the Colonels trainer, one of his responsibilities was to give the game ball to the officials for their inspection. "It was almost always the oldest ball that would be taken off the ball rack for use in the game," says Gardner.

To further point out how much under control Dampier played, one would have to look no further than his personal foul statistics. For his 728 Colonels career games, he committed a total of 1,633 fouls. That's slightly more than two a game.

And on closer inspection he only fouled out of three games. Three games! Unbelievable! Compare that to Carrier's 16 foul-outs in 334 games.

But what about technical fouls?

"I only got one, ever," he recalls. "John Vanak called it on me and it was later rescinded."

When Gene Rhodes had his near boycott episode when Colonels players signed a petition wanting the coach gone, Dampier managed to distance himself from it all by not signing anything. "It just didn't feel right," he said years later.

Probably the most controversial situation Dampier found himself in occurred shortly after Frank Ramsey had taken over as head coach in 1970 following the dismissal of Rhodes and the two-game coaching career of Alex Groza.

Ramsey had recently completed a Hall-of-Fame career with the Celtics, and most of his coaching knowledge would come from two of the all-time biggest names in coaching, Adolph Rupp and Red Auerbach. Never having coached before, any practice, game plans, strategies and anything else about running a pro-basketball team would have to come from his experience as a player with those coaches. Therefore, it was probably a legitimate question when one of the local Louisville sportswriters asked Dampier about Ramsey as a coach.

"He asked me if Ramsey is still learning as a coach," says Dampier. "I kept saying, 'I'm not going to answer that. He kept on and on asking me, and finally I said, 'yes.'"

Dampier actually simplified, and even downplayed the situation that had occurred involving the quote in talking about it several years later.

Gardner had his take on it.

He recalls there had been quite an uproar in the newspapers the day before Dampier's quote appeared. And although it was indeed his quote, it was printed as an "unidentified source." The day before, head trainer Bill Antonini had been dismissed from the Colonels by Ramsey following a road trip. The ex-trainer had blasted Ramsey after the firing pretty good, so the coach and general manager Mike Storen were just a bit sensitive about anything being written or said concerning the Colonels organization.

The coach and G.M. called a meeting to discuss a few of the comments in the paper. "They wanted to know who the source was," says Gardner. "When no one admitted to it, they refused to end the meeting until somebody fessed-up. It lasted over two hours."

Finally Dampier stepped up. "Ramsey and Storen told me not to worry about it and said there would be no repercussions," said Dampier. "But, I know the next game I was replaced as captain."

Dampier's ABA memories are many.

"I remember the night Johnny Givens ran up into the stands after some guy that threw an egg on the floor," he said in describing an incident involving the first Colonels coach in a game at the Convention Center.

Although Givens was relieved as coach after a 5-12 start in the ABA, Dampier remembers Givens telling Cotton Nash after one of the losses, "If you play like you did tonight we won't win another game." Nash then told him, "If you coach like you did tonight we won't win another game."

And then there was Joe Mullaney.

"I really liked him, but I really didn't like playing for him," Dampier said. "The only thing he talked about was basketball, never anything else. And during a game he continuously walked up and down in front of the bench screaming, 'What are you doing to me?'"

Dampier recalled a night when Babe McCarthy had been over to his house for a party.

"He was pulled over by the police on the way home," laughs Dampier. "Hoping they'd let him go, he told the police that he had been to Louie Dampier's house, like that was going to help him with the police."

There's even a story he tells after Rupp joined Ellie Brown and her all-female board as Vice-President of the Colonels.

"We were on the road and Dan (Issel) and I met Coach Rupp in the hotel bar," he said. "Coach Rupp ordered a bloody Mary and Dan said, "Coach, I thought you were a bourbon man? Coach told us the doctor told him to quit drinking the hard stuff."

Another UK connection to the ABA was Cliff Hagan. Anyone who knows anything about basketball in Kentucky knows Hagan and Ramsey are considered to be among the best to ever play for the Big Blue.

Although playing at UK a little more than a decade apart, Dampier and Hagan knew each other as members of an elite brotherhood of University of Kentucky All-Americans. A mutual respect for what each had accomplished in not only their collegiate, but professional careers as well, was to be expected.

That's why years later Dampier still is not sure about a comment Hagan made to him prior to a Colonels game in Lexington at Memorial Coliseum against Hagan's Dallas team.

"He told me I needed to shave my mustache," recalls Dampier. "Said it's not the All-American look, and then during the game as I was cutting across the middle on offense, he jumped out and put a forearm in my neck. I just didn't understand it. It was totally unnecessary, and I thought why is one of UK's guys doing this to another one?"

Like everyone else, Dampier was shocked when he learned the Colonels were not going to be included in the NBA expansion. He never had really gotten over the departure of Issel the year before and now, after nine years with the same team, he was not ready to give up basketball. Still playing at a high level, he hoped to now match his skills against other guards in the NBA.

Dampier had always been loyal to the Colonels, and although he could probably have jumped to the old league along the way, he never really thought about doing it. "I was happy in Louisville and never wanted to negotiate with any of the NBA teams," he said.

But now he would, for certain, be playing somewhere else. He had been playing basketball in the state of Kentucky from 1963 through 1976, and maybe, just maybe, he might be going back to his home state of Indiana to play for the Pacers. The one-time "traitor," as he was called when the Colonels traveled to Indianapolis, really wanted to play out his career there.

"Yeah, I really wanted to play there," he said. "I called Bobby Leonard (Pacer's coach), but he told me they wanted a big guy, so when it came their turn they took Wil Jones."

Forget the fact that Dampier had once scored 54 points against the Pacers. At that time it was the ABA single game record.

Dampier's disappointment didn't last long, however. He was picked by San Antonio, a team he was very familiar with, obviously from all of their ABA encounters.

Doug Moe, a longtime ABA player and now the coach of San Antonio, had earned Dampier's respect over the years as one of the "hardest working guys in the ABA," and in turn, he knew the little Colonel would be an asset for his teams' effort in transitioning into the NBA.

"I was really glad I went to a former ABA team," says Dampier of the team that paid $25,000 for his draft rights. "I knew them and they knew me. I didn't have to prove myself all over again."

Former Colonels teammate Mike Gale and friend Billy Paultz were two Spurs players Dampier knew quite well, so at least the move to the Texas town would perhaps be a little less stressful after all of his years of living in Louisville and Lexington, and just a few miles from family he had in Indiana.

Dampier's three years in San Antonio caught him on the downhill slide of his best basketball. But by then he had become the ultimate team player.

For his entire career, Louie Dampier's skills, even as good as his statistics were, were often overlooked. From his college days at the University of Kentucky, playing alongside with the likes of Pat Riley, Larry Conley, Tommy Kron and Thad Jaracz, Dampier was the epitome of consistency. He passed, shot, rebounded, and even defended. Playing for Adolph Rupp, who was often reluctant to pass on praise to individuals, Dampier received the ultimate compliment from his coach after he graduated. The legendary coach said Dampier was the greatest shooter he had ever seen. And who is the best shooter Dampier has seen? Decades later, without hesitating, he answered, "Darel Carrier."

David Vance recalled watching Dampier and Carrier in practice. "They played HORSE from behind the 3-point line, he said. "And it was something to see, bombs, one after the other."

The respect his coaches, teammates, and opponents had for him was unparalleled. "Louie Dampier was as good a clutch player as I've ever seen. He was phenomenal when it came to taking and making the shot when the game was on the line," former Coach Hubie Brown said.

Dave Vance had his take on Dampier and the fact that he had such a productive career. "It seemed like before every season there would be conversation about this player or that player coming in and replacing Louie. But none of them did," offered Vance. "And you know why they didn't, because none of them could shoot like Louie."

In the Colonels formative years, Dampier and Carrier were all about shooting, especially the three. But as the Colonels upgraded their inside talent over the years, ultimately bringing in the likes of Issel, Gilmore and Wil Jones, Dampier's game evolved from a shooter to playmaker. But remember what Hubie Brown said: "When the Colonels needed a basket, it was in Louie's hands."

It was his ability to adjust his game that allowed him to have what should be a Hall-of-Fame career. And possibly some day it will be.

Dampier's shot was so pure that it was easy for him to detect a rim that might have been just a little too high or a little too low.

"When a goal wasn't right, he would have me measure it," says Gardner. "And when he asked me, it was always off somewhere. You've got to keep in mind that back then in the early days some of the teams put their 3-point line down with tape and sometimes shoe polish. It was pretty common for something to be off."

Without question, Dampier's better days were behind him when he got to San Antonio. By then he recognized that the NBA was more like a business and not as enjoyable as the ABA.

In his three seasons stint with the Spurs, Dampier played in 232 games, averaging 6.7 points, a far cry from his Colonels days. His field goal percentage for those games was 49 percent. Blatantly missing from his stats were 3-point goals. There were none, as the NBA was a few years away from implementing that shot.

So in 1979, Louie Dampier's basketball playing days were over, but not necessarily his basketball days.

Returning to Louisville, his adopted hometown, he entered private business. But in 1998, his phone rang and it was Dan Issel, who had become general manager of the Denver Nuggets.

Dampier was on his way to Denver, not to play, but to coach.

CHAPTER SIX
A HILLTOPPER CONNECTION

DAREL CARRIER

A basketball purist, particularly of the ABA, cannot talk about the Colonels without mentioning Darel Carrier. He has the distinction of being the third player signed by the Colonels in 1967, soon after the Gregorys paid for the rights to start a professional basketball team.

From the outset of his basketball career, when as a high school freshman playing against Sunfish he scored 64 points for Bristow, a small school just outside of Bowling Green. Carrier's thought process on the basketball court was shoot first, pass later.

It's almost like he was born shooting a basketball, and by the time he left high school he had scored 3,148 points, and was being heavily recruited by many of the collegiate basketball powerhouses. But for Darel and his family it was a package deal. Twin brother Harel, not as tall and certainly not the shooter his brother was, was touted for his defense and passing ability. Western Kentucky coach Ed Diddle was more than happy to oblige both Carriers with scholarships.

Individually at Western, Carrier had an outstanding career. As a sophomore he was on an NCAA team that included All-American Bobby Rascoe, Charlie Osborne and Harry Todd. And although his junior and senior years were two of the worst records ever posted in the school's history, going 5-16 in each, his individual stats were good enough for him to be listed on several All-American teams.

Carrier, like many stars in that era, decided after college to opt out of trying out for an NBA team, but instead signed on with the Bartlesville Phillips 66 Oilers in the AAU League. Here, basketball employees played against top flight competition during the season, and in off-season trained for a secure job with the company when their playing days were over. The Oilers already had Rascoe, as well as Glendale, Kentucky, native Jimmy Hagan, who had developed into a high scoring All-American while playing for Coach Johnny Oldham at Tennessee Tech in 1960.

Carrier picked up with the Oilers where he left off at Western, throwing up big numbers and even being selected for the Pan American Games.

But when the new ABA league started up and Carrier found out there would be a team in Kentucky, he forgot all about job security and headed back home.

Joe Gregory, always a basketball fan, was well aware of Darel Carrier and insisted that if there were good Hilltopper players out there, he wanted to do everything possible to make them a strong presence on his Kentucky Colonels team.

Carrier's initial contact with the Colonels came from Joe Hullett, who had been brought in to help quickly assemble a professional team. Hullett asked Carrier who else on the Phillips Oilers might be willing to make a move. "I brought Kendall Rhine with me," Carrier says of the 6'10" center that had played college ball at Rice University in Texas. "I also made them aware that Rascoe could still play, and they signed him."

Make no mistake about it, Carrier from the beginning occupied a special place in the hearts of Joe and Mamie Gregory. In their eyes he could do no wrong. Carrier and Rhine, in fact, lived on the Gregorys' property. "I was a farm boy from Bristow," said Carrier. "And it suited me just fine to run their part of the farm during the off-season. I did whatever they needed, and they took care of me. I enjoyed being around their million dollar dogs and million dollar horses."

One of those not real happy about Carrier's relationship with the owners of the Colonels was Gene Rhodes, who had taken over for fired coach Johnny Givens.

"Gene resented me knowing and getting along so well with them" said Carrier, who like Rhodes and Givens had played for Diddle at Western. "Gene and I were a lot alike. We were both hard-nose, but he kept making comments about me and the Gregorys."

Carrier says Rhodes never seemed to be happy with him, even recalling the night against Miami in 1969 when he scored 53 points, a franchise record at the time. "He sat me out half of one quarter," he said. "Gene was a good coach, but just couldn't relate to the players. We stayed upset with him and the way he would act in the dressing room, kicking and throwing things around."

Carrier did in fact have somewhat of an unusual relationship with Joe and Mamie Gregory, even to the point of them personally handling his contract. "I always had a no-cut contract," he said. "They pretty much took care of everything. It even included a gold Pontiac Grand Prix from Swope Pontiac."

Not only was Carrier a fan-favorite, but also Mamie's all-time favorite player. "The love-of-my life," she laughingly recalled years later.

To further point out Carriers place in the hearts of the Gregorys, you only had to look at what took place during a Colonels practice session. It was 1967 and former Murray State standout, Stew Johnson, who played for Cal Luther, was having some early-season success as a scorer and rebounder. Just as in games, tempers often flared in practice, and on this particular day, the former Murray and Western players were going at it pretty good. Johnson at 6'9" and Carrier at 6'3" had a built-in rivalry from their Ohio Valley Conference days, but it still was a surprise when Johnson suddenly threw a wild haymaker that caught Carrier in the head, resulting in a trip to the hospital to be stitched up.

For Johnson, it was the beginning of the end of his Colonels days. He was quickly traded to the New Jersey Americans in a straight player deal for Jim Caldwell.

Of course there are always two sides to a scuffle, and then there's the real reason. Carrier, never known to be one to tip-toe through the tulips, was a rough-and-tumble guard who liked to mix it up. Perhaps if it had been any owners other than the Gregorys, it might have been considered just another rough practice.

And then there was the time the Colonels played the Pacers in Indianapolis. Hardin McLane had been a successful high school coach at Elizabethtown (Kentucky) Catholic, and the Gregorys hired him to be a part of the organization's public relations team. He and his wife, Marilyn, traveled by car with Joe and Mamie up the road to see the two rivals play. As often happened at an

ABA game, a fight broke out. "We're sitting there with Joe and Mamie, and Darel Carrier is right in the middle of it," McLane recalls. "Mamie grabs my arm and says 'Hardin get out there and help Darel.' I said, 'Mamie, you don't pay me enough to go out there.'"

But once the Gregorys sold the team to the Wendell Cherry group things began to change.

Carrier's last contract with the Colonels was negotiated through general manager Mike Storen. But it didn't start out that way. "Bruce Miller was handling Issel's contract, and mine, too," Carrier said. "I had been holding out for a better contract, so Storen, Miller and I met about it. Storen and I worked it out ourselves without Miller's help, so I fired him right there on the spot."

Carrier had begun to suffer some back problems at this stage of his career, and as a result of the contract he had with the Colonels, when it was all said and done he had played an impressive five years while being paid for six.

Rick Mount, a former Indiana high school Mr. Basketball and Purdue All-American, was brought in from Indiana to replace Carrier after his back injury was too much to overcome.

Years later Carrier still thinks about that first year with the Colonels. And although he liked Givens as a coach, he felt like he lacked the skills required at the professional level of basketball.

There was a time when the team had to take matters into their own hands.

"We were getting ready to play at New Jersey," Carrier laughed. "We all got together in the parking lot at the hotel and decided to come up with a couple of our own plays. Bobby (Rascoe) and I set up a play we used with the Phillips Oilers. Givens didn't know any of this, but during the game we would holler out "special" and run it. We got some baskets off of it and pretty soon Johnny was yelling for us to run the special."

Following Rhodes' departure as coach in spite of a 10-5 record, Carrier seemed to thrive under new coach Frank Ramsey. "He believed in me," says Carrier. "He told me if I missed my first ten to keep shooting, because he knew I'd make the next ten."

It's here that Carrier likes to point out that though his reputation had been made as a shooter, it was defense that he delighted in talking about as a pro.

There was one night in particular that got a little testy for Carrier. The night before, on April 23, 1971, the Colonels beat the Virginia Squires 115-107 in what was said at the time to be the biggest win in franchise history. This gave the Colonels a 3-2 lead in these best-of-7 Eastern Division finals. The two teams returned the following night to Freedom Hall and game six.

The game, keep in mind, was the following night. No days off here, even when you traveled. The Colonels won as Issel scored 36 points and grabbed 21 boards. Did it surprise anyone that the game was interrupted by a fight between Goose Ligon and the Squires' Jim Eakins?

Carrier and former North Carolina great Charlie Scott also had words, harsh words. "He started pushing," Carrier told *Courier-Journal* writer Dick Beardsley. "So I told him to knock it off or I'd knock the %@?!X out of him."

Carrier continued, "So he started screaming, 'but you're holding and throwing elbows, and so I said 'Charlie the next time that happens, you tell me and I'll tell the official and see what he can do for you.

"I went over to the sideline to see if I should pop him. But I told Coach Ramsey, "He's already all shook up, so why pop him?"

From there the Colonels went to the ABA finals at Utah, where they lost in seven games. Years later Carrier recalled that even though his team lost, he was most proud of the defensive effort he had against Utah sharpshooter Glen Combs.

Combs, the son of legendary Carr Creek High School coach Morten Combs, had been a Kentucky All-Stater who played his college ball at Virginia Tech. Though not quite on par with the likes of Carrier and Dampier as a marksman, he was not far behind, and when he got on a roll he was very difficult to contain. "I liked to try to shut down the other team's best shooters," he said. "I would ask our coaches to let me guard certain players."

Carrier and his teammates had a difficult relationship with Warren Jabali, formerly known as Warren Armstrong. Jabali was an exceptional talent. Though only 6'2", he was always a scoring threat and ferocious rebounder. However, he had a difficult time getting along with teammates and coaches. "We would try to talk to him, and all he would do is just stare back at you," Carrier said. "I'll never forget Gene Rhodes trying to get Jabali to go into one of the games. He just sat there looking at Gene and never moving. Rhodes hollered out that he couldn't coach this guy."

Not long after, Jabali was traded to another of several teams he played for in the league. But in spite of Jabali's defiance, years later he was voted one of ABA's all-time best 30 players. Even though he created quite a stir with teammates and in the community, Jabali was never officially listed as a Kentucky Colonel.

Those who attended Colonel games in the early days at the Convention Center remember the oversized gong with Marathon printed on it. The gong and its sound became a big part of the game, especially when Carrier and Dampier would successfully launch one of their rainbow three pointers.

"We got 20 gallons of gas from Marathon for every three-point basket," said Carrier. "I told Louie we'd never have to buy a gallon of gas the rest of our lives. But they decided to give some of it to the rest of the team and that was all right with us."

As good as Carrier and Dampier were on the court, you might expect that there was a business deal just waiting to happen, one that would take the duo's popularity and convert it into advertising.

"A California firm contacted me and wanted to hook up with Louie and me for some promotions," remembered Carrier. "They were going to pay, of course. I told Mike Storen about it and he said why should I deal with them when he could get me a commercial in Louisville and not take a cut or anything?"

Storen, who had come to the Colonels as the general manager from the Indiana Pacers, had also worked with the Cincinnati Royals in the NBA. He knew his way around professional basketball, so Carrier left it up to him to land him a promotional contract.

Sure enough Storen delivered. But so did Fall City Beer. When Carrier came home one afternoon, he found cases upon cases of beer stacked on his front porch. "I never drank a beer in my life," he said. "I've always tried to do the right thing as a player. I couldn't tell people to drink beer and then go out and do basketball camps with kids. Fall City brought their big old truck and loaded it all up and hauled it off." So much for the commercial venture.

BOBBY RASCOE

Bobby Rascoe is one of the all-time great names in the history of basketball in Kentucky. From his high school days at Daviess County through his All-American years at Western Kentucky, he excelled at the highest level. So when he signed to play on that inaugural Kentucky Colonels team in 1967, it only added to the commitment Colonels management had made toward bringing in talented players with a local connection.

Rascoe was one of Mr. Diddle's boys at Western Kentucky. His career there places him among the best to ever play. In fact, his career per game point average ranks 4th of all-time. And when Diddle proclaimed that Bobby Rascoe was the most perfect player he had ever coached, it only added to just how talented the 6'4" guard really was.

A book, *Championship Basketball by 12 Great Coaches*, compiled and edited by Hardin McLane, says it all on pages 24-25.

Here's how Coach Diddle described Rascoe: "He did not have the physical equipment that a great player must have. He had very bad feet; he was not a very large boy; he did not have great speed. But he came to play, and he was a coach's dream. He wanted to be great. When Rascoe stepped on the basketball court, he exemplified the perfect basketball player."

Rascoe's 1958 Daviess County had lost to a St. X team, coached by Gene Rhodes, in the finals of the state championship, and many believed that Rascoe should have been the state's Mr. Basketball. Two other outstanding players, Harry Todd, from Earlington, and Ralph Richardson, from Russell County, were named co-Mr. Basketball for the first and only time in the history of the award.

Deciding to forego the NBA, Rascoe signed with AAU Phillips 66 Oilers in Bartletsville, Oklahoma, after leaving Western in 1962. For four years he played against some of the best basketball talent throughout the world, before deciding to retire from basketball and work with Phillips full time. During the team's off season he had gone through the company's trainee program and decided he was ready to give up a lifetime of playing basketball.

Well, not quite.

"Darel Carrier called me. He and Kendall Rhine had played with me on the Oiler team," Rascoe said. "Darel said they were going to sign and play for a new team, the Kentucky Colonels."

By now Rascoe had been out of the game a little more than a year, and even though his best, most competitive years may have been behind him, the allure of going back home and playing professional basketball was too much to remain in the corporate world.

A phone call from new coach, Johnny Givens, asked Rascoe if he would come to Louisville to tryout. This tryout would be different from some of the others the Colonels had. This wasn't one of those 30, 40, 50 guys going through basic passing, dribbling, and shooting drills. Yes, this tryout would not be like the others.

"We went up to the YMCA in Louisville," recalls Rascoe. "It was going to be a two-on-two tryout. Darel had already signed a contract with them, and he said he wanted to make me look good so I would make the team. I can't remember who I played with, but Darel's partner was Givens. I think we played a couple of games to 24."

Team owner, Joe Gregory, stood looking over the railing in the upstairs balcony of the gym.

Although Rascoe was somewhat rusty, not having played in over a year, he was still impressive enough for the Colonels to offer him a contract.

"Bill Motsch, Gregory and Givens were talking about giving me a contract that was $2,500 less than Darel and Kendall were going to make, plus they had a two year, no cut," Rascoe said. "They had a $15,000 no-cut, and what was interesting was that Joe Gregory came to me and told me to ask for the same as Darel and Kendall … and he was the owner. I said I'd take $13,500 and a two year no-cut, and that's what they gave me."

Rascoe says the Gregorys had actually talked to Gene Rhodes before Givens was hired, and when Givens came out of the starting gate with a 5-12 record, the former professional teammate of George Mikan was doomed as the Colonels coach, becoming the first fired coach in the ABA.

"I always heard they broke the news to Givens in the men's restroom," said Rascoe. "He said he was blindsided by it, and he might have been. The players actually knew it before Johnny did."

Rascoe recalled that Gregory had come to him and asked what and who he thought would be a good choice to coach. "I knew they had talked to Rhodes," he said. "And I suggested him because he was a good coach."

But as much as Rascoe liked Rhodes as a coach, he didn't particularly care for his style in dealing with adult professional players. "He treated us more like kids," he recalled. "He knew the game but his treatment sometimes was like he was dealing with a high school team."

Things began to go south for Rhodes when several of the players signed a petition against him. By this time the Gregorys, who had had their run-ins with Rhodes, decided to sell the team. But before they did, Joe Gregory went to Rascoe and told him to get a new contract before the sale was finalized. "I told them I'd sign another contract if I can be retained with Colonels even if they cut me as a player," he said.

As a part time starter, he had sometime been described as one of the fastest slow guys in the ABA. Often he relied on just plain good old basketball instincts to get by.

Nevertheless, he had some big games.

By the time the third year rolled around the Colonels had traded Rascoe to the Carolina Cougars. Former Wake Forest legend Bones McKinney was coaching the team, and it was loaded with players with a North Carolina connection. This was commonplace throughout the ABA. Territorial rights was the term used when granting teams first opportunity to sign a player who had collegiately played for a team in the area of the ABA franchise.

The Cougars had former Duke All-American Bob Verga, and former North Carolina Tar Heel standouts Doug Moe and Larry Brown, who would both leave their marks in the ABA before they were through as both players and coaches.

"I went over there for the pre-season workouts, about three weeks," Rascoe said. "They cut me. I had a contract for my third year guaranteed by the Colonels, so I went back to Louisville.

"Joe Gregory wanted me to be a player and assistant coach. He told me to tell Rhodes, but I never said anything to him about it."

Rascoe was now back with the Colonels, and one of those pre-season exhibitions coming up was against Carolina. "I really had it in for them after the way they cut me," Rascoe laughed. "I went out and scored 34 points against them. After the game McKinney came over to me and said he wanted me back with Carolina."

But by now the Gregory's had sold the team to the Wendell Cherry-John Y. Brown group, and six games into the third season Rascoe was once again cut.

He could have probably gone back to Carolina, but there were no guarantees there. He was guaranteed, however, of having some sort of job with the Colonels for the remainder of the season.

"I moved up in the office and worked in publicity," he offered. "And whenever someone on the team was hurt, Rhodes used me in practice."

As an original Kentucky Colonel he was a part of something totally new to Louisville, professional basketball. Trial and error was often the rule of the day. It was, however, the gimmick game involving female jockey Penny Ann Early that got Rascoe in more photos than any other time during his two years. It was the 1968-69 season. "Her only play was to inbound the ball to me," he laughed. "I immediately called timeout and she was out of the game."

FIRST SEASON
1967-68
by Lloyd Gardner

Regular Season Standings

EASTERN DIVISION	W—L
Pittsburgh Pipers	54-24
Minnesota Muskies	50-28
Indiana Pacers	38-40
Kentucky Colonels	36-42
New Jersey Americans	36-42

WESTERN DIVISION	W—L
New Orleans Buccaneers	48-30
Dallas Chaparrals	46-32
Denver Rockets	45-33
Houston Mavericks	29-49
Anaheim Amigos	25-53
Dallas Chaps	22-56

The very first game in the ABA, American Basketball Association, was played on October 13, 1967… yes, it was on Friday the 13th. That game will go down in sports history as the start of a league that was at times good, bad, and ugly, but sometimes great! Nine seasons later only three of the eleven teams remained in the cities where they originated … Louisville, Indianapolis and Denver.

In that first game the Oakland Oaks defeated the Anaheim Amigos 132-129 in the Oakland Coliseum before a dismal crowd of 4,828. Write it down, Willie Porter scored the first points ever recorded in the scorebooks of the ABA when he tipped in a missed shot at the 12:56 mark in the first quarter.

It was only fitting that one day later, October 14, 1967, two states with great basketball traditions would square off before a sellout crowd of 10,835 in Indianapolis. The Indiana Pacers hosted the Kentucky Colonels. Mike Storen, the Pacers General Manager, sold 1,700 tickets for $100. Not $100 each, but all 1,700 tickets for $100.00. The actual capacity at the Indiana State Fairgrounds Coliseum was 9,135. On that opening night the Colonels were coached by Johnny Givens, and the Pacers by Larry Staverman. The Pacers came out on top by defeating the Colonels 117-95. Both Roger Brown of the Pacers and Stew Johnson of the Colonels led their teams in scoring with 24 points. It was Mamie Gregory's birthday, and she recalls that before the tip-off the band played "Mamie" in celebration of her special day.

The opening night lineup for the Colonels was Darel Carrier and Larry Conley at guards, Cotton Nash and Johnson at forwards, Kendall Rhine at center. For Conley it was the only game of his professional career, as he left for military training the following day.

Following Johnson in scoring was Carrier with 22 and Randy Mahaffey off the bench with 12.

The official roster on opening night for the Kentucky Colonels, #10 Louie Dampier, #41 Kendall Rhine, #22 Jim Ligon, #24 Stew Johnson, #25 Randy Mahaffey, #32 Dave Gaines, #34 Bill Bradley, #35 Darel Carrier, #40 Larry Conley, #44 Cotton Nash, #45 Bobby Rascoe, #50 Howard Bayne, #52 Orb Bowling.

The next night the two teams squared off again, this time in Louisville at Freedom Hall. Five thousand advance tickets were sold, and Colonels management was hoping for 12,000 fans. However, the 10,427 that did show up saw the Pacers win again, 106-99.

The Friday night game at Freedom Hall had lots of competition for the sports dollar. Friday nights in Louisville had been high school football, and on this particular night, when the Colonels played, there were 10 games in the city and two more in Jefferson County. And one of those games was played only 500 yards away at the Fairgrounds. The St. X – DeSales football game drew 5,000 fans. By some estimates 30,000 spectators watched basketball and football in Jefferson County that night.

On January 9, 1968, the ABA held the league's first All-Star game in Indianapolis. Dampier, Carrier and Mahaffey represented the Kentucky Colonels.

Denver's Larry Jones was the first player in league history to eclipse the 50 points mark when he scored 52 on November 28, 1967, in Denver's 126-108 win over Oakland. On March 22, 1968, the last scheduled regular season game, Dampier broke Jones' record by scoring an amazing 54 points. Louie made 19 of 36 field goal attempts.

After playing 72 regular season games, the Kentucky Colonels and the New Jersey Americans had an identical record of 36-42. The two teams were to meet on New Jersey's home court in the Teaneck Armory. But because the circus was in town, the game was moved to Commack Arena on Long Island, New York. Unfortunately for the Americans, after a long conversation with Commissioner George Mikan, the game was forfeited because of unsafe playing conditions. The Colonels then flew to Minneapolis to start the Eastern Division semifinals. The Muskies won the five game series, 3-2.

With 13 games left in the season Colonel owner Joe Gregory decided to publicly discuss his financials involving his ABA team. Although his team was in last place of the Eastern Division, Gregory used two words: "quite satisfactory." With he and wife Mamie owning 85% of the team's stock, he let it be known that the team was not for sale even though there had been several inquiries.

"At the outset, I felt an average attendance of 3,500 would have allowed us to break even financially," he was quoted as saying. "But our expenses were more than we figured. So our current average of 3,200 will leave us about $100,000 in the red." That home season average was third best in the first year of the ABA.

Gregory went on to say he thought the Colonels performed up to their ability, but that it was important to reach out and get the best talent they could for next season.

Although Commissioner Mikan had been against it, league owners had voted to allow territorial draft rights only in the first round. And it was no secret who Gregory, and everyone else in Louisville, wanted for next year's team, Wes Unseld.

"We're in a predicament," Gregory said. "We're at the mercy of the ballplayers as well as the NBA. I can't see anything less than a three-year contract for Unseld." Although by today's standards three-year, no cuts are run-of-the-mill, back then it was a stretch, as only a few Colonels had two-year deals.

Early in the year Oakland Oaks coach Bruce Hale let it be known he was on a mission to get rid of the red-white-blue ball. "We don't like it," he said in referring to the coaches, "And neither do the players."

Hale also wanted to move the 3-point line a bit closer. "Why can't we make it easier for the referee to call and easier for the shooters to hit?"

He wanted the line reduced from 25-feet to 22-feet a line that parallels the 10-second line, except for following the arc of the foul circle. "That three-foot difference is a great handicap," he added.

Hale's conclusion was that the fans like the 3-point shot better than anything else, and therefore the league should make it more a part of the game.

Cliff Hagan, player-coach of the Dallas Chaparrals and a big, big name in Kentucky basketball, scored the winning basket at the horn in 104-102 win over Colonels in Louisville. He had 19 points while playing only a half. Many of the 4,210 fans at Convention Center cheered every time he scored that night. A group from Owensboro, Hagan's home town, held a pre-game appreciation ceremony honoring Hagan and another Owensboro native, Colonels player Bobby Rascoe.

It was no secret that many opposing coaches and players thought Hagan got lots of breaks from the referee because not only was he a player-coach but he was also the oldest player in the league at 36.

At one point during the 1967-68 season Hagan had fouled out of only five games, but had been ejected twice by referees on the double-technical foul rule. Hagan said he was under pressure from ABA headquarters to cut down the technicals. Rules permitted the ABA commissioner to suspend Hagan if he was ejected one more time. But the Owensboro native said he wouldn't be intimidated because technicals just add a little something to the game. Referees were often uncertain to hit Hagan with a technical as a player or a coach. Players received a $25 fine, while coaches were fined slightly more.

As the season ended, New Jersey owner Art Brown, upset over his team's forfeit to the Colonels for an unplayable floor in that first round playoff game between his team and the Colonels, indicated he would push for Mikan's removal as commissioner at the league's Los Angeles meeting April 27.

CHAPTER SEVEN
WHERE THERE'S SMOKE, THERE'S FIRE

GENE RHODES

Gene Rhodes was never described as passive. From his days of playing basketball alongside Ralph Beard at Male High School in 1946, through four years at Western under Ed Diddle, he laid the groundwork for a successful coaching career. At St. Xavier High School his team won the 1958 state title, and then while coaching at his old school, Male High, another opportunity came.

When Johnny Oldham replaced Diddle at Western in 1965, he tapped Rhodes to be one of his assistants. It was from there that he moved to the Colonels, replacing his former Hilltopper teammate, Johnny Givens, early in the first Colonels season.

From the very beginning of the franchise, Rhodes was the Gregory's first choice to be the coach of the Colonels. His reputation as a coach and popularity in Louisville made him a logical pick. Added to it all was that he was now on the coaching staff of a top-flight college program at Western Kentucky.

Any offer from the Gregorys would have to be a good one because he was involved with his college alma mater, and who knows, perhaps one day he would be Western's head coach.

When the phone rang at Rhodes' Bowling Green home it was Joe Hullett, telling Rhodes about the Colonels and asking him if he would talk to them about becoming the team's coach. Soon he met with Hullett and Bill Motsch, a Louisville CPA and a close associate with the Gregorys. From the outset Motsch admitted that he knew very little about basketball, even though he would have the title of general manager of the Colonels.

When Rhodes returned to the Western campus, he was thinking seriously about the job, even to the point that he beckoned the graduating Lloyd Gardner, and asked him if he would like to be his trainer, equipment manager and travel secretary.

Rhodes was interested in the job, but demanded a two year contract with the money put in escrow. That was the apparent deal breaker. Rhodes would stay at Western and the Gregorys turned their attention to hiring Johnny Givens.

A few months later, with the Colonels off to a 5-12 start, once again, behind the scenes, Rhodes was approached. This time it clicked.

Word circulated that Rhodes had made a deal with Oldham that if the Colonels didn't make it he could have his old job back at Western. "That would have been difficult to do," Oldham said years later. "If I filled his position there would have been no place I could have put him.

66

"But I'll tell you one thing," Oldham continued. "If I had an opening I would hire him in a minute. He was a great basketball coach. I never had that burning intensity as a coach like Gene did, so we made a good combination."

Although Rhodes was appreciative of the Gregorys hiring him, he was not overjoyed with their courtside behavior. "For owners they were just too vocal at the games," said Rhodes. "Always yelling at coaches, players, and trying to tell me who needed to play more. I really felt some of the players had gotten too close to the owners."

Rhodes' first priority was to improve the talent on his ball club. He knew he needed to overcome management's lack of basketball knowledge, and in order to do that he had to surround himself with basketball people.

"One of the first things I did was bring in Ralph Beard and Bill Reiss," Rhodes said. "They knew the game and I trusted them. They scouted players and offered advice, and with what we put together we had a good draft after my first year."

The Colonels improved enough that first year to tie for fourth place in the Eastern Division with New Jersey. Money was tight, not only for the Colonels, but for the league as well, when the team boarded the plane for a trip to New Jersey's Commack Arena for a one game playoff.

When the Colonels arrived at the arena it was not a pretty picture. "I was so tense," Rhodes recalled. "When I saw all of the workers out there repairing the floor I couldn't believe it." Not only was it the floor in need of repair, but the goals as well. And all of this before a league play-off game!

A call was made to Eddie Mikan, head of ABA officials, from the officiating crew there at Commack. Eddie was the brother of Commissioner George Mikan, and after a brief phone discussion the floor was deemed unplayable, resulting in a forfeit win for the Colonels. All of that money spent to get there, in a league strapped for cash, and the result was a forfeit. No ticket sales, no concession, no nothing.

Back on the plane, the team headed straight to Minneapolis where they would play Minnesota, and lose a five game series, 3-2.

The following year Rhodes was named to coach the East team in the league's All-Star game held at Freedom Hall in Louisville. How his coaching duty came about was a bit unusual to say the least.

"I was at home the night before the game and it was 10 o'clock when my phone rang," remembers Rhodes. "It was George Mikan and he told me he wanted me to coach the East team. There had been an incident he said. Vince Cazzetta, the Pittsburgh coach, was supposed to coach the team, but had gotten drunk and slugged the owner."

The East team, which included Carrier, Dampier and Ligon, lost to the West 133-127.

In Rhode's third year the Gregorys decided to get out of basketball and get back to their true love — show dogs.

The new owner group was headed up by Wendell Cherry and included John Y. Brown, Stuart Jay, David Grissom and David Jones. Soon they hired general manager Mike Storen away from Indiana. Rhodes was excited because he knew Storen was a basketball man. Before working with the Pacers he had been with the Cincinnati Royals in the NBA, so the experience he brought with him was enough for him to be named president and general manager of the Colonels. If that wasn't enough, former UK great Alex Groza, who had played with Beard in college, was hired as the team's new business manager.

As the 1970-71 season rolled around things began to twist and turn for Rhodes, as stories began to surface about team turmoil, even to the point of a player walk-out. Although the average fan might have thought it happened suddenly, it had actually started simmering shortly after Rhodes arrival three years earlier.

Dave Kindred wrote in the *Courier-Journal* that last year, eight of the ten Colonels players signed a petition asking that Rhodes be dismissed. They talked about harsh practices lasting far too long, and often ending with tiring teammates fighting each other. Rhode's curfew policies were not in line with what the Colonels players felt they should endure as professional athletes.

It was later learned that Dampier and Bud Olsen had refused to sign the petition.

Storen became agitated by run-ins Rhodes had with forwards Cincy Powell and Jim Ligon, Kindred wrote. And then there was Warren Armstrong, who later became known as Warren Jabali. It was known that Armstrong pushed individualism as a proud black man.

To prove just how radical Jabali had become, there was the time Howard Wright, a rookie from Austin Peay, after taking a shower, put on his white cotton underwear and walked into the locker room. Now keep in mind that Wright was also black. Jabali ripped Wright's underwear off of him, screaming that they were made of cotton and that he shouldn't be wearing anything his slave ancestors had to pick in the field.

Soon Storen sent Jabali packing before he ever played a regular season game.

While Powell, Ligon and Jabali were black, Rhodes also created a stir with some of his comments to a couple of his white players.

In Carrier's case, Kindred reported that Rhodes would play up the sharpshooter's friendly relationship with former team owners Joe and Mamie Gregory, sometime telling him "you don't have the Gregorys around to help you anymore."

Kindred also wrote in a column that Rhodes told Mike Pratt in his rookie year: "Sonny boy, we're going to try you at forward today." "That's what all our fan mail says. 'Try Pratt at forward,' so we will sonny boy." Pratt played forward four minutes that day, Kindred wrote.

Rhodes never lacked for a fiery, sometimes confrontational personality when it came to coaching basketball. There had even been a time while coaching at St. X during the 1957-58 season when he became so upset with a call that he jerked the official's whistle from his neck and threw it in his face. For that, Rhodes was suspended for two weeks from coaching.

But when Rhodes was fired by Storen after three winning seasons, and a 10-5 early season record in 1970, anyone who knew the color of an ABA basketball knew the situation had developed into far more than wins and losses.

When asked why Rhodes was let go, Storen was quoted as saying, "It would do irreparable damage to Rhodes to elaborate on the reasons."

The record shows that the Colonels were setting a torrid pace, winning eight of their last nine games with Rhodes as head coach. With so much at stake, it would seem that the coach and players could put any differences aside for the good of the team.

According to Rhodes, Storen became more withdrawn, even to the point the pair quit talking.

"Earl Cox at the *Courier-Journal* and I were friends." Rhodes said. "He disliked pro ball. With him it was high school first and college second."

Cox had gotten ahold of a story, so he and Rhodes had lunch one day to talk. "Earl asked me if I knew what was going on," said Rhodes. "I didn't. He said they were waiting for me to lose a game so they could fire me.

"Wendell Cherry was really calling the shots over Storen. He thought I was not prestigious enough. I had played at Western and not UK.

"Earl told me they had hired Ramsey, so I went to Storen and told him it would be my last game. It was reported I had lost control of the team."

So, on November 11, 1970 with a 10-5 record, winning nine of his last ten games, Gene Rhodes was fired. He knew it was coming, and with 17 seconds left and the Colonels leading the Virginia Squires 127-118, Rhodes left his seat and headed to press row. "Thank you, thank you, thank you," he said to every person sitting there.

As the final horn sounded with a 128-123 Colonel win, he was out the back door of Freedom Hall, disappearing into the Louisville night.

From the outset Rhodes' style of running his ball club didn't sit well with many of the players. His locker room rants that on occasion included kicking over a table full of drinks, with often salty language, didn't go over big with many of the guys who considered themselves professionals. Their feeling was that it might work with high school and college kids, the yelling and screaming, but not with professional basketball players.

Rhodes, on the other hand, saw it differently. "In high school or college, you can at least talk to your players and tell them what they should be doing," Rhodes was quoted in the *Courier-Journal* as saying. "But these prima donnas I got, you can't tell them anything."

From the beginning of workouts in June 1968, the team was deemed Rhodes' team. It was his choice, the draft and all; the offensive and defensive sets were his entirely. No carryovers.

Courier-Journal reporter Tev Laudeman wrote that Rhodes, before his first game as Colonels coach, would try to make it in the ABA the same way he made it in high school and college, coaching with patience and persistent teaching, by exercising discipline and control, and by using what some of his old coaching rivals and his former players say is an immense technical knowledge of the game.

His responsibility of coaching Kentucky's only professional major league team in any sport, although perhaps not overwhelming, was none-the-less pressure packed.

Rhodes was a proud man. He thought he had done everything expected of him. Yes, he was well aware that coaches in the ABA moved around like a revolving door; he also had heard the old saying that every coach waits to get fired. It's just that he never expected to be one of them.

"When I was first hired, I sold tickets, spoke to civic groups, promoted everywhere, and I even tried to win over Earl Cox, who I found out was upset with the Colonels about not getting road game statistics to his paper."

Frank Ramsey, the new coach, liked Rhodes, and Rhodes liked Ramsey. The two of them met to discuss player personnel, but after that, Rhodes disappeared from the Louisville basketball scene.

Ramsey had made it clear that he didn't want to be the reason Rhodes was let go. He insisted on that. So during the time it took to work his contract out, Groza stepped in to coach two games, and won them both.

Even though he was on salary for the remainder of the season, Rhodes didn't do anything or go anywhere for a time. "I had never been through such agony," recalls Rhodes. "Louisville was my hometown, but I didn't see a game after that. I didn't want to be seen as a nuisance. I had worked hard and was really disappointed."

Rhodes, in fact, moved back to Bowling Green, not to coach at Western, but to take a job with Jostens, a company that sold high school and college rings. Bowling Green was comfortable, and he still had lots of friends there, but it wasn't Louisville.

In the meantime, Rhodes had been in contact with a former high school player of his at St. X, George O'Brien, who had become a Louisville attorney. They both talked about the good old days and then got around to discussing how Rhodes had been wronged by the Colonels. A suit was soon filed. Rhodes says it was settled out-of-court to everyone's satisfaction.

John Y. Brown and his wife Ellie had purchased the team from the Wendell Cherry group in July 1973. When Mike Storen resigned to become ABA commissioner, and Adolph Rupp was named Vice President of the Board, of which Ellie Brown was chairman, the entire Colonels landscape was about to change once again.

"Ralph Beard called me in Bowling Green and said John Y. would like to talk to me," remembers Rhodes in talking about the Colonels general manager position. "I drove to Louisville to talk to him. Nothing was decided that day. He said I had to pass a screening by Ellie."

In July of 1973 in somewhat of a bigger twist, the Colonels had actually been purchased by a Cincinnati group led by Bill DeWitt. That's why 10 games were played in the Ohio city. It turned out to be a disaster. Instead of a home-type crowd rooting for the Colonels, they often cheered louder for the opposition, especially Dr. J. Five games were also played in Lexington.

"John Y., like a knight in shining armor, stepped in and bought the team," Rhodes said.

So there it was, the old musical chair game. Storen was gone and Rhodes was back replacing the man who fired him as general manager. Ramsey had coached only one year and retired back to Madisonville.

Joe Mullaney, who followed Ramsey, had left the Colonels to take the same position at Utah.

With Rhodes now actively involved again in his beloved Louisville, it didn't take long for him to help Brown hire a head coach.

"John Y. even suggested to me that I do the coaching," laughed Rhodes, years later. "I said no and even suggested Bud Olsen, (a former University of Louisville star and former Colonel). He knew the team and the town."

In the meantime Babe McCarthy had gotten out of pro coaching and had just accepted the coaching job at the University of Georgia in Athens. He was a well-respected coach, and returning to the Southeastern Conference where he had coached before at Mississippi State, would be familiar territory.

But it was not to be. Rhodes and McCarthy had talked a time back about Babe joining the Colonels as their coach. He knew the ABA and it, too, would be familiar.

"At first when we talked it was nothing serious," Rhodes said. "He had just told Georgia he would be their coach. And then he called me back a short time later and said, 'You know, I might be interested.'"

The deal was starting to simmer. The Browns, John Y. and Ellie were already in Chicago, so Rhodes flew up from Louisville and McCarthy flew in from Athens, Georgia. "John Y. was really excited about Babe," said Rhodes. "He remembered Babe from his Mississippi State days."

The deal by now was boiling and was completed in Chicago. McCarthy wanted a three-year contract, but John Y. offered two. They settled on two, and Babe McCarthy was the new coach of the Kentucky Colonels for 1973-74.

As could only happen in the ABA, Joe Mullaney, now at Utah, and Babe McCarthy just completing his first year were named Co-Coach of the Year for 1972-73.

But only as the Colonels could do it, McCarthy was fired at the conclusion of the season.

In game one of the first round of the playoffs on April 1, 1974, the Colonels defeated the Carolina Cougars. Game two was scheduled to be played in Freedom Hall on April 4.

Something was about to happen that would be etched in the minds of Louisvillians for a very long time.

"I recall being in the office that afternoon," says Gardner, "And Gene came in on a gloomy day and said, 'I don't know what it's going to do out there, but I hope it's over before the game tonight.' Well it happened. The tornado of 1974 hit the roof of Freedom Hall.

"I had been out on the Freedom Hall floor shooting around while waiting for the ball boys to come in and set up the locker rooms. I had instructed the ball boys, all teenagers except the older Jay Bauer, to take the Carolina uniforms (which we had washed) to their locker room and lay them out on chairs in front of the lockers. I had just taken a shower and put on a pair of gym shorts when I heard this unbelievable roar. It sounded like a freight train in the hallway outside our locker room. I could feel the pressure on my head like it was going to cave in. I had never been in a tornado, but I knew that it wasn't anything good. I yelled at the ball boys, 'Get under the table.' For the first time ever, five teenage boys followed my directions without questioning me. Dust and dirt were taking over the hallway, so I ran down to where it went out into the arena. Before closing the door I looked out, and ceiling tiles, roofing and even chairs were being tossed about. By the time I got back to the locker room, it was over. I walked out into the arena and a huge portion of the roof had been blown off and the results were lying on the game floor. After that, I often thought how lucky I was. Just thirty minutes before I had been out there shooting baskets.

"Freedom Hall that day claimed the first hit of that massive twister. The destruction was felt from Louisville to northern Ohio. I immediately called our office and told them of the damage and assured them that there wasn't going to be a home game in Freedom Hall for the rest of the season. I recall the Cougar players telling me that they stood in their rooms in the nearby Executive Inn and watched the arena take a hit," he said.

With this disaster came scheduling changes in the entire playoff itinerary. Game two was moved to Greensboro, North Carolina on April 5. Game three was played in Charlotte on April 6, and game four was played in University of Kentucky Memorial Coliseum in Lexington, Kentucky on April 8. Kentucky won the seven game series 4-0 over the Carolina Cougars.

Then disaster hit the Colonels. In an eight day span, the Colonels lost four straight games to Dr. J's New York Nets. The Colonels lost the first two games in Nassau Coliseum in Uniondale, N.Y. Because of the damage to Freedom Hall, the Colonels were forced to play game three in Louisville's Convention Center, and Gardner says it was one for the ages, one he would never forget. With about fifteen seconds remaining and the score tied 87-87, New York took a timeout and set up a play for guess who? The Doc. He got the ball, took it to the middle of the floor, weaving and bobbing, and in total control, as Dr. J always was. As the clock was winding down, he jab stepped, faked, and headed toward the foul line. As the Colonels tried to hover over him and force a pass, Doc quickly crossed over to the right and let it fly, off the board and through the net. Once again the Doc put a nail in another team's coffin. Game four was played in Memorial Coliseum, and the Nets won. The season was over; the Colonels lost four games in a row. The Nets went on to win the ABA Championship by defeating the Utah Stars 4-1.

Professional sports are a tough business, and make no mistake about it, it was strictly business. Forget about relationships, friendships and emotions. It's all out the window. It didn't take long for the smooth talking, southern accented McCarthy to fall out of favor. As popular as he was, the bottom line is winning championships.

"When John Y. decided to fire Babe, he went to several in Colonels management and tried to get everyone to agree with him that Babe needed to be fired," said Rhodes. "This way he could say we all decided on it."

Shortly after McCarthy was let go by the Colonels, he became ill. Gardner, the Colonels jack-of-all-trades guy, drove from Louisville to Tupelo, Mississippi to see the former coach in the hospital.

He was gravely ill with prostate cancer, and soon after Gardner's visit, and six months after being fired from the Colonels, Babe McCarthy was dead.

Gardner remembers: "On several occasions during that season, Babe would tell me before the game, '"Have Dr. Ellis stick around after the game with his rubber glove."'

Rhodes went to Babe's funeral, the only Colonels representative from the team to attend.

"The Colonels didn't pay my way," Rhodes said. "I paid my own way because I felt like I really needed to be there. I really felt bad because I had pulled Babe away from a good college job at the University of Georgia."

Gardner, who was close to all of the coaches, remembered that, although it was after the fact, John Y. offered to pay all of Babe's bills.

Hubie Brown made his professional head coaching debut with the Colonels in the 1974-75 season. Few people remembered that he had been interviewed for the job before Babe was hired.

There were some similarities between the new coach and Rhodes. Both were for the most part no nonsense, cut-through-the-chase kind of guys. When it came to being intense, however, it was a draw.

The big advantage Brown had over Rhodes was experience. Coming to Louisville from the Milwaukee Bucks, where he had been an assistant coach, Brown knew how to deal with professional players, the older guys. He knew how to push the right buttons when it came to motivation.

Rhodes, on the other hand, had been a high school coach, albeit a great one, and had spent a couple of years as a college assistant. His experience with the professional game was non-existent, but still he won.

In another day and time Gene Rhodes would have been a hall-of-fame coach at the pro level. He was that good.

"It was business," says Rhodes in discussing the very unpopular sale of Issel. "John Y. was a hard-ass when it came to business. I really questioned the Issel deal, but John Y. banked everything on Gilmore for the future of the team. He sold Dan and got his money back."

The next season, 1975-76, ABA teams began to fold, go by the wayside, but the Colonels were still plenty good even without Big Dan. As for Rhodes, his title was changed to Vice President of Operations, and Dave Vance, who had been a key operations guy in the front office, became the team's general manager.

That was okay with Rhodes. It was business, and business meant not only winning, but selling tickets. Fans in seats were everything. They paid to park, bought food, drinks and merchandise. That's what business was about.

When the handsome Wendell Ladner was with the team, Rhodes says Ellie used his good looks to the fullest. "Ellie and her board would take Wendell to teas, luncheons, art shows and style shows and use him to sell tickets," Rhodes said.

"John Y. would come in my office and couldn't understand why every seat in Freedom Hall was not sold as a season ticket," Rhodes said. "He was very frustrated about the lack of ticket sales. He was so driven."

By the time John and Ellie had decided to close the door on the ABA Kentucky Colonels, things were not good between Rhodes and the team's owner.

"When it was near the end, we had parted ways," Rhodes remembers. "I really didn't have a say in anything, and looking back on it, I probably never did."

Gene Rhodes had quite a history with basketball in Louisville. He will forever be linked with the Kentucky Colonels.

He had tried to get former Western Kentucky All-American Jim McDaniels to join the Colonels from the NBA Seattle team. Rhodes pleaded with Big Mac to "come home where the people love you." McDaniels finally did come home that last season.

Rhodes made an effort to get former Western star Greg Smith to become a Colonel. Smith had just finished a nice career with the NBA Milwaukee Bucks and the Portland Trail Blazers. He was out of the game and wanted no part of the ABA.

As the book closed for Rhodes and everyone else with the team's organization, John Y. Brown had made another shrewd business decision. Putting everything else aside, Rhodes remembers parting words from Brown.

"Ellie and I have done our civic duty." "That's a quote," said Rhodes.

HARDIN McLANE

Hardin McLane only spent a little more than one year with the Colonels, but what a year it was. Enough memories for a lifetime.

McLane was coaching basketball at Elizabethtown Catholic, where he had been since 1958, when he was named to coach the 1968 Kentucky High School All-Stars in their annual summer game against Indiana. His 10-year record at the small Catholic school was an amazing 264-66 and included a 1961 Louisville Invitational Tournament championship, which at the time was considered the strongest high school tournament in Kentucky other than the state tournament. That win included a semi-finals victory over St. X and its future Mr. Basketball star Mike Silliman. In the finals, they won over Christian County and Bob "Snake" Grace, who went on to star at Vanderbilt.

It's interesting to note that McLane's assistant during his last year at E'town Catholic was Mike Polio, who went on to a very successful collegiate coaching career.

It was at these all-star practices that McLane first came in contact with Joe and Mamie Gregory.

"They would come out to our practices at the Masonic Home Gym just to see the players who down the road might make future Colonels players," recalls McLane. "We got to know each other and they came to like me."

It probably didn't hurt McLane's stock when his Kentucky team swept both games over Indiana. At least on paper, a more talented Indiana team was expected to win. The Hoosier Mr. Basketball was Billy Shepherd, who later played three years in the ABA. Don Buse played ten years in the NBA and ABA. Bob Ford went to Purdue and played one year in the ABA, and Jim Price starred at U of L before playing in the NBA for nine seasons.

Kentucky's team was led by Ron Thomas from Thomas Jefferson High School. Of course, he later became a star for the Colonels, but that year with the Kentucky all-stars he elevated his game to score 20 and 14 points, respectively, to lead all Kentucky scoring. Compared to Indiana's talent, McLane's squad was a bunch of no-names. Terry Davis was Mr. Basketball, and his two-game total of one field goal in 14 tries was almost like not showing up. But Shepherd, his counterpart for Indiana, was not much better.

Other Kentucky all-stars were Jerry Dunn, Henry Bacon, Randy Noll, Stan Key, Billy Burton, Granville Bunton, Gary Waddell and Larry Carter.

Ultimately, the Gregorys offered McLane a job with the Colonels, not to coach, but to work in promotions. "Heck, I was making $7,500 at E'town Catholic and I knew they were going to be closing the school pretty soon, so when they offered me $15,000, I went," McLane said.

Soon he was sporting a new silver colored four-door Ford Fairlane from Hull-Dobbs Ford with green lettering on the door spelling out "Kentucky Colonels."

"Joe and Mamie gave my wife, Marilyn, and me a dog named Calvin Murphy." (Murphy had been an All-American player at Niagara College before playing in the NBA. He once held the record for 78 straight free throws.) McLane laughed, "We, of course, were still living in E'town and they wanted us to move into their home with them. But our kids were so small that it just would have been difficult to do. The Gregorys were so good to us, even letting us spend a week at their Bal Harbor home in Florida. It had its own private dock and everything you could imagine."

Decades later, Colonels and Gregory memories still flood McLane's brain.

He recalls that the Gregorys had a car phone, years before there was such thing as a cell phone. And then there was the time Mamie went car shopping.

"She drove a pick-up truck down to V.V. Cooke Chevy," McLane said. "She saw a Corvette she liked and pulled over and bought it on the spot. She wrote a check for it right then. The salesman couldn't believe it, and of course, he called the bank. The bank told the salesman that he could take a check on her up to $52 million."

"True story," says McLane.

Then there was that game against the Pacers at the Fairgrounds in Indianapolis, where Mamie wanted Hardin to "help Darel out" when Carrier got into a fight. That incident had to have caused McLane flashbacks to the previous year when his high school all-star team was police-escorted from the floor at Hinkle Fieldhouse when, with 52 seconds remaining and Kentucky on top 61-56, the referees declared the game over after Indiana fans pelted the floor with coins, cardboard fans, cups and even a plastic ketchup bottle. "It hit the floor and it looked like there was blood everywhere," McLane laughed.

During McLane's time with the Colonels it fell to him and Alex Groza to do most of the public speaking about the team. That part of his job he enjoyed. He also cherished the times he, Groza and Ralph Beard would spend over lunch talking basketball at the Blue Boar Cafeteria, only a short walk from their second floor offices at the Convention Center.

"It was just so enjoyable being with Ralph, Gene, Alex, and Joe and Mamie," he said. "And I know a lot has been said and written about Joe and Mamie and their actions at all of the games, but I can say I never saw either of them angry or mad, just excited."

There was one promotion in particular that McLane remembers that went nowhere. Years later he still seems surprised it didn't happen. "There was what was called back then the Greater Nine Chevrolet Dealers of Louisville. We offered them 7,000 seats, 3,500 in each end, for 25 cents a ticket. The total promo would have cost them $1,750, but they wouldn't do it," he said.

Finally, in a relatively short period of time, it quit being fun for McLane.

"It just got to be too much, never seeing my wife and kids," he offered. "My job was to entertain writers and I was not a drinker and I just didn't enjoy that part of it. Charlie Mastin did a better job at that part than I did. If I had been good at socializing and entertaining, I'd have stayed with the Colonels."

When looking back on Colonels history, and the fact that the team went through seven coaches in nine years, the one name that didn't surface to coach the team was Hardin McLane.

Second Season
1968-69
by Lloyd Gardner

Regular Season Standings

EASTERN DIVISION	W—L
Indiana Pacers	44-34
Miami Floridians	43-35
Kentucky Colonels	42-36
Minnesota Pipers	36-42
New York Nets	17-61

WESTERN DIVISION	W—L
Oakland Oaks	60-18
New Orleans Buccaneers	46-32
Denver Rockets	44-34
Dallas Chaparrals	41-37
Los Angeles Stars	33-55
Houston Mavericks	23-65

Only the strong survive, and a few of the weak. In the inaugural season of the ABA there were eleven teams. The second season saw four teams relocate with new names and new logos. The Anaheim Amigos became the Los Angeles Stars. The New Jersey Americans became the New York Nets. The Minnesota Muskies became the Miami Floridians. For some unknown reason, after winning the first ABA Championship, Gabe Rubin packed up his bags along with league MVP Connie Hawkins and moved the Pittsburgh Pipers to Minnesota, following a franchise that had already failed.

The 1968-69 season opener for the ABA was on October 18. The Indiana Pacers hosted the Oakland Oaks. The Oaks proved that crime does pay when they stole Rick Barry from the San Francisco Warriors. Why did he cross the Bay to play for the Oaks? Number one, he would be playing for his father-in-law, Bruce Hale. Hale was also his college coach when Rick played for University of Miami, Florida. Number two, he was given a big paycheck and stock in the club, which eventually became worthless. Oakland beat the Pacers 144-133. Barry led all scorers with 36 points, packed his bags and headed down I-65 to ruin the Colonels opener the next night. Barry introduced himself to an ABA record crowd of 13,067 Colonels fans in Freedom Hall by tossing in 46 points as the home team lost 134-113. The underhanded free throw shooting (89%) Rick Barry is the only player to ever lead the NCAA (37.4), the ABA (29.4) and the NBA (35.6) in scoring. Louie Dampier paced the Colonels that night with 26. The arrogant, outspoken, but very intense Barry became the face of the ABA.

On November 27, 1968, on the New York Nets home court the Minnesota Pipers Connie Hawkins broke Louie Dampier's ABA single game scoring record (54) by scoring 57 points. That was the same night Penny Ann Early made history in Louisville.

On February 7, 1969, the Colonels were once again playing the Oakland Oaks and Rick Barry in the Convention Center. Back in late December Barry had sustained a serious knee injury and missed much of the season, including the All-Star game, but now he was back. After Barry went 23-23 at the free throw line, the Colonels lost to the Oaks 124-122 in overtime.

In the early days of the ABA, the biggest battles with the NBA were not fought on the hardwood, but on signing players. In a time when every ABA team was trying to survive, signing big time local talent was of utmost importance. Some teams were more stable than others; some teams were surviving paycheck to paycheck. Before the season ended, it was announced that the Houston franchise would move to North Carolina and become the Carolina Cougars for the 1969-70 season. On most nights in Houston, the combined score of the two teams was greater than the attendance. On one night, only 89 spectators showed-up to watch the Mavericks. Other teams were unloading players in an effort to make payroll and pay the bills. Although the Colonels were one of franchises that were somewhat stable, nothing was more important than upgrading your talent on the floor. One of the ways the ABA was accomplishing this was through deferred payments known as the Dolgoff Plan.

After a good college career and a brief pro career, Ralph Dolgoff settled down to a career in accounting, where he made his greatest contributions to basketball. When the ABA challenged the supremacy of the NBA, they sought to build the league with talented players. Because the ABA owners did not have the kind of money NBA owners did, Dolgoff devised a deferred compensation package. The Plan required an ABA owner to buy an annuity for a player that would be paid to the player over a twenty-year period, beginning when the player reached age 41. The deal would then be publicized for its annuity value, plus the actual cash salary.

In 1969, the Colonels closed out their final "home game" in an odd sort of way. Well, even though it was played at the Convention Center, it was not really a home game after all. Playing before the smallest home crowd in the team's two-year history, they defeated the Minnesota Pipers 109-101 in front of only 873 fans.

Dick Fenlon wrote that the Colonels management couldn't have cared less, because the game resulted from a postponement of an earlier snowed-out game at Minnesota and was a "home game" for the Pipers. Because of this, the Colonels received the standard fifteen percent visitor's share of the paid gate, which amounted to slightly more than nothing.

It was quirky situations like this that set the ABA apart. Where was the logic in not promoting a game like this? What about concession sales — food, drinks, T-shirts, programs — and what about the parking fees that locals could benefit from when the crowds showed up downtown?

The game was reported as a nothing game in the *Courier-Journal*.

The ABA in two short years had become a sort of a wild west style of play where pretty much anything went. Players fought players, players fought fans, fans fought fans, referees fought owners, players fought coaches, (sometimes their own), and in one case, a coach almost fought an owner of the opposing team.

Minnesota was in town playing the Colonels in the Convention Center. Their coach, Jim Pollard, had taken a good bit of a verbal attack, he said, from Colonels owner Mamie Gregory. When he had had enough, he reportedly told her if she said anything else to him, he was going to take her out in the middle of the floor and spank her. For sure it makes a good story, but knowing how things were in the early days of the ABA, it is very believable.

In another oddity, the ABA decided to experiment in mid-season by allowing teams to play a zone defense, which had previously been outlawed. If you can believe it, and why not, it would include only games involving teams not in contention for the playoffs, or that had no bearing on league standings.

Rhodes was opposed to legalizing the zone; Babe McCarthy, who often used a zone when coaching at Mississippi State,

Complete Preview of All 14 NBA Teams

PRO BASKETBALL ILLUSTRATED 1968-69

Baylor-Chamberlain-West: Can Three Superstars Unite?

What Dave Bing Had To Learn

Can The ABA Survive?

John Havlicek: The Guts Of The Celtics

What The Experts Say About Bill Bradley

countered that no coach in his right mind would use a zone against the Colonels...not while they have shooters like Louie Dampier and Darel Carrier.

Once again the Colonels were eliminated from the playoff in the first round. The Pacers won the seven game series 4-3.

CHAPTER EIGHT
LOUISVILLE'S FAB FIVE

NEW OWNER GROUP

It almost seemed like a no-brainer when a group of young professional men from Louisville came forward in April 1969, and purchased the majority of stock in the Kentucky Colonels.

After all, on the surface it seemed that most of the heavy lifting had been done, and with two years under their belts, the Colonels looked good enough for this group to step in and take the team to a bigger stage, maybe even the NBA.

Forget the fact that, by Joe and Mamie Gregory's own admission, they had lost money. The mindset was that they didn't know, businesswise, what they were doing, and in an odd sort of way the Colonels had been successful in spite of the Gregorys.

Figuratively speaking, it was time to turn the keys to the building over to someone else. In actuality and on paper, the new owners gave immediate credibility to, not only what the Gregorys had achieved, but also where they could take this ABA franchise.

H. Wendell Cherry, president of Extendicare; David A. Jones, chairman of Extendicare; John Y. Brown, KFC; Stuart P. Jay, president of General Educational Services; and J. David Grissom, attorney, were the principals in the new purchase.

According to John Y. Brown, he bought into the Colonels not just to make money, but since "Kentucky is the greatest basketball state in the nation, I'd like to get the satisfaction from a top notch pro team that we all get from our college and high school teams."

It was agreed at the time of the sale that the Gregorys and Cherry's group would not disclose any particulars of the deal, including purchase price. The Gregorys, however, did hang on to some minority stock in the team.

For sure no one was talking, and although Joe and Mamie had lost a reported $150,000 a year in their two years of ownership, it was assumed that this amount was what caused them to sell. You've got to believe that Joe Gregory's comment about selling out to some "real businessmen" showed he felt the sell was in the best interest of the team and Louisville.

Mamie had her own take on things.

"I hate cold weather," she said at the time. "I plan to spend most of my time in the future in Florida."

Even though the ABA was only two years old, team ownerships and city locations took on the appearance of a badly organized game of musical chairs. When the music stopped, would there be a chair for Louisville?

For certain there were many of the proverbial hoops to jump through when it came to getting much of anything approved through ABA headquarters in New York. Since the inaugural 1967-68 season, ABA franchises had moved from Pittsburgh to Minnesota, back to Pittsburgh, Oakland to Washington, D.C., Houston to Carolina, Anaheim to Los Angeles, New Jersey to New York and Minnesota to Miami.

When would the music stop?

Most Louisvillians thought that the music had indeed stopped when the local business world's "fabulous five" was now in charge of the state's only professional sports team.

Combined, the young guns were in leadership positions of corporations worth almost a billion dollars, and with an average age of 35, it looked like they were ready to take the Colonels to another level of success. Since, by their own admissions, they weren't in it strictly for a financial return, their basketball loyalty and the excitement of being owners of a professional sports team boded well for the city of Louisville.

How many times has it happened, especially in Kentucky, that individuals and groups bought into an ownership of a race horse? Without question, horses are the most risky sports investment of all, but the pride of ownership of a Kentucky thoroughbred is often too much to pass up. Now, so was a pro-basketball team.

Whether it was the truth or not, former Kentucky Wildcat basketball coach, Joe B. Hall, once told a story about when he considered getting into the horse racing business.

"I went out to one of the farms in Lexington to look at a horse," Hall recalled. "The groom brought it out. One ear was a little bent over, there was a slight sway in the back, and one foot looked a little odd. But, other than that it was a beautiful horse. I asked the owner," Hall continued, "now if I buy this horse, can I race him? 'Yes,' the owner said, 'And there's a good chance you'll beat him.'"

So goes the story with most thoroughbred ventures. But professional sports teams were different, and the opportunities were few and far between.

For sure the Gregorys had tilled the earth, planted the seeds and withstood some dry spells during their first two years.

Although Bill Motsch had a reputation for being a good CPA in Louisville, his professional life gave him no real credibility in being the executive director of a professional basketball team.

And Burr Long, a lifetime friend of Joe Gregory's, who took on the role as treasurer, had no experience with sports teams. His qualifications were that he grew up with Joe in Cloverport, went to Western Kentucky State College, and became a trusted advisor.

As for Bill Boone, he probably knew more about the sports world than anyone else in the Kentucky Colonels organization. At the age of 33, he served as the team's legal counsel as well as focusing his private practice on sports law. One of his clients was Louisville PGA golfer Bobby Nichols, who was also a Colonels stockholder.

Other than Joe and Mamie, Charlie Mastin had been the organization's most visible member. Most Louisvillians already knew him before he joined the Colonels. For four years his face and voice were seen and heard as the Sports Director for WHAS radio and TV. Being from Irvine, Kentucky, he had attended Eastern Kentucky State College where he also broadcast some of their

Cliff Hagan, a former University of Kentucky All-American, was a player/coach of the Dallas Chaparrals.

Hardin McLane, Director of Public Relations

Charlie Mastin, Business Manager

Burr Long, Treasurer

Assistant Coach William (Buddy) Cate, 1967-1968.

John Givens was the first head coach of the Kentucky Colonels. He was fired.

Joseph N. Hullett, Promotion Manager

William Motch, Executive Director

Indiana General Manager Mike Storen and wife, Hannah, talk with ABA executives.

The day the Kentucky Colonels hired Lloyd Gardner. Alex Groza left, Gardner right.

Mike Storen and Chairman of the Board Wendell Cherry.

ABA's First Commissioner George Mikan

Mike Storen introduces Frank Ramsey as Colonels head coach, 1970-71.

Mike Storen and wife, Hannah.

Joe and Mamie Gregory and children, Joseph and Evelyn.

Mr. and Mrs. Joseph E. Gregory and Ziggy (mascot).

An usher helps a fan find his seat.

Penny Ann Early takes one dribble!

Timer Donnie Beckhart, Official Scorer Charles M. Ruter and Penny Ann Early as she checks into the game.

Left to right: Hardin McLain holding Michelle McLain, Marilyn McLain, Pat Boone, Mamie Gregory, George Mikan, Joe Gregory, Mike Storen and Thurlo McCrady.

Mayor Frank W. Burks and Colonels fans welcome the team home after the 1971 Championship with the Utah Stars.

Kentucky Colonels Scout Ralph Beard.

Kentucky Colonels secretaries Bev Scott and Alice Miller.

Miami Floridian Ball Girl

Nancy Ligon, Goose Ligon, Ruth Anne Ellis, Sandy Gardner, Lloyd Gardner. Arrival home after seventh game in Utah, 1971.

Coach Gene Rhodes, Randy Mahaffey, Jim Caldwell, Darel Carrier and Bobby Rascoe at presentation of a basketball goal to the Cerebral Palsy School.

The Official Table...Rated as "Tops" by game officials, coaches, players and fans is this "Official Table" at all Kentucky Colonels home basketball games. These four men with many years of experience take great pride in giving the teams and the fans a quick and accurate account of the game at all times. The men are seated left to right: Donnie Beckhart, 30 second clock operator; Charles M. Ruter, scorer; John Tong, the table chief and public address announcer and Richard "Rosie" Rozei, timer. Standing is Ed Mikan, ABA Supervisor of officials.

Kentucky Colonels

AMERICAN BASKETBALL
ASSOCIATION

DAN ISSEL

LOUIE DAMPIER

MIKE GALE

GENE LITTLES

RICK MOUNT

JIMMY O'BRIEN

Kendall Rhine

Manny Leaks

Exhibition – Baltimore Bullets, 1971-72: #53 Artis Gilmore (he wore #54 in exhibition games), #25 Walt Simon.
Bullets: #41 Wes Unseld, Kevin Loughery.

#10 Louie Dampier (shooting), #54 Gene Moore, #10 Glen Combs (Dallas Chaparrals) and #12 Ron Boone.

Wayne Chapman

Gene Moore

Jim Caldwell   *Bill Bradley*

Louie Dampier, Gene Rhodes and Darel Carrier.

#54 Gene Moore, #42 Lonnie Wright (Denver Rockets), #35 Darel Carrier.

#40 Tommy Kron (with ball) and #4 Walt Simon (New York Nets).

Stew Johnson

Bobby Rascoe

Kentucky Colonels Louie Dampier rebounds as East All-Star teammates #24 Bob Netolicky and Mel Daniels look on.

#10 Louie Dampier (shooting), #40 Tommy Kron, and Randy Mahaffey (New York Nets).

#35 Darel Carrier and #20 Steve Chubin (Los Angeles Stars).

Sam Smith

Wilbert Frazier

Bill Reiss. He was hired by Gene Rhodes as a Team Scout along with Ralph Beard.

#14 Anothony Jones, #12 Art Heyman, #32 John Washington (Minnesota Muskies), 1968-69.

Cotton Nash

Jim "Goose" Ligon

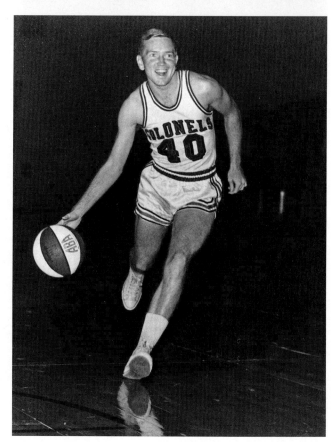

Larry Conley

Orb Bowling

Howard Bayne

Dan Hester

AW Davis

Rubin Russell

George Tinsley

basketball games. Many considered him, along with Joe Hullett, the most knowledgeable sports guys in the organization.

Mastin's aggressive personality fit in well with what those early day promotions needed. Good or bad, it seemed he was involved in far more than his job description of Director of Public Relations called for.

Cherry, one of the new owners, had earlier passed on an opportunity to be involved with the Louisville team. Three years before, he traveled to Los Angeles to learn more about the formation of the upstart American Basketball Association.

As a young attorney, he had been asked to make the trip by a client of his who was interested in the new league. Cherry reported back and was quoted by sports columnist Dave Kindred as telling his client, "The ABA is sheer, absolute nonsense. Only an idiot would get involved."

When the new owners held their first press conference that night, Wendell Cherry, as the team's new president, stepped up to tell a bit about the new organization, their plans, and "to do whatever is necessary to attract and sign truly outstanding players."

Cherry dropped names: Dan Issel, Pete Maravich, Rick Mount and Calvin Murphy.

"We want it clearly understood that we are ready to negotiate with any NBA star playing out his option. We have made a total financial commitment to bring top-quality basketball to the country's basketball capital, and we are confident that our investment will be well rewarded," he said.

Where have you gone Penny Ann Early?

Perhaps her only association now with this group is saying "giddy-up" to one of the horses the new group might own.

Unfortunately, professionalism and dollars don't always equate to pro sports success, but it does at least present a better opportunity.

This group didn't personally scout future players as the Gregorys did at the 1968 Olympics in Mexico City. They wouldn't be offering up their personal automobiles, either, to future players to sign a contract, as Gregory did when he made his $6,000 red Corvette a part of the deal if a player would sign.

The owners were up front in that their involvement with the Colonels was strictly personal, and they were investing only as individuals. In no way was it connected with the high profile businesses they headed up.

All they had to do to look like geniuses was to sit back, sign great players, attract larger crowds, sign a lucrative television package, and wait for a merger with the NBA. Oh, and don't forget, win!

BUD OLSEN

You won't find the name Enoch Eli Olsen III on any Kentucky Colonels rosters during the team's nine-year existence in the American Basketball Association. You will, however, find Bud Olsen's name, albeit for only one season, playing for the Colonels during the 1969-70 season.

The 6'8" Olsen had been in and around Louisville since 1958 when he came to U of L to play basketball for coaches Peck Hickman and John Dromo. He had been a top-flight recruit out of

Belmont High School in Dayton, Ohio, and when he graduated from Louisville in 1962, he had established himself as one of the school's all-time best players. His 44 points against Kentucky Wesleyan is still a Cardinal road game scoring record.

Olsen was good enough to attract NBA teams, but stayed focused on his goal of playing in the 1964 Olympics. He opted first to play for the Akron Goodyears in order to maintain his amateur status. From there he went to Chicago in the American Basketball League.

"I was making $1,000 a month, but the problem was the season was only five months long," he says, "And then the Cincinnati Royals drafted me."

Olsen was overall the 15th player picked in the 1962-63 draft, and the Royals made him their number two pick behind Ohio State All-American Jerry Lucas. "I received a $1,500 bonus and a contract for $10,500," he recalled.

Olsen's road roommate with the Royals was one of the NBA's all-timers, Jack Twyman. After a three-year stint, the Royals traded Olsen to the San Francisco Warriors for Art Hayman and Connie Dirken, plus dollars.

"There's something about being traded in pro sports that makes you feel like you've been fired," Olsen said. "At least it did for me."

Olsen was with the Warriors for two years, playing with the likes of Rick Barry, Clyde Lee, Fred Hetzel, Jeff Mullins, and Nate Thurmand. Although Olsen was considered small for an NBA center, his chief roll was as Thurmand's back-up.

"We were loaded," Olsen says. "But so was the team we lost to in the NBA Finals, the Philadelphia 76ers. They had Wilt (Chamberlain), Hal Greer, Billy Cunningham and Chet Walker."

When the NBA expanded in the 1966-67 season, Olsen went to Seattle, where he played for a couple of years for coach Al Bianchi.

"I was in the best shape of my life," Olsen recalled. "And then all of a sudden I hit a brick wall. I was a starter, and because I tried to play while I was sick, I just couldn't get back to where I was, and I lost all my confidence. Without confidence you don't have much as a basketball player."

Olsen then tried to catch on with the Milwaukee Bucks, coached by Larry Costello. "I didn't have a no-cut contract and was soon out of a job," he said. "But I did get an offer to be the assistant basketball coach at the University of Wisconsin."

Olsen still felt like he had some basketball left in him, and although he had established himself as a "journeyman," players like him were important to a basketball team. Playing most of his pro career as an undersized inside player, he was capable of coming off the bench and contributing solid minutes. He knew the game fundamentally, and his reputation as an exceptional passer had allowed him to participate at the highest level of basketball for longer than some had predicted.

But his days were numbered. "I got a call from Red Auerbach at Boston," Olsen recalled. "He wanted to pick me up. I moved my family up to Boston thinking this was a great opportunity for me." Seven games later he was cut.

"I was through with basketball," he said. "So I came back to Louisville. But guess what? I get another call, this time from coach Paul Seymour at Detroit. So I go up there and came down with the mumps . . . in the hospital and everything. I was sick for two months."

Now back home in Louisville, and for all practical purposes, he had resigned himself to the fact that his NBA playing days were indeed over.

But not so fast.

The lure of playing for the Kentucky Colonels was too much for him to ignore. The Colonels were getting ready for their third year. Gene Rhodes was the coach, and the team had a new ownership group of Louisville businessmen.

Olsen made the 1969-70 Colonels team. With Ligon, Dampier, Carrier and Gene Moore forming the nucleus of the team, Olsen felt like he could find a role where he would contribute. George Tinsley and Sam Smith, a pair of Kentucky Wesleyan products, were solid, and so was Wayne Chapman, a Western Kentucky grad, and former Kentucky star Tommy Kron.

Olsen played in 84 games that season, averaging 16 minutes, 4.1 points, 4.5 rebounds and 3 assists, he was a solid backup to Moore.

By now, he had decided he was finished as a player.

But he was not about to leave Louisville, his adopted home town. He never lost the warmth of Louisville, always knowing it was his comfort zone. His brother, Bill Olsen, had also attended U of L, playing baseball, and later serving as an assistant basketball coach to Denny Crum. Then for several years brother Bill was the school's Director of Athletics.

Olsen wasn't going anywhere. He had been around some of the biggest names in the game. An eight-year pro career had given Olsen an insight into the game you only get from being there and doing it. Never being a superstar, and with lots of bench time, it allowed him a perspective that some of the great players don't get.

And through it all, he says years later, Gene Rhodes was the best X and O coach he was ever associated with.

"I stayed on as a scout on a part-time basis with the Colonels," said Olsen. "I was doing some TV color for Howard Hoffman who did the play-by-play for WLKY-TV. Alex Groza and I were both doing it. I remember Frank Ramsey when he was the coach didn't want me to listen in on the huddle during timeouts when I was giving sideline reports."

After Ramsey's one year of coaching the Colonels, Joe Mullaney came in and Storen called Olsen to see if he was interested in being an assistant to Mullaney. He thought about it, recognizing that the Kentucky Colonels were on the verge of putting together a very good basketball team. So, even though Olsen wouldn't be playing, Storen had presented him an opportunity to stay involved with the team.

The Colonels had added Dan Issel, Walt Simon, Cincy Powell and Les Hunter the year before, and although Mike Gale had just been added, the big news was the signing of Jacksonville All-American Artis Gilmore. It was Gilmore who really got Olsen excited about being able to work with someone who possessed unlimited potential.

"I gave up a successful chemical sales job to be an assistant," Olsen said years later. "Gilmore initially was not skilled … you know the picks, low post moves, he had to get closer to the basket to make better moves."

When Mullaney left after the season, Olsen felt like he might have the opportunity to be the next Colonels coach.

"I thought I'd get the job." Olsen said. "Lots of people were calling John Y. on my behalf. After a while they still hadn't hired anyone, and I was putting the rookies through their paces. I even tried to get Rhodes, who had become the G.M. to take it, but then they hired Babe, and he hired me as his assistant.

"Babe ran a shuffle offense," said Olsen. "It involved all five players and was not easy to teach. Just when the team was getting to know it, John Y. traded two of our starters. I told John it was awful; we were in first place at the time and it destroyed our chemistry."

"Babe got fired at the end of the year," Olsen said. "We had a pretty good year, but lost four straight in the playoffs."

Once again Olsen wanted the head coaching job, even interviewed for it, but instead Hubie Brown was brought in from the Milwaukee Bucks, where he had been an assistant.

"John Y. called me before they hired Hubie and talked to me about the position," he said. "He didn't want me politicking for the job. When John Y. called to tell me he hired Hubie, he said the reason was that he had been the co-head coach at Milwaukee. He then said he wanted me to be Hubie's assistant. I said absolutely not!"

Years later Olsen says that decision was probably a big mistake. "I let my pride get in the way," he says. "If I had gone with Hubie, things could have been different for me. I would have probably been an NBA coach."

John Y. Brown had quite a bit of clout throughout the ABA, and in an effort to keep Olsen involved in basketball, the owner went to him and asked if he would like to be in charge of officials and security in the ABA?

Brown and Olsen flew to New York to talk to the league's office about it. "I remember we were walking down the street and John Y. asked me if I liked hot dogs. We went over to one of the street hot dog stands and after getting them, John Y. said, 'Bud, pay for it because you can expense it out. He paid for my airline ticket, but not my hot dog," Olsen laughed.

Olsen did in fact become head of officials and security.

Always concerned about the image of officials, the ABA did a good job of getting some of the NBA's best referees to switch leagues. Olsen knew them from a player's perspective as well as a coach's.

"I gave my speech to them," he says, "letting them know what was expected and so forth. We just needed to be aware of the game's integrity. Looking back on everything, if I was ever going to fix a game, it would not have been through the players, but the referees.

"John Y. was the one who got the ABA games included in publicized point spreads. I was asked by a writer if putting out the point spread helped attendance at the games. He told me to answer truthfully. I said it did. People in New York apparently thought they were the only ones who gambled."

Hubie had quite a reputation among league officials. His off-color language was known throughout the ABA, and was easily heard when less than big crowds showed up for the games. Van Vance, the Colonels radio broadcaster, tells of one time when Hubie's wife even called the radio station for them to get word to Hubie to quit cussing because she could hear him on the radio.

"I told the referees they didn't have to take his cussing, and all of his bad language," Olsen said. "And Hubie called me in to talk at his office in the Executive Inn. He was screaming at me about what I'd said to the officials. I just told him he didn't need to do what he was doing, and that I didn't have to take this from him, and basically we never spoke again."

When the ABA folded, Olsen went to work for Pat Williams and the Philadelphia 76ers as a scout.

MIKE STOREN

Mike Storen left little doubt everywhere he worked in sports that he was "a by-the-book" kind of guy. And for the most part those who worked with him and for him, knew where they stood when it came to operating a professional basketball organization.

When Storen left the NBA Cincinnati Royals to go to work for the newly formed ABA Indiana Pacers as the vice-president and general manager in 1967, it didn't take him long to figure out the lay of the land. He also quickly figured out in that first year that for his team to be successful it would probably have to include a fierce rivalry with that other ABA team just down the road – the Kentucky Colonels.

Storen, like his counterparts in Louisville, knew that anytime Kentucky and Indiana played against each other it sold tickets, and one thing he was very good at was selling tickets. During his three years with the Pacers, his team led the ABA in attendance all three years.

Early on, it was Storen's belief that the Pacers and Colonels were going to end up being the best two teams in the league, and it seemed such a waste for them to both be in the Eastern Division. His thinking was that Indiana needed to move to the Western Division. It would make for a much more exciting ABA final, and besides, the fans and teams could travel back and forth by cars and busses. Ultimately, in Mike Storen style, he was thinking about the financial savings.

Following the 1969-70 Pacers ABA championship, Storen received a call from Wendell Cherry informing him that a group of five investors had just purchased the Kentucky Colonels. Cherry went on to say he would like to meet with Storen in Louisville.

"The way the call sounded was that they just wanted to ask me some questions about our success," said Storen. "I met them at the Seelbach Hotel, and the first thing I asked was what can I do for you? As I remember, David Grissom and David Jones were also there."

What Storen hadn't counted on was a job offer, but that's exactly what he got. "They wanted me to be their president and general manager, plus the offer included an equal share of stock in the team's ownership," he recalled. "I told them I really needed to see the books and records of their sales and attendance history."

Storen pulled out a yellow legal pad and began to take notes, serious notes. They told him to write out what he needed in order to take them up on their offer.

"They were very professional and generous," offered Storen. "Even to the point that I was to get a certain percentage of any increase in attendance. Their numbers were based on attendance at the downtown Convention Center. In the back of my mind I'm thinking attendance at Freedom Hall. Later on I remembered a sellout there during the playoffs and was thinking 'I'm getting a piece of this!'"

The Seelbach Hotel meeting had begun in one of the suites at 7 p.m. and eight hours later, when the meeting ended at 3 a.m., Storen had turned the five-person ownership group into six.

At the age of 34, less than a week after his Indiana Pacers won an ABA Championship, Mike Storen was a Kentucky Colonel.

Storen said that Dick Tinkham, the head man with the Pacers, was very good about it all and understood his reasons for leaving. "It wasn't one of those, you match this or that," says Storen. "We didn't get into all of that. After all, I had left them with a championship."

Almost immediately, a firestorm erupted between Storen and Rhodes, which resulted in Rhodes' firing. It was not what Storen said were his reasons, but what was not said. The media ran with it, thus leading to a Rhodes lawsuit against the Colonels and Storen for more than $2 million. Rhodes settled the case out-of-court.

Storen says he had little to do with signing Dan Issel. Although, at the time, it was the most important thing the team had ever done. He says 90% of the work of obtaining Issel was done by the time he arrived from Indiana. "The owners were Kentucky grads who had great ties with UK," he said.

Alex Groza had taken over the coaching duties after Rhodes' departure, but only for two games, time enough for details to be worked out with Frank Ramsey. "To his credit, Frank would not talk to us about the job as long as someone had it," said Storen. "When Gene was let go, Frank was my target. I didn't have a contingency plan, because I knew I was going to get him."

Another pretty slick move that only Storen could pull off benefited both the Colonels and Pacers at the same time.

"When I accepted the position with Kentucky, I was still working with Indiana. From the Indiana position, I wrote a contract proposing the Pacers and Colonels play an eight game exhibition series across Indiana and Kentucky with both teams traveling on the same bus. I sent it to 'Dear General Manager' (Kentucky). When I got to the Kentucky job, I signed the contract and sent it back to Indiana," he laughed. "My name was on both ends of the contract."

The following year Storen and the other teams had declared an all-out war in signing the best college talent they could get their hands on. "Our league developed a strategy to sign the best we could," said Storen years later. "We were in a war, and it was decided that the team willing to spend the most money should get their man.

"That year the two best players coming out were Artis Gilmore and Jim McDaniels, and we felt like Gilmore was what we needed," Storen said. "Miami had finished last in our league and had the draft rights to him, but we went to a league meeting and created a strategy with a goal of getting him to Kentucky. It worked, and we signed Artis before the ABA or NBA draft."

With Gilmore signed, and Ramsey gone after one year, by his own choice, the Colonels had to have a coach. Storen knew it had to be a good one, ideally a coach with quality experience.

The Colonels were coming off of an ABA final with Ramsey and Storen, and though they lost, they were beginning to increase the depth of their stable of talent, and Storen wanted to make sure he had a jockey capable of bringing the team home first.

Joe Mullaney had just been let go with the Los Angeles Lakers, but that didn't seem to matter with Storen. Mullaney's reputation was solid. An outstanding coaching career at Providence

College, and then the experience with the Lakers, made him Storen's choice to be the Colonels next coach.

While Ramsey had taken a more easy-going approach, sometime staying in Madisonville to take care of business instead of attending each and every practice, Mullaney brought a little more discipline to the scene.

And Mullaney was Storen's hire all the way!

The Colonels got off to a roaring start under Mullaney, and the fact that Louisville was also playing host to the league's fifth ABA and All-Stars game in Freedom Hall on January 29, 1972, caused Storen to want to line up a top-notch speaker. He did so in a nationally radio commentator Paul Harvey.

"I think it was $5,000 we paid him, but I really thought he didn't live up to the expectations," recalled Storen of the banquet that took place at the Convention Center.

Storen, being Storen, went to Harvey's hotel room the next day to talk to the radio icon, in a professional way, of course.

A few days later Storen received a check from Harvey for $2,500.

The fact that the Colonels went 68-16 in his first year really made Storen look like a genius. The Colonels were a lock for their first ABA title. Or so it seemed, but a not-so-funny thing happened on the way to the Eastern Division playoffs.

Normally, or even logically, in a seeded four team format, one would play four, and two would play three.

But anyone who knows anything about the ABA knew normal or logical were not part of the league's vocabulary.

Instead of playing Miami, who was number four, and against whom the Colonels were 10-0 in the regular season, they were paired against a very good number three-seeded New York, Rick Barry – led team.

The Colonels were 7-4 against the Nets during the season, but the New York team ended the season strong, and whoever they played would be in for a battle.

Once again the Colonels were denied. Coming off of a dream season with the highest of hopes, the team suffered the lowest of blows, losing to the Nets in six games.

Everyone was looking for excuses. Darel Carrier did not play at all during the series because of a back injury. But still one would expect with the likes of Issel, Gilmore and Dampier, it would be enough to overcome the Nets. But it wasn't.

The *Louisville Times* sports editor wanted Dan Issel to write an expose' in his paper about what was wrong with the team. Not taking too kindly to this, Storen in turn requested that reporter Jim Terhune write a story in the Colonels game program about what all was wrong with his paper's sports department.

It wasn't long until John Y. and Ellie Brown stepped up and purchased the majority of the Colonels stock in order to keep the team from being sold and moved to Cincinnati. That's when Storen became very uneasy about his role in the team's day-to-day operations.

At the press conference announcing the purchase, John Y. said he was turning the team over to Ellie and she was going to run the team with an all-women board of directors.

At first Storen didn't take it seriously and he asked John Y. what it was all about. "It's okay if the ladies want to sell season tickets or whatever, but...."

John Y. talked to Storen about the power of women and how they were an untapped resource in sports marketing. "I told John, please understand, I'm not going to talk to Ellie and the board about running this team. He said 'yes I was.' I chose to resign. It was a philosophical difference."

And if Storen was gone, Mullaney wouldn't be far behind. He too, didn't like the fact that John Y. and the ladies would be more or less telling him how to ply his trade — coaching.

Storen and Mullaney's relationship developed beyond the game of basketball. They became close personal friends, and with Storen no longer in Louisville, and Mullaney not sure where management was headed, he decided to take the Utah coaching job. Mullaney was a basketball guy and he wanted to work for one, not a bunch of ladies.

It didn't take Storen long to land on his feet either. Five weeks after departing the Colonels, he was the new Commissioner of the ABA.

Few in basketball were surprised, because one thing was for sure, Mike Storen, like him or not, could make things happen. Even John Y. knew this.

Storen made some noise. Traveling over 100,000 miles from cities to towns and from towns to cities; he talked with each team, the players, management, owner and media, getting a handle on what could make the ABA better. He developed criteria, one that even included how players and coaches would, not should, stand during the pre-game National Anthem. Whenever his rules were not followed there were fines.

But Storen still wanted to run a basketball team. And when he saw an opportunity, he became part-owner of the Memphis Tams, whose name he changed to the Sounds.

His partners were entertainer Isaac Hayes and Holiday Inn founder, Kemmons Wilson. "It was a struggle," says Storen. "I remember Issac Hayes was really behind on his payments to the team. I kept calling and calling, but could not reach him. Finally I got him on the phone and he said if I'd come by his office that night he would have $100,000 for me. Now keep in mind, I had never actually met him in person. I'd just seen all of those pictures, with the heavy chains and looking a lot like Mr. T. I pictured him as a real big guy, you know, maybe 6'4". But when I arrived at his office that night, there he was, maybe 5'10", in jeans, tennis shoes and a T-shirt. He had the money, $100,000 in cash in a brown grocery bag. I left with it, but quickly decided I didn't need to be walking out into a dark parking lot with $100,000 in cash on me, so I turned around and went back to Isaac's office. I told him if it was okay, I'd come back in the morning to get the money. The next day Isaac was gone and we never got the $100,000 from him."

Storen tells of the time while still at Indiana that he was retained by the league to create a strategy to attract Lew Alcindor to the ABA.

"We called it Operation Kingfish," says Storen. "I hired a psychiatrist and psychologist to develop questions that would give us a profile to better understand how we might go about signing him. It was pretty much a personality profile. We hired a private investigator to investigate him and his family, their financials, everything. We had a notebook four inches thick. The end result was that he, and not his big backer at UCLA, Sam Gilbert, would make his own decisions."

But how did these so-called investigations get close enough to gather their profile information? Supposedly they posed as newspapermen interviewing him. "We needed to pay attention to what he said. We found out Alcindor liked the underdog, which helped the ABA," Storen continued.

All of the teams, according to Storen, put up $100,000 each. A $1 million certified check was going to be the enticement to go along with an ABA contract. New Jersey's Nets were going to be the team to sign the New York native.

"We met in New York City for his decision," Storen said. "ABA Commissioner George Mikan, Dick Tinkham, Net owner Arthur Brown and I were there. Arthur Brown met with Alcindor and didn't even give him the check. He said he didn't need to, that he was going to get him signed without the check. He said the meeting went so well he didn't need the check. We went crazy."

Lew Alcindor signed with the Milwaukee Bucks of the NBA, but to this day Storen thinks the ABA's offer was better.

"We were absolutely close to signing Alcindor," Storen said.

And then there's Storen's connection to the fabled red, white and blue basketball. When George Mikan agreed to be the ABA's first commissioner, whatever he wanted he usually got. His name and the respect he had earned as an all-time NBA great went a long way in garnering support for the fledgling league. One of the new wrinkles Mikan wanted was a red, white and blue basketball. He may not have demanded the multi-colored ball, but he left little doubt of where he stood on the issue.

While many of the players, coaches, and even the owners, wanted the brown standard issue ball that had always been used, Mikan stood firm and tall, all 6'10" of him. He was adamant in separating the ABA from the NBA, and the ball surely would be a strong statement.

Storen was also in favor of the colored ball of which the old-guard NBA was already poking fun at. "At Indiana I got Marathon Oil involved in a promotion with the new ball," says Storen. "They ordered half a million of them to give away across the state with a gas purchase." The balls were shipped to a warehouse in New Jersey, deflated to make the process easier. Then they were shipped to the individual Marathon Oil stations throughout Indiana. Customers would receive the basketballs in a deflated condition.

"Then you know what happened?" Storen asked, already knowing the answer. "Keep in mind these were cheap balls, made in Taiwan, and when the customers blew them up on the commercial pumps at the station, they would over-inflate, making them bigger than the rim. You could drive all over Indiana and see a red, white and blue basketball sitting on all of those outside goals."

Storen went on to get the selling rights for the ABA ball. He found out you can't trademark a color pattern, but he could get the ball with the ABA logo. The ball was popular. Every kid wanted one when they saw it. Storen would have been in tall cotton if the ABA had not folded, but when it did, so did the ball. How ironic it is that today in the NBA's 3-point competition at the All-Star game, the red, white and blue ball in the rack is referred to as the money ball.

FRANK RAMSEY

It was destined for Frank Ramsey to one day be involved with the ABA Kentucky Colonels. After all, his nickname was "The Kentucky Colonel" when he played with the Celtics. Although Ramsey only coached a single season for the Colonels, he did, indeed, make his mark.

As a basketball icon in Kentucky that began with an all-state selection at Madisonville High School, and then at UK where he teamed with Cliff Hagan and Lou Tsioropoulos to win an NCAA title in 1951, Ramsey was a first round draft choice by the Celtics in 1954. He played his entire career for them. His time with Boston is considered by some to have been the golden era of professional basketball. It sure was golden for Ramsey! Being labeled the first great sixth man of basketball, he not only was, but played with some of the biggest names in the game's history. Winning NBA championships in 1957, 59', 60', 61', 62', 63', and 64', and playing with Bob Cousy, Bill Sharman, Sam Jones, K.C. Jones, Bill Russell, Tom Heinsohn, and John Havlicek, it is called one of the all-time sports dynasties.

Ramsey was inducted into the Naismith Basketball Hall of Fame in 1982, and some sport trivia experts may not know that it was Ramsey who scored the very first basket in Freedom Hall while playing for a military team at Fort Knox in 1956. This was before Western played the official dedication game against San Francisco that same year. U of L did not begin playing their games at Freedom Hall until later.

He had been around Boston coach Red Auerbach for all those years. Auerbach, considered a coaches' coach, evidently rubbed off on most of his great players, as many coached at one level or another following their playing days.

"I had always wondered if I could coach," Ramsey said years later while sitting behind his desk at his Dixon Bank in western Kentucky where he is its president. "Red had even talked to me about coaching with the Celtics."

When Mike Storen and his Wendell Cherry group of owners began throwing names out there to replace the recently fired Gene Rhodes, Ramsey's name came to the top. John Y. and Frank had been classmates at UK, so there was an added connection other than him just being a great player.

"Storen said he'd like to talk to me, so he drove down to Madisonville and I drove over from Dixon and met him there," Ramsey recalls. "The timing was fairly good for me right then. I had just sold one of my nursing homes, so I was willing to at least talk."

Ramsey had seen the Colonels play before, and he did know some of their players. Even though the NBA had a shot clock similar to the ABA's, what he wasn't sure about was the upstart league's 3-point shot. If he took the job, he quickly realized he would be coaching two of the best long-range shooters the game has ever seen in Darel Carrier and Louie Dampier.

"I told Mike Storen that Gene (Rhodes) was a friend of mine and I was concerned that they were firing him to hire me." Ramsey said. "He told me that was not the case, that getting rid of Gene had nothing to do with hiring me. I didn't want Gene's job."

Following brief negotiations, Storen and Ramsey settled on a one-year deal. That's all Ramsey wanted, win or lose.

Even though Ramsey had a permanent room at Stouffer's Inn in downtown Louisville, he spent little time there. "I'd drive up for practice and drive back home on the same day," says Ramsey. "Sometimes they had a plane available to get me back and forth."

The laid-back Ramsey had his own style of coaching, but on occasion implemented techniques, philosophies, styles, and mannerisms of the two coaches he had spent most of his playing days under, Adolph Rupp and Red Auerbach.

When Rhodes was dismissed as the Colonels coach, he had an impressive 10-5 start in the 1970-71 season. When Colonels front office man, Alex Groza, stepped in and won his only two games as a head coach, Ramsey was handed a team with a 12-5 start.

Ramsey's pre-game actions often included pulling up a chair in the middle of the locker room and talking to the players while they were getting into their uniforms. There would even be times when he took over for trainer, Gardner, and taped the ankles of some of the Colonels, simply because he wanted it done his way.

Some Colonels insiders said Ramsey's discipline standards had not been up to those of Rhodes', mostly because he spent much of his off-court time back home in Dixon. Still he implemented a travel technique that cut down on many of the late night escapades before team flights. He scheduled the first available flights out in the morning, going to or coming home. There were certain players that this slowed down, but others it didn't.

Ramsey's regular season coaching record was an unimpressive 32-35, but everything he had thought about and talked about to his team finally found a home in the playoffs.

Did it ever!

As expected, the Colonels defeated the Floridians in the opening round. The powerful Virginia Squires were the second round foes, and their glossy 55-29 record made them a favorite to beat Ramsey's team. Al Bianchi's team was led by Doug Moe and co-ABA rookie of-the-year Charlie Scott.

The Colonels, however, behind their own co-rookie-of-the year, Dan Issel, won in six games to advance to the ABA title game against Utah and their coach, Bill Sharman, a former teammate of Ramsey's with the Celtics.

Zelmo Beaty of Utah was a force to contend with. His 63 points against Pittsburgh will always be the ABA record. At 6'7" he could do it all.

Out of Prairie View College, Beaty initially played with the NBA Hawks, first when they were in St. Louis and then in Atlanta, before sitting out the required one year before playing for the Utah Stars. He was 31-years-old by the time he reached the ABA in 1970. Beaty was the second player, behind Rick Barry, to jump leagues, and could have easily been the poster child for why NBA players fought vehemently against any merger between the two leagues. Making $37,000 a year with the Hawks, he then signed a four year contract with the Stars for $250,000 per year.

Willie Wise, Red Robbins, Merv Jackson, Ron Boone, and Carr Creek native Glen Combs rounded out the other players for Utah.

Utah had just won a seven game playoff over Indiana and, with a league-best 58-26 record, would be a solid choice over the Colonels.

Several Colonels players went to Ramsey with concern about Salt Lake City's high altitude and the lack of oxygen for those unaccustomed to playing there. No problem, said Ramsey.

Whiffing ammonia always helped clear the head he reasoned, but he would have an oxygen tank near the team's bench that would help with all of that thin air stuff.

Kentucky pushed the Stars to a seventh game final where they lost 131-121 at Utah. Beaty was spectacular, scoring 36 points and gathering 16 rebounds; Wise did his share with 22 points and 20 rebounds.

Issel led the Colonels in scoring with 41.

Colonels players had found comfort in the nearby oxygen tank. The relief it gave them during timeouts and substitutions allowed them to overcome the high altitude. Only after the playoffs did Ramsey reveal to the team that nothing was in the tank.

"Frank told me to take the oxygen tank with us," says Gardner. "I told him it was empty. He said take it anyway."

Today, Ramsey sits behind his desk in Dixon, far removed from the adulation of University of Kentucky fans, with only memories of those incredible days of watching Red Auerbach actually lighting up a cigar on the Celtic bench when he knew his team had it won, which was most of the time.

Visitors to Hopkins County might be disappointed in not seeing photos of Ramsey's glory days. Instead, his brown paneled walls are the resting place for two Ray Harm prints, one a deer and the other an eagle. A stuffed Kentucky Lynx Wildcat that was shot with a bow on a farm he owns in Webster County protrudes from one of the walls. Another wall has several family pictures that includes one showing the remains of a 2005 tornado that completely destroyed the Ramsey home, leaving only two chimneys standing, one in the center of the house and the other at the end. Ramsey feels very lucky to have survived. He was the only one home when it hit and lived to tell about it by hunkering down in a closet that backed up to the centrally located fireplace. With the exception of a few minor scratches on his face caused by falling brick, he was able to step out of the closet unscathed. Gone are most of his keepsakes and treasures, some blown into other states. The photo on his wall is a constant reminder of his good fortune, and it had nothing to do with basketball.

You have to look close in his office to find the only thing that connects him to the Boston Celtics. It's a piece of the parquet flooring from the old Boston Garden.

On one of the bookcases is an ABA book, but on closer examination it is an American Bankers Association publication and not one from the American Basketball Association.

"After that season I had to make a decision about whether to continue to coach or not," Ramsey says. I had my family back in Madisonville and several businesses also.

"The owners wanted to talk to me about next year, so I flew to Louisville to talk to them about coming back. We had lunch and talked about it at the Executive Inn," Ramsey recalled.

Ramsey, for the most part had had a good experience with the first year of coaching. With the exception of his differences with trainer Bill Antonini, and a little bad press here and there, he had a Colonels team that played in the ABA championship game.

"The ABA, and especially the Colonels with Darel and Louie, was a completely different style than the NBA because of the 3-point shot," he said. "Back then the NBA had military veterans. These guys liked to smoke and have a beer now and then. In fact Heinsohn (Tom) had to have a couple of cigarettes at the half, and I'd usually start the third quarter."

Ramsey says today it's totally different from when he played with the Celtics and coached the Colonels. "It's the attitude," he says. "They now seem selfish."

He chuckles when talking about little things like meal money back then when teams were on the road. "With the Celtics, we got $7 a day to eat. Seven dollars a day," he repeats. I think with the Colonels it had gone up to $10 or $12."

But those were the days, and Ramsey knows it. Satisfied that one year of coaching was enough, he returned to his little piece of heaven back in Dixon, content that he would never have to say "what if."

Only one win from winning a professional basketball championship had been enough.

JOHN Y. HAMILTON

It was 1972 and John Young Hamilton had just graduated from DePauw University in Greencastle, Indiana. At 21 years of age, he wasn't quite sure what he wanted to do in the real world. He was sure, however, that he really liked basketball. After all, he had been a decent player a few years before at Country Day High School in Louisville, and the fact that the Kentucky Colonels were going strong gave him a far-fetched notion that maybe, just maybe, he could get a job with them.

"The Colonels had just signed Artis," remembers Hamilton. "Everyone in town was excited, so I just went to Mike Storen's office and told him I had lived here all my life and that I'll do anything you want if you'll give me a job. I told him he didn't even have to pay me."

Not having to pay someone to work for the Colonels must have been music to Storen's ears. But the team's general manager did a little better than that.

"He said I could sell tickets on a commission-only basis," Hamilton continued. "I really got after it. I started on the top floor of every tall building in Louisville and worked my way down, floor by floor. I was selling more tickets than anyone in the organization. I kicked all of their asses on ticket sales."

Hamilton's efforts also caught the eye of David Vance, who at the time was the team's director of publicity.

"David took me under his wing and taught me the ropes," says Hamilton. "What a life it was back then. We would fly on the Ollie Bird to the games and back. And later on, when David became general manager, I moved up to publicity director. I was only a year and a half out of college."

Hamilton's responsibility was to take care of the media. One of those occasions was when a fledgling television network came to Louisville to broadcast a game between the Colonels and Nets back to Long Island.

"It was HBO and their sportscaster was Marv Albert," Hamilton said. "They told us they wanted to do a two or three minute interview with Hubie Brown's wife, Claire. She had gone out and had her hair fixed that day all in preparation for the interview. Then, at the last minute, HBO decided they wanted to interview the wife of Jan Van Breda Kolff. Now keep in mind that Claire was a very attractive lady, but one of the HBO guys saw Jan's wife who was just out of college, and on a scale of 1 to 10, a 10 plus. She was beautiful."

HBO's decision not to interview Claire Brown immediately put Hamilton between a rock and a hard place.

"I had to go tell her she wasn't going to be interviewed," laughs Hamilton, years later. "I went to her seat, and kneeling down on one knee, gave her the news. She was not happy and neither was I. But time was my ally. It took her two weeks to get over it, but that night I really got the stare."

Hamilton also recalled the night the St. Louis Spirits came to town. "They had a wild bunch on that team," he chuckled. "Marvin Barnes, Freddie Lewis and a young 23-year-old broadcaster. It was my job to help him a little. I remember he had his on-air commercials written out on index cards and my job was to hold them up for him when it was time. His name was Bob Costas."

There was also a trip to St. Louis that became one of the legendary stories within the Colonels organization.

The Colonels were playing game four of the playoffs there and had chartered a plane to take the staff, wives, and owners to see the game. Every seat was filled. After the game, John Y. decided to bring his friend "Jimmy the Greek" back to Louisville for the remainder of the playoffs. There was only one problem: the plane was full. After several minutes of discussion, Brown told Hamilton to hide in the plane's bathroom for the trip home. After the plane was airborne, Hamilton decided to peek out of the bathroom door. He barely opened it, but when he did, his eyes made contact with a stewardess seated in a nearby jump seat. She immediately notified the cockpit, and the plane did a 180 degree turn and headed back to St. Louis. All of this time, Ellie was spitting venom at her husband for putting Hamilton in this situation. At the terminal, local police were waiting and immediately handcuffed Hamilton and escorted him from the plane. As they walked across the tarmac, Hamilton kept asking security if they could loosen the cuffs. "They hurt like hell," he said. He could also see the Colonels contingency staring out the window. All the while, Brown was trying to talk the police into releasing their suspected stowaway, guaranteeing them he would put Hamilton in a hotel for the night and give him money to fly home the next day.

"They took me to a small holding room where John Y. finally convinced them of his plan," said Hamilton. Brown gave Hamilton $200 cash out of his pocket and told him to get a room at the airport and buy a ticket back to Louisville.

Hamilton now works at Three Chimney's Farm in Lexington where he is the blood stock agent, buying and selling horses. It's also where Big Brown, the renowned racehorse hangs out. "When Big Brown ran in the Preakness a few years back, I got up to Baltimore, and Costas was doing the broadcast. We renewed an old friendship."

Hamilton, like anyone else who crossed paths with Wendell Ladner, has a story to tell. Like most others it involved a pretty lady. "Wendell was supposed to speak to a group of people at 1 p.m. that day, and I knew if I didn't go pick him up, he would never get there. That's just the way it was with him," says Hamilton. "He was living in the Vieux Carre Apartments at the time. Anyway, I go knock on his door, waited a minute, and when the door opens there is this pretty blonde standing there, buck naked. I just stood there, and then here comes Wendell around the corner with a big grin on his face. At least I got him to his speaking engagement."

Hamilton was around when the other John Y. gave everyone the news that the Kentucky Colonels were no more. It was a shock. "He said he would take care of every one of us," remembers Hamilton. "He said he could get me a job with the San Francisco Warriors. Heck, I was only 25-years-old and the thought of moving to San Francisco just didn't fit at the time. I've wondered what would have happened if I had."

THIRD SEASON
1969-70
by Lloyd Gardner

Regular Season Standings

EASTERN DIVISION	W—L
Indiana Pacers	59-25
Kentucky Colonels	45-39
Carolina Cougars	42-42
New York Nets	39-45
Pittsburgh Pipers	29-55
Miami Floridians	23-61

WESTERN DIVISION	W—L
Denver Rockets	51-33
Dallas Chaparrals	45-39
Washington Caps	44-40
Los Angeles Stars	43-41
New Orleans Buccaneers	42-42

Commissioner Mikan stepped down and Jack Dolph took over. Dolph had been the director of sports for the CBS Television Network for over 10 years and had spent 19 years with the network.

On April 15, 1969, Joe and Mamie Gregory sold the Kentucky Colonels to Wendell Cherry, David Grissom, John Y. Brown, David Jones and Stuart Jay.

Mike Storen left the Indiana Pacers to become the Colonels general manager.

In August 1968, four of the NBA's best officials jumped to the ABA. John Vanak, Norm Drucker, Earl Strom and Joe Gushue had their salaries more than doubled, plus benefits with the move.

Out with the old and in with the new. Connie Hawkins left the Pittsburgh Pipers/Minnesota Pipers/Pittsburgh Condors to play for the Phoenix Suns. Spencer Haywood, a sophomore at the University of Detroit, became the first college player to leave college and become a pro when he signed with the Denver Rockets. This was the first known "hardship case."

The Los Angeles Stars raided the NBA once again when they signed the Atlanta Hawks all-star Zelmo Beaty. The NBA made Beaty sit out a year, but gave the Stars the option to pay $75,000 so he would be released to play ball. Times were hard and teams were losing money, so they turned down the offer.

For the third year in a row the Kentucky Colonels lost their home opener. The first year it was to the Pacers, then the Oakland Oaks (now the Washington Caps) and this year to the Miami Floridians, 110-106.

127

It was common for the ABA to hold secret drafts. The league would do almost anything to get a jump on the NBA. In December, the ABA held a draft of players coming out of college. Extraordinary college players were the number one target. Pete Maravich was selected by Carolina, where he had lived as a youngster when his dad, Press, coached at North Carolina State before going to LSU. Indiana grabbed Rick Mount, and Dallas nabbed Dan Issel. So how did Kentucky secure the rights to Issel? They paid $25,000 for those rights.

Of course, every season the big game for the Colonels was any time they played there biggest rival, the Pacers. Those Colonels-Pacers encounters were always special to Indiana native Dampier. Rarely did he have an off shooting night, but there was one in particular against the Pacers on November 15, 1969, at the Convention Center. Louie played 39 minutes that night. He was one for eleven from the field that included 0-2 from his specialty, the 3-point basket. The sellout crowd of more than 6,000 saw Indiana win 115-111 in overtime. Darel Carrier's 38 points and Goose Ligon's 17 points and 23 rebounds were almost enough to make up for Dampier's off night.

As often happened in a Colonels-Pacers game, it was the off-court antics that only added to the rivalry. As Indiana guard Roger Brown headed to the locker room, someone tossed a full cup of beer on him, causing Pacers Coach Bob Leonard to scream into a microphone while doing a post-game interview being broadcast back to Indianapolis.

"See how they treat us down here in Kentucky," Leonard yelled. "That's what we have to put up with down here. But we'll get 'em when they come back to Indianapolis."

Later Leonard said, "It really is quite a rivalry we're building with the Colonels, and that's good for the league."

The ABA All-Star Game that year was played in Indianapolis, but without a lot of drama. Commissioner Dolph negotiated a deal with CBS to broadcast several ABA selected games as well as the All-Star Game. There was just one problem. The game was scheduled to be played on Tuesday, January 27, 1970, in Charlotte, North Carolina, but CBS demanded the game be played on Sunday the 25th. To make matters worse, the Charlotte Coliseum was already booked on that date. It was extremely important for the ABA to get the national exposure that a live telecast would offer, so in a last minute decision the game was switched to Indianapolis.

After all of the efforts to change the venue, the game was still in jeopardy. The players, under the advice of the NBA players that had jumped to the ABA, wanted a Players' Association. With all the elite players in the league united in Indy for the game, they demanded that the owners recognize their ABA Players' Association. After hours of negotiating and less than an hour before the game, an agreement was reached. Now the players had some bargaining power of their own.

In the game, Dampier, Carrier and Gene Moore represented the Bluegrass state, and Spencer Haywood was named the all-star MVP.

On February 22, Carrier burned the nets for 53 points against Miami, but 14 days later Dampier rattled the rim with nine 3's and tallied 55 against the Dallas Chaparrals.

In the Eastern Division semifinals, Kentucky defeated the Nets 4-3, but then lost in the Eastern Division finals to the Pacers four games to one.

CHAPTER NINE
STAND UP WHEN A LADY
ENTERS THE ROOM

JOHN Y. BROWN

For most of his life, John Y. Brown, seemed to get more enjoyment out of the chase than from the prize that awaited him at the end.

As an owner, he was involved with the Colonels for six and a half of their nine-year existence.

Growing up in Lexington and graduating from Lafayette High School, John Y. had been exposed to politics and sports most of his early life. His father, John Young Brown, Sr., had served in the state legislature, U.S. Congress, and had even ran for governor and for the U.S. Senate at one time. He was also a close friend of Adolph Rupp. In fact, the senior Brown tried to help recruit Wayland's King Kelly Coleman to UK in 1956, even arranging a meeting at his home in Lexington between Rupp and Coleman.

John Y., while still in high school, would on occasion go over to the UK campus and get into a few early day frat house poker games. But once he was enrolled there, where he was a teammate on the golf team of future PGA great Gay Brewer, the poker games became commonplace. That's where he solidified a friendship with Frank Ramsey.

Years later, Brown says he's not sure how he made it through college and especially law school. "I had ADD (attention deficit disorder)," he said. "I'm still not sure what I learned and didn't. I had a girlfriend, played poker and sold encyclopedias. I didn't realize until I was 28 that it was all about the money."

It was reported that he earned $60,000 a year while in law school selling Encyclopedia Britannica's across the state. In the meantime, he married Ellie Durall during his last year of law school in 1960.

For a short time John Y. practiced law with his dad, but soon discovered in 1964 that he wanted more. He put together a group of investors, and purchased Kentucky Fried Chicken for $2 million from Harland Sanders.

"I just had to keep going," he recalls. "We didn't know what an organizational chart was in our operation. We just did what needed to be done. I had 19 people reporting to me and they were all millionaires because of KFC."

Previously the closest thing to the food business for Brown was that he had eaten in a restaurant, and Ellie, while in college, had worked in one. "I never knew anything about the food business before Kentucky Fried Chicken," he said.

With that said, and the fact that he sold his interest in KFC in 1971 for a reported $285 million, John Y. had been recognized as a fast-food phenomenon. Harvard's School of Business recognized him as one of the top businessmen of the 20th century. Along with McDonald's Ray Kroc, John Y. Brown, Jr., had received credit for helping to build America's fast-food business.

"Colonel Sanders was the dreamer and Johnny the prime mover, who together achieved perhaps the most astonishing financial success of this century, or any other century in the world of business," offered John Y. Brown, Sr. several years ago.

He was 38years old.

By his own admission he became easily bored. So when Louisvillian Wendell Cherry approached him in 1970, about becoming part of a group to purchase the Kentucky Colonels from Joe and Mamie Gregory, he was quickly on board. The group included David Grissom, Stuart Jay, and David Jones. Although some records indicate that newly acquired general manager Mike Storen was a part of the group, Brown says the former Indiana Pacers GM never had any stock in the Colonels.

With Storen running the day-to-day operation, Gene Rhodes was dismissed as the team's coach, and soon after, Frank Ramsey was hired. "People thought I was the one who got Frank to come in, but that was Wendell's deal," says Brown.

"Frank and I had been friends, remember even before I went to UK, during my senior year of high school, and later, when I ran for governor, I got three small donations from him. He's a friend, but he was cheap," Brown laughed.

How the Browns came to own the Colonels seemed all too simple. Following the 1972-73 season, the group sold out to a Cincinnati group headed by Bill DeWitt. The plan was to play games in both Louisville and Cincinnati. However, there were some who felt once the Ohio city built a new arena, the Colonels would move there permanently.

One of those who didn't want to see the team leave town was John Y. and Ellie's 10-year-old son, John Y. Brown, III.

"We were at breakfast and he told Ellie and me he didn't want the Colonels to quit playing in Louisville, so we decided then and there to buy the team and keep it here," Brown said.

"When we bought the team I told Ellie she owned it," Brown says. "Walter Kennedy (NBA Commissioner) told me 53% of the fans who came to the games were women. She never questioned one time that she couldn't do it. I didn't know until 30 years later how much she loved it."

For some time John Y. had thought that Muhammad Ali had been a bit neglected by the city of Louisville. However, back in 1971 there were still some ill sentiments toward the boxer's refusal to be drafted into the army. John Y., however, felt differently.

"I thought we needed to recognize Ali for all he had done," Brown said. "Here was a guy from Louisville, known all over the world, yet our city was slow to embrace him."

The Browns invited Ali to a Colonels game. They wanted him to know how much he was appreciated. A downtown parade the day of the game for the boxing champion was even staged. In Brown's opinion, it helped soften the edge between Ali and the city. "We made a big deal out of it, and it was," Brown says years later. "I'll never forget how Mayor Harvey Sloane tried to slip in and get all the credit for it."

Mullaney didn't relish having to work with all women, and for sure Storen didn't. "Storen's ego was bigger than the team," Brown said. "I remember back before Ellie and I bought the team and I was involved with Wendell and them. We had just lost a half million dollars that year. Storen was giving a report about the season and everyone was congratulating him. I said I'd never heard of someone being congratulated for losing a half million dollars a year."

Brown says not only was the ABA losing money, but so was the NBA. "I talked to all the ABA owners and most of them in the NBA," he offered. "They wanted to get together, except for Jack Kent Cook (Los Angeles Lakers). He was one arrogant guy."

All the while, Brown had been named honorary chairman of the National Democratic Party, and along with future NBA Commissioner Larry O'Brien, had co-chaired a national Democratic telethon to help get the party out of debt.

For sure at this point in his life Brown was not bored. He didn't have time to be.

Years later Brown laughed when looking back at the Colonels venture. "Ellie thought I was such a genius with KFC and all, and then she found out how dumb I was."

Ellie, while making the national media circuit because of her status of being the female owner of a professional basketball team, was often asked what she knew about running a basketball team. "Not much," she said. "But my husband didn't know much about chickens and he did all right."

Babe McCarthy followed Mullaney as coach, and although for the 1973-74 season his Colonels team record was 53-31, they lost in the second round to the New York Nets and Dr. J. McCarthy was out. Who to hire next was a dilemma. Brown knew he had to get it right this time.

Wayne Embry, a former NBA star with connections to the old Cincinnati Royals and Milwaukee Bucks was high on Bucks' assistant Hubie Brown.

"Embry said he was a good coach, but hard to get along with," Brown said. "I interviewed Hubie at the airport sitting in my car. He wasn't a warm person, not much of a personality, but I wanted Ellie to talk to him, so I turned him over to her. She liked him and hired him."

One of the things John Y. and Ellie also did was to bring Adolph Rupp into the Colonels organization. Though the former UK coaching icon had early on badmouthed the league before being hired by the ABA Memphis franchise, his name in Kentucky meant instant credibility.

"My dad was close to him," recalled Brown. "And when they were getting ready to retire him at UK, I took Colonel Sanders with me to a board of trustees meeting to try to get Rupp's job saved. So when we had a chance, I just asked him to be a part of the team."

Whenever Rupp was at a Colonels game, his presence never went unnoticed. "Adolph would get up to go to the restroom and get a standing ovation," Lloyd Gardner recalled. Hubie turned to me and said, 'He's the only guy in the nation who could go take a piss and the crowd would cheer.'"

Hubie Brown came to Louisville and did what he was hired to do, and what those before him couldn't do — win an ABA championship in 1975.

But no sooner was the ice melting around the champagne than John Y. was at it again. This time he was asking anyone who would listen if they thought the Colonels could beat Golden State (the NBA champs) in a challenge game. "It was like we couldn't enjoy the championship we had just won," said David Vance, the Colonels general manager at the time.

Gardner even remembers a $1 million challenge game that Brown talked about. "It was mentioned about the game being winner-takes-all and playing it in Las Vegas," he said. Brown, however, says he would never spend that kind of money on a game, and doesn't really remember such a challenge.

It was said that ABA Commissioner Dave DeBusschere had issued the challenge to the NBA Champion Golden State Warriors in a $1,000,000 winner-take-all *series*. The money would come from major television network sponsorship.

Merger talks were still ongoing between the two leagues, but by now some of the teams had individually set out in an attempt to strike their own deals with the NBA. Two of those teams were Denver and New York. Reportedly, Kentucky had been approached about doing the same. But John Y., being president of the league, refused to consider it. When it got right down to it, at the time the biggest stumbling block was the cost of the NBA's entry fee, $6 million.

"When we hired Hubie, I told him we're not going to lose $1 million a year," remembered Brown. "But we still lost money after winning the title. So I talked it over with him about selling Artis or Dan. We both said we would be okay with Artis. He was a game changer. Dan was a center, playing an out of position forward. We were dealing in a dying enterprise with owners in and out, just not very stable. I was encouraged at the time that we were going to get a merger. We sold Dan, and Hubie was okay with it. Later he turned the tables on me and said he couldn't believe we got rid of him. I don't regret it to this day. It's something we had to do. We were losing money. But, you know, I just wasn't going to get into a pissing contest with Hubie over it."

The following year, with Issel gone, not only didn't it feel the same, it wasn't the same. There was a scene in the Secretariat movie where Penny Tweedy's brother demanded her to sell Big Red in order to keep their horse farm afloat, but she stood fast, refusing to give in. Her intuitions kicked in and the rest is history. Many believe that was the same situation faced by John Y. And what a coincidence that the beginning of the end of his stable was when he sold his horse, Dan "The Horse" Issel.

John Y. admits that Ellie did, indeed, take exception to the Issel deal. "Oh, that was just a one night thing," John Y. chuckled years later. "She threw a glass at me all the way across the room, but she missed."

Brown still insists that losing Issel had nothing to do with the Colonels not being in the NBA. According to Brown, no ABA owner in the league's history ever made money. Player's salaries escalated in a bidding war and the fact that no television revenues were available all added to its demise.

"It was about the money," he said. "In the end, the four ABA teams (San Antonio, New York, Indiana, and Denver) wanted to buy me out. They offered $2 million.

"I asked Ellie what she thought. I told her it sounded fair to me. I told them we would sell on one condition, and that was they didn't pay anyone else more than they paid us."

The Browns were in Chicago, and John Y. remembers Ellie and he waiting for several hours outside of a hotel meeting room for a financial decision by several ABA owners on what to offer the Browns in order for them to disband the Kentucky Colonels.

"Finally Angelo (Drossos, San Antonio owner) comes out and says, 'would ya take $3.4 million?' Now keep in mind we were satisfied with the $2 million that had been talked about earlier," Brown said. "They didn't say a word about TV rights, and that's what the St. Louis guys got to go away. Those guys held them up."

The so-called heist he was referring to was the deal St. Louis owners Ozzie and Danny Silna and partner Don Schupak cut with the four other ABA teams.

As Brown had requested, St. Louis was not paid more than he was to go away. The $2.2 million they received was substantially less, but what wasn't on the table was the 1/7 of a share of future television money annually from each of the four ABA teams. But there was more. It was to be in perpetuity. And since 1976 the TV contracts and payouts have run into the hundreds of millions with no end in sight.

Even though the New York Nets took the offer to become an NBA franchise, its owner, Roy Boe, offered that it was the demise of the Nets as its fans knew them.

The cost to Boe had been close to $5 million when it was all added up, but then there was an annual territorial infringement payment to the Knicks of $480,000 that would last for 10 years. On top of that, Dr. J was making something like $350,000. Boe had to do something. So, like John Y. did with Dan Issel, he dangled his franchise player Dr. J out there for sale.

The Philadelphia 76ers offered $3 million, and Boe, in order to pay his bills, took it. The Nets were in, but in doing so, it destroyed the team's short-term future.

Looking back on it, John Y. says he had compassion for the other owners. "The only teams who paid their way in the ABA were Indianapolis, Louisville and San Antonio," he says. "It was wild, like a bunch of cowboys operating wild. My business mentality was not to continue putting that kind of money into something that had no future. I'd do it the same way if I had it to do over."

There was one deal, in retrospect, Brown would not do over again. It was the Wendell Ladner and Mike Gale trade to the Nets for guard John Roche.

"I'm not sure why I did it," Brown confesses. "I think I thought Louie (Dampier) was at the end of his career ... but he just kept going."

While both Ellie and John Y. deny that the departure of Dan Issel directly led to their divorce in 1977, they both said it made for contentious times.

There were written stories with John Y. saying he and Ellie were fed up with pro basketball, deciding it was not the type of business they wanted to be involved in. So, after hearing that, it would be easy to understand why fans didn't take kindly to it when Brown went out and bought the NBA Buffalo Braves.

Could it be that once the Colonels were gone Brown quickly began looking for another rainbow to chase?

"I got into the Braves for $10,000 down and a $1.5 million loan," Brown says. "I sold Bob McAdoo for $3 million to the New York Knicks."

For all practical purposes he had pulled off a deal that only John Y. could do.

With some of Louisville's civic leaders pleading with Brown to move his NBA team from Buffalo to Louisville, Brown asked for the locals to put their money where their mouths were. Reportedly he said if 20 individuals each committed $100,000 he would consider it. But years later, Brown says he doesn't remember it quite like that. "That was Bruce Miller who tried to do that," Brown says. "Bruce has been a friend for a long time, but that was not me; it was him who might have tried to do it."

But Brown was not through. In 1978 he made the trade of a lifetime, not for players, but for a team. It just happened to involve one of the most storied sports teams in history, the Boston Celtics.

"I was close to moving the Buffalo team to Minnesota," says Brown. "They had already sold 5,000 season tickets."

But then Brown learned that one of Boston's owners, Irv Levin, might be interested in trading his interest for the Buffalo franchise so he could then move it to San Diego, in his home state of California.

"I swapped straight up Buffalo for Boston, if you can believe it. Probably the best business deal I ever made," says Brown.

Gardner even had his chance at being a part of the Celtics. "John Y. offered me the job as the team's trainer," he says. "I told him that Ray Melchori, the trainer there, did a great job, and if it meant he was going to fire Ray, I wouldn't take it."

However, Brown and Celtic president Red Auerbach butted heads from the beginning.

"Red was a legend and he acted like it," said Brown. "He had made fun of the ABA over the years, and then we made some trades he didn't like when I bought the Celtics."

Keep in mind that this was the same Auerbach who said his league would never have a 3-point basket, and he was also quoted as saying Julius Erving is a nice kid, but not a great player.

Auerbach pleaded his case to the other Celtic owner about what Brown was doing, even threatening to move over to the Knicks. Brown, once again enjoying the chase of owning the Boston Celtics, decided there was something else to do. So he sold his interest to Harry Mangurian in 1979.

Businesswise, Brown had a reputation for keeping several balls in the air at the same time. His ability to juggle things around, more often than not, kept him from becoming bored.

There was Lum's, a beer and hot dog chain, Ollie's Trolley, John Y's Chicken, Kenny Rogers Roast Beef, Miami Subs, Texas Roadhouse and Roadhouse Grill, all eating establishments that John Y. and some of his associates hoped to parlay into the success he enjoyed with Kentucky Fried Chicken.

Not long ago Brown made a trip to China representing Alltech, a Kentucky-based company that was the major sponsor for the World Equestrian Games staged in Lexington in 2010. "I was introduced as the co-founder of Kentucky Fried Chicken. You would have thought I was Henry Ford," he said in pointing out the restaurant's popularity.

John Y. might have lost interest in several of his businesses along the way, but it was a hobby, one that he acquired early in life, that he always seemed to find time for, and that was a good poker game. With a well-earned reputation as a jet-setting high roller, John Y. Brown was on a first name basis with several greeters and doormen at Las Vegas casinos.

His star-power, although perhaps not quite as bright as some of the entertainers he hung with, was nevertheless well-known. "I kicked around with Jimmy the Greek (Snyder) a lot," says Brown. "I loved sports and betting on them."

Years later Brown still expresses a fondness for his old gambling pal, even though when Snyder died in 1996 their relationship was not on the best of terms.

"He did some PR work for me," recalls Brown. "And he wasn't the big-time gambler or mafia-type guy everyone thought he was. He was harmless. In fact, I helped get Jimmy the TV show."

The show Brown was referring to was the CBS Sports show, "The NFL Today," that featured Snyder, Brent Musburger, Irv Cross, and the former 1971 Miss America, Phyllis George. George's presence made her one of the first females to have a prominent role in a nationally televised sports show, and she caught the eye of the nation.

She also caught the eye of John Y. Brown, who had recently been divorced from Ellie, his wife of 17 years.

"I saw her on TV and said, 'She's someone I'd like to meet,'" recalled Brown.

Not just anyone could say "I want to meet Phyllis George" and do it, but Brown could, and did.

With his connections from the telethons and Las Vegas, getting an introduction was no problem, and years later while sitting in his Lexington townhouse surrounded by framed photos of himself with the likes of Presidents Jimmy Carter, Ronald Reagan and Bill Clinton, he described his somewhat uneventful first date with her.

"I went to pick her up at the Beverly Wilshire Hotel in Los Angeles," he said. "I ran into Howard Cosell in the lobby. After talking awhile he said he had not met Phyllis, but would like to do so, so I went up to her room and brought her back to the hotel's lounge to meet Howard. For the rest of the evening he talked, and she hung on every word he said. If that wasn't enough, Warren Beatty came over and joined us. By now I was really overmatched."

Brown says he was able to save face when a little later he introduced Phyllis to Ali. "She was able to interview him and get a scoop on an up and coming match the champ had scheduled," Brown said.

Apparently Brown wasn't overmatched too much, because in March 1979 the two married.

Some thought it might be a Las Vegas wedding. After all, John Y. was a frequent visitor, and it was both Phyllis and John's friend, Jimmy the Greek, who had taken credit for the couple's meeting. Years later John Y. laughed when recalling that he had actually received a $100,000 invoice from him for making the introduction.

The two were married by Norman Vincent Peale in New York's St. Patrick's Cathedral. Among the hundreds in attendance were Andy Williams, Walter Cronkite, Milton Berle and Bert Parks.

Six months later, he and his new wife embarked on another of John Y.'s rainbow treks, the governorship of Kentucky.

It was a campaign sprint. Not having time to do much fundraising or to drive across Kentucky, John Y. used much of his own millions, and with a former Miss America on his arm, helicopered from one end of the state to the other.

Out of it came one of the all-time great political ads. It captured a Kentucky farmer speaking to a rally and caught on camera saying, "I'd a whole lot rather him be a millionaire a comin' in than a goin' out." With that commercial, John Y.'s millions seemed to resonate with both the haves and have-nots across Kentucky.

Gardner recalled years later that one Buffalo newspaper reporter who had not been a John Y. supporter through all of the dealings with the NBA team there wrote that if Brown became Kentucky's governor, the nation might end up with 49 states.

John Y. and Phyllis won the Democratic primary and defeated Republican Louie Nunn in the general election. From 1979 to 1983, he served as Kentucky's 55th governor.

But in spite of the "Super Bowl-everyday" life John Y. described, the couple divorced in 1998.

Decades later John Y. Brown says he never knew that many people loved the Colonels like they did.

"I'm so proud of the championship we won," he says. "But I just didn't fully appreciate it until I came back for the Derby Parade a few years ago when members of the team were grand marshals. I was so proud of Ellie and what she did with the team. It wasn't like KFC, not like this was my company and I built it. The team belonged to the community, and Ellie was the high spot."

ELLIE BROWN

Ellie Brown's name comes up quite a bit whenever there's any kind of talk about the Kentucky Colonels. There were times when she seemed to know her place, but not always, as there were those that thought women had no place in running a professional basketball team.

The Browns, as Gene Rhodes described it, were like knights in shining armor riding in and saving the city when they bought the team in early July 1973.

From the beginning, Ellie wanted to be involved, but figured she could really make a difference by putting together several of her high society friends and literally going door-to-door in the business community selling season tickets. The Browns and everyone else in the Colonels organization knew tickets were the life-blood of the team.

"We had a group of high powered women," she says years later. "Maxine Lutz was one of them, and she could have run General Electric. They had great ideas, and we started making money on things we'd lost on before."

In addition to Lutz, the board included Billie Claire Kurfees, Nancy Jones, Kay Morrissey, Joni Coleman, Sissy Jenkins, Mary Taylor, Patsy Baker, Faith Lyles, and Mary Baird.

"We did a lot of things the men wouldn't even think of doing," Ellie Brown said back then. "We walked up and down the street selling tickets. We even planned a baby-sitting service at Freedom Hall during the games."

Unlike Mamie Gregory before her, Ellie knew something about basketball. Growing up in Central City she had been a cheerleader for the Golden Tide before graduating in 1957. She had cheered for Coach Delmas Gish, and his star player Corky Withrow, it seemed like forever, because Central City had been a state powerhouse for years.

And then she went to the University of Kentucky where she met John Y. They saw the great Adolph Rupp teams, including the 1958 national championship team, the Fiddlin' Five.

How could she not like basketball? And now here she was deeply involved in running a pro team. "We had a great team when John and I got the team," she said about the Colonels. "It's just that there didn't seem to be much community support."

She was right on both accounts. The Colonels had finished second in the eastern division with a 56-28 record before losing to Indiana in the seventh game for the championship, and those season ticket numbers being sold in and around Louisville were not where they needed to be.

Ellie says before she knew it, she was in charge. At least it seemed.

Ellie felt it was her duty to touch base with other teams, not only in the ABA, but in the NBA as well.

"All of the owners were terrific," she recalled. "They offered advice and encouragement. The only one who wouldn't call me back was Red Auerbach (Boston Celtics)."

"John went to California to do the National Democratic Party Telethon," she says. "And I was left to run the team."

Ellie Brown quickly became the darling of the media. There was Club 21 in New York City and interviews with Haywood Hale Broun, Howard Cosell and Frank Gifford. The national press, and even the locals, had jumped on her bandwagon. Newspapers, televisions, magazine and radio were all talking about the lady in Louisville who was president of one of the best professional basketball teams in America. Dinah Shore talked to her, as did all of the network morning shows, and she even stumped the panel on, "What's My Line," a popular T.V. show.

"I called all of the heads of banks and corporations, and they came on board with ticket buys," she said. "The response was amazing. We toured the state in many of the towns, telling our story and selling tickets. We started at the crack of dawn and finished late at night."

One of the techniques the ladies used when they could was to take some of the players with them.

"All of the ladies wanted to see Wendell Ladner," she laughed. "And Artis (Gilmore), Dan (Issel), and Louie (Dampier) did an amazing job of helping us out. We spoke to civic clubs everywhere. We even had teas and coffees in people's homes around Louisville."

With Ellie as chairwoman of the board, the Colonels were still searching for an edge, something over the top that could carry the team to statewide notoriety. And as quick as you could say the baron of basketball, there he was.

At the age of 72, Adolph Rupp was brought in to serve as vice-chairman of the board.

Legendary owner and promoter Charlie O'Finley had hired Rupp as president of his ABA Memphis team a year or so before. Yes, the ABA Memphis Tams. At the age of 65 Rupp had been forced into retirement by the University of Kentucky, and wanting to do anything to stay in basketball, his vulnerability made him easy prey for Charlie O. and Memphis.

"We thought Coach Rupp would give us that edge," says Ellie. "And besides, he was connected to Dan and Louie. He did anything we asked and would go anywhere we asked."

Just a few days after the Browns bought controlling interest in the team, general manager Mike Storen tendered his resignation. Storen had done some great things for the Colonels and his professionalism gave the team some front office legitimacy. But still, there was a notable distance between him and the fans.

In spite of the lawsuit by Rhodes against the Colonels when he was fired, all was forgiven when John and Ellie brought him back, this time as general manager, replacing the man who had fired him.

Looking back on it all in discussing why Storen would leave such a successful team, Ellie Brown simply said, "Mike may have had trouble working for a group of women."

The next year when Mullaney decided to move on to coach at Utah, it was up to Ellie to bring in a new coach. She yielded much of this decision to Rhodes, who convinced Babe McCarthy this was where he needed to be.

But unfortunately for Babe, in spite of a respectable 53-31 record and a second place eastern division finish, the Colonels lost four straight in the second round of the Eastern Division Finals playoffs to New York. As soon as the season ended, McCarthy was fired.

A lot was going on at the top of the heap with the Colonels. Was Ellie actually making the calls when it came to Storen, Rhodes, and McCarthy? And was she the one who convinced Rupp to join up? The scuttlebutt was that John Y. still kept a very close watch on everything, but years later Ellie Brown says she did, in fact, have a say.

"The best thing I ever did was hire Hubie," she said in talking about bringing in Hubie Brown. "We actually interviewed him at our home. He was impressive; he was a star. He told us his plan and he did it."

Hubie Brown had actually been interviewed by the Colonels before McCarthy was hired, but this time he got the nod over Al Bianchi, Doug Moe, and local favorite Bud Olsen.

Ellie even took in a few Colonels practices. After all, if she was going to talk the talk, she was entitled to walk the walk, and that included a Hubie Brown practice.

"I was told that Hubie said I could come, but be prepared because he wasn't going to clean up his language. Later he even had basketball clinics just for women, and they went great."

But what about all of those trades that took place while Ellie was supposedly running the show? Did she sign off on them? What was her role in it all? "John and I had a lot of disagreements over some of them," she reflected. "I think the coach should have had a little more say in it all."

Ellie says the Dan Issel deal was the beginning of the end.

"If I could go back, I wouldn't have gotten rid of Mike Gale, Wendell Ladner or Dan Issel," she says years later. It was the selling of Issel that brought the house down, and Ellie is not at all pleased at how it was handled.

"Dan was at the harness track when I called him," she said. "I should have been face to face with him and not on a phone call, but John operated on such impulse back then, so I called Dan. I've never really had a chance to talk one on one to him. I would have liked to have done that. After all, we were a Kentucky based team and he was such a part of it."

Ellie kept emphasizing all of the opposing opinions she and John had through it all, even saying that the fans reaction over Issel completely caught her husband off guard. "He was totally unprepared for it," she said.

But finally it was over.

"We really thought we had succeeded," she said. "We won a championship. We were going 24/7, but it still didn't seem like work. When it was all over, I was really disappointed. "But here it is more than 35 years later, and we're still writing about them. We're still celebrating them. The Colonels, they were really special."

David Vance

For six years David Vance was a part of the Kentucky Colonels management team. In the beginning, in 1970, his main responsibility was the media, anything that had to do with publicity, in other words getting the word out.

Vance grew up in Franklin County, Kentucky, and attended college at Morehead State and Eastern Kentucky, and in 1970, was seemingly satisfied with his job as Director of News and Public Relations at Eastern, when his phone rang. It was Mike Storen of the Kentucky Colonels.

"He said he had heard about me from Cawood Ledford," Vance says. "Said he was looking for a media person and I was it. He made an offer of $14,000 a year and I was headed to Louisville."

Vance was a go-getter type, doing whatever it took to get his or anybody else's job done. It wasn't long before his title was changed to Assistant General Manager, still doing, of course, all of the things he had done with the other title. That's the way it was done in a fledgling professional basketball team where every penny was looked at and often counted twice.

Years later Vance says, "Working with the Colonels was one of the true blessings of my life." And that comes from a man who has now been in the horse business for more than 30 years. Today, Vance is working as a consultant to the thoroughbred industry, mostly in Latin America.

Vance has many memories of his Colonels days, which include those games played in Cincinnati. "The crowds were okay," he said. "But we played a couple of bad games there, one of which was against Dr. J. They ended up cheering for him and not us. Then there was the time I went on a morning radio show asking, pleading, for the fans to come out to the game. I assured them it would be very entertaining. They came out all right, and we were down to Larry Brown and his Carolina Cougar team at the half by 40."

In 1975, Vance, at the age of 31, was named as the Colonels General Manager, making him the youngest GM in all of pro basketball.

Vance remembers well the conflict between John Y. and wife, Ellie, over the departure of Dan Issel.

"Ellie definitely didn't want to sell Dan to Baltimore, but John was a smart businessman and financially felt he needed to do it, so he went ahead and did it," Vance explained. "He had decided between Artis and Dan. It was heart versus mind, and he thought he made a decision that was in the best interest of the team. John for sure underestimated Dan's popularity in Kentucky."

David Vance, who was there when it all ended, has his take on the wild and crazy ending of the Kentucky Colonels. It came fast and totally unexpected to most.

"John Y. is a savvy business man," says Vance. "He definitely was not closed out of the merger with the NBA. He decided after the merger not to go with the NBA. He had his own plan."

All of a sudden Brown, in a seemingly short period of time, had gone from folding the Kentucky Colonels in the ABA, to owning one of the most storied professional franchises in the history of sports.

But from his beginning with Boston it was a tumultuous relationship with the often abusive Celtic general manager, Arnold "Red" Auerbach. John Y. had his way, and for sure Auerbach had his.

"John Y. called me and told me he was having problems with Red," said Vance. "The Boston media had gotten hold of it all and had sided with Red, naturally. He wanted me to be the general manager of the Celtics, but by this time I had become the president of Latonia race track, and he couldn't pay me what I was making there."

Speaking of Auerbach, Vance remembers some of the pointed shots the NBA Hall of Fame coach took at the ABA. According to Auerbach, "The red, white and blue ball belongs on the nose of a seal and the 3-point shot is abuse of the game."

Decades later, there are other things Vance says he will never forget.

"Every year we tried to draft a quick little guard to take Louie's place," he says. "But we never did."

As for Artis Gilmore, Vance says he was something special, and still hasn't received the recognition he deserves. Artis, all-time in pro-basketball, ranks 14th in scoring and 15th in rebounding," says Vance. "And he is the sole reason blocked shots is now an official stat in the NBA, NCAA and high school. I remember the game we started stating it. It was his rookie year against Virginia. At that point I went to the stat crew at Freedom Hall and said, "let's do it." Utah then included the blocked shots in theirs, and then the rest of the league picked it up."

Vance loved talking about the 7'2" Gilmore. But who wouldn't. He recalled when Alex Groza, a big man himself, picked Artis up when he arrived in Louisville to be introduced to Colonels fans at Freedom Hall. Not only was his signing a big deal in Louisville, but also throughout the ABA, as he was one of the big names to have been wrestled away from the NBA.

"Alex took him to a store and bought him some clothes." Vance said. "It was the first tie that he had ever owned.

Artis was introduced at halftime that night, and the 12,000 fans went wild.

Anyone in the Colonels front office would have to have had their heads in the sand not to know that John Y. had problems with his coaches, at least personality-wise.

"When John Y. decided to get rid of McCarthy, he started looking everywhere," said Vance. "We talked to Al Bianchi and Bill Musselman, who was coaching at the University of Minnesota at the time. We even met with Lake Kelley."

Kelley was at Austin Peay in Clarksville, Tennessee, and his claim to fame at that point was coaching New York playground legend Fly Williams. Perhaps the thinking here was that if Kelly could handle a player with Williams' reputation, he could take care of some of the other characters in the ABA.

But the Colonels settled on Hubie Brown, and Vance says the former Milwaukee Buck assistant had his stuff together when he was interviewed and ultimately hired.

"He knew what was expected of him," Vance said. "He knew he had to win."

But Vance said that from the outset the personalities of John Y. and Hubie just didn't mesh.

"Everyone always thought John Y. just shot from the hip," Vance offered. "But I saw it a bit differently. I think he was just always testing the water to see what was out there. He was always asking those questions like 'what if this, what if that,' just seeing what others thought."

Of course Vance, like everyone else, was crazy about Wendell Ladner. Much of Ladner's legend was built on unplanned events. However, Vance had one that was planned.

"Burt Reynolds had recently done a photo spread for *Cosmopolitan Magazine*," Vance remembers. "It was one of those sexy layouts that showed him wearing pretty much nothing."

Ladner, who resembled Reynolds, but perhaps even more handsome, triggered an idea for Vance to do a poster with the popular player lying on his side, clad only in his uniform trunks holding an ABA basketball.

"The poster sold out in one day," said Vance. "He was single at the time and women just loved him.

Vance had become close enough to Ladner to serve as a pallbearer at his funeral following a plane crash in 1975.

Chapter Ten
A Horse and an A-Train

Dan Issel

When Dan Issel signed an ABA contract in 1970 to become a Kentucky Colonel, not only did it give the team legitimacy, it also led to the changing of the team's uniform color scheme.

It had to be more than a coincidence that the chartreuse green uniforms disappeared in favor of blue and white ones that looked very similar to those worn by Issel when he was a Kentucky Wildcat.

The fact that the group of Colonels owners had close ties to the University of Kentucky probably also played a part in the change.

Arriving the same time as Issel was former Wildcat teammate, Mike Pratt, and new coach, Frank Ramsey. So, along with Dampier, there was, indeed, a Kentucky flavor.

At 6'9" and 240-pounds, Dan "The Horse" was a big man who could crash the boards and also step out and shoot. By the time he had finished his three year varsity career at UK he had become the school's all-time leading scorer with 2,138 points, even with no 3-point goal.

The Detroit Pistons made Issel their first choice in the NBA draft and the Dallas Chapparels had the rights to him in the ABA. But from the outset, Issel made it clear that if he played in the ABA at all, it would be with the Kentucky Colonels.

"Mondo Angulucci, an attorney in Lexington, made some inquiries on my behalf," Issel said. "The Colonels knew where we stood, and I loved living in Kentucky. I'm not sure how it all came about, but the Colonels ended up with the draft rights."

Angulucci was a friend of Rupp's, and according to Issel's UK teammate, Pratt, Rupp had put the attorney in contact with his two players and told him to look out for them.

Issel, like all of the other collegiate stars of the day the ABA was trying to sign, inked an ABA contract before the NBA had even held their official draft.

The top six All-Americans in 1970 along with Issel were Calvin Murphy, Niagara; Rick Mount, Purdue; Charlie Scott, North Carolina; Pete Maravich, LSU; and Bob Lanier, St. Bonaventure. Three of them, Issel, Scott and Mount, signed with the ABA. It was definitely a coup for the new league. It also meant the ABA was not going away anytime soon.

By the ABA's own admission, they wanted to draft players as early as possible. They held secret drafts, while at the same time discussing the best way to get a certain player to a certain team. It was almost like, be damned of the rules, get the best college players anyway you could.

Most people would be hard pressed to recall the first player the ABA drafted before his college eligibility was completed. What is commonplace today was not even thought about in the 60s. But leave it to the ABA to have changed all that.

Spencer Haywood had been a 1968 Olympian, and after his sophomore year at the University of Detroit, he wanted to play at the next level, the pros. The NBA required that in order for a player to be eligible, he must wait until his class graduated, so this presented the ABA's Denver Nuggets with a perfect opening to implement what was called a "hardship case." In other words, a player's personal life, dictated by their finances and family situation, would allow him to leave college, regardless of the year of school, and sign a professional basketball contract with the ABA.

Why shouldn't a student have the right to earn a living, even if he was a college basketball player? After all, a student, regardless of year, could go to work in the corporate world without repercussions.

But, wouldn't you know it, a year later Haywood was in the NBA playing for the Seattle Supersonics, despite their eligibility rules.

Although Issel had completed his four-year college career, he was a big time target of the ABA, so when the Colonels hustled Issel and Pratt out of Kentucky to Fort Lauderdale to hide them, the league had gone into a protective mode.

Issel roared into professional basketball much like he roared out of the college game. Not missing a beat, he led the ABA in scoring with an average of 29.9 points a game, plus averaging 13.2 rebounds. Along with Charlie Scott, he was the league's co-Rookie of the Year, and just when you thought it couldn't get any better, Issel came back the next year after moving to forward from center and averaged 30.6 points. He was first team All-ABA and won the 1972 All-Star game MVP award. Issel became the first ABA player to score 5,000 points over two seasons.

Issel's roommate on the road that first year with the Colonels had been Darel Carrier, but after that, the remainder of his Colonels days he roomed with Louie Dampier.

Any discussion of the Colonels glory days always includes Dan Issel. He was not only a great player, but one of the most popular players in the state's history. From the mountains in the east, to the lakes in the west, Issel's name meant basketball.

His Colonels statistics were off the charts, and his teaming with Gilmore gave the team an inside presence that few teams could match, even in the NBA. What had for several years been the most obvious weakness of the ABA — lacking big, dominating inside talent — had now begun to go the other way. At least for the Kentucky Colonels.

Issel referred to the Colonels next coach, Babe McCarthy, as easy going. "But he jumped on you when he needed to," remembers Issel. "We were at Memphis and had just been beaten bad. Babe came in the dressing room and said, 'Boys, the sun don't shine on the same dog's butt everyday'."

It was Hubie Brown's style that Issel remembered. "His prep work and being ready to play was the best I ever played for," he said.

One of the most talked about events in the Colonels nine-year history occurred following the teams' one and only ABA championship in 1975. When John Y. and Ellie sold Dan, some said it was the beginning of the end of the Colonels.

Issel says he even heard about the possibility of a trade involving him when he was playing some exhibition games in Japan following the season. And then by his own admission, he says, he talked to the Phoenix Suns of the NBA when it looked like the ABA was, in his words, on a "downhill slide."

"I talked to Phoenix, but that was all," he said. "I couldn't pull the trigger. I loved Kentucky so much."

By now most know that Dan got the news of his sale by the Colonels by way of a phone call from John Y. and Ellie.

"I answered and Ellie told me it was one of the hardest things she'd ever done, and that I had been sold to the Baltimore Claws," Issel said. "I told her I had a no-trade clause in my contract, and then she put John on the phone."

At the harness track it had only been a few minutes before that Issel had run into Stuart Jay, one of the former Colonels owners.

"Stuart and I were talking and he said that Louie, Artis and I ought to buy the team from John Y., and shortly after I was paged to the phone."

Issel, however, decided to check the Baltimore situation out, and when he arrived there it was not good. Neither were the things being said in Louisville about Issel's sudden departure, and especially about John Y.

"The Baltimore franchise had been given by the ABA to two guys who didn't know what was going on," Issel offered. "A few days later I got a call in my hotel room in Baltimore from John Y. He said if I would say some good things about him, he'd get me to Denver. I said, 'Yes, I will,' and then he said, 'Come on down to my room.' He was already in the same hotel."

Anyone who ever saw Issel play in person couldn't help but notice the missing front teeth. As rugged as his play was, with flying elbows and swinging fists, it would be easy to see how some teeth could go missing, but in his case it was in the 8th grade.

"It was the first day of school and I was running laps in the gym," he said. "My feet slipped and my teeth hit the floor first."

It's difficult to talk with Issel and not talk some about his old college coach. "I was so fortunate that I got close to Coach Rupp after I left UK," he says. He would come out to the house after some of the games. He was so special in my life."

Rupp was at Issel's home one night after a game. "He and his driver, Claude Vaughan, stopped by," he recalled. "I offered Coach Rupp some bourbon, but he said the doctor told him to lay off the hard stuff because of his diabetes, but did I have some vodka?"

Issel did in fact end up at Denver and continued to be one of the best in the game. When his career ended following the 1984-85 season, he had scored more than 27,000 points in the combined ABA and NBA. Later, in 1992, he became the Nuggets head coach, where he once again hooked up with Dampier as one of his assistants.

Dan Issel was inducted into the Basketball Hall of Fame in 1993.

Artis Gilmore

Artis Gilmore was a dominate player. In college he led his Jacksonville team to the NCAA championship game in 1970 before losing to UCLA. He is one of only five players to average at least 20 points and 20 rebounds for a career, and his 22.7 career rebounds per game is an NCAA record. From 1971 to 1976, Gilmore was a Colonel, and along with Julius Erving, was perhaps the most dominating player in the league. In 1975, he was the ABA Playoff MVP as his Colonels team won a professional basketball championship.

The Colonels set their sights on Gilmore early, and although the ABA Miami Floridians wanted him, they were in no financial position to make it happen. But the Colonels were. The ABA's front office did everything in its power to put teams in position to sign players as early as possible, so the Colonels had the league's blessing to go after him, and their efforts were rewarded.

And they did, and they did.

Gilmore's impact was immediate. Moving the 6'9" Issel out of the middle to forward, and bringing in a 7'2" player that looked like he was 7'5" gave the Colonels a double-whammy on both ends of the court. In his first year he was not only the Rookie of the Year, but also the ABA's Most Valuable Player.

For the Colonels he was a five time All-Star, five time All-ABA first team, five-time ABA All-Defensive team, 1974 ABA All-Star Game MVP, and 1975 ABA Playoff MVP. Of course, he is a member of the all-time ABA team. And if that wasn't enough, he set an ABA record for career field goal percentage at 55.7%, and career blocked shots with 750. Add to this, a single game record of 40 rebounds.

When the Kentucky Colonels called it quits and folded their team at the conclusion of the 1975-76 season, the Chicago Bulls targeted Gilmore in the dispersal draft. There was strong evidence that Bulls' ownership was against admitting the Colonels into the league because they wanted the rights to Gilmore. It had been Chicago who had the draft rights to him back in 1971, but lost out to the Colonels. This time they were not going to be denied.

Though he did not post the almost unbelievable numbers he did in the ABA, still he was good enough to be a six time NBA all-star in a career with the Bulls, Spurs, and Celtics, as well as the NBA career leader in field goal percentage with 59.9%. He led the league in field goal percentage four straight years.

For his combined career in the two leagues Gilmore ranks in the top ten in rebounds, blocked shots and minutes played. Point-wise he ranks in the top 25 with just under 25,000. Almost overlooked in it all is his durability. During one stretch, he played in 670 consecutive games.

For Gilmore, his reason for being a Colonel was the financial security it gave him. The $1.5 million contract was easily one of the highest ever signed by a professional basketball player at the time.

Gilmore was familiar with Kentucky, and with Freedom Hall in particular. His Jacksonville team had eliminated an Issel-led Kentucky team in the NCAA in 1970. Then in December of 1970, he faced off against the other best big man in college, Jim McDaniels and his Western Kentucky team.

Jacksonville lost that night, but it would not be the last Gilmore saw of Freedom Hall, not by a long shot.

The Colonels championship season, says Gilmore, was definitely the highlight of his career, but he also is proud of his second season. "The second year with the Colonels, I got married," he says. And I'm still married to the same lady.

MIKE PRATT

When UK lost to Jacksonville in the 1970 NCAA tournament, it ended a storied career for Issel and teammates Mike Pratt and Mike Casey. Issel and Pratt were named to most All-American teams, while Casey's professional future was clouded by a broken leg he had suffered a couple of years before. He never quite reached the heights that had been predicted for him because of the injury.

However, the dynamic duo of Issel and Pratt were to be a package deal.

"As soon as we lost to Jacksonville, Adolph (Rupp) called Mondo Angulucci, a friend of his, and told him to look after Dan and me," said Pratt.

Not long after, the pair was in Louisville, overnighting at the Stouffer Inn on 2nd and Broadway.

"John Waiters was a friend of the owners of the Colonels," Pratt continued. "We went out to his house and the next thing I know we were on our way to Fort Lauderdale because they didn't want the NBA to find us. I'm not even sure whose house we were at back then, but we stayed about a week."

Pratt's first coach with the Colonels was Rhodes. "He coached a lot like Rupp in that era, and I learned from him," he said. "But I always felt he may have had a little something against UK people."

Pratt remembered when the Colonels won the Eastern Division that year by defeating Virginia in Louisville. "We had a big party upstairs at Freedom Hall. My dad was there and he got to meet Alex Groza," said Pratt. "He might as well have met Mickey Mantle. That was a big deal for my dad."

Pratt that year was a part of what he called the "Goon Squad," some of the guys who were not always starters.

"I'll never forget it. I'm on the floor with the Goon Squad. I think that night it was me, Les Hunter, Walt Simon, Howard Wright, and Tom Hagan," Pratt says. "All of a sudden I see Rhodes shaking hands with everyone on press row, and then he runs out the tunnel at the end of the floor. I'm thinking, what the hell is going on and where is he going?"

That, of course, was the night Rhodes coached his last game, and unbeknownst to the team had been fired earlier in the day. "Mike Storen comes in the dressing room after the game and tells us Groza will be our coach," he said.

"Alex won his first game at Virginia," says Pratt. "We were on a bus headed to Raleigh and Alex tells the driver to pull over at a convenience store. Bill Antonini, the trainer, runs in and buys two cases of beer. We win the next night over the Carolina Cougars and fly home."

Groza had won the only two games he coached.

"Ramsey was our new coach," Pratt said. "He wanted everyone to weigh a certain weight. He ran his team a lot like it was when he was at Boston. He played his bench. I remember he called me in and told me I needed to make something happen, especially on defense.

"Frank didn't want anyone telling him how to coach or do anything. If he had stayed on, the Colonels would have won a championship with him."

Like many of those who played for the Colonels, Pratt has great memories, especially one that involved Danny Hester. "His nickname was "Freak Mama," laughed Pratt. Back then he wore beads and flowered shirts. He drove Frank crazy with what he wore.

"We were in Pittsburgh, and Hester was always fussing and fighting, so Frank puts him in the game to take care of John Brisker. When he ran by the bench to go in the game, Frank yells for Hester to give him his beads before he checked in. Anyway, he could never get Brisker where he could hit him, so Frank takes him out and hands Hester his beads back as he heads to the bench."

Pratt tells of the little head games that Walt Simon and Les Hunter used to play with coach Joe Mullaney. "When Mullaney would walk in front of them pacing up and down during a game, they would act like they were asleep," he said. "Once the coach was talking to Jimmy O'Brien and me, and both Simon and Hunter, sitting right next to us, were pretending to be sound asleep. They didn't really like Mullaney and didn't give a damn."

By the time the 1972-73 season rolled around, Pratt, without a guaranteed contract, was cut following an exhibition game against the Pacers. He spent two years working for Converse before joining Lee Rose's staff at the University of North Carolina at Charlotte in 1975.

Pratt became UNCC's head coach for four years after Rose departed to coach at Purdue in 1978.

Today he is the radio color analyst for UK.

WAYNE CHAPMAN

Wayne Chapman was a Colonel for two years. He played at Western Kentucky for John Oldham and some of his great Hilltopper teams that included Clem Haskins, Dwight and Greg Smith, Butch Kaufman, and Steve Cunningham. Chapman, in 1968, was named the Co-Ohio Valley Conferences' Player of the Year with East Tennessee's Harley Swift.

At 6'6", the Daviess County native was versatile enough to play guard or forward, so it only made sense when the Colonels made him a top draft choice in 1969. After all, coach Gene Rhodes knew him well. Rhodes had been an assistant on the Western staff when Chapman was there.

"I loved the ABA" says Chapman. "With the exception of a few big men, the ABA was a better league than the NBA.

"I enjoyed the fact that Louie and I got to reunite. We played on the freshman team at UK before I transferred to Western."

The ABA was wild and crazy times, he remembers. "There was always a fight back then, and I never will forget a big fight in Indianapolis at the Fairgrounds. Players, fans, everyone was going at it, and I look up and there's Joe and Mamie Gregory out in the middle of the court right in the middle of it all."

Chapman spent two years with the Colonels before being traded to Denver.

"I arrived at the Denver airport," he says. "And there were all of these people around the gate, photographers, reporters, and all. I thought, Wow! What a reception. This is a pretty nice welcome." Soon, however, he realized that the commotion was not about him at all, but instead,

Denver star Spencer Haywood had just announced that he was jumping leagues, leaving Denver and heading for the NBA.

"I was coming in and Haywood was heading out," Chapman laughed.

LES HUNTER

For players like Les "Big Game" Hunter, the ABA was a reprieve from a death sentence. The death sentence being never playing professional basketball again.

Hunter, coming out of Pearl High School in Nashville, Tennessee, had been recruited to Loyola of Chicago by George Ireland, where in 1963 his team defeated Cincinnati on a last second put-back by Vic Rouse on Hunter's missed shot to win the NCAA Championship in Freedom Hall.

Originally drafted by the Detroit Pistons and traded to the Baltimore Bullets, he played in only 24 games that first year, averaging just 1.8 points a game. As quickly as he came into pro basketball, he was out of it. For the next two years he was on the outside looking in, that is until the ABA arrived.

"The NBA didn't wait back then for a player to develop," says Hunter. "There were only eight teams and just 10 guys on each team, so if you weren't ready to play in the NBA when you got there, they didn't wait for your development. The ABA was a blessing."

Hunter played two years with the Minnesota franchise that became the Miami Floridians, and then he was traded to the New York Nets for the 1969-70 season.

"As soon as they got Rick Barry I was gone," he said.

Hunter became a Colonel.

"I had known Storen from my year in the NBA at Baltimore," he said. "He worked, I believe, in their ticket sales."

"Gene Rhodes had his own lingo," recalled Hunter of his first Colonels coach. "Wall-off, wall-off, wall-off he'd yell. Walt Simon and I came over from the Nets and I remember us saying 'what the hell is wall-off?' Well, it was Gene's lingo for a screen."

His thoughts of Ramsey were of a coach that was very laid back. "He had a quiet confidence about him. He had his way of letting you know he had done it before," Hunter says. "He could tell you that you screwed up in a good sort of way. He made everyone around him feel comfortable."

And what about Mullaney?

"I didn't really care for Joe as a coach," Hunter offered. "I'm not sure how much the team really respected him. Oh, he knew the game, but there were always excuses. He always talked about Elgin (Baylor) and when he coached him with the Lakers. He said Elgin was so good offensively that he didn't have to play good defense. Some of us knew that he was referring to Dan, who some thought didn't always play good defensively. As great as Dan was, it just seemed Joe made excuses for him.

"I think players saw insecurity in Joe. He would make these funny faces and talked to himself constantly pacing up and down during a game."

When Jim Pollard gave Hunter that tryout with his ABA Minnesota team back in 1967, it was after he had contacted Babe McCarthy, then coaching at New Orleans. McCarthy had seen Hunter before, in fact coaching against him when his Mississippi State lost a second round NCAA game against Loyola at East Lansing, Michigan, in 1963.

"You know I always had a little grudge against Babe for not even giving me a tryout at New Orleans. He knew I could play," Hunter said.

Hunter, along with Colonels teammate Darel Carrier, ended up with Memphis the following year. Carrier had had some back problems with the Colonels and when they brought in Rick Mount to replace him, he went to Memphis.

"Darel had a torn Achilles tendon," recalled Hunter. "Bob Bass (Memphis coach) tried to get Darel to play with it and he couldn't."

Carrier picks the story up: "They sent me to a foot doctor and he told me the problem. Then they sent me to an orthopedic. Man, they took this long needle and filled me up in my heel and put me in a hot tub. Heck, soon my bad foot felt as good as the other one. I thought I was ready to play … but I wasn't. Memphis cut me loose and didn't even want to pay me."

Hunter says Carrier sued for the money they owed him and won. "I was a witness for Darel that they tried to get him to play when he wasn't ready."

CINCY POWELL

Cincy Powell was a Colonel for two years, 1971-'72, but during that period he officially played for four different coaches: Rhodes, Groza, Ramsey and Mullaney. He came to the Colonels by way of Dallas, and Cincy not being one to hide his feelings or his comments, was fairly vocal about his dislike of Cliff Hagan, the Dallas player-coach, who was a very popular Kentuckian of the Chaparrals.

"When Cliff was in the game, he ran an offense that was geared to only one thing, and I mean one thing, and that was him shooting," says Powell. "I got tired of just setting screens for him. In fact, when they let Hagan go at Dallas, he blamed some of it on me."

Powell came to the Colonels under the Storen regime, who in an effort to move beyond a guard oriented team began to look for forwards that could score and complement the newly signed Issel.

With Rhodes running the team, the intense coach was often at odds with some of Storen's new signees.

"Gene was a control guy," said Powell. "And when I came along with Warren Jabali and Mike Pratt, none of us kept our comments to ourselves. There were a couple of times we told Rhodes we were gone. I know he didn't care for me and wanted me out of there."

When Rhodes was let go by Storen, and Groza's two game coaching stint was no more than the blink of an eye, Frank Ramsey arrived on the coaching scene. For the Baton Rouge, Louisiana, native who played his college ball at the University of Portland in Oregon, it was like fresh air.

"He was one of the best coaches I've ever had," he said of Ramsey. "I respect him so much. With Frank we had basically three plays, sort of like the Celtic teams he played on. He demanded three things from me: rebound, look down the floor to pass, and be tough."

When Ramsey's one and only season of coaching ended with the loss to Utah in the ABA finals, Powell recalled the Colonels team party celebrating a successful year.

"Frank pulled me aside and told me he was proud of the season I had," offered Powell, who had 19 points and 20 rebounds in the final game against Utah. "He then told me he had gotten a call from his old friend Cliff Hagan early in the season telling him to cut my ass. Ramsey was his own man. He was as fair as anyone I've ever known, and everyone played hard for him."

During that 1970-71 season, Powell recalled a night in Memphis after a Colonels game.

"Goose (Ligon) liked to go clubbin' after the games," Powell laughed. "And there was one of those country-western places he'd heard about. He wanted some of us to go with him. We told him it wouldn't be a good idea for him since this was a mostly white club, and that it would probably only mean trouble. Well, Goose says, 'nobody tells me where I can't go.' So he heads out. When he got back he had been whipped up on pretty good."

Joe Mullaney followed Ramsey as the Colonels coach, and went 68-16, an ABA record. But it was that first round playoff loss to the Nets that Powell still vividly remembers decades later.

"I still can't believe it," he says. "Mullaney was supposed to be a defensive guru, and his plan was to force everything to the left. Here we were forcing John Roche (Net guard) who was left handed, to the left ... his strength. I'm trying to guard Rick Barry, and then I'd have to drop off of him to pick up Roche, who would then drop it to Barry. Issel wouldn't come over to check Barry because Mullaney didn't want him to get in foul trouble."

So when the season was over the team had only one thing remaining to do, and that was to vote who would receive the different shares of playoff money. Playoff money, and who got it, was strictly a team decision, and when the early voting failed to include Mullaney, general manager Mike Storen was incensed.

"I didn't want to, and neither did Darel (Carrier). There were several others," says Powell. "But Mike locked us in the locker room until we voted Joe a full share."

Cincinnatus Powell was the name given to him by his grandfather. "He insisted on it," Powell says. "Cincinnatus was a soldier back in the Roman days in Caesar's army."

Powell has always been a good talker, quick with his tongue as well as his feet. In fact, back in college he had been a state speaking contest winner, and a national oratorical finalist. So it only made sense when Storen came to him with the idea to do a Fall City Beer commercial for television.

"He wanted Dan to do it, but his agent said no," Powell laughed. "So, I did it. It was me in the kitchen getting a beer out of the refrigerator, I'd pop it open and pour it, and then I said something like 'have a beer.' Well every time I'd miss a foul shot, the fans would holler, 'Cincy, go have another beer.'"

Powell liked Storen. "He was really pushy ... but good at what he did. I picked up on his body language pretty quick. When he told a lie, his neck jerked to the right ... sort of like a twitch," chuckled Powell.

WALT SIMON

Walt Simon hailed from New York City, but although a pretty fair basketball player, he was overlooked by the so-called named schools, and went south to play college ball for Benedict College in South Carolina. There he had the chance to develop his game while growing a couple of inches.

Simon attracted enough attention to be drafted by the New York Knicks in the seventh round in 1965, but was quickly sent packing. Still wanting to play, he signed on with the Eastern League, a league made up mostly of guys who couldn't cut it in the NBA.

But like so many young men back then who felt like they still had game, when the ABA came calling in 1967, he was ready.

The New Jersey Americans, who became the New York Nets, latched on to the 6'6" Simon, and two years later he was an ABA All-Star scoring 18 points in the game, and averaging over 21 points for the season. He often said he was the first player to ever sign an ABA contract.

In 1970 Simon became a Kentucky Colonels, where he played at a high level until retiring at the end of the 1974 season.

Simon never reached All-Star status again, but once again he had proven what many already knew, that without the ABA, who knows what path Simon or his life might have taken. Not only did he have a stellar ABA career, scoring 6,414 points in seven seasons, but he had made such an impression on John Y. Brown and his Kentucky Fried Chicken business that 1973-74 season Simon hung it up for good, he had a job. The result was 22 years of working his way up the ladder to become KFC's vice-president of franchising. It was reported that Simon was the first black to become a vice-president of a Fortune 500 company.

Simon was so recognized in Louisville that he was sought after to serve on boards and committees, among them the Kentucky Derby Festival, chairman of the Louisville Urban League, and a member of the board of trustees at the University of Louisville. He even found time to serve on the board of trustees at his old school back in South Carolina, Benedict College.

Seemingly, Walt Simon had everything, financial security, fame, family, and even for a short time after his playing days, working with Van Vance on the Colonels radio broadcast. But then sometime in early 1997, a tumor was discovered on his brain, and on October 13, he was dead.

For sure he had taken his second chance to play basketball in the ABA and made the most of it in more ways than one.

BIRD AVERITT

William Rodney Averitt, better known as "Bird," not because of his soaring ability, but because of his slight-of-frame as a youth, could play the game.

Many colleges in Kentucky failed to recruit the dazzling left-hander out of Hopkinsville, Kentucky. Few noticed when Fred Overton, the assistant coach at Pepperdine University, in Malibu, California, slipped in and took him west. They did perk up a bit, however, when as a freshman Averitt rang up 44 and 43 points respectively in two games against a UCLA frosh team that included Bill Walton and Keith Wilkes.

"I was from Crofton, not far from Hopkinsville, and was home over the holidays," recalls Overton. "I went over to one of those Christmas tournaments they had back then. I think Bird scored over 50 that night against Madisonville. I was blown away at how good he was, and that no one was recruiting him. We flew him out and he signed in March."

Decades later, Jim Richards, who had a long history at Western Kentucky University as an assistant and head coach of the Hilltoppers, is still at a loss as to how the high scoring Averitt got out of the state, particularly away from Western or Murray State.

"I guess Fred (Overton) just did a better selling job than we all did," Richards laughed in talking about his longtime friend who later became the head coach at Murray State University.

"Actually the only school in Kentucky that recruited me at all was Kentucky State," Averitt says. "I rode the bus from Hopkinsville to Frankfort. I had layovers and stops in between. It took forever, and when I got to Frankfort, the bus station was closed. No one was there to meet me, so I walked to campus.

"Pepperdine was great. I had never been out of Kentucky before they flew me out to visit. Heck, I had only been to Louisville when we played in the state tournament and then for the Kentucky-Indiana all-star game."

Averitt played for coach Gary Coleson at Pepperdine, and he recalls that in addition to Overton, Sonny Smith, who would later become the head coach at Auburn, was also on the staff.

Before Averitt was finished at Pepperdine, he led the nation in scoring in 1973 with a 33.9 average. But like the Kentucky colleges before, the NBA passed on him, and he was signed by the ABA San Antonio Spurs for the 1973-74 season. Then with Hubie Brown on board as the Colonels new coach, Averitt came over from the Spurs in exchange for some cash and a draft choice.

"Hubie was a great coach, but we had our differences now and then," Averitt recalled. "I wasn't the most disciplined player in the world back then. I was sort of a jokester, always cutting-up and laughing, and coach didn't always like that. But I loved him as a coach. We had the same goal, and that was to win."

When the Colonels finally did win in 1975, Averitt was a key part.

"The team came up short all those years before I got there," he said. "And it was great that we could win the championship not only for ourselves, but for Louisville and Kentucky as well."

When John Y. shut the team down following the 1975-76 season, the Buffalo Braves of the NBA selected Averitt through the dispersal draft for the sum of $125,000.

When he left basketball in 1978, and moved back to Hopkinsville, the money he was owed from John Y. through the Colonels and the Buffalo Braves in an odd sort of way ended up in the lap of the Boston Celtics. Though Averitt never played a game for the Celtics, John Y. had made his contract part of the deal he made when he swapped his Buffalo team for Irv Levin's Celtics. But when Brown departed Boston, he also left Averitt's "you'll get paid later" deferred cash contracts with them.

Averitt was to collect $1,500 every two weeks from the time he was waived out of the NBA in 1978 until he turned 53 years of age in 2006.

In the meantime, a car accident in 1995 left Bird partially disabled. A broken neck that required a steel plate and a severely injured right arm keeps him somewhat confined in his Hopkinsville home, not far from where he grew up.

FOURTH SEASON
1970-71
by Lloyd Gardner

Regular Season Standings

EASTERN DIVISION	W—L
Virginia Squires	55-29
Kentucky Colonels	44-40
New York Nets	40-44
Miami Floridians	37-47
Pittsburgh Pipers	36-48
Carolina Cougars	34-50

WESTERN DIVISION	W—L
Indiana Pacers	58-26
Utah Stars	57-27
Memphis Pros	41-43
Texas Chaparrals	30-54
Denver Rockets	30-54

In June, Commissioner Jack Dolph ordered the Colonels to send Jim "Goose" Ligon and Bud Olsen to the Texas Chaparrals as compensation because the Colonels had signed their draft choice, Bobby Croft. Ligon and Olsen didn't want to go to Dallas. Storen once again proved why he was the ABA's best "wheeler-dealer." In the back of his mind must have been the thought that Issel would play the pivot, thus making Gene Moore expendable. So on July 6, 1970, Storen sent Moore and a 1971 second round draft choice to the Texans, and Ligon and Olsen stayed at home. That wasn't the biggest surprise. Somehow he swindled them out of the league's sixth leading scorer (20.1) at the forward position, Cincy Powell.

On October 14, 1970, Storen continued his restructuring by acquiring Walt Simon from the New York Nets for a future draft choice.

Storen also negotiated a new three-year radio deal with WHAS and television contract with WLKY. He secured as many dates as were available to play in the city's big house, Freedom Hall.

In a real tragedy on January 6, 1971, referee Andy Hershock, 43, collapsed at the Island Garden in West Hempsted, New York, while officiating a game between Memphis and New York. He was a four year veteran of the league and father of 11 children. Hershock complained of dizziness late in the first quarter and then suddenly collapsed near the Memphis bench. Less than 20 minutes later, he was pronounced dead. The game was played to its conclusion, and New York won, 110-101.

The ABA raised money for the Hershock family through donations from the individual clubs, the referees and the fans. Mike, for the most part was a no-nonsense general manager, but he could also be very compassionate. He organized a double-header between Indiana and Pittsburgh, and Kentucky and New York that was played in Freedom Hall in March. The gate receipts were donated to the struggling Hershock family.

In April of 1971, Colonels fans were surprised when they were introduced to a new signee, Artis Gilmore. Mike had wanted the Big A to wear #7 because Bill Russell of the Celtics had worn the hell out of the #6. After pictures were made, Artis immediately started negotiating for #53, his number at Jacksonville University. As everyone knows, the big fella won this encounter. His next request was that he could wear Adidas shoes instead of the Converse which the team was presently wearing. Storen went to work and negotiated an ABA contract making adidas the "Official Shoe of the ABA." Before Artis ever tied his adidas shoes for an ABA practice or game, he had already made an impact on the league.

Dampier, on February 11, broke the professional basketball record for most consecutive free throws when he swished his 58th basket.

On February 13, 1971, after dropping two games at Virginia and returning home on a late night flight, Colonels trainer, Bill Antonini, got off the plane and went to the *Courier-Journal/Louisville Times* and blasted Ramsey. Antonini had been a trainer for former coach Gene Rhodes at St. Xavier High School in Louisville, and he really never got over the firing of Gene. He claimed that the Colonels, under Ramsey, lacked direction, and that the team had a black-white problem. Antonini also alleged that Ramsey attended few practices and didn't know what to do. When writers for the *Courier* and the *Times* interviewed the players, 100% of them denied that the Colonels had a racial problem.

It didn't take long for me to learn a very big lesson. At my first practice I walked into the locker room and said, "You boys turn in your practice equipment so I can send it to the laundry." It took about two seconds before I got ripped, and I mean ripped, for calling them "boys."

Practice that day ended about 5 p.m. and Storen and Ramsey ordered the players to the locker room for a meeting. Storen immediately ordered me to wait outside. Frank and Mike wanted to know who didn't want their name revealed when they made the statement to *The Louisville Times*. "He's learning as he coaches, and maybe that's why some of the players feel they don't have confidence in him. A lot of times when we do need a play, he asked us what should be done rather than coming up with his own play. But this falls back on the fact he's still learning," the anonymous source said. Storen had told the players that, we would not leave this locker room until the person that made this statement stood up and admitted it. I sat in the hallway for over two hours. Finally the door opened. It was told to me that Louie got tired of waiting so he stood up and took the blame … it was after 7 p.m.

The Colonels didn't win a high percentage of their games in Indianapolis against the Pacers, but when we did, the ride back to Louisville was a blast. I always had a couple of cases of beer and sodas on the bus. Reminiscing about old times was usually the topic. Mike Storen frequently rode the bus with us, and he always had the best stories.

One of Mike's greatest stories was one that I will never forget. Mike had called Jimmy Rayl in to discuss his poor performance the previous night. Before going into detail about what happened, I need to tell you how different teams handled roommates on road trips. With the Colonels, once you had a roommate, as long as things worked out, the same two players would room together until one of them was dismissed, traded or had to miss a trip because of other circumstances.

The Pacers had signed a known menace, 7-foot Reggie Harding, because the team was in need of a center due to injuries. One morning the team was checking out of the hotel when they noticed that their 5'9" guard, Jimmy "Tweetie Bird" Rayl, was sleeping in the lobby. When asked why he wasn't in his room, he explained that Reggie Harding was his roommate and that he was scared to stay in the room with him. It was late, the night before a game in New Orleans. Jimmy had been sleeping for several hours when Reggie came into the dark room. Jimmy was sleeping soundly when Reggie walked over to his bed and placed a gun to his temple and said, "Tweetie Bird, I heard you didn't like niggers." Jimmy sat up in his bed, tried to come to his senses, and talk Reggie into giving him the revolver. After a short discussion Reggie gave Jimmy his weapon. Jimmy emptied the chamber, walked over to a window, opened it and threw the bullets onto a warehouse below. Jimmy went back to bed. A short time later, Rayl heard Reggie moving about the room. Reggie went back to Jimmy and once again placed the revolver on his temple and said, "Jimmy you don't think I just brought six bullets do you?" Jimmy got up, packed his bags and moved to the lobby.

Needless to say, the next night Tweetie Bird had a horrendous shooting night going 1-14. When the team arrived home, Storen summoned Rayl to his office to discuss his dismal performance. When he explained his encounter with Reggie, Mike quickly excused Tweetie Bird.

After numerous fines (somewhere in the neighborhood of $4,000), problems with teammates, coaches and management, the Pacers released Reggie before the playoffs began. The final straw came when Reggie, while doing a radio show said, "If I had a gun I'd shoot Mike Storen...," and Mike knew that he had a gun; Tweetie Bird had told him.

Storen also told this story about Reggie. Reggie grew up in a small community in Detroit, Michigan. As the story goes, the 7-foot Harding put on a ski mask and went into the neighborhood liquor store at gunpoint and said, "This is a stick-up; give me your money." The clerk said, "Reggie, what are you doing? Take off the mask and go home." "I'm not Reggie," Reggie replied.

You must know that Dan Hester was a free spirit … he wanted to be called Freak Momma. On one occasion two nuns came to the office and asked if they could get an autographed ball for an auction at a local Catholic picnic. I had a ball autographed, and on the Monday after the picnic, the two nuns returned, in tears, and asked to see Mr. Storen. They proceeded to his office and said that someone had written an obscene word on the ball. She showed the ball to Mike and he realized that Hester had written "Freak Momma" on the ball, but you can use your imagination as to what the word "Freak" looked like when written with a ballpoint pen. There were no Sharpies at that time. Storen called me in and told me to send Hester to his office as soon as practice was over. Mike told him that if he ever signed another article using those words he would fine him heavily.

The Colonels had defeated the Floridians 4-2 in the first round of the playoffs. Cincy Powell had gotten into several confrontations and a fight with Ira Harge in one game. It seemed that Cincy or Goose was always getting into fights.

We were in Richmond, Virginia, for game one of the Eastern Division Championship. The team was in the locker room preparing for the game. Coach Ramsey always sat in the locker room while the team got dressed and taped. He was the only coach in the seven that I worked for that stayed in the locker room while the players got dressed. Most coaches came in just in time for a pregame meeting. Hubie Brown and Stan Albeck were always in the locker room putting the game plan on the chalk board. Hubie took the Colonels, and Stan always took the opposing team.

After everyone was dressed and seated, Frank said, "It seems like every game somebody is getting into a fight. Tonight, if one of our players gets in a fight, I want every one of you to get off that bench and help your teammate. If I look over and see you on the bench, I'm going to fine you $125. When I played for the Celtics, "Red" would always tell us to grab the opponent. Don't ever grab your own teammate because that sets them up to get hit, so grab an opponent and somebody hit him.

It was early in the game when Cincy got into a fight … I don't know who. It was right in front of our bench. Seconds later, I saw Frank grab Neil Johnson, who was one of, if not the most, muscular players in all of professional basketball, and one of the meanest. In a game against the Denver Rockets, Johnson delivered a blow to Warren Jabali that referee John Vanak called the most devastating punch he'd ever seen on the court. It was my first year back with the Colonels, and I didn't know a lot about Neil. Well, Frank was holding him and I said to myself, "I'd better hit him or Frank's going to fine me." I took a swing … to this day I don't know whether I connected or not. The next thing I can remember is that I was seated on our bench and the Squires' trainer, Chopper Travaglini, was standing over me telling me that my job was to keep the fans off of the floor and not to get involved with players. I can remember looking up and here comes Charlie Scott, Ray Scott and George Carter. Thanks to Chopper, he sent them back to their own bench. I will never forget that night. I took the last cab from the arena back to the hotel, hoping Neil wasn't waiting for me. When I got to the hotel, it was my custom to stop by the bar and see if any of our players were in there. As I walked in, somebody tapped me on the shoulder. It was Neil Johnson. He said, 'let's have a beer.' I never drank beer, but that night I loved having a beer with the Squires' enforcer. After that encounter, our players called me Pink Floyd Patterson.

The Kentucky Colonels had finished 11 games behind Virginia in the Eastern Division during the 1970-71 regular season. The Colonels defeated Florida and Virginia to reach the ABA Championship Series against the Western Division Champs, the Utah Stars.

1971 ABA Championship

Utah Stars (57-27) vs. Kentucky Colonels (44-40)
May 3 at Utah 136, Kentucky 117
May 5 at Utah 138, Kentucky 125
May 7 at Kentucky 116, Utah 110
May 8 at Kentucky 129, Utah 125 (OT)
May 2 at Utah 137, Kentucky 127
May 15 at Kentucky 105, Utah 102
May 18 at Utah 131, Kentucky 121
Stars won Championship, 4-3

Who knows whether or not we could have won the championship if Goose had been healthy? He was having bad low back spasms. He was getting treatments as often as he could. I even had a massage therapist in Salt Lake City who worked on him when we were out of town. I will give Goose credit, he did everything possible … he even took injections in his lower back before every game in an effort to help us win. Dr. Rudy Ellis, our team doctor, traveled with us and gave the injections to try and stop the spasms. The needle was about 3" long and as round as a pencil lead.

It is a common practice in professional sports for the trainer to have his own room on the road. Toward the end of the season, Frank and Mike asked me to room with Hester on the road.

They thought his free spirit behavior might change. Well it didn't. One night in Utah he came in about 2 a.m. I was long gone hours before. I heard this wheezing, sucking sound. I rolled over and there was Dan, a soldier and a girl sitting on his bed smoking a joint. I had no idea what they were doing. I had never been around marijuana, and I turned back over and went back to sleep.

The team flew out to Salt Lake City on May 17. The owners chartered a plane and everyone in the front office, the team doctors, and the coaches, trainer, and player's wives were invited to attend the championship game. Fifteen seats were left open so the entire entourage could fly home together.

Prior to the game, a party had been planned in a local hotel. Unfortunately, the Colonels lost the seventh game and the Utah Stars behind Zelmo Beaty won the ABA championship. Although we lost the game, the team still had a lot to celebrate.

As everyone was enjoying the food, beverage and reminiscing about the past season, a family squabble broke out. Goose Ligon and his wife Nancy were seated at a table with me and my former wife, Sandy, and several other players. Goose got up and went to get a drink. After being gone for a few minutes, Nancy noticed this young lady had her arms around Goose. Nancy, red faced with anger, got up and confronted the mistress. Nancy said, "Get your damn hands off my husband." The young lady replied. "He's not your husband; he's been divorced for six months." With that, Nancy put a haymaker on her jaw. A fight broke out like an old time barroom brawl. There was hair rolling around like tumbleweed and each swinging furiously at the other. Turn out the lights, the party's over. Needless to say, the party was over, but the fight wasn't. As everyone was catching cabs back to the hotel, one of the Colonels office staff invited the young lady to spend some time with him. As the cab pulled up to the hotel and they were getting out, the Ligon cab stopped right next to them, and guess what? The mistress was in that cab and they squared off once again in the parking lot of the Travel Lodge.

At the end of the season Ramsey resigned for business and professional reasons, back in Madisonville, and so, on June 21, 1971, Joe Mullaney became the fifth head coach of the Kentucky Colonels.

FIFTH SEASON
1971-72
by Lloyd Gardner

Regular Season Standings

EASTERN DIVISION	W—L
Kentucky Colonels	68-16
Virginia Squires	45-39
New York Nets	44-40
The Floridians	36-48
Carolina Cougars	35-49
Pittsburgh Pipers	25-59

WESTERN DIVISION	W—L
Utah Stars	60-24
Indiana Pacers	47-37
Dallas Chaparrals	42-42
Denver Rockets	34-50
Memphis Pros	26-58

Before coming to the Colonels, Joe Mullaney's contract had been terminated by the Los Angeles Lakers when he failed to win a championship with Wilt Chamberlain, Jerry West and Elgin Baylor. In 1969-70, the injury-plagued Lakers had lost the NBA Championship to the New York Knicks 4-3. Then in 1970-71, his Lakers lost in the Western Division Championship to Kareem Abdul-Jabbar and the Milwaukee Bucks, who went on to win the NBA Championship.

The Colonels draft picks included Artis Gilmore, John Roche and Mike Gale, who all signed. But two others, Fred Brown and Larry Steele, signed with the Seattle Supersonics and Portland Trail Blazers of the NBA, respectively. The Colonels then sold Roche to the New York Nets. Gilmore, like Issel, signed a contract for 10 years and $1.5 million.

Chopper Travaglini was the trainer for the Virginia Squires during basketball season, and the trainer for the Charleston Charlies during baseball season. The Charlies came to Louisville to play the Louisville Colonels (baseball). They stayed at the Executive Inn, where our offices were located. Chopper always came down to visit, and on this day, he stopped by to tell us about the Squires' rookie camp that had just ended several days before. Puffing on a cigarette, he said in his raspy voice, "We had this guy sign a contract and come to rookie camp. Boy is he a player! He is going to be great some day … his name is Julius Erving." This was the first time anyone had ever heard of Julius Erving. We thought, this guy can't really change the ABA, can he?

For the first time in ABA history all 11 franchises remained in the same locality. In an effort to boost season ticket sales and interest in the team, Mike Storen organized a rookie camp at the Masonic Home Gym where 23 players were allowed to try-out. Among them were University of

157

Kentucky standout Mike Casey, Louisville Seneca High School star Mike Redd, Louisville's Jerry King, Eastern Kentucky's Boyd Lynch and Elizabeth City's (NC) Mike Gale. On June 3, 1971, 19 of the players suited-up and squared-off and played two exhibition games at Bellarmine College. Only nine of the 23 were invited back in September. Once camp started, the innovative Storen showcased the team by traveling to Burkesville and Lebanon, Kentucky, and nearby Sellersburg and Seymore, Indiana. The rookies went to Indianapolis for a game against the Pacers' rookies and their sensations George J. McGinnis and Darnell Hillman. They made a return trip to Louisville the next night. Some of the exhibition games were rookies vs. veterans, and once some cuts were made, the players would be divided into two teams.

For the first time, in 1971, the ABA played exhibition games against the NBA. On September 21, 1971, the very first matchup between the two leagues took place in Dallas, Texas. The Bucks prevailed over the Dallas Chaparrals, in a close one, 106-103. Kareem Abdul-Jabbar scored 32 points, but it was a jumper from 15 feet with 11 seconds left on the clock by McCoy McLemore that sealed the victory.

On September 22, 1971, in front of 13,821 fans at Freedom Hall, the Kentucky Colonels took on Louisville native and University of Louisville All-American Wes Unseld and the Baltimore Bullets. At one point during the game the Bullets' Stan Love got hit in the throat and knocked down in front of our bench. He was choking and was about to swallow his tongue. I rushed onto the court and quickly forced two of my fingers into his mouth to grab his tongue. He almost bit them off. I had bite marks and indentations on my fingers for several days, but it was the only thing I could do. The Colonels prevailed 111-85. It was the Big A's (Artis Gilmore) first big test as he finished with 16 points, 16 rebounds and seven blocked shots in 37 minutes. Issel topped all scorers with 24 points, along with eight rebounds. All 15 players scored for Kentucky. In 28 minutes, Wes Unseld hauled in eight rebounds along with seven points. Four of those points coming on goaltending calls on Gilmore. With the win, the Colonels became the first ABA team to defeat an NBA team.

Darel Carrier did not play. Although he was practicing, he did not play because he was holding out for a new contract. Players could practice, but could not play in games without a contract. Mike Storen was a teacher of the business. On one occasion, in a summer staff meeting, he had everyone study and learn the obligations of all parties involved in an "Official American Basketball Association Uniform Player Contract." We were in the locker room and Darel was asking his teammates what "playing out his option" meant, and how did it work. I was the only person in the room that knew the answer. It means in short, "If a player plays out his option year, he will be paid not less than 90% of the amount of his salary the preceding year." After telling Darel this, I also told him that his salary or medical expenses would not be covered in case of injury. He signed the next day.

On October 8, 1971, all eyes of professional basketball were on the Kentucky Colonels. In what many consider the most anticipated matchup in the four year history of the ABA was about to take place in Louisville's Freedom Hall. I will never forget the buzz, excitement, and enthusiasm that entered that arena as soon as the gates opened. It would be a marquee game, a game that would truly show the world just how competitive the ABA teams could be. It was a matchup compared to the Yankees and the Red Sox, the Colts and the Jets or Ali vs. Frazier. It was Artis Gilmore, our rookie, literally going head to head with their veteran and NBA MVP, Kareem Abdul-Jabbar and the defending Champions of the NBA, the Milwaukee Bucks. But there was more; they had the "Big O," and we had "Little Louie," but we also had "The Horse," Dan Issel. It was a standing room only crowd announced at 18,000, and they were standing and cheering their hearts out. The atmosphere alone was worth the price of admission ($6.00 and $5.00). When the final stats were tallied, it had Abdul-Jabbar with 30 points and 20 rebounds. Gilmore had 18 points, 16 rebounds and five blocked shots. Dan Issel led all scorers with 34 points. The biggest spread of the game was six points. The final score, Bucks 99-Colonels 93.

In the first game of this two night double header, the Virginia Squires with some guy named Julius Erving and last year's co-rookie of the year, Charlie Scott (Issel won it with him), played the Memphis Pros and the much anticipated rookie Johnny Neumann.

Mike Storen backed down from no one. The next night the Colonels faced off against the powerful New York Knicks. Led by Walt Frazier, Willis Reed, Dave DeBusschere, and Jerry Lucas, the local fans went home disappointed with a 112-100 loss.

It seems as though the regular season would never start. The NBA games were very electrifying, but all these scrimmages and games away from home wear you out. Practice in the mornings and leaving in mid-afternoon for a game, getting home late and starting over early the next day. This goes on for 30 days, with no days off. If you don't have a game, you have two practices a day.

Exhibition games, even though you make every effort to win, are really played to find out which players will make the team and which ones will move on. There have been a lot of times where a better player was released simply because you had to keep a lesser talented player with a no-cut contract. Believe me, this happened a lot.

Now it's time to shift gears, pick it up a notch, every game counts. It was October 16, 1971, and the Colonels opened regular season play against Rick Barry and the New York Nets. In Artis Gilmore's debut, he led all scorers with 29 points and led the team to a 107-98 victory.

On January 14, 1972, the Kentucky Colonels defeated the Dallas Chaparrals, and the Indiana Pacers beat the Memphis Pros in a doubleheader played in Toronto, Canada. The games were not the big story. First of all, the wind chill was 66° below zero. When the teams went through customs the next morning, the free spending, cocky Neumann had purchased some expensive items. When customs at the airport asked him what he had bought and what was in his suitcase, he refused to open it. Needless to say, Neumann was detained for several hours.

The city of Louisville, along with the Kentucky Colonels, hosted the 5th ABA All-Star game in Freedom Hall on January 29, 1972. The banquet was held in Louisville's Convention Center. Famed speaker Paul Harvey was the keynote speaker. It was a perfect setting for him to use a variation of his world famous saying. He opened with, "Hello American Basketball Association."

Artis, Dan and Louie were voted onto the East team, and because the Colonels were in first place, Joe Mullaney was named the head coach, Bud Olsen assistant coach, and I was trainer as well as the host trainer. The host trainer was in charge of getting all the uniforms made, practice facilities scheduled, and all other team related duties.

The game itself became a blowout in the fourth quarter. The East squad defeated the West 142-115. Fifteen thousand, seven hundred and thirty fans stood and cheered as Dan was named the MVP (21 points and 9 rebounds) by one vote over Bluegrass native and Carolina Cougar, Jim McDaniels. McDaniels, a former Western All-American had scored 18 of his 24 points in the fourth quarter. He also had 11 rebounds.

On February 9, 1972, just eleven days after his remarkable All-Star performance, McDaniels was AWOL for a game against the Kentucky Colonels in Charlotte, N.C. He had jumped leagues and signed with Seattle in the NBA.

In mid-February, the Pittsburgh Condors hosted the Memphis Pros. Before the game, as a promotion to encourage fans to attend the game, Muhammad Ali had a boxing exhibition. There was only one problem, after Ali had completed his appearance, most fans left the arena.

After learning that someone had stolen nearly $800 from the novelty stand funds out of the Colonels office in the Executive Inn, Mike Storen summoned a security expert to give everyone in the front office a lie detector test. One by one each of the employees were hooked up to the machine and asked a series of questions. Everyone was asked the same questions that were given to us prior to being wired to the monitor. The questions were asked in advance, so that it would give you time to think about your answers. I, along with everyone else, passed the test, but I was told by the examiner that one question indicated that most of us didn't know who did it, but we had an idea of who might have stolen the money. Most of us knew that one of our employees liked to play the horses and go to Churchill Downs, and there was some thought that he had gambling debts. Thank goodness that person also passed the examination. We didn't find the thief, but the test was quite an experience.

After 84 games, the hometown Colonels had the best regular season mark ever recorded in ABA history sporting a 68-16 (.810) record. The Los Angeles Lakers were 69-13 (.828) that same year and held that record until the Chicago Bulls, led by Michael Jordan, accomplished a record 72-10 (.841) season in1995-96. In 1991-92 the Bulls were 67-15 (.817). The Colonels ABA record is still the fourth best regular season record ever recorded in professional basketball.

Unfortunately, the ABA that year matched the first place team, Kentucky, against the third place team, the New York Nets. Why the Colonel's didn't play the fourth place team, as would normally have happened, no one understands to this day.

Game one was played in Louisville's Convention Center because Freedom Hall was already booked. In that game I witnessed one of the greatest dunks I have ever seen in my life. I will never forget it. In the third quarter, 6'2" Ollie Taylor dribbled down the middle of the floor. When he reached the free throw line, Artis Gilmore was standing in front of the basket … up, up, and away. Taylor leaps over Artis and slam dunks the basketball. Taylor had always been known for his great jumping ability, but no one saw this coming. Wow!

In the series, the Colonels simply could not stop Rick Barry and John Roche. It seemed they scored at will. In that first game, Barry had a game high of 50 points while Roche contributed 31. Gilmore's 30 points and Issel's 26 couldn't offset the performance by the Nets' duo.

I also remember, that year it became a team tradition any time a player was traded, put on waivers, or released, someone on the team would lead a song to the tune of Abraham, Martin and John. "Has anybody here, seen my old friend (Player's name), Can you tell me where he's gone? He couldn't remember the plays, so they put him on waivers, and I just looked around and he was gone."

<u>Kentucky Colonels (68-16) vs. New York Nets (44-40)</u>
April 1, New York 122 at Kentucky 108
April 4, New York 105, at Kentucky 90
April 5, Kentucky 105, at New York 99
April 7, at New York 100, Kentucky 92
April 8, at Kentucky 109, New York 93
April 10, at New York 101, Kentucky 96
Nets won series, 4-2

This picture was taken the day Artis signed with the Kentucky Colonels and was introduced at a Colonels' game.

Pierre Russell

Referee John Vanak watches as #32 Dr. J and #30 Al Skinner doube team San Antonio Spurs' guard Jonas Silas.

Claude Virden drives the baseline.

#12 Ron King

#22 Wil Jones, 1974-75

Allen Murphy

#9 Walt Szczerbiak

#53 Artis Gilmore and #24 Rick Barry (New York Nets).

#2 Walt Simon, Darnell Hillman and Donnie Freeman, both Indiana Pacers.

Playboy Bunny at the Andy Henshock Benefit. This was the "team" coached by Van Vance.

1972 All-Star Don Criqui and Jack Dolph.

1972 All-Star Colonels table.

Playboy Bunnies

#10 Louie Dampier, #35 Ron King and #23 Chuck Williams (San Diego Conquistadors).

#33 Mike Pratt, #5 Sam Smith and Texas Chaparrals #12 Ron Boone, #33 Rich Jones and #55 Gene Moore.

New York Nets' #13 John Roche falls against leg of Kentucky Colonels' #33 Mike Pratt during the Eastern Division ABA semifinal playoff game at Nassau Coliseum in Uniondale, New York. Roche maintained control of the ball and passed off to a teammate. Watching are Colonels #10 Lou Dampier and #44 Dan Issel. New York won, 101-96, to also win the best-of-seven series with a 4-2 record.

Board of Directors, back row: Joni Coleman, Mary Baird, Kay Morrissey, Billie Kurfee, Sissy Jenkins, Patsy Baker. Front row: Maxine Lutz, Ellie Brown, Adolph Rupp and Nancy Jones.

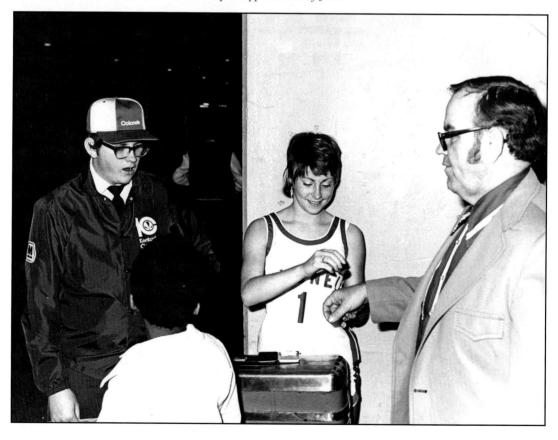

Ticket takers and ushers welcome the fans to Freedom Hall.

1970-71 owners, left to right: Stuart Jay, Wendell Cherry, David Grissom, David Jones and John Y. Brown Jr.

David Vance presents the Ladner family a picture of Wendell as the Kentucky Colonels honor the life of Wendell Ladner in a special ceremony after his tragic death in an airplane crash.

#24 Rick Barry (New York Nets) and #33 Mike Pratt.

Artis Gilmore shooting over Lew Alcindor.

#3 Joe Hamilton challenges Virginia Squires' #30 George Irvine.

During a game in Freedom Hall, Ellie Brown honors Muhammad Ali after his win over George Foreman in Zaire.

Ellie Brown, Board Chairman of the Kentucky Colonels of American Basketball Association, holds a basketball during a get acquainted visit to New York. The young Louisville matron, wife of John Y. Brown, President of Kentucky Fried Chicken, is the only woman board chairman of a major sports franchise.

Owner Ellie Brown and Kentucky Governor Julian M. Carroll gather at center court after the 1975 Championship game.

John and Ellie Brown

#44 Dan Issel

Walt Simon and Dan Issel

Dan Issel, Wendell Ladner and Coach Babe McCarthy watch from the bench.

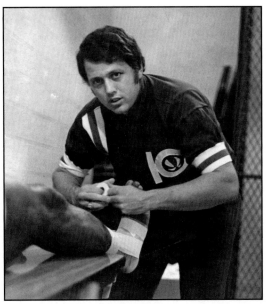

Trainer Lloyd Gardner and Wendell Ladner the night
he went over the water cooler.

Lloyd Gardner

Lloyd Gardner, Referee Bob Serafin, assistant coach Bud Olsen and Rick Mount.

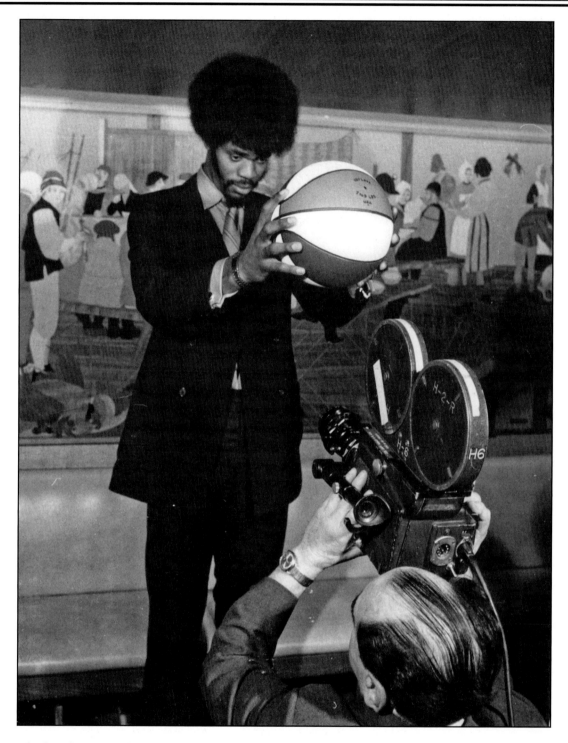

The day after Artis Gilmore signed with the Kentucky Colonels he appeared at a press conference at Toots Shor Restaurant in New York City, March 17, 1971.

Coach Hubie Brown and trainer Lloyd "Pink" Gardner.

Mike Storen and 1971-72 All-Star MVP Award won by Dan Issel.

Head Coach Joe Mullaney, 1971-72 and 1972-73.

Hubie Brown, former coach of the Kentucky Colonels of the American Basketball Association, was named coach of the Atlanta Hawks of the National Basketball Association. He stands with hands on hips as he met with the news media. He replaced Cotton Fitzsimmons, who was fired by the Hawks with seven games remaining in a 29-53 campaign.

Coach Babe McCarthy, 1973-74.

Assistant Coach Stan Albeck, 1974-76.

Mike Pratt, Dan Issel and trainer Lloyd "Pink" Gardner pop the cork after the Kentucky Colonels clinch the Eastern Division Championship in 1971.

Coach Hubie Brown is introduced as head coach by Ellie Brown.

Head Coach Frank Ramsey, 1970-71.

John Y. Brown Jr.

Billy Chamberlain (Phoenix Action)

#53 Artis Gilmore and #33 Kareem Abdul-Jabbar (Milwaukee Bucks).

Mike Pratt and lockeroom attendant Jay Bauer.

Colonels secretaries, left to right: Barbara Comstock, Alice Miller (office manager), Kathy Holder and Pam Schaftlein Thomas (typing).

Cheerleader in action.

Kneeling, left to right: Angela Neff, Judy Corbett, Phyllis Mefford and Janice Sego. Standing: Betty Swain, Mary Lee Bryant, Ann Lindsay, Debbie Dahl, Barbara Korfhage (choreographer), Brenda Winders, Karen Beil, Donna Grubbs and Sylvana Monroe.

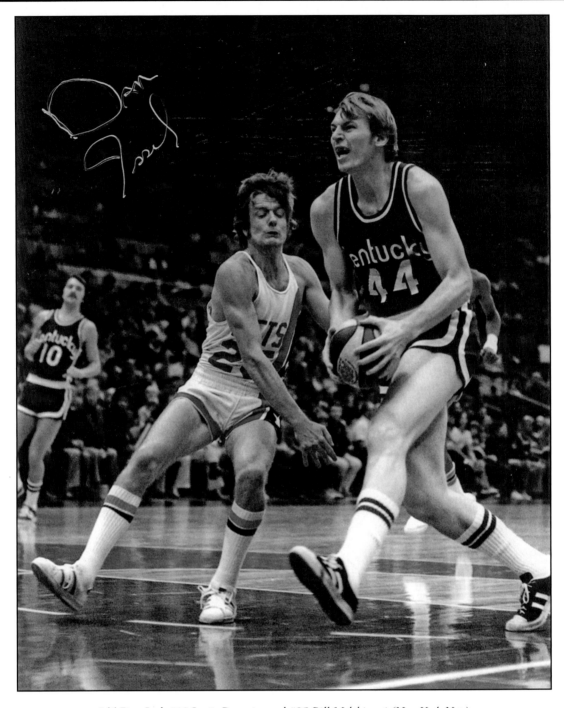

#44 Dan Issel, #10 Louie Dampier and #25 Bill Melchionni (New York Nets).

John Y. Hamilton, Sales/Promotions, Director of Publicity/Public Relations

Gordon Crawford, Director of Promotions

When you think of Bobby Nichols . . . certainly basketball is not the sport that comes to mind. This sweet-swinging native Louisvillian is one of the biggest names on the professional golf tour. Winner of numerous tournaments . . . Bobby's "big one" came in 1964 when he captured the PGA Title . . . one of the four major trophies the pros covet. His interest in the Colonels is something else again. He attends every game his touring schedule permits. But his interest goes beyond just being a stock-holding fan. During one discussion about a trade last year, Bobby's ears perked up. He liked the maneuver being considered. He offered to fly to the city where the player the Colonels wanted was playing (taking time off from a scheduled tour appearance), play a round of golf with the General Manager, and try to entice him into making the trade.

Bobby is major league in every respect and his involvement with the Colonels presents an image that money can't buy. The Colonels are proud that he is a part of the organization

WAVE-TV & radio broadcaster Ed Kallay, the first voice of the Colonels.

Professional golfer Bobby Nichols, stockholder.

Bumper Sticker

All-Star Banquet Ticket

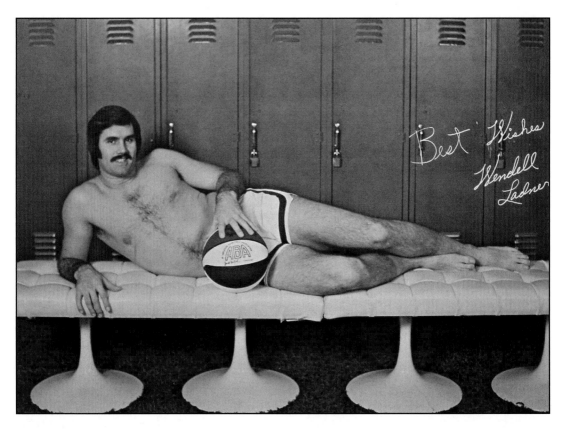

Burt Reynolds' picture on the front of Cosmopolitan Magazine *had nothing on the Kentucky Colonels Wendell Ladner.*

Chapter Eleven
More Than Just Basketball

Gordon Crawford

It takes much more to put on a professional basketball game than two teams showing up. Go to a game and look around. See how many people you can identify who are actually involved in one capacity or another with the logistics and operation of the game.

In the early years of the ABA it was often trial and error, not only with the Colonels, but even more so with the rest of the league.

Some teams would even wait to the last minute to put down the 3-point line in their arenas. Keep in mind that at that time the 3-point basket had not been implemented in colleges and high schools, and in all fairness many teams in the league often did not get access to their arenas until a few hours before tipoff. This led to inaccurate tape-jobs for the lines, and often times the height of the goals was not correct. On occasion, portable floors were assembled incorrectly, often leading to lots of mishandled dribbles.

There was a time when the Colonels played games in the Convention Center downtown, in Freedom Hall at the Fairgrounds, a few in Cincinnati at the Armory-Fieldhouse, and, yes, even in Lexington at Memorial Coliseum. It fell on the Colonels organization to make sure the game was set up to professional basketball standards.

In 1969, Gordon Crawford was in his early 30s and working at Brown-Forman in Louisville. He had a more than decent job, moving up the corporate ladder as an assistant brand advertising manager for Old Forester and Usher Green Stripe Scotch.

After graduating from U of L in 1960, where he played baseball, he landed the job with Brown-Forman that he thought could last forever.

But there was something missing.

It took a college all-star basketball game between graduating seniors from Kentucky schools playing against the best from Tennessee to jolt him into a career change.

"I wasn't a big fan of the Colonels at first," says Crawford. "I wasn't even really sure they were going to make it."

But that all changed when he went to see that all-star game in Freedom Hall.

"There were about 14,000 people in there," Crawford recalls. "And most of them had come to see Dan Issel, Mike Pratt, and Claude Virden from Murray. A light went on. I knew they were going to be playing for the Colonels, plus the team had new owners and they had just hired Mike Storen to run things. I knew then they were going to be viable."

Crawford set out to get his foot in the door, asking around to anyone who knew the owners or Storen. Finally he just went up to Storen at a practice game and introduced himself and told him he wanted to work for the Colonels.

Storen told him all positions were full at the time, but he just might have a commission only job that would involve season tickets and group sales.

"I gave up a good job with Brown-Forman to go with the Colonels for commission only," he laughed.

The following year the door opened a bit wider, when Joe Hullett, who had been in on the ground floor with the Colonels, left the organization.

It was Hullett who had first contacted Joe and Mamie about the ABA franchise and over the years had become well-known in Louisville for his involvement in sporting events. But there was a personality clash between him and new general manager Storen, according to Crawford.

"Joe was sort of a free-spirit, and liked doing things his way," he recalled. "And Mike was very disciplined and wanted it his way. They just didn't mesh."

So with the departure of Hullett, Storen offered Crawford a full-time position. Then the following year when Alex Groza left the Colonels to join the ABA San Diego Sails, Crawford moved up again, assuming many of Groza's duties.

And, indeed, his duties were many. "Mike Storen watched every dime he spent, and he expected that from me," laughed Crawford. "In fact he was cheap."

With Storen being a former Marine, Crawford quickly had his marching orders. By now, as the team's director of promotions, he was responsible for ushers, ticket sellers, police security, ticket takers, pep bands, the National Anthem, color guards, cheerleaders, halftime entertainment, and many times, pre-game shows.

For the average fan, all of these responsibilities are just taken for granted, but someone has to make sure it happens.

Away from the basketball court there was another operation going on; merchandising for the Colonels was big. Not only did it bring in revenue, but it got the team's logo out there on the red, white and blue souvenir basketballs as well as t-shirts and sweatshirts.

One of the bands Crawford hired was Bill Lippy and his Fog Bound Five. They had been contracted to perform at 20 of the Colonels 40 home games.

"They would walk completely around the court playing their music before Freedom Hall reconfigured the arena," says Crawford. "Bill was a real estate appraiser in the area, and I will never forget that he had his home ripped apart in the tornado of 1973."

Crawford recalls that one of the best shows he had was one he discovered by accident. "I went out to Freedom Hall on a Friday night to work on some Colonels tickets. The Globetrotters were going to play that night, and I saw some guys practicing on unicycles," he said. "They were called the World Wheelers out of New York, and there were ten of them. What a show they put on! They were amazing, and I signed them for a few halftimes. We didn't pay hardly anything for them."

There was also the Breckinridge Job Corp Percussion Marching Group, even receiving a standing ovation on the night they performed. "They stomped on the floor with those big boots of theirs," he recalls. "The Fairground Board was worried about them ruining the floor and didn't want them to perform again, but they put on a memorable show."

Crawford figures that from 1969 through 1975 he was responsible for 280 halftime shows.

Among them was one on March 12, 1976. It was a "50s Night," and WKLO's Bo Brady emceed an after-the-game sock hop in the Freedom Hall ballroom. It wasn't enough that the Colonels were hosting the New York Nets, Dr. J, and the return of former Colonel Ted McClain. And then add to this the local Monarchs singing group, who provided music for a halftime hula-hoop contest. And this was just one game.

Another particular promotion was called "Guaranteed Win Night," and although it put a little pressure on the Colonels, it did draw attention. This particular game was a February 15 encounter against the Pacers. If the Colonels didn't win, the ticket stub would be good for entry at the next home game. Luckily the Colonels won.

Then there was "Farmer's Night," an event coordinated with the Rural Electric Co-ops and Kentucky Farm Bureau. Give-a-ways included tractors, tires, feed, and barn paint.

On March 21, 1976, the Virginia Squires were in Louisville, but that's the night the Playboy Bunnies from Cincinnati also came to town. The Bunnies were to "play," and that was a stretch, against a team of local radio personalities. Colonels broadcaster Van Vance coached the Bunny team against the Louisville Media All-Stars, coached by Sue Anne Vance, Van's wife. The team included Bob Domine, Vince DeSalvo, Paul Rogers, Wayne Perky, Bo Brady, Joe Fletcher, Gary Burbank and Tom Dooley. Years later, lots of people remember the game, but not the score. Who knows, perhaps Penny Ann Early had paved the way for this game years before.

One of the more popular promotions at Colonels games was advertised as the Hi-Pro Doubleheader and included a high school game preceding the Colonels game. Not only did Louisville teams play, but also some of the top rated schoolboy teams across the state. The coaches loved bringing their kids to Freedom Hall. Not only did it give them an opportunity to play in a big-time atmosphere, but also to play on a legitimate full size court in the same building that the state tournament was played on back then.

Media coverage had always been a challenge. Some years, it seemed, were better than others. At the time Colonels management never felt like it was enough, but with all things considered, it might not have been so bad after all.

Over the nine years of the Colonels existence, lots of words were written, good and bad, about the franchise. Many of the articles were matter-of-fact, either an advance story of an up and coming game, or one covering the results of a recent one.

Of course, it was the local media, the *Courier-Journal* and the *Times* that provided the majority of the ink. However, area newspapers also provided their share of coverage as well.

The Colonels also provided plenty of fodder for the newspaper's columnists to give their opinions. Players, owners, management, and the ABA in general often made for entertaining, if not controversial commentary.

Here is a list of some of the local writers and broadcasters who covered the Colonels: Earl Ruby, Dave Kindred, Tev Laudeman, David C. Adams, Dean Eagle, Earl Cox, Johnny Carrico, Marvin N. Gay, Jr., Lou Younken, Gary Schultz, George Rorrer, Dick Fenlon, Denny Dressman,

Dick Beardsley, John Flynn, Jim Terhune, Keith F. Overpeck, Leslie Whitley, C. Ray Hall, Mike Barry, Billy Reed, Ed Kalley, Van Vance, Cawood Ledford, Paul Rogers, Bob Domine, Howard Hoffman, and Dave Conrad.

At courtside on almost every home game night there would be as many as four writers from Louisville's two major newspapers, the morning *Courier-Journal* and the afternoon *Louisville Times*. Over the nine-year Colonels existence there were 20 different writers from these two papers who covered the Colonels, but on any given night Kindred, Fenlon, Rorrer and Overpeck could be seen on press row. So could Jim Parks of the *Louisville Defender*, and writers from the *Charlestown Courier, Jefferson Reporter, New Albany Tribune, Shively Newsweek, Highland Old Towner, County Gentleman*, and the *Prospect News*.

From Mike Storen through Gene Rhodes, through David Vance and John Y. Hamilton, a major effort was made to put together a radio network not just in the Louisville area, but across Kentucky as well.

At one time or another Colonels games were heard over WHAS's 100,000 watts into more than 40 states, and in Kentucky it was WBLG Lexington, WLBJ Bowling Green, WSAC Fort Knox, WKLB Hindman, WDHR Pikeville, WOVO Glasgow, WLOL Munfordville, WYGO Corbin, WYWY Barbourville, and WMMG Brandenburg.

Pat Richardson remembers the calls she would get from Crawford. She was the sponsor of the Drill Corp at Seneca High School in the early '70s.

"Gordon would call me sometimes at the last minute to do a halftime show, and that was okay," she said. "We looked for every opportunity to perform that we could. We had 41 girls from grades 10 through 12. It was fun going to the games."

Crawford had lots of Catholic grade school promotions with league teams playing before the Colonels took the court.

"People would come to see them, family and friends," Crawford says. "Of course they would have to buy a ticket, and the teams made a dollar off of each ticket they sold."

One of those preliminary games that stand out was when Duvalle Junior High played. Their star player was Darrell Griffith, who went on to be one of the all-time greats at U of L, and later an NBA star.

Another person who remembers playing before the Colonels game is Ken Robinson, a 1962 Manual High School graduate. He had played intramural basketball with his Sigma Chi fraternity at UK and wasn't ready to quit playing when he moved back to Louisville to work.

"I played in an adult league and we played at Freedom Hall two or three times before the Colonels games," he says. "The court seemed so big compared to what I was used to playing on."

And just like Crawford had hoped, Robinson's wife, Iris, family and a few friends bought tickets.

Years later, long after the Colonels were no more, Robinson found himself playing in the same league with former Colonels stars Louie Dampier and Bud Olsen.

In looking back on it all, Crawford says there was "lots of last minute stuff" that went on with promotions. "John Y. would have some of his Hollywood connection friends coming in from time to time," he said. "He came in one day and said singer Andy Williams was coming to town. He told us to sell tickets to the high schools, anywhere, give them away if we had to, just get people to the game. He always had something going on with people coming to the games.

In his first two years he was with the Colonels, Crawford says the cheerleaders were just pretty girls who would sit on the sidelines and clap when the team made a basket. The third year there were tryouts set up by sponsor Barbara Korfaghe, and Crawford says not only were the girls pretty, they could also dance.

The dance team was called the Goal Tenders, and Crawford says one of the girls, Karen Beil, was so good she would do a solo. Later, he said, she had a cameo spot in a movie.

He also remembers a talented 12-year-old named Karen Kraft who sang Patsy Cline-type country music songs.

It didn't have a thing to do with any of Crawford's pre-game or halftime shows, but he recalls that general manager Mike Storen wanted the press tables only on one side of the court.

"He wanted the fans on one side to have their seats that would be right next to the floor, without anything in front of them," he said. "Sometimes it was a problem because of all of the media."

Speaking of the media, Crawford chuckles when recalling his association with the *Courier-Journal* and *Louisville Times*.

"Everyone had to pay for parking at Freedom Hall unless you had a special parking decal," he said. "I offered them the decal, but they refused. They wouldn't take free parking. I guess they felt it would compromise their objectivity."

When the Colonels finally folded in 1976, Crawford used his connection with former team owners Wendell Cherry and David Jones. They had previously sold their interest in order to devote more time to their Humana Company, and Crawford worked there until he retired.

CHAPTER TWELVE
IF THEY SAID IT, YOU CAN BELIEVE IT

ED KALLAY

Whenever Ed Kallay showed up for anything in Louisville, it was a big deal. So when the sports director at WAVE radio and television showed up to broadcast Colonels games in 1967 everyone knew it was a big deal.

During the 1967-68 season, Kallay faced a 78 game schedule, plus any playoffs. On top of that, he did double duty for the University of Louisville and their 24 regular season games and two more in the National Invitational Tournament that season.

All told there were 109 games that season and Kallay saw 97 of them. The reason for not seeing them all was due to a conflict in the Cardinals and Colonels schedules.

There was no disputing the fact that Kallay was a "homer." He wouldn't have it any other way, and his continual digs at ABA officiating kept listeners riled up, much like they would be if they were actually at the game.

Kallay jumped on board early with the Colonels, even to the point of immersing himself into the team by convincing management and coach Johnny Givens to let him be a part of the team's exhibition roster.

In those beginning years with the Colonels, Kallay's personality often mirrored whether his team had won or lost. It was easy to tell, because those games became a part of him.

Kallay was an amazing game caller. How he did it was really something special to see. For those who occasionally took their eyes off of the game, and watched Kallay at courtside were perhaps clueless as to how many things he had going on in the small space that had been assigned to him on press row. He was definitely different from most other broadcasters.

Not only was he keeping game statistics, and doing play-by-play, but he was also filming some of the game at the same time. Later, his film would be rushed back to WAVE to be shown on nightly sports. Remember, there was no internet, no e-mail, and not a whole lot of things in 1967. He was a one-man show, as were many of the sports broadcasters during that time.

Today, a broadcast might include a couple of engineers, a spotter, and a color man.

A listener in those early Colonels days didn't have to wait long to get Kallay's opinion or find out what he thought of the game; he regarded his own opinion very highly.

There was nothing 9-to-5 about Ed Kallay. About as close to a schedule as he would get would be when he hosted one of Louisville's most popular TV kiddie shows. It was called "Funny Flickers," and took place at the Magic Forest. He went by the name of Uncle Ed.

There was even a documentary, "The Littlest Colonel," that showed Kallay in contract negotiations with the team's management, going through a practice, and even playing in one of the exhibition games.

Not only was it a publicity gimmick, it could have been an early sign of things to come. Does Penny Ann Early ring a bell?

Kallay probably never really got the credit he deserved in the early days. For that matter, WAVE probably didn't either. They both were somewhat overshadowed by high powered WHAS and their sports personalities that included Van Vance and Cawood Ledford.

WAVE, however, certainly had their moments in history. In 1949, it was WAVE-TV that televised the first live broadcast of the Kentucky Derby won by Ponder, and then in 1953 they did the first live broadcast of the Kentucky-Tennessee football game.

It was Kallay who hosted an amateur boxing show in the mid-50s that sometime featured a cocky, 12-year-old named Cassius Clay. Kallay was among the very first to tell us about this gifted youngster who would later become Muhammad Ali.

For sure Kallay had his moments. To make sure they lived on after he died in1977, at the age of 60, the University of Louisville presents an annual Ed Kallay award, the highest honor given to a senior student athlete.

Van Vance

Growing up in Barren County, near the small town of Park City at the edge of Kentucky's cave country, Van Vance fancied himself a pretty fair basketball player. Others had given him the nickname of Hawkeye, which would be a compliment to any youngster who liked to shoot. And he did.

Lee Robertson, Vance's high school coach, thought enough of him to encourage him to travel a few miles south to Bowling Green and try out for the Hilltoppers after he graduated in 1952. It wasn't just any team, mind you; it was one of Ed Diddle's best.

Before he got to Western, Robertson recalled that Vance had some other talent besides basketball.

"We had a football banquet after Van's junior year," recalls Robertson. "Not only was he the MVP of the 6-man football conference, he was also the entertainment that night. First he sang the song like Bing Crosby would sing it, then like Perry Como, and then like Frank Sinatra. Van then told the crowd 'now here's the way Hawkeye sings it.'" Years later Vance says, with a laugh, the song might have been "Old Man River."

Before his junior year of high school, Vance moved from the farm to the city, moving into one of the 12 rooms at the Cavern Motel owned by his aunt in downtown Park City.

Vance was always ambitious. As a 17-year-old while he was at WKAY radio studio in Glasgow recording a speech he wrote, "I Speak for Democracy," station manager Jack Eversole heard him and offered him a job on the spot. And then when Eversole moved over to WKCT in Bowling Green, Vance joined him while attending Western.

"I emceed a Saturday afternoon talent show at WKCT," says Vance. "I'd do a little singing myself. But one day I taped myself, and when I heard my voice, I never sang again."

Vance actually lived in Diddle Dorm, the coach's on-campus house where all of the players lived at the time.

"When I got to Western, they had some great players, Tom Marshall, Art Spoelstra, Dan King, and Dickie White were some, and they were ranked number nine in the nation," Vance recalled.

"I told Coach Diddle my heart really wasn't in basketball and that I wanted to get into radio," he said. "I had begun doing some things with WKCT in Bowling Green. He let me stay in Diddle Dorm the rest of the semester. Back then Coach did a nightly bed check on all his players. Of course, I wasn't there, and he'd leave me a note letting me know that I missed bed check."

In 1957 Vance found his way to WHAS radio in Louisville, where in the beginning it was not all sports, but anywhere they needed him. He worked alongside Cawood Ledford who he described as "the best ever."

Vance finally moved into sports full time.

Several years later opportunity knocked for WHAS to get the broadcast rights for all of the Kentucky Colonels games. At the time, WAVE radio had broadcast rights and their man, Ed Kallay, was a legend of sorts in Louisville.

It was before the 1970-71 season when Ed Shadburne, an executive at WHAS, made the decision to go after the Colonels business, recalled Vance. It looked like the team was for real, with solid community support that included the new ownership group. The fact that they had made a commitment to go after UK stars Dan Issel and Mike Pratt further heightened WHAS's interest in Colonels basketball.

"That first year, WHAS had the rights. Cawood and I would alternate games," Vance said. "But we also carried all of the UK games, and the Colonels games would be broadcast on delay following their game."

Colonels management the following season let it be known they would like to have one broadcaster who could be identified with the team. That man was Van Vance.

Although Vance was an employee of WHAS and not the Colonels, his attachment to the front office, and the players in particular, was evident. "Of course I wanted the Colonels to win," he offered. "But I stayed away from the "we stuff." I didn't want to be called a homer."

Vance remembers that one night, Mike Storen came over to him before a game and said, "If we're not playing well tonight, why don't you say the other team is playing great defense?

"When I was critical of the team on the air, the Browns (John Y. and Ellie) were okay with it," said Vance. "They said if we're playing bad, say it."

But Vance concedes that there was one time in particular that John Y. was not happy with what Vance had reported on a broadcast. It was nothing negative about the team, but more so about John Y., the owner.

"I reported on the air that Virginia Squires' broadcaster Marty Brennaman had said the trade the Colonels made to get John Roche in return for Mike Gale and Wendell Ladner was the worst trade ever in professional basketball," Vance said. "And just before I was going on the air the following night, John Y. came running over to me very upset with what he had been told I said.

"I told him I only repeated what Brennaman had said, and that wasn't necessarily how I felt. After I explained it all, he was okay."

Vance remembers that John Y. had a small group of people that he really respected and listened to. They often would tell Brown what they had heard on radio or seen on television, not always getting it right.

Among John Y.'s close confidents were said to have been football hall-of-famer Paul Hornung, a Louisvillian; Harry and Larry Jones, brothers who had played football for Paul "Bear" Bryant at UK at the same time Brown was a student there; and Thumper Coleman, whose wife Joanie was on Ellie Brown's board of directors.

During his years with WHAS and the Colonels, Vance might have known more about the day-to-day inner workings of the organization than anyone else, including management. Players talked a lot to him, some confiding their personal lives as well as the professional side. And because of this, Vance often came up with lots of the so-called "scoops."

Back in the early days of the Colonels, Louisville had two newspapers, the morning *Courier-Journal* and afternoon *Louisville Times*. Earl Cox was on the verge of replacing long time sports editor Earl Ruby, who was retiring. Cox was an outstanding writer, and even when not writing an editorial-type article, his opinions often leaked through as straight up sports reporting. Readers loved Cox's style of reporting. He was not afraid to take a position, and he seemed to thrive on occasional controversy. Even though the Bingham family owned both newspapers and WHAS radio and TV, it didn't mean those working for the separate entities took vacations together, not at all.

Vance recalls that Cox didn't really get on the Colonels bandwagon from the beginning, but that he was a Gene Rhodes supporter, going back to his St. X high school coaching days.

"I had a great relationship with Gene, as I did with all of the coaches," said Vance. "But he was so intense, and when John Y. let Gene go, it really made Earl mad. He really didn't have much to do with the Colonels after that."

Just to prove the point that the radio guys didn't always get along with the newspaper guys, there was the night of the 1974 All-Star game in Salt Lake City. The Colonels had Gilmore, Issel and Dampier playing for the East team. "I interviewed Ellie Brown at halftime, Vance said. "And what I remember most is that she said it's a shame our hometown newspaper didn't think enough about our team to send a writer."

The next morning Vance recalled that Wayne Perky, a popular WHAS radio host, called Cox on the phone live. "Earl said he didn't send anyone to cover the game because he didn't think it was important enough," Vance said.

It was apparent Cox didn't appreciate the call.

Vance tells of the time John Y. would always ask his friends and those around the Colonels what they would do in certain situations?

"John Y. was always asking people close to him for advice," laughed Vance. "But the truth was he already knew what he wanted to do. He was just looking for those that would agree."

One of those he asked was none other than Cox, and Vance says Cox told Brown he needed to bring Gene Rhodes back. He did. But this time Rhodes re-joined the Colonels as the general manager, and not as the coach. That was in 1973, and Babe McCarthy was running the team. With Rhodes on board again, Cox was in a little better frame of mind about the Colonels.

It was Vance, with a little bit of a dig, who reported on his afternoon sports radio show a few years later that Earl Cox had been replaced as sports editor at the *Courier-Journal*, and that Cox would become a columnist.

When Rhodes was let go the first time, word on the street was that John Y. wanted more of a UK image with the head coach. Rhodes had even said so as well.

"I think the Browns really did want a UK flavor to the team," said Vance. "So when Frank Ramsey replaced Rhodes, and later Adolph Rupp joined the board of directors, they were headed in that direction."

But the reality for Rhodes was that there was some discontent among his team that had reached the media, so if John Y. wanted to replace him, this gave him one more reason.

The Colonels had scheduled a handful of games in Lexington in addition to the ones they were playing in Cincinnati. "Joe B. had just taken over for Adolph at UK, and you know Adolph didn't leave on his own free will," Vance said in referring to Joe B. Hall who followed Rupp as the Wildcat head coach. "And Joe B. didn't really relish the thought of competing with the Colonels in Lexington."

Could it have been a way for Rupp to get in one last jab at his former university?

Vance fondly recalled the night the Colonels defeated the Pacers at Freedom Hall to win their only ABA title.

"Harry and Nancy Jones were close friends of the Browns, and they were having a victory party at their home," Vance said. "Everyone was there, John Y.'s friends, the players, their wives, all of the Colonels people. But John Y. just couldn't relax and enjoy the moment. He was already thinking about next year.

"John was so good at working a crowd and he was working this one. He asked me "What if I challenged San Francisco (the NBA Champions), Rick Barry, Jeff Mullins, and Nate Thurmond. Do you think I ought to do it?"

"I said, 'John let's enjoy this win.' Then he asked me if I thought we could beat them?"

"We played them the next season in an exhibition game, Vance said. "We didn't have Issel and still won 93-90."

Following the championship season, John Y. made a decision that shook the ABA basketball world, but most of all it shook Louisville, and all of Kentucky's basketball fans.

Regarding the sale of Issel, Vance said, "John felt like he was actually saving the team. I don't think he really got over it and all of the fans' negative reaction. He was stung by all of the criticism."

"We had been hearing about the NBA merger possibility for some time," recalled Vance. We just knew that Indiana and Kentucky would be two of the teams. John Y. felt that the NBA should pay us to join them and not us pay them. He felt very strongly about how good his team was, and that it would be an asset to the NBA."

Brown was good friends with Larry O'Brien of the NBA front office, and both were heavily involved with the National Democratic Party, so most of the Colonels in-crowd felt like he had a lock on NBA inclusion.

It was not to be.

One year after the city of Louisville had been so consumed with a professional basketball championship, it was all over.

"Lots of people in Louisville just knew that John Y. would move the NBA team he bought to Louisville," Vance said in referring to the Buffalo Brave team he purchased for half of the $3 million dollars he had been paid for folding up the Colonels. "People were calling him, encouraging him to do it. I even called him. He asked me 'where are all the movers and shakers?' They're not calling."

That was the end of that.

Vance had a nice career with the Colonels, even winning Kentucky Sportscaster of the Year in 1975 and 1976. "I couldn't believe it when I won," Vance laughed. "It was always Cawood. And then Ralph Hacker, his color man would be second, and one year John Ferguson, a sideline reporter at the time, finished third in the voting. It was a real honor."

Even though Vance would no longer call Colonels basketball, he became the voice of the Louisville Cardinals from 1981-92, broadcasting three Final Fours in his first five years.

DICK PALMER

When Dick Palmer called his first ABA game in 1970, it was the first professional basketball game he had ever seen. He was doing an audition tape to become the play-by-play announcer for the Memphis Pros, who had just moved their franchise from New Orleans.

"It was an exhibition game in Martin, Tennessee, between Memphis and Dallas," says Palmer. "I had known their coach, Babe McCarthy, before he started in the ABA. I did some advertising work for him when he was promoting an NBA exhibition game several years before in Jackson, Tennessee for Bailey Howell, who played for him at Mississippi State and was then playing for the Celtics."

Palmer sent his dry-run tape to WREC in Memphis, and when the team took the floor, he was sitting courtside broadcasting the first for-real professional basketball game in the city's history, in front of 13,000 fans. The loss to the New York Nets did nothing to help build attendance for the Pros' next home game two days later.

"We hosted the Colonels two days later," says Palmer. "And got a 109-99 win, but only just over 1,000 showed up for the game."

In December 1970, Palmer made his first trip to Freedom Hall with Memphis, and once again the Pros won. "It made it two straight over the Colonels," he says of the 110-106 win. "And a win at Freedom Hall was very rare for us."

Palmer says there was already a natural rivalry going on between Memphis State and the University of Louisville teams, so nothing less was expected between the cities' two ABA teams. "I still remember the silver-haired PA announcer at Freedom Hall and his flowery introduction of Babe before every game we played," said Palmer.

Of course he was speaking of John Tong.

"He was a fixture there for many years," Palmer continued. "He would say something like, 'and the head coach of the Pros, that dapper and dashing Southern gentleman from Baldwyn, Mississippi ... Babe McCarthy.'"

Palmer said the Pros made the playoffs that first year in Memphis, but lost four straight to the Pacers.

The next three years in Memphis were a struggle. The league had to rescue the team from the owners who brought the team from New Orleans, and before the second season began, stock was sold to keep the team afloat. Just prior to the third season, 1972-73, when it appeared the team was ready to fold, Charles O. Finley, the controversial baseball maverick, stepped in and bought the team. By then McCarthy had moved on to Dallas, and Bob Bass was the Pros' coach.

In spite of Finley's baseball-type promotions, the fans still stayed away. But only as Charlie O. could do it, he had one more trick up his sleeve.

"He dropped a bombshell with the announcement that Adolph Rupp was coming out of retirement to become the team's president." Palmer said.

"Coach Rupp was a joy to be around," he said. "Because you never knew what was coming. I recall setting up a halftime interview during a home game and noticed as I looked down press row during the second quarter that he seemed to be nodding off during the game. But when he got to the mic, he told me in detail everything that happened, should have happened, and didn't happen in the whole first half. I was amazed.

"Our trainer, Don Sparks was sort of assigned to take care of coach Rupp when he was in Memphis, and Sparky said Rupp had a favorite catfish restaurant that he wanted to go to every time he was in town. I wish I would have made one of those outings with them."

Rupp didn't make many road trips with the team back then, but Palmer remembers one in particular.

"We played somebody in St. Paul, and he went along. St. Paul was thinking about getting a franchise, so the league moved a game there. We were sitting around listening to Rupp tell Kentucky stories during happy hour the day before the game. He was trying to impress upon Coach Bass the importance of setting screens, and I can still hear him now ... 'I tell my players, you go out there and set a hard screen ... I want to see sparks fly from your ass ... and if the referee calls a foul on you, just look over at me and smile ... because that one's on me.'"

"He then ordered a martini, and when the waiter came over for another round, Rupp told him, "Son, tell your bartender I want a martini with some vodka in it this time!"

Palmer says Rupp was amazed at the freedom the players had.

"I would never let my players wander around airports like that . . . they'd all be lost and miss the flight," he said.

Palmer, like many of the other broadcasters in the ABA, "worked solo" on the road, but they tried to be helpful to each other.

"Van Vance at Kentucky, Terry Stembridge at Dallas, and Bill Howard at Utah, in particular, were really nice to me that first year," he says.

As bad as the 1972-73 season was for Memphis, Palmer says funny stories still happened.

"We were at Freedom Hall and played awful and lost by about 30," says Palmer. "Bass was in a nasty mood in the locker room. We had a 7-foot center named Luther Rackley, an NBA reject. Rackley started whistling "Taps" in there, and Bass went bonkers and fined him something like $500 for that little gag."

Joe Mullaney

Playing at Holy Cross in the same backcourt with Bob Cousy and winning an NCAA title in 1947, Joe Mullaney went to work after college in the FBI. But soon he heard the calling; basketball was in his blood. After a brief stint at Norwich College in Vermont, he took over at Providence College in 1955. His teams were so successful that in 1969 he became the head coach of the Los Angeles Lakers.

As successful as he was, he still could not win an NBA championship and soon he was out of a job. But not for long.

The Colonels came calling, and Mullaney was their man. Much like his days with the Lakers, the talent was there, and he was expected to do more than just win. It was an ABA title that he was expected to bring to Louisville. Nothing less would be accepted.

The 1971-72 Colonels team posted a 68-16 record, the best ever in the ABA. They lost, however, in the first round of the Eastern Division playoffs to the Nets.

The following year the Colonels were a very respectable 56-28, but still no championship.

Mullaney's basketball resume was good enough that he would never be out of the game for long. So when he left the Colonels, he coached the Utah Stars in 1973-74 to a record of 51-33, but lost once again to the Nets 4-1 in the ABA finals. He was there only one season when the Stars folded.

Mullaney quickly caught on with the Memphis Sounds for the 1974-75 season until they, too, called it quits. And then at mid-season of the 1975-76 season, he was brought in to coach the St. Louis Spirit. It would seem at this point in Mullaney's career, he would know what was coming. And he did.

At the end of the season the ABA was no more.

Mullaney became associated with the NBA again, this time with the Buffalo Braves. John Y. Brown, the team's new owner, re-hired Mullaney for the 1976-77 year.

A few years later Mullaney returned to where it all really began for him, Providence College. He coached there from 1981-85 before retiring. He died of cancer on March 8, 2000, at the age of 74.

SIXTH SEASON
1972-73
by Lloyd Gardner

Regular Season Standings

EASTERN DIVISION	W—L
Carolina Cougars	57-27
Kentucky Colonels	56-28
Virginia Squires	42-42
New York Nets	30-54
Memphis Tams	24-60

WESTERN DIVISION	W—L
Utah Stars	55-29
Indiana Pacers	51-33
Denver Rockets	47-37
San Diego Conquistadors	30-54
Dallas Chaparrals	28-56

It was a long hot summer. Losing in the first round of the playoffs after an ABA best ever 68-16 regular season record left a bitter taste in our mouths. Disappointing yes, but with Artis, Dan, and Louie, Colonels fans still felt that a championship was inevitable.

Prior to the season, the Pittsburgh Condors and the Miami Floridians took down the nets, packed their bags and closed the door. The Memphis franchise that had always been in financial disarray was about to follow to the exit door, too. That's when Oakland A's (baseball) owner, Charlie O. Finley, bailed Memphis out. Finley's first move was to remove the name Pros. He had a contest and paid the winner $2,500. The name selected was TAMS. This name was chosen because Charlie O. thought he could draw fans from Tennessee, Arkansas, and Mississippi. The team logo would use their colors on a tam-o-shanter. Babe McCarthy packed his bags and headed to Dallas with Bob Bass. Just as he had done in Oakland, Finley bought all new white, green and gold uniforms with all tops and trunks interchangeable. He also offered to pay any of his employees $300 if they grew a mustache.

One of the few times in ABA history the league had an expansion team, the San Diego Conquistadors, better known as the Q's. Leonard Bloom had purchased the team, and each ABA team was to make three players available for a dispersal draft. If a team's player got drafted, that club could pull back one of their other players. Bloom's first big move was to raid the Colonels office and hire Alex Groza as the General Manager. Groza's appointment as GM was highly endorsed by Mike Storen. The Q's then hired K.C. Jones, a former Boston Celtic, as their first coach.

The Colonels' Les Hunter was chosen by the Q's in the dispersal draft. In August the Colonels traded Cincy Powell to Utah for a 1973 draft choice and cash. Mike Storen took the cash and bought Rick Mount from the Indiana Pacers for $250,000.

The Pacers first choice for coach in the beginning was said to be Oscar Robertson, at the time still putting up big numbers in almost every category with the Cincinnati Royals. The Pacers were going to offer him $125,000 to jump to his hometown team as a player-coach.

With Robertson getting an early taste of what bidding for his talent might feel like, he had enough influence and connections to get lawyers and judges involved to block any so-called merger between the NBA and ABA. The NBA Players Association filed a suit that became known as "the Oscar Robertson Suit" in order to prevent the merger of the two leagues as a monopoly that would be an antitrust violation. Any merger, of course, would drive down player's salaries.

When the ABA appeared on the scene, it was like dollars falling out of the sky. For sure most of the players in both leagues never in their wildest dreams thought they would make so much money for playing basketball.

Even though on September 8, 1972, the U.S. Senate Antitrust Subcommittee voted to allow a merger of the two leagues, the Oscar Robertson suit hung around for almost another four years before finally being settled in February 1976.

On September 23, 1972, the Kentucky Colonels played the Atlanta Hawks in an exhibition game in Frankfort, Kentucky. Very few people knew or realized that Dr. J had jumped from the ABA to the NBA Atlanta Hawks. He left the Virginia Squires and had attended training camp with the Hawks in Savannah, Georgia. "Pistol" Pete Maravich was also on that team.

After the game in Frankfort I had a plane waiting in Lexington to fly us to Atlanta for a rematch on Sunday afternoon. It was very late at night and Artis and I were in the last cab together headed to the hotel in downtown Atlanta. Artis asked me if I would go out with him to get something to eat when we arrived at the hotel. I told him I would. The cabby was listening to the local news on his radio. At one point the broadcaster said, "Atlanta police are looking for 7'2" Thomas Payne on a rape charge." Artis looked at me and said, "Pink, I ain't goin' nowhere, how many 7'2" black guys are gonna be walkin the streets of Atlanta at 2 a.m. in the morning? Not me!" Payne, of course, had played at UK a few years earlier.

The ABA/NBA games would be played under ABA rules using a red, white and blue basketball one half, and under NBA rules with an NBA ball the second half. The first game in Frankfort, the Hawks defeated the Colonels 112-109. Dr. J was wearing #54 with white high top Converse All-Stars.

The second game in Atlanta was played at the Alexander Memorial Coliseum on the Georgia Tech campus. The three-point line was painted with white shoe polish. The Colonels fell behind by 24 points at one time, but ended up winning the game 104-103.

For Dr. J, the real issue was not money. The issue was that the Hawks did not have the right to sign him two days before the NBA draft in 1972, in which the Milwaukee Bucks owned the draft rights to the Doc. NBA Commissioner Walter Kennedy slapped a record fine of $25,000 on the Hawks for playing him in the two games against Kentucky. The Hawks ignored the Commissioner and played Dr. J in a third game against the ABA Carolina Cougars. After three games, a three judge panel ruled that the Doc had to honor his prior contract with the ABA Virginia Squires, and Dr. J returned to the ABA.

The Colonels traveled to Phoenix on September 30, 1972, to play the Suns. In the third quarter of that game, the NBA referee called a technical foul on me. Just as he hit me, I looked directly across the floor and Mike Storen was irate; he hit the press table so hard the telephone went about two feet high and fell to the floor. I wasn't anxious to come face to face with him after the game. Thank goodness the Colonels won the game 120-118.

On October 1, 1972, the Milwaukee Bucks made a return visit to Freedom Hall. Kareem Abdul-Jabbar and Oscar Robertson tallied 20 points each and the Colonels went down in defeat 131-100. On October 6, the Suns paid a visit to Louisville and defeated the hometown team 103-91. The Colonels closed the exhibition games against the NBA the next night with another loss. The Baltimore Bullets prevailed in a close one, 95-93.

Before the season started, two court orders were issued. Rick Barry was ordered to honor his contract with the NBA Golden State Warriors. Billy Cunningham was ordered to leave the Philadelphia 76ers and play for the Carolina Cougars.

The Kentucky Colonels opened regular season play in the new Nassau Coliseum in Hempstead, New York. Although Rick Barry had returned to the NBA, John Roche once again put a dagger in the Colonels back by scoring a game high 32 points, leading the Nets to a 114-90.

On October 14, 1972, without Julius Erving, the Virginia Squires visited Louisville's Freedom Hall for the Colonels home opener. Former Colonel, Jim "Goose" Ligon, paced the Squires with 20 points, but the Virginians were no match for the home team. With six players in double figures, led by Issel's 28 and Gilmore's 27, the Colonels prevailed 130-110.

On January 9, the Colonels' Claude Virden, a part-time starter who had played at Murray State, the same school that produced Stew Johnson, was going in for a wide open layup when he fell to the floor and grabbed his knee. Our team doctor, Dr. Rudy Ellis and I rushed to his aide. He had torn his ACL (anterior cruciate ligament), medical meniscus, and medial collateral ligament. The next morning I went into surgery with Dr. Ellis and Dr. Walter Badenhausen. This was a career ending injury for Virden.

On January 19, 1973, the Colonels traded Bill Chamberlain, a North Carolina Tar Heel, to the Memphis Tams for Wendell Ladner. When Wendell arrived at the airport, he went to an airport phone and called our office, which was in the Executive Inn. When an office secretary answered the phone, Wendell said, "I need someone to come to the airport and take me to the X-e-cute-ive Inn."

Wendell was from Necaise Crossing, Mississippi. He didn't use many suffixes in his speech. He was one of my favorite players of all time. Being from the south, you might think Wendell was prejudiced, but he wasn't. Off the court he got along with everybody, the color of your skin didn't matter. Wendell was always concerned about his appearance; he always wanted to impress the women. Many times he would ask me in the huddle during a timeout, "Is my hair messed up?" At halftime, Wendell would sprint to the locker room, get his hair dryer and hairspray and fix his hair before the rest of the team would arrive. Another saying familiar to his teammates was, "I get all piss off." He would often use only part of a word.

We were flying to Norfolk, Virginia with a plane change in Washington, D.C. National Airport. As we were landing, Wendell asked Dan, who was in the seat in front of him, "What's that down there?" Dan, looking at the Washington Monument, said, "That's the Washington Post." Wendell, still gazing at the historic D.C. area said, "Well, is that the Lincoln Memorandum?"

With Virden injured, we were down to nine players. That was not enough to scrimmage in practice, so we picked up former U of L player Ron Thomas. Ron had been working selling used cars.

Most of us could never figure out why Rick Mount played basketball. He really didn't like it. He would rather be back home in Lafayette, Indiana, hunting and fishing. His dream was to be a salesman or representative selling and demonstrating guns, rods and reels.

After a game, most players go out and get something to eat or hit a local pub, but not Rick. One night we were in Norfolk, Virginia, and when we got back to the hotel, the "Rocket" was in the hallway practicing his casting. He had bought a brand new "Shakespeare" rod and reel.

Joe Mullaney had flown to Salt Lake City two days early to scout the Stars, and Bud Olsen handled practice. Most people don't know that the trainer/travel secretary was always in charge of the team from the end of practice until the team was dressed and ready for a pregame meeting. As always, I was in charge of getting everybody in our entourage to the team's destination.

We always took the first flight out in the morning. If a team missed a game, there was a $5,000 fine. If you were late, it was a $3,000 fine assessed by the ABA Commissioner. If you took the first available flight and you didn't arrive on time, there wasn't any penalty.

On February 6, 1973, the ABA All-Star Game was held in the Salt Palace in Salt Lake City, Utah before 12,556 fans. The West team's Warren Jabali was named the MVP after scoring 16 points in the fourth quarter in a come-from-behind win. The night before, comedian Bill Cosby entertained the ABA players, coaches and fans in the Salt Palace. Dan Issel, Artis Gilmore, and Louie Dampier were selected to the East team.

Because of fog at the airport in Salt Lake City and bad weather in Chicago, the Kentucky contingency didn't arrive home until late. About 75 people were waiting at the Duncan Memorial Chapel that is located in a cemetery in Crestwood, Kentucky, where Van Vance and Sue Ann Lyons were to be married. The chapel was built in 1936 by Alexander Duncan as a memorial to his wife, Flora Ross Duncan. Duncan and his wife are entombed in the chancel of the chapel. It was misting rain, the temperature was in the mid-30s, and the Chapel didn't have any heat in the winter or air conditioning in the summer. The nuptials were to start at 7 p.m., and the plane didn't land until about 9 p.m., and the Chapel was about 35 miles from the Louisville airport. Van Vance and our Public Relations Director, David Vance (no relation), jumped into a car and headed to the cemetery. To make matters worse, Van was in a cast due to an ankle injury he had suffered playing tennis.

After the wedding, Van and Sue Ann rented a honeymoon suite at a hotel in southern Indiana. It was a floating cabin on a small lake beside the main hotel. You had to be taken to your accommodations by boat. It got so windy that the cabin was bobbing up and down. Van got so seasick that before the sun came up, he had to call someone to "bring the boat and get me out of here."

Last year, Charlie Scott of the ABA Virginia Squires jumped to the Phoenix Suns of the NBA. The NBA came in very quietly, stole him and got out of town. They were trying to get as many ABA All-Stars as they could.

On February 10, 1973, the Kentucky Colonels were playing the Virginia Squires on the Virginia Commonwealth campus in Richmond. The Colonels had checked-in at a Holiday Inn that afternoon. About 4:30 p.m., Dan Issel called my room and said that he was sick and running a fever. I immediately went to his room and took his temperature, and it was over 102 degrees. I told him to stay in bed, drink plenty of fluids and I would check with him before we left for the game.

I always gave the team a wake-up call 30 minutes before the bus left for the game so that I know everyone is awake. Sometimes they didn't answer the phone, they just showed-up in the lobby. When the team gathered in the lobby, Artis and Pierre Russell were nowhere to be found. They roomed together. Rumors started floating around within the team that maybe the NBA had come in and stolen Artis and took Pierre with them. After calling their room numerous times and beating on the door, the team finally left for the arena. No one had any idea where they were. After taking us to the arena, the hotel manager was going crazy trying to help us find them.

I would tape an ankle, go out to the press table, call the hotel, and call their room. Finally, it reached a point that I had to call Dan Issel and tell him that he had to get up, even though he was running a high fever, and come and sit on the bench. Why, because the league had a rule that you **MUST HAVE EIGHT PLAYERS ON THE BENCH TO START THE GAME**. Even though he was very sick, he got dressed and I notified the hotel manager that he would need a ride over to the arena as soon as possible.

Dan got up, got dressed and went to the elevator. When the elevator door opened, Artis and Pierre were on the elevator and Artis said to Dan, "Hey big fella, I thought we were late." Dan replied, "You are late; the game starts in 10 minutes." Dan got off the elevator and went back to bed. Artis and Pierre got to the game three minutes before tip-off.

The girl working the front desk had changed their room because their heat didn't work. She never recorded the room change anywhere, and they were still sleeping because they didn't get the normal wake-up call.

This may not seem like a problem to you, but when the NBA is trying to steal your players, there were tense moments thinking that someone might be kidnapping the league's top big man.

That same night, Artis turned his ankle and I took him to the emergency room and had it x-rayed. I also had it put in a cast because we had a game the next night in Louisville, and I heard him ask a couple of the players if they wanted to go out and eat. By putting his foot in a cast, it forced him to get back to his room as soon as possible. I called on Dr. Rudy Ellis, our team physician, and made arrangements to see him in his office as soon as we could get there from the airport.

When we got to the Louisville airport, Artis told me to go to the parking lot and I could drive him down to the doctor's office. Well, that was an experience in itself. Artis had a straight stick Corvette. In order to start the car you had to have the clutch all the way to the floor. Now that was a problem! Artis, being so tall, had the seat put way back into the rear wheel well, and I had to lie down to get the engine started. Dr. Ellis removed the cast and Artis played that night and had 24 points.

On Sunday, February 25, 1973, the Colonels played an afternoon game against the Denver Rockets and lost 87-86. Because we had Monday off, we slept in and took a midmorning flight to Salt Lake City. When I arrived at the hotel I was getting the players keys when one of the desk clerks handed me a pink message slip. It read, "Lloyd, call home." I called home and there was no answer, so I called my aunt's house. My mother had been diagnosed with cancer in January, and she was too sick to make the ride back and forth to the hospital from Fairdale for radiation treatments, so she was at her sister's house near St. Joseph's hospital. I asked Dan and Louie to go to my room with me. I was certain that my mother had passed. When I called my aunt's house and she answered the phone I said, 'Let me talk to dad.' She handed the phone to my brother Paul. He said Mr. Mullins (our neighbor for 25 years) found dad dead in bed this morning. I couldn't believe it. Mom had cancer and dad seemed healthy at age 68. Every morning dad got up and took my mother to the hospital for treatments. He didn't show-up, so they called Mr. Mullins to go check on him. When Mr. Mullins opened his door to go to our house he noticed that there wasn't any smoke coming out of the chimney (we had a coal furnace). He went over to the house (he had a key), knocked on the door and found dad in bed. He just died in his sleep.

I talked to Dan and Louie and then I went to Joe's room and told him I was going home. I sat on the bed and called the airlines and made a reservation for the next flight out heading home. It was bitter cold and snowing. I picked up my bags, and headed to the airport for the long trip home. I went through Chicago and arrived in Louisville late that night.

There were no signs of any struggle. My dad was the hardest working man I ever knew. As kids, my brother and I were taught how to work. We had huge gardens, a few cows and a large yard to cut with a push mower. He hated Adolph Rupp (because he won so much); he liked sports but didn't have a lot of time to watch. He always allowed me to go to practices, but never really watched me play football when I played for Fairdale. He never thought I was any good. He went to one game, Fairdale's first ever at the new school, and I started at right guard.

Every week he would remind me to not be too disappointed if I didn't get to play. Although I started every varsity game my junior and senior year, he never went to another game. As a basketball manager he always let me take the time needed to do my job the right way. Now my mother, that was a different story. She loved sports, especially basketball. She was on the Fairdale girls' team (at the old school) that won the Fifth Region in 1933. Even though I didn't play basketball, she went to every high school game.

Once my mother got cancer, I visited her every day that we weren't on the road. Life changes so quickly. Everybody was together Christmas, but after she went to the doctor in mid-January she never returned to our home in Fairdale.

The team played in Salt Lake City on Tuesday night and I would go out to my car at the funeral home and check on the score. The team came home the next day. That night, Wednesday, every person in the Colonels organization came to the funeral home. Several members of the office staff came to the funeral. My mother was in a wheel chair.

I had four tickets on the fourth row right behind the Colonels bench. My mother was there with my wife, Sandy, about 90% of the time. She loved the game of basketball and she was so proud of what I had accomplished. My brother Paul wasn't really into sports. All through high school, college and the pros he thought I was wasting my time. He went to one game a year, if my cousin who lived next door to him wanted to go.

The Colonels opened the playoffs against the Virginia Squires with Dr. J and the Iceman, George Gervin. Gervin had been playing at Eastern Michigan when he was involved in an altercation, and was dismissed from the team. There were only 31 games left in the regular season when he requested a tryout with the Squires. Rumors circulated around the ABA that he made 22 out of 25 three point shots.

To everyone's surprise, the Colonels ended the series in five games 4-1.

The Colonels would now face the Carolina Cougars for the Eastern Division Championship and earn the right to play for the ABA Championship for the second time in three years. The Cougars were loaded with talent. Billy "The Kangaroo Kid" Cunningham, "Jump' in" Joe Caldwell, Mack Calvin and rookie coach Larry Brown were primed and ready to challenge any and all teams for a championship ring.

In the second game, Mike "Philly Dog" Gale got elbowed in the eye, which resulted in a broken occipital bone and had surgery two days later. He would miss the remaining games against Carolina.

As Babe McCarthy once said, Wendell doesn't know the meaning of the word fear. That was never more evident than on April 21, 1973, in Game 6 of a second round playoff game against the Carolina Cougars in Freedom Hall. Wendell always played with reckless abandon, always diving after loose balls, jumping over press tables and always hoping that he would come down in the lap of some beautiful young lady. Well, on this night he met his match ... well, almost. With 3:09 left in the game and the Colonels with a sizeable lead, Wendell went airborne over the Cougars bench, crashing into a five gallon glass water cooler. I jumped from my seat, with Dr. Rudy Ellis right behind me, and headed to the other end of the floor. Can you imagine what blood looks like in five gallons of water? It looked like five gallons of blood. I had grabbed a towel as I headed down the floor and immediately wrapped Wendell's arm in it. The back of his jersey was already sopping up the blood coming from the cuts on his back. I helped him to the locker room, and Dr. Ellis and I wrapped him up. He wanted to go back out and play. Dr. Ellis said no. We took him to the hospital and stitched him up, 37 stitches in all. There were 25 on his forearm and 12 scattered on his back, plus a lot of small cuts too small to stitch-up. Kentucky won that game 119-100. The next day, and from that day on, the glass coolers were replaced with plastic water coolers.

It took me over an hour to steri-strip his stitches and wounds, but Wendell never missed a practice or a game. Three days later, when Ladner played again, fans noticed blood on his legs. The stitches were fine, he just refused to change his blood-stained socks until the playoffs ended. Every game was a brutal battle. On April 24, 1973, Kentucky won Game 7 in the Charlotte Coliseum 107-96, thus earning a trip to the Championship series against the powerful Indiana Pacers.

It was called the I-65 series. It's only 110 miles from Louisville to Indianapolis. The Pacers and the Colonels were without a doubt the biggest rivals in the ABA. With Louie Dampier and Rick Mount, both Hoosiers, on the team, it just raised the intensity of this match-up that much more.

Game One was played in Freedom Hall on April 28, 1973, and was televised on national television. It was only fitting that this game would feature a controversial play. Kentucky was leading 100-97 with 1:09 left in the game. The always reliable Roger Brown hit a three-pointer for the Pacers and the game went into overtime.

It was late in the extra period when our Jimmy O'Brien missed a short jumper, but followed his shot and grabbed his own rebound and scored, putting the Colonels up by two. But the crowd of 12,119 was so loud that the buzzer on the 30-second clock couldn't be heard. After the referees met and consulted with the 30-second clock timekeeper, Tom Curley, he took the basket away. Jimmy Clark, the alternate official, was seated next to Curley and he had told Clark that the buzzer had sounded.

In the final 20 seconds Freddie Lewis hit a shot and canned two free throws for a 111-107 victory. Lewis finished with 29 points and 13 assists. Dan Issel had 33 points and 20 rebounds to lead the Colonels.

The next day Mike Storen called Tom Curley and asked him to stop by his office. As most people were, he was petrified by the phone call. Not looking forward to facing Mike, much less after he had to admit that the shot-clock had gone off, possibly costing the Colonels the game. With shaky knees Tom went to the meeting. Mike told him, "I just wanted to tell you that I thank you for being honest and you are the kind of person that I want working for this organization." Was Curley relieved? Yes he was.

Game two was once again at Freedom Hall on April 30. The Colonels jumped out to an early 18 point lead before the Pacers behind the play of George McGinnis tied the score at 85. By outscoring Indiana 35-22 in the fourth quarter, the Colonels prevailed 114-102. The Pacers simply could not do anything to contain the Big A and Dan as 13,406 fans witnessed Artis finishing with an amazing 29 points, 26 rebounds and 7 blocked shots. Dan had 28 points and 12 rebounds.

Game three moved north on I-65 to the Indiana State Fairgrounds Coliseum. Once again Artis dominated the paint before an unruly crowd. He proved once again that the lane was under enemy control. The big man finished with 28 points, 18 rebounds and seven blocked shots.

Final score, Kentucky 92 – Indiana 88, advantage Kentucky 2-1. The Colonels regained home court advantage.

Game four was as physical as the first three. Would you expect anything different? The Colonels led 70-68 late in the third quarter, but Roger Brown wiped that out with two quick baskets and the Pacers led 74-70 after three quarters. Even with Gilmore in foul trouble and Issel having a poor shooting night, the game was still nip and tuck. The Colonels never took the lead again after falling behind in the third quarter. The final score was Indiana 90-Kentucky 86. The series was tied 2-2.

Game five at Freedom Hall was a game that got away from us. With 1:40 left in the game, Kentucky was leading 85-80 when Artis picked up his sixth foul and headed to the bench. Somehow, someway, we lost 89-86. Everyone in the arena was stunned, including the Pacers. Instead of going up three games to two, with two games to win one, the Colonels found themselves down 3-2. Our backs were indeed against the wall.

Game six was back in Indianapolis. For the first time in the series, one of the teams shot over 50%. The Colonels burned the nets for 52%, and we led 55-43 at the half. Indiana made a run, cutting the lead to two before we went on a 16-1 run. With five players in double figures, and three with over 22 points (Gilmore 29 points, 21 rebounds, Dampier 25 and Issel 22, the Colonels won by the largest margin in the series, 109-93. We were tied 3-3.

Game seven was held in Freedom Hall on Saturday, May 12, 1973. The Pacers led 42-41 at the half, but that was as close as it would get. George McGinnis got hot and the Colonels went cold. Kentucky set an ABA record for the fewest points in a quarter when they scored only 11 in the 12 minutes. The Pacers led 66-53 going into the fourth quarter and the closest Kentucky could get was seven. Pop the cork, spray the champagne. With the 88-81 win, the Pacers became the first team in ABA history to win three championships, and the Colonels became the only team to lose their second championship in three years, to the Utah Stars in 1971, and now to the Pacers.

It was Sunday, May 13, and it was Mother's Day. Our little pooch bit my 34-month-old son Chad. We had to take him to the hospital. We took him to St. Joseph, the same hospital where my mother was being treated for cancer. As I was getting on the elevator, they were taking her off. She was in a lot of pain and they were taking her down to run some tests. Little did I know that would be the last time I saw her alive. Monday morning about 6:30 a.m., the hospital called and told us we needed to come as soon as possible. We arrived about seven o'clock, but it was too late. She was a true Colonels fan and it seems like she just held on to see if we could win that championship ring.

It's ironic that both my parents died on a Monday, and both were buried on a Thursday, just 11 weeks apart. It has always been said that when God closes one door, he opens another. Thirty-four days later, joy once again filled our hearts with the birth of our second son, Jason.

SEVENTH SEASON
1973-74
by Lloyd Gardner

Regular Season Standings

EASTERN DIVISION	W—L
New York Nets	55-29
Kentucky Colonels	53-31
Carolina Cougars	47-37
Virginia Squires	28-56
Memphis Tams	21-63

WESTERN DIVISION	W—L
Utah Stars	51-33
Indiana Pacers	46-38
San Antonio Spurs	45-39
Denver Rockets	37-47
San Diego Conquistadors	37-47

Mike Storen believed that the owners were to be seen and not heard. Well, not very much or very often anyway. Under his direction, owners were not allowed in the dressing room and could not talk to the coaches about personnel. They were also banned from "hanging out" with the players and staff, and finding a seat at the press table was prohibited. To help control his ownership's involvement, Storen was the host of most team parties where everyone intermingled. He threw some awesome parties, and most of the time his wife, Hannah, would make small gifts for the guests. Whenever the team made great accomplishments, he would roll out the carpet for the organization. There wasn't anything about Mike Storen that wasn't first class, but he was in control. I missed Mike. He taught everyone on the staff the business of sports. That's why our business manager, Alex Groza, became the general manager for San Diego Q's and our sales manager, Jack Ankerson, became the general manager for the San Antonio Spurs and the Virginia Squires. His former trainer with the Indiana Pacers and Chicago Bears became the business manager for the Spurs. A lot of people didn't like Mike, but I don't dislike somebody just because you do. A lot of my close friends didn't like Mike.

When the Browns indicated to Storen that they were going to call the shots, he bailed out. Within weeks, Mike was named the Commissioner of the ABA, and, in a sense, he was still in control.

Not far behind Storen was head coach Joe Mullaney. Joe indicated that he didn't want to work for a man that knew more about frying chicken than basketball.

It was then that John Y. and Ellie filled the seat of the departed Storen with the person that he had fired, Gene Rhodes.

On September 5, 1973, I was working at my desk in the Colonels office preparing for camp to start when the phone rang. I picked it up and the party on the other end said in a slow southern draw, "Is Gene (Rhodes) there?" I said, "Who is this?" He replied, "The man who is to meet Gene in Chicago." I thought it was Babe McCarthy and he was trying to disguise his voice.

Two days later, assistant coach Bud Olsen started our camp at Bellarmine College for rookies and any veterans that wanted to come. Bud wanted to be the head coach, but they hadn't named him at this point. After practice, Rhodes called me into his office and asked me if I had leaked the McCarthy possibility to Cawood Ledford. I told him no. I don't know where he got the scoop, but it wasn't me.

A press conference was held at the Executive Inn on September 10, and Babe McCarthy was named the Colonels fourth coach in four years. If I were to describe Babe, I would simply say that he was a real southern gentleman, with that drawl. He could wear a white shirt and tie for 24 hours and it still looked as fresh as it did when he put it on. Babe always looked like he was out of GQ magazine.

Tryout camps and preseason exhibitions are more work for the trainer than anybody on the staff. With 15-20 players, two practices a day, taping ankles, scheduling airlines, busses and hotel confirmations for exhibition games, player per diem to be paid, three point lines to be put on courts, 30 second clocks packed, laundry, laundry and more laundry, game uniforms, and all the nagging injuries, a typical day would be 18-20 hours long.

It was September 21, and we had been in camp for two weeks and we would have our first exhibition game against the NBA Houston Rockets. We were now down to a manageable 13 players. It took all day to move from Bellarmine College back to Freedom Hall. With Gilmore leading the way with 22 points and 18 rebounds, the Colonels defeated the Rockets 110-102. Rudy Tomjanovich led all scorers with 32.

The next night Kentucky hosted coach Bob Cousy and the Kansas City – Omaha Kings. The Colonels prevailed behind Dan Issel's 23 points, Dampier's 22 and Rick Mount's 21. Nate "Tiny" Archibald and John Bloch each had 19 for the Kings.

The Colonels left on the 24th for three exhibition games. The first was in Lafayette, Louisiana where the Q's #1 draft choice, Dwight Lamar, had attended Southwestern Louisiana College. We played in Blackham Hall, a livestock, open air arena. The portable floor was placed on the dirt surface and the conditions were so bad that we dressed and taped at the hotel. There were so many bugs flying around that they turned almost all the lights off during timeouts.

We left the next day for Tulsa, Oklahoma for a game against the Spurs at Oral Roberts University on the 26th. The next morning it was up and out. We were heading for another game at the University of Virginia in Charlottesville. Barry Parkhill was a rookie on the Squires' roster, and he had just graduated from UV.

In professional basketball you practice, travel and practice, or shoot around every day. There are very few days that one of these doesn't occur. It was off to Owensboro on September 30th for a game against the New York Nets. Our exhibition ended in a game in Marion, Indiana, against the Pacers. Jimmy Clark, the ABA official who called a "T" when I hollered "foul," kicked me out of the game. Artis then got hit in the eye and was bleeding. Babe was furious. Clark told Babe I could come back out and take care of him. Babe then told him, "You kicked him out, now he can stay out. You take care of him." Artis ended up with several cuts and a big shiner. The next day I sent him to an eye specialist.

The day before the 1973-74 season opener, the players held a meeting and voted to strike. It was feared that the season would be delayed, but somehow the Players Association and the Commissioner, Mike Storen, worked things out.

Kentucky started the season with an 11-1 record. After the Colonels got their 11th win against Babe's former team, the Memphis Tams, Issel asked Babe, "When was the last time you were 11-1?" Babe replied, "When I was in grade school."

On October 19, the Colonels drubbed the Carolina Cougars 121-109. Larry Brown got three technical fouls and an early exit. The next morning Carolina and Kentucky were on the same flight back to Louisville for a rematch that Carolina won 105-102, our first loss.

Wilt Chamberlain brought his San Diego Conquistadors (3-6) to Freedom Hall on October 24. Leonard Bloom had signed Wilt to a personal service contract as a player/coach. Wilt still had a one year option on his contract with the Los Angeles Lakers. He actually played in four exhibition games before a court order forced him off the court and on the bench as a coach. Wilt wasn't always around for practices and sometimes he missed games. On occasion he would arrive at halftime. Assistant coach and a basketball mastermind, Stan Albeck, held the team together and should get all the credit for any wins the team had. Wilt had his own dress code. He usually wore a long, tail-out, wild pullover shirt with sandals. His wardrobe did change somewhat after a meeting with Storen, the commissioner.

Wilt's first visit wasn't much of a game. The Colonels trounced the Q's 146-105. Kentucky had eight players in double figures.

In November, Kentucky played three games in Cincinnati, one in Lexington, one in Bowling Green, and five in Freedom Hall. All were considered home games. They also played four on the road. On November 18, we lost again to Carolina. All three of our losses (12-3) were to the Cougars.

As I have mentioned before, Wendell didn't know the meaning of the words fear or pain. When he walked on the court, practice or game, he played with wreckless abandon. He was having some low back pain and after a few days Dr. Rudy Ellis told me that he would get me an appointment with Dr. Robins and have his prostate checked. I took Wendell to the doctor and after a thorough examination he told Wendell that he had an infection. Dr. Robins said, "Wendell, it's no big deal, you have an infection in your prostate and you need to cut back on your alcohol and sex." Wendell said, "Alcohol is not a problem because I drink very little anyway, but what you mean about cutting back on sex?" Dr. Robins said, "Just cut back on sex." Wendell looked at me and asked me three times, "Pink, what did he mean cut back on sex?" I said, "Just cut back on sex." Finally, as we were getting nowhere Dr. Robins said, "Well, Wendell, how often do you have sex?" Wendell replied, "About five, six time a day." A shocked, red faced Dr. Robins told Wendell that if he wanted to fight this infection he would have to put his sexual activities on hold.

After a game one night Wendell asked Dr. Rudy Ellis to drain some fluid off his knee. Doc used this needle about 4" long and about as round as the lead of a pencil. Unknowingly, Artis came in and went to his locker to get a camera that he had in his gym bag. He wanted to get a picture of this! Just as Artis got the camera out, Ellis had finished the aspiration and pulled the needle out. Artis laughed and said, "Awe shucks. I wanted a picture of that." So what does Wendell do? He said, "Doc, put the needle back in so Big A can get a picture."

In a game at Diddle Arena in Bowling Green, the official, Jess Kersey, passed out at halftime. I took his blood pressure and it was 140/100, and his temperature was 100.4. We lost to Carolina again. Our record was 15-5 with four losses to the Cougars. When we got back that night, Babe told me that we were going to put Ron King on waivers the next day.

We played Indiana at Cincinnati on November 30. I got a "T" when I asked referee Ken Sussman, "Are you going to ride the team bus home with Indiana?" He was from Beech Grove, Indiana. We lost the game 107-104.

The team spent the night and we took the "Olliebird" for a game in Charlotte. Once again the Cougars beat Kentucky 120-113. The Colonels were 16-8 for the season, but a miserable 1-5 against Carolina.

The "Olliebird" was a Gulfstream prop jet that John Y. leased from William H. May, owner/ president of Brighton Engineering in Frankfort, Kentucky. We flew to all games on the east coast in this 15 passenger plane. We only went west of the Mississippi River once and that was to San Antonio. The head winds were just too much going west. It saved a lot of money, time, and wear and tear on the body. We could play the game, get on the bus and head home. I would have food prepared that we would stop and pick-up on the way to the airport.

We could usually be home and in our own beds by one or two o'clock in the morning, the time the players usually wound down anyway. There were plush reclining seats, couch, bar, card table, and most important, lots of leg room.

December 5, we practiced at Bellarmine College. Wendell hyper-extended his left foot and broke the fifth metatarsal. The next day he asked me if he could go to Cincinnati to see his friend, Ken Avery. He was a linebacker for the Bengals. They had both attended Southern Mississippi. We were playing there on the 7th, so he wanted to meet us there and go to the game on Sunday.

We lost to the Nets 102-84. The Cincinnati crowd cheered for Dr. J., and did he put on a show. After the game we went back to Stouffer's Inn and had dinner with our wives. Bob Hope was at the table next to us (Dan, Louie, and Kenny Anderson, the Bengals' quarterback). He came over and chatted with us for a short time. The next day, Dan, Louie, Bud and I, along with our wives, went to the Bengals game. Ken Anderson grew up in Batavia, Illinois, and his

backyard and Dan's back yard joined at the property line. He furnished the tickets for all of us.

We played at San Antonio, flew back to Cincinnati for a game against Memphis, then played at Denver and San Diego. We arrived home at 5 p.m. on the 17th, and needed to be at John Y. and Ellie's house for a Christmas Party at 6:30. They gave us each champagne coolers as a gift. Babe got wiped out. Our record was now 20-10 after an 11-1 start.

It was December 21, 1973, and the Colonels had not played a home game in Freedom Hall since November 17. That was 15 games and 41 days away from the friendly confines of Freedom Hall. When we started this venture, our record was 13-3. When we got back to Louisville, we were

20-11. Nine of those games were on our opponents' courts, and six were considered home games for us.

We lost to Utah at home and flew to Utah the next day. Issel missed the second game of his career with a sprained ankle. We lost on the road once again. We flew to San Diego on December 23 and beat the Q's 123-120. They can't stop anybody and nobody can stop them. Issel played despite the bad ankle and was the leading scorer with 31. Our plane left at 12:05 am December 24. I wanted to get us home for Christmas Eve. We flew all night. Babe allowed the players to have a drink on the plane...something not allowed in the past. We arrived home at 9:30 am.

Alex Groza told me before the game that a big trade might be in the works. It went this way: Red Robbins and Chuck Williams to Memphis for Randy Denton and John Baum to San Diego; Denton to Carolina for Jim Chones; Chones to Houston for Jack Marin; Marin to Los Angeles so Wilt can play for the Q's.

We practiced on Christmas Day at five o'clock in preparation for the Pacers on the 26th. We beat Indiana by two and Gene and John Y. had a smile on their face for the first time in months.

With the New Year well under way, we began a 10-day road trip I will never forget. It all started on January 23, 1974, after a 106-99 loss to the San Diego Conquistadors. As I was leaving the locker room to go home and pack, I stopped and told Babe that I would see him at the airport in the morning. As I walked up to him I heard him say, "John (J.Y. Brown), if I can't stop you from trading Winnie (Ladner) then I can't stop you, but don't trade Mike Gale."

The next night we lost to the San Antonio Spurs 93-84, and after the game Van Vance and I went out to eat with Wendell. That was a mistake; both of us knew that if Wendell had a chance, he would end up with a fine lady … well it happened, and Van and I got stuck waiting until 3:30 a.m. for Wendell. Why, I don't know, but Winnie made us stay with him.

When I got back to the hotel, my message light was flashing off and on. When I called the operator, she told me to call Babe. I immediately called his room and he asked me if I knew where Wendell was? I told him that he was in his room. Before I hung up, with a rasping, teary voice, he told me that John Y. had traded Wendell and Mike to the New York Nets for John Roche. I called Wendell and Mike and told both of them to go up to Babe's room. Wendell cried like a baby and "Philly Dog" was in disbelief. It was now 4 o'clock in the morning and I had to get Mike and Wendell a plane ticket to New York and try to find John Roche and get him to meet us in Salt Lake City for a game on January 25. I looked at an ABA master schedule and noticed that the Spurs were going to New York for a game with the Nets, so I called their trainer and got Wendell and Mike on the same flight. They would give them a ride to Long Island. I had to make their reservations and prepay tickets for them. In between calls, I tried to call John Roche. I must have tried 100 times and I never got an answer. Knowing John, he probably didn't want to answer the phone. That morning Wendell and Mike rode the team bus to the airport with us. They met the Spurs and we said good-bye. It was a very emotional parting. Our players were without words. We were losing our enforcer and the best defensive guard in the ABA in Mike Gale. This was probably the worst trade ever made in the history of the ABA. We not only lost two great players, but two great people. The happiest person in the ABA was Doctor J. He said, "Now I have the enforcer; Wendell could have ended my career at any time."

On January 28, 1974, Babe, Bud, Dan, Artis, Louie and I flew to Norfolk, Virginia, for the ABA All-Star game. I sent the rest of the team back to Louisville. Babe and Bud were the coaches and I was the trainer because the team that was in first place on January 1 in each division earned that honor.

I was fortunate enough to be the trainer for the All-Star game for the second time, but not without some negotiating. The players on the winning team received $500 each. The losing players received $300. The trainers received $100. All the trainers in the league had a conference call with ABA Commissioner Mike Storen asking for $300, the same as the losing team received. He refused to budge. I didn't have a choice as to what to do; I had to do what the rest of the trainers agreed on. Fritz Massman was the Nets' trainer and the head of the ABA trainers, and after talking with everyone involved, we all agreed that we would do it for the players.

There was a banquet at noon the day of the game and Joe Namath was the guest speaker and we got robbed, $5,000 for 10 minutes. Before the banquet, Warren Jabali called all of the black players and told them to boycott the banquet. He was very upset because the gifts given by the host team were not acceptable. It is expected that the host city put nice gifts in the rooms of all team members before they arrive. Artis and Doctor J. ignored Jabali's request and went to the banquet anyway.

The East team beat the West team 128-112. Artis Gilmore was named the MVP despite 29 points by Swen Nater. After the game, I was working in the locker room and Doc walked up to me and said, "Give me your hand." I took his closed palm hand and he slapped a silver dollar in my hand. He said, "Give that back to me." He reached in his pocket and pulled out $300. He had collected the money from every player and coach so that I would get the matching $300. That's just how the Doctor operated.

Shortly after that, all the black players from the West team came in our locker room and told me to leave. The meeting was very short, about three minutes. Later, Artis told me that Jabali wanted to know why he and Julius went to the meeting, with that, Dr. J., who was putting his pants on, said "When I was growing up, my mother taught me the difference between right and wrong, and today I did what was right." Meeting over! When the Doc spoke, people listened.

After the game, all the Colonels contingent, that included our wives and John Y. and Ellie, went back to the hotel for the post game party. We were all sitting around talking when John Y. walked up and said, "How would you guys like to have Red Robbins and Chuck Williams on the team?" Few remarks were made. Everyone knew that on the other side of this room John Y. was making a deal with the San Diego Q's owner. A few minutes later he came back and said that he had traded Jimmy O'Brien for Red and Chuck. Both of these guys were great players and individuals, but so was O.B. In all, I took names off of three warm-up shooting shirts and one jersey. Without a return trip back to Louisville, we had a six player transaction on this road trip. My how things had changed since I walked out of Freedom Hall on January 23.

After 10 days on the road, three new players and the departure of three players, we all flew back to Louisville.

A few days later, on a cold, snowy day in New York, 1,516 fans showed up in Nassau Coliseum to see the Colonels win 123-91. Issel and Roche were the leading scorers in the game, but that wasn't the big story. Artis Gilmore wrote the headlines on this day as he grabbed an ABA career record 40 rebounds: 34 defensive and six offensive.

After the game, we boarded the bus and headed to the airport. The wind was blowing, the snow was beginning to drift, and the temperatures were dropping. We were using the Olliebird so there were no flights to miss, we just needed weather that would allow us to takeoff.

We waited and waited, and finally our pilot, Charlie Clay, told me to find a hotel for the night. We checked into the Hilton Inn Airport.

I got up early the next morning and had breakfast with John Y. He told us that he had spent the night with Howard Cosell and the head of ABC's Sports Division, Roone Arledge. Arledge told Brown that if we got into the ABA finals, ABC would televise the games.

Issel got his 10,000th point in a win over the Carolina Cougars on February 10. It took him just 3 ½ seasons to accomplish this milestone. Once again I had the champagne iced down to celebrate. Adolph Rupp came into the locker room to take part in the celebration. Rupp told Dan, "You have to get it when I can't take a drink. Damn you." Apparently Coach Rupp had been on doctor's orders not to drink.

Dr. Raymond Shea had joined Dr. Ellis' staff and was covering his first game for the Colonels as our team

OFFICIAL ABA BOX SCORE:

Kentucky Colonels vs New York Nets — DATE 2-3-74
SITE Nassau Coliseum — OFFICIALS Walt Rooney, Jack Madden — ATT 14,516

No.	Visiting Team — Kentucky Colonels	Position	Minutes	2-Point Field Goals M	A	3-Point Field Goals M	A	Free Throws M	A	Rebounds Off.	Def.	Team	Assists	Errors	Fouls	Total Points
25	Jim Bradley	F	22	3	5	0	0	2	2	1	7	8	1	4	2	8
44	Dan Issel	F	38	9	22	0	0	8	9	4	5	9	0	3	1	26
53	Artis Gilmore	C	42	9	15	0	0	3	5	6	34	40	9	7	2	21
10	Lou Dampier	G	29	6	11	0	0	0	0	0	0		5	1	2	12
11	John Roche	G	29	9	14	0	1	8	8	1			2	4	5	26
2	Walt Simon	F	11	2	5	0	0	0	0	0	1		1	4	2	4
3	Joe Hamilton	G	20	3	6	2	2	0	0	2	1		1	3	0	12
8	Ron Thomas	F	14	3	6	0	0	0	0	1	6		0	0	2	6
9	Red Robbins	F	13	1	8	0	0	0	0	3	1	4	0	1	0	2
15	Chuck Williams	G	19	1	2	0	0	0	0	0	1		5	3	0	2
22	Collis Jones	F	4	1	2	0	0	2	3	0	1		0	0	1	4
	TOTALS		240	47	96	2	3	23	27	18	58	76	24	30	17	123

PERCENTAGES .490 .667 .852 — TEAM REBS. 5 — DEAD BALLS 2
TOTAL FG PCT. .495 — TOT. REBS. 81

No.	Home Team — New York Nets	Position	Minutes	2-Point Field Goals M	A	3-Point Field Goals M	A	Free Throws M	A	Rebounds Off.	Def.	Team	Assists	Errors	Fouls	Total Points
32	Julius Erving	F	35	7	20	2	2	1	1	4	3	7	5	3	2	21
35	Larry Kenon	F	30	7	17	0	0	0	1	5	7	12	0	1	1	14
40	Willie Sojourner	C	18	2	12	0	0	0	0	2	5	7	1	0	5	4
12	Mike Gale	G	34	2	10	0	1	2	2	4	4	8	6	0	4	6
23	John Williamson	G	30	9	22	0	0	2	3	4	1	5	1	3	3	20
4	Wendell Ladner	F	32	2	8	2	7	0	0	1	4	5	3	2	6	10
5	Billy Paultz	C	18	4	10	0	0	0	2	2	2	4	1	1	2	8
15	Billy Schaeffer	F	15	1	4	0	1	0	0	2	2	4	0	1	0	2
25	Bill Melchionni	G	23	1	7	0	3	0	0	1	2	3	4	2	2	2
44	Jim O'Brien	F	5	1	3	0	0	2	3	1	0	1	0	2	0	4
	TOTALS		240	36	113	4	14	7	12	26	30	56	21	15	25	91

PERCENTAGES .319 .286 .583 — TEAM REBS. — DEAD BALLS 2
TOTAL FG PCT. .323 — TOT. REBS. 61

BLOCKED SHOTS: Roche 1, Bradley 2, Issel 1, Gilmore 7, Hamilton 1; Erving 3, Ladner 1, Gale 1, Schaeffer 1

Goal Tending: Schaeffer 1

STEALS: Issel, Williams, Bradley, Simon, Robbins, Jones; Gale 4, Williamson 3, Paultz, Ladner 2, Schaeffer 1, Kenon 1, Melchionni, Sojourner

	1	2	3	4		Total
Kentucky	25	34	33	31		123
New York	25	20	27	19		91

REMARKS: Artis Gilmore's 40 rebounds is new ABA record, breaking George McGinnis record.

Stats sheet showing Artis Gilmore's incredible performance of 40 rebounds in one game.

doctor. He earned his money on that very first night. Joe Hamilton had an open dislocation on his right index finger, Jim Bradley stretched a ligament in his knee, and Red Robbins stepped on a nail walking to his car. What a way to start!

It was a Sunday afternoon, March 7, 1974. The Colonels were playing the Squires in the Norfolk Scope. A fight broke out near the Virginia bench between Artis and Roger Brown (7' 0"/ Kansas). As I learned from Chopper Travaglini during my encounter with Neil Johnson, it was my job to help keep fans off the floor and away from the players and the action.

As I ran to the other end of the court, I saw this elderly lady, about 65-years-old, heading onto the floor to "help" her team...the Squires. As I approached her I said, "Lady, you better get your ass off the floor before you get hurt." She has this rather large purse hanging on her right elbow. The fighting stopped, the arena went deadly silent and at that very moment she swung her right arm loaded with her purse and pow, she hit me right across the face. She then attempted to get me on the rewind when a policeman grabbed her. I did not retaliate. I was always taught never to hit a female, much less a little old lady. After the game someone from the Squire office told me that the woman was one of their biggest fans and that she was fighting cancer. They introduced me to her and we became friends. I always made it a point to talk with her when we played in Virginia. By the way, she was all over RIck Barry when he came to town.

McCarthy and the Colonels had completed an outstanding season with a 53-31 record

Kentucky then won the first round seven game series 4-0 over the Carolina Cougars, and then disaster hit. In an eight day span the Colonels lost four straight games to Julius Erving's New York Nets. The Colonels lost the first two games in Nassau Coliseum in Uniondale, N.Y. Because of tornado damage to Freedom Hall on April 8, the Colonels were forced to play game three in Louisville's Convention Center and lost. Game four was played in Memorial Coliseum in Lexington, and the Nets won. Season over.

We lost four games in a row and the Nets went on to win the ABA Championship by defeating the Utah Stars 4-1.

1973-74

Chapter Thirteen
The Southern Gentleman

Babe McCarthy

The 1973-74 season was typical as players, coaches and general managers moved from one franchise to another. In the ABA it was a continuous game of musical chairs. Of course, this season the Colonels were right in the middle of it all.

The average fan was trying to figure out what was up in a league engulfed in wholesale changes every year. Not only did the league owners vote Storen in as the ABA commissioner when he left the Colonels, but John Y. recycled former coach Gene Rhodes as the team's new GM. He replaced the man who had fired him.

In the name of Ziggy, what was going on?

And to top it all off John Y. and Rhodes hired an old Kentucky nemesis to both the Kentucky Wildcats, when he coached at Mississippi State, and of course, the ABA Colonels. In spite of the smooth talking Babe McCarthy's back-handed comments about the Colonels, for some strange reason he was still liked by lots of the fans. Besides that, the guy could coach.

But before he came to the Colonels, James H. "Babe" McCarthy – always seemed to have a way of sticking the needle in Kentucky basketball fans.

First there was the fight his player Leland Mitchell had with a Colonels fan at the Convention Center. Dean Eagle wrote in his "Press Box" column that some of these fights compared to some boxing-wrestling matches that had taken place in the Convention Center. McCarthy was reported to have instructed Mitchell to "go knock his head off."

It's interesting to note that this was the first Colonels game in the Convention Center when the player's benches had been on the sideline. Before that, they had been positioned at each end of the floor. The ABA rule did, in fact, state that benches were to be at courtside. The new location put the players closer to the fans, or as Eagle stated in his column, "virtually sitting in the laps of the fans."

The fight that night marred the coaching debut of Rhodes, who had just replaced the fired Givens.

It was ironic that a story directly below Eagle's column, detailing Dampier's completion of army duty was headlined in 36-point type with the words: "Dampier Going to 'War' for Colonels."

But then there was a visit by the Colonels to play the New Orleans Bucs in tiny Loyola Fieldhouse, because the floor was also used by the college. Babe had a special substance for applying the 25-font line denoting the ABA three-point shot.

During warm-up, Darel Carrier tried to zero in on the basket, but for some strange reason his shot was a bit short, no, make that considerably short. Carrier knew something was wrong when teammate 6'10" Jim Cardwell, who hadn't attempted a 3-point shot in 20 ABA games, backed up behind the line and canned four straight.

Sure enough, the line had been painted closer to 30 feet than 25.

Of course Babe apologized, as any southern gentleman would do, even offered to let the Colonels use the other end of the floor for both halves. It just so happened that the Bucs shot fewer threes than any team in the league, so Babe figured it didn't matter which end his team shot at.

In the meantime, when you think you've seen and heard it all, Adolph Rupp, that's right THE Adolph Rupp, for a short period of time had been hired as president of the Memphis franchise.

But by June 1973, Rupp was gone from Memphis, leaving behind some unkind words about the ABA in general. "Bush league," he called it. "Nothing first class."

In a league where no one should be surprised when the absurd or ridiculous happened, it seemed routine business when John Y.'s wife, Ellie, announced in the fall of the same year that Rupp was joining the Colonels board of directors as its vice-president.

Mullaney headed west to Utah, where he had a cadre of talent. There he was working for a basketball guy, Vince Boryla, the GM who hired him, and Babe was expected to do what Mullaney hadn't been able to do, win a championship.

But first the Colonels had to get past their division rival, New York Nets, and that hadn't always been easy. The Nets had been around since the ABA's beginning, and although they had seemed to give the Colonels trouble, they were never really considered a league power. In fact, quite the opposite. Rick Berry lasted two years with the Nets and then jumped back to his original NBA team, Golden State. When the 1973-74 season rolled around, though, the Nets began to transform into a contender. Dr. J came over from Virginia, and former NBA'er Kevin Loughery took over as head coach at the age of 33.

Suddenly those early days and all of the jokes about this team had been forgotten. Key players for the Nets were Mike Gale and Wendell Ladner, former Colonels. There were also Billy Paultz, Larry Kenon, Bill Melchionni, Jim O'Brien, Brian Taylor, John Williamson and Willie Sojourner.

The Nets weren't just good, they were very good. Breezing past Virginia in the first playoff four games to one, they then met Babe and the Colonels, who had just disposed of Carolina 4-0.

For Kentucky, it was a nightmare. Losing the first two games in New York, they returned to Freedom Hall, down, but still with hope.

When Dr. J. banked in a 15-footer off the wrong foot, not only did it win game three, but it buried pretty much any hopes the Colonels had for an ABA title. They lost the following night in an almost unimaginable sweep at the hands of the New York Nets.

Gilmore was first team all-ABA, while Issel and Dampier were named to the second five. To top it all, McCarthy and Mullaney (now at Utah) were named the league's Co-Coach of the Year.

With what many observers felt was the best talent in all of pro-basketball, including the NBA, Babe McCarthy was fired.

Naturally, Lloyd Gardner was there to see all of the inner workings of the Colonels organization, not necessarily understanding it, but still having an opinion. Now, decades later, he does have more understanding of those workings, but does not necessarily agree with them.

"I got paid to do my job and I did it," he says. "It wasn't my role to hire or fire, to trade players, or to choose who to play. Just the nature of being a team, traveling together, and winning and losing together, we all developed feelings and emotions for each other from the top on down."

Gardner's emotions are usually front and center, regardless of what he is doing. In fact some of his friends have even compared his personality to that of Coach Ed Diddle, for whom he served as student manager for two years at Western Kentucky University.

"When I see Pink I can't help but think of Coach Diddle," says Wes Strader, the legendary former "Voice of the Hilltoppers." "His mannerisms, especially when he tells a Diddle story, are just like him."

Gardner shows those Diddle-like emotions when talking about a lot of his friends, but especially when it comes to Babe: "It wasn't unusual for Babe to say to me at a shoot around on game days, "'Pink, call Dr. Ellis and tell him to bring his gloves. I need him to check my prostate.'"

"A few weeks after he was fired, I got word that Babe was in the hospital, and I went to see him," said Gardner. "He wasn't having a good day. I stayed by his side for about an hour, and just before I left he told me, "'Pink, when that day comes, my son will probably call you for some money. Whatever you do, don't give him any.'"

Just weeks after Babe went into the hospital, John and Ellie called the family and told them they wanted to take care of his hospital and doctor bills. Babe struggled for nine months in and out of the hospital, and on March 12, 1975, at age 51, Babe took his final breath. He was buried in his hometown of Baldwyn, Mississippi. David Vance, assistant general manager, said it best, "The main thing to remember about Babe that everybody knows is that he contributed to basketball. I can think of only a handful of men like Babe who had such a refreshing outlook on life that it really had a contagious effect on others."

Vance's words rang loud. But you have to go back to Babe's coaching days at Mississippi State to see just how loud they really were.

McCarthy attended Mississippi State as a student, and for the most part his only association with basketball was playing for his fraternity intramural team. Like most students at the time, he went to see some of the Bulldog games, usually to see the likes of Kentucky when they visited Starkville.

He coached a junior high team for a while before going to work as a salesman in the oil business. Then out of the blue came an opportunity to coach at his alma mater.

Much has been written about Babe's escapades at Mississippi State, but the bottom line as to why UK fans developed a hatred for him was that he was able to hold his own, and then some, against their beloved Wildcats.

Perhaps Babe's finest hour came when he helped devise a plan after winning the SEC title in 1963 to get his team out of Mississippi in order to play against a predominantly all-black Loyola of Chicago team in the NCAA tournament in East Lansing, Michigan.

The three-time SEC Coach of the Year defied an injunction that prohibited his team from playing, but McCarthy, who had been ordered to turn down two previous NCAA bids, this time had the support of the school's president, Dean Colvard and the athletic director, Wade Walker.

State senator Billy Mitts, who had been student body president in his college days as well as a cheerleader at Mississippi State, led the efforts to block the schools participation, and with the backing of Governor Ross Barnett, if they had their way, Babe and his team would stay home.

But McCarthy had already set a diversion into motion so as to be conveniently out of reach when any official documents were delivered to the school.

First, Colvard, the president, was in Alabama on business; McCarthy, Walker, and a few others, drove to Memphis and then flew to Nashville; at the same time McCarthy sent his freshmen team to the airport posing as the varsity; meanwhile, the varsity was hiding out in a campus dorm room until the following morning, when they flew to Nashville on a private plane, where they hooked up with their coach. Together, they all flew to East Lansing, where they lost to eventual NCAA champions Loyola 61-51. All was not lost, however, when the Bulldogs defeated Bowling Green University and their All-American Nate Thurmond in the consolation game of the regional.

McCarthy's efforts proved to be a social turning point in race relations involving sports teams from the deep south. His legacy was much more than his outstanding career won-lost record.

Chapter Fourteen
From a Diamond to a Court

Hubie Brown

In Hubie Brown's early years it was baseball, not basketball, where he thought his future might be.

Hubie and his dad had one of those relationships that might show up only in a movie. Though they both liked all sports in general, it was baseball that froze those shared memories in time.

"I called my dad Chief, because that's what he also called me," chuckled Hubie. You've got to remember back then, baseball was *THE* sport. Professional basketball and football were not nearly what they are today.

"My dad and I did everything together. Every Sunday we'd go and catch the train in Elizabeth (N.J.) and go to the city to see a baseball game, either the Giants at the Polo Grounds or the Yankees at Yankee Stadium. We were baseball guys. We got there early enough to see both teams take infield and batting practice, and then take in a double-header. We just couldn't get enough. That was my dad's recreation and my development into sports."

Hubie became an outstanding catcher in high school and at Niagara University, where he also excelled in basketball. Following a brief stint in the old Eastern Professional Baseball League, he latched on to his first basketball coaching job at St. Mary Academy in Little Falls, N.Y. Nine years later he took his first college job as an assistant at William and Mary.

From there he began his climb through the coaching ranks that have led to a Hall of Fame career, but it was those early days coaching high school ball that gave Hubie experience he never could have gained anywhere else.

"Coaches today get jobs because of their names, and these coaches are short term unless they surround themselves with really good coaches who have lots of experience," he pointed out.

Brown spent four years with Vic Bubas at Duke before moving into the pro ranks as an assistant to Larry Costello with the Milwaukee Bucks. After only one year with the Bucks, he was contacted by both the Colonels and Spurs in the ABA. "I knew nothing about the ABA, but I also knew I wasn't ready for a head coaching job either," Brown said. "But the next year we lost in the NBA finals to Boston. I thought I was ready now."

Again, Brown was contacted by the Colonels. Babe McCarthy had departed the Colonels, not in the best health and also failing to win the big one.

"I remember meeting with John Y., Ellie and David Vance at the Executive Inn," he said. "We had dinner and discussed the team and a contract. They offered me a three year deal, $45,000 the first year, $50,000 the second, and $55,000 the third."

It was June 1974 and officially Hubie Brown had become the Colonels seventh coach in seven years. With this said, it would appear that the organization was a franchise in turmoil. Normally, a turnover of head coaches doesn't speak well for the success of a team. However, in spite of this, the team from Kentucky was one of the most successful in all of professional basketball, including the NBA. Their talent, winning record, attendance, and finances seemed to be in order, and with Brown at the helm, they had, once again, a legitimate chance to win that elusive championship.

Hubie set about to hire a top-notch assistant, one with some experience, and that coach would be Stan Albeck.

"I contacted Stan and met him at the Chicago airport," said Brown. "He had been at Northern Michigan and then with the Denver Rockets."

Brown was not the only new face with the Colonels. Marv Roberts, Bird Averitt, Wil Jones, Ted McClain, and Gene Littles were now on the team's 10-man roster. That means half the team was new, usually not a good recipe for success. In spite of this, Brown says, "This was the best team I ever coached as a head coach. People always overlook what this team did in that one year. We only had ten guys, but we got off to a great start. In February we lost Issel to a shin injury and Gene Littles to a pleurisy illness."

Brown says the Colonels that year were truly a great offensive team. "We averaged 108 points and only gave up 92," he recalled. "We were good in the half court, in the fast break and could shoot the threes. Our defense wasn't bad either, especially McClain. He broke the league's steal record that year."

As the 1974-75 season wound down, the Colonels found themselves in a real battle. On paper it looked almost impossible to overcome the Nets. They had answered the call and closed out the season in a rush.

"We ended the season with a 22-3 stretch run," he said, still amazed after all of these years. "We even put the 22-3 number on our championship rings."

A championship for the Colonels was everything they had imagined. It brought notoriety to the city and publicity to the team. It also brought credibility to the coaching resume of Hubie Brown. He had put his time in, virtually an unknown outside of basketball's inner circle. But here he was, in one year accomplishing what no others had done with the Colonels. Some had come close, for sure, but none had grabbed the ring.

He was in his element, surrounded by basketball people. Gene Rhodes, who Hubie described as a very sound basketball man; Ralph Beard, the team's scout; and David Vance, helping Rhodes keep the front office in order. And all the while as he remembers, "Ellie and her group were active and out in front of everything going on with the team.

"We just had a very good group of basketball people in our operation," Hubie said.

But as perfect as the world seemed for the Kentucky Colonels, a few cracks started to appear.

"I was contacted by John Y. and Ellie about a meeting with Issel and his agent (J. Bruce Miller)," recalls Brown. "There was talk that Dan might want to be traded. I was shocked. Why did he want to be traded? We had just won a championship."

Hubie continued, "In our style of play, we went through the center position first and he (Issel) was used to scoring more points. It was a point of contention between Issel and his agent. And then when Artis was the MVP in the championship, this may have caused the idea of Dan wanting to be traded."

Little if anything had ever been reported on the meeting that Hubie described. For all of these years it seemed that John Y. Brown solely took it upon himself to sell, not trade Issel, in order to recoup some of his losses in running a professional basketball team. Perhaps the door had been opened just a bit, and John Y., being the savvy businessman that he was, felt he had more to gain with a sell instead of a trade.

When Issel was sold to Denver, by way of Baltimore, it left the Colonels roster down to only one white player, Louie Dampier, and Brown recalled some picketing by the KKK.

"It was near the trade deadline and we were going to add some players to the team anyway," Brown said in referring to the 10-man roster he had the year before. "Their picketing didn't last long."

The 1975-76 roster added Jan Van Breda Kolff, Jimmy Dan Connor, Johnny Neumann, and Kevin Joyce, all of whom were white.

The season was somewhat of a downer compared to the previous year. After a hot start in the preseason exhibitions, the Colonels had a 7-2 record against NBA teams. But with a host of new faces, and Issel no longer around, the team slipped to a 46-38 mark. They finished fourth in the Eastern Division and won a best of three playoffs against Indiana before losing four games to three to Denver and Issel in the semi-finals. For the first time in his nine year career, Dampier had failed to make the all-star game.

The season was not what everyone with the Colonels had hoped for. Of course the rumors and conversation had picked up full speed about a forthcoming merger of the ABA and NBA. It was going to finally happen. But no one, most of all Hubie Brown, was prepared for what was to happen next.

"I felt all along we were going into the NBA," remembers Brown. "But when John Y. said he was folding the team, I was shocked. This meant unemployment."

In two years Hubie had built a successful reputation. Anyone who knew him and watched him work had a strong suspicion he wouldn't have to wait long for a job. And he didn't. Ted Turner and his Atlanta Hawks team came calling, and quickly Hubie was in the NBA, with or without the Kentucky Colonels.

"Ted Turner bought the Braves (baseball) and the Hawks, and a bankrupt T.V. station in Atlanta," said Brown. "He put old movies, baseball and basketball games on the station."

With cable television beginning to take root across America, Turner was on the cutting edge of the communication industry and his teams and movies were a national hit.

Decades later Hubie laughs when he recalled that the often unpredictable Turner even tried to persuade him not only to coach the Hawks, but also manage the Braves during the same season.

"He was only going to pay me what I was making with the Hawks," Brown said. "He said if I did both jobs it was a surefire way of getting in the Hall of Fame."

The story seemed so bizarre and outlandish that today Hubie doesn't enjoy talking about it.

When the merger between the two leagues finally happened, Brown says he will never forget that first all-star game. "The game was full of former players from the ABA, ten to be exact," he says. "Dr. J. was the MVP, and TOPPS Gum Company gave him a check and the trophy. He took the trophy and put it over his head and said, 'I would be remiss if I accepted this award for myself. I accept it for the ten guys in this game who were told we couldn't play this game.'"

"Powerful words," says Brown. "But that's the kind of class Julius Erving had."

Looking back through a career in basketball from someone who really wanted to be a baseball man, Hubie says he is respectful of the fact that John Y. and Ellie gave him a chance to coach the Colonels and for the most part allowed him to coach the team without a great deal of interference.

"When it comes to evaluation of talent, trades and cuts, of course there is going to be a difference of opinions with management and ownership," he points out. "But they did everything in their power to get us players."

Few people living today are respected as much as Hubie Brown when it comes to basketball knowledge. From his 37-year involvement with the famed Howard Garfinkle Five Star Basketball Camp to becoming an elite NBA television analyst, he has seen it all, most of which he understands. The August 12, 2011 induction of Artis Gilmore into the Naismith Basketball Hall of Fame finally put to rest one of Hubie's biggest issues.

"It was absolutely staggering that he was not put in sooner," says Brown with fire in his voice. "His points, rebounds, games played and everything else are Hall of Fame numbers."

And what about Louie Dampier? "He's one of the greatest shooters I've ever been around ... and not just 3-point shots," says Brown. "Remember, I had not been around the 3-point shot until I came to the Colonels. They can all talk about Artis and Dan, but Louie was our closer. I have great respect for him as a professional ... that's my highest compliment to a player. He was prime time."

Hubie is still a bit miffed over Louisville's lack of an NBA team.

"It seems way back then that Louisville and Atlanta were vying for the label as Gateway of the South," he says. "I think Louisville might have had a population of about 400,000 and Atlanta 750,000." Today Atlanta has about five million people in the area. When the NBA didn't come to Louisville, it closed the door on a lot of things for the city. It was disappointing to me and for all of those people who supported the team all those years.

"The Browns had the deal, and it's a shame the way it turned out," he concluded in talking about the Colonels being the team left behind.

Lloyd Gardner has his memories of Hubie's final days with the Colonels:

"Personally, I think all of the rumors about the merger and player trades played a major role in his departure. As a trainer I was in a position that allowed me to hear the players talk, spent numerous hours with the coaches evaluating team matters, and many hours in the front office communicating with the staff on future plans. As a matter of fact, the trainers had more access to more individuals in the organization than anybody else. I literally heard everybody's side of the story. If someone had a gripe or complaint, I heard it. If somebody needed something, they usually asked me for help. If I heard something that needed to be relayed to an individual that would alleviate a problem, I passed it on. If I heard something that I needed to keep confidential, I kept my mouth shut. That's why I kept my job; I knew when to talk and I knew when to keep my mouth shut.

"In the past season, Hubie, Stan and I were always discussing the atmosphere and morale of the team and the franchise. This year the team was in constant chaos, mostly because of rumors and uncertainty. It seemed like everything was day-to-day."

On Tuesday, May 11, 1976, just twelve days after Denver eliminated Kentucky from the playoffs, Brown signed a contract with the NBA Atlanta Hawks. He left a franchise that had much better talent to go to an NBA team that had been in the division cellar for some time. In his press conference he said, "I'm taking a positive attitude from day one. I feel I'm entitled to take an optimistic approach because I feel I can get the job done."

Brown's contract was believed to be between $75,000 and $100,000.

EIGHTH SEASON
1974-75
by Lloyd Gardner

It was mid-June, Babe McCarthy had been fired and had returned home to Baldwyn, Mississippi. Gene Rhodes and Ellie Brown had asked me to have lunch with a prospective coach. I must say, I have never met anyone that intimidated me like Hubie Brown did. I wasn't sure how the players would react to his expectation every day. I even had doubts of how I could meet his standards. He knew exactly what he wanted and how he wanted to get there. After working for the laid back Babe, I knew that his philosophy was going to be a complete turnaround. Hubie's philosophy was to be accountable, follow the rules and earn your paycheck. I often heard him say "don't steal your money."

Tedd Munchak sold the Carolina Cougars to a group of New York businessmen headed by Harry Weltman and brothers Daniel and Ozzie Silna, and then replaced Mike Storen as the ABA Commissioner. They moved the franchise to St. Louis and became the Spirits of St. Louis. Only two of the Cougars reported to St. Louis. Ted McClain and Marvin Roberts were acquired by the Colonels.

Storen then took the $170,000 he picked up for his share of the Kentucky Colonels when he departed and took over Charley O. Finley's financially troubled Memphis Tams and changed the name to the Sounds. Storen immediately hired his friend Joe Mullaney (Utah) to coach the team.

When Hubie hired Stan Albeck as his assistant, it was apparent that their coaching demeanor was as different as the colors of the ABA ball and the NBA ball. Hubie was very intense, while Stan was rather mellow. I don't know of anybody in the league that didn't respect Stan's perception of the game. One of the things that Hubie wanted Stan to do was chart every offensive play. What play was it, what was the outcome, did we score or not, chart every fast break and second shots by both teams. Fast break and second shots often produce easy baskets and they should be prevented when possible. He would also be in charge of scouting the opponent and, along with Hubie, go over the defensive game plan at shoot-arounds. He would also put the opponent's plays and how many times they scored on that play on the chalkboard before every game. How Stan did this I will never know.

I spent so much time with Hubie and Stan that we became very close quickly. They always had my back. Almost every day in August or September the three of us would meet and I would pull out game tapes from the past. We would get red-eyed from watching so many game tapes; my fingers were sore from hitting the rewind controls. Hubie wanted to see every team and every player in the league and what style of offense and defense they played. In his spare time, Hubie was off to Los Angeles to watch the Southern California Pro Summer League, where several ABA teams were participating.

Hubie felt that if we were going to use a full court press, we would need to play ten players every night. This was unheard of in basketball at any level. Jim O'Brien, founder of *Street & Smith's Basketball* magazine and a writer for the *New York Post*, criticized Brown's rotation system early in the year. He said Hubie would never win a championship playing ten players every night.

For all the coaches that I worked for, Hubie was the only coach with a playbook. The very first page was a table of contents, and a list of over 45 plays that the team would use throughout the season. Page one was a letter stating the expectation of the team. Page two was **CLUB REGULATIONS AND FINES — IF VIOLATED.**

The fines were garnished from the player's paycheck and were earmarked in a special account. The money belonged to the players and not the organization. At the end of the season, the players would meet and distribute the money.

My first task was to have a board made so that I could list every team, with a removable card listing the team's roster. When Hubie and Stan walked in the door to their office, they could see what players were with what teams and what position they played. If a player was traded, we simply moved the card. It was also used when looking at possible trades. It was my responsibility to keep it up to date.

As the trainer, I always kept track of player fouls, fouls in the quarter and timeouts. Hubie gave me another responsibility. I had to keep track of how many shots Issel, Gilmore and Dampier had each quarter. His philosophy was that these three players had to take the majority of the shots. It was important for me to let him know how many shots each player had taken so that he could keep the shots distributed equally.

Bird Averitt had just completed a summer tour that would have made AAA proud. After driving four days from Hopkinsville to Los Angeles to compete in the Summer Pro League his agent, Tom Meehan, called him and told him that the Kentucky Colonels had purchased him from

CLUB REGULATIONS AND FINES - IF VIOLATED

RULE	FINE
1. Each player must take notebook on all road trips – during exhibition play. Team meetings will be held during this time period.	$ 50.00
Replacement for lost notebook.	$ 250.00
2. If a player misses a scheduled flight departure, charter or commercial – Be at airport at least one-half hour before departure.	Player will pay his own transportation expenses.
3. On all road trips, players will dress neatly – Also be neatly dressed around hotel lobbies.	$ 50.00
4. On road trips – (a) Night before a game – curfew at 12:30; (b) If no scheduled game the following night, curfew is 2:00 a.m.	1st Offense - $ 250.00 2nd Offense – Double
5. A) Bus departures, hotel departures, practice times.	$ 5.00 for each late minute starting at 6th minute
B) Reporting on time in locker room for all games – 1. All players will be in locker room 1 HOUR and 15 MINUTES before game time.	First 15 Min. $ 50.00 15-30 Min. – $ 100.00 30-60 Min. – $ 150.00
2. All players will be dressed, taped, etc. 50 minutes before each game for pre-game meeting in seats.	$ 50.00
C) Missed practice – unless permission granted by Coach.	$ 250.00
D) Missed game – unless permission granted by Coach.	$ 500.00
6. No smoking in game or practice arenas.	$ 50.00
7. No drinking will be allowed in hotel bars where we stay on all road trips, exhibition and regular schedule, or on any commercial flights.	1st Offense - $ 250.00 2nd Offense - $ 500.00
8. Issued equipment bags must be used for all games. No laundry bags or pillow cases.	$ 50.00
9. Appointments must be kept with trainer at designated time, for treatment of all injuries.	1st Offense - $ 50.00 2nd Offense – Double
10. No fraternizing with opponents prior to any league game. Following the game it is perfectly okay. The night of a game, let's get our minds on winning. This is your "Bread and Butter."	1st Offense - $ 50.00 2nd Offense – Double
11. No player is allowed to leave practice gym without permission from Head Coach.	$ 50.00

CLUB REGULATIONS, cont.

RULE	FINE
12. At all practices – whether at home or on the road – all players will dress at practice site, unless instructed otherwise by the Coach.	$ 50.00
13. Girls in room on game day (EXPLAIN).	$ 250.00
14. Card Playing – no money showing at any time on commercial flights.	$ 250.00
15. Missing uniform at game time causing a player to forfeit playing time.	$ 250.00

We hope that no fines have to be imposed during the entire season. If each player is doing his job, this will be accomplished. We do not fine anyone, you fine yourself for lack of responsibility as a professional athlete. Let's discipline ourselves as men for respect of our teammates and the fine profession we represent as professional athletes.

the Spurs and he needed to fly back to Louisville and sign a new contract. The next day he flew to Louisville, signed the contract, and boarded a plane and flew back to Los Angeles for a 16-game summer schedule. To end the summer, Artis, Wil Jones and Bird went on a 10-day tour that took them to Hawaii, Tokyo, Sapporo, and Osaka. The four games were ABA players vs. NBA players. After the Pacific tour, Bird returned to Hopkinsville to visit his family and put an engagement ring on the finger of his high school sweetheart, Jackie Hale. In the meantime, Artis spent his last few days before practice scuba diving in the Bahamas. Can you imagine a 7'2" scuba diver?

On September 20, twelve veterans and four rookies reported to Knights Hall on the Bellarmine campus to compete for a spot on the Colonels 11-man roster. The Colonels would have two-a-day practices at 10 a.m. and 7 p.m. until October 17. You could feel the tension when Hubie walked into the gym. One thing you didn't want to do was piss Hubie off. He didn't handle lethargy or daydreaming very well. It didn't take long before everyone knew that things had changed. There was a new man in town and his mind was in high gear every minute. One thing I do know is that the players knew that we had not won a championship in the past and that we had somebody here that demanded that we perform every day. The enthusiasm Hubie and Stan brought to the team was contagious. Believe me, I was given new responsibilities and was expected to turn it up a notch like everybody else. Our new, young publicity director, John Hamilton, was petrified of Hubie. At times it seemed that he would turn as white as a ghost when Hubie was around him. For the first couple of months, everyone in the office, except the secretaries, was on pins and needles.

At the very first team meeting, two days before camp started, Hubie told the players to "take this playbook home and know the basics of the Triangle Offense." Not a minute was wasted! "I hope the playbook doesn't scare anybody," said Brown. "If they miss anything in practice they can just look it up." Milwaukee had been the only team in the NBA to have a playbook, but now we had one.

With Hubie, there isn't any situation in basketball that he hasn't analyzed down to the basics. When there are technical point to make, Hubie physically demonstrates exactly what he means.

I had two small tasks to take care of before the team took the floor for pregame warm-ups: First, put Dan Issel's three front teeth (partial plate) in a small container and put them in my medical kit, and second, stand on a chair as Artis and Dan walked out and pop their backs.

The team always left the locker room 30 minutes before tip-off. Hubie, Stan and I would stay back. I would go out at the 10-minute mark, but before I did, the three of us would ALWAYS shake hands and say, "There's nothing to it but to do it."

Finally, the exhibition season came to an end with a 93-75 win over the Chicago Bulls at the Convention Center, ending an exhausting eight game stretch in thirteen days.

The 1974-75, 84-game regular season opened on October 18, with a win against the Denver Nuggets 117-99. Hubie's aggressive, trapping defense was the key to victory. The Colonels would play 10 of their first 12 games at home.

Let's make one thing perfectly clear: Bird Averitt plays hard all the time. In practice, he soaks two sweat suits. In games, I put two towels on the sideline near the bench, one is wet so the players can clean the bottom of their shoes, the other is so Bird can throw-up on his way down the floor. That's exactly what he did against his former team, the Spurs. He was running down the floor, stopped, threw-up and kept going. He was a great addition to our team.

The Colonels would win their first four games before losing to the newly formed Spirits of St. Louis 91-86 as rookie sensation, and often troubled, Marvin Barnes poured in 25 points.

It was off to Indianapolis for the Colonels fourth games in four days. After shooting a lackluster 37% against the Spirits, the Colonels blistered the nets, shooting 59.8% and handing Indiana its third loss in four games. Kentucky is now 5-1 and has the best record in the ABA. The game also marked the first time that WHAS would simulcast an away game. The game was carried on WHAS-11 and WHAS 840 radio. As usual, Van Vance did the play-by-play and former Colonel Walt Simon was the color commentator.

It was now time for the Colonels to make a decision about reducing the size of the roster from 12 players to 11. After negotiating most of the night trying to make a deal, general manager Gene Rhodes and coach Hubie Brown agreed to keep John Roche on the disabled list. Roche expressed his displeasure at this move. It was obvious that Red Robbins and Roche are the best candidates to be moved.

With wins against Virginia, Memphis, Utah and the Nets, the Colonels improved to 10-1. Joe Hamilton had been put on waivers, enabling the Colonels to get down to the 11-player limit. John Roche was taken off the injured reserved list and reactivated. The Utah game was played in the University of Kentucky's Memorial Coliseum in Lexington, and the fans were introduced to Moses Malone. Moses was the first player to go from high school directly to the pros. With the departure of ABA All-Star Zelmo Beaty, coach Bucky Buckwalter was forced to play his youngster immediately. His transaction from the prep games to the big time surprised many nonbelievers. The very shy and withdrawn Malone had an immediate impact on the ABA.

For the second time in five days, Kentucky faced the defending ABA champion New York Nets, this time in Memorial Coliseum. This was a game that defied all odds. Down by seven points with 30 seconds remaining in overtime, the Colonels pulled out the win in two overtimes.

E.A. Diddle Arena in Bowling Green was the site of Kentucky's 15th win of the season, as they defeated the San Diego Q's 109-100. It seems that the Colonels were setting a pattern, not one that Hubie Brown liked — win at home and lose on the road. The Spirits Maurice Lucas and Marvin Barnes scored 30 and 28 points respectively to hand the Colonels another road loss. Averitt was taken to the hospital with a cut to his upper left eyelid and a scratched cornea after a collision with Freddie Lewis.

The Colonels, with a 25-10 record, were now 5-9 on the road and 20-1 at home as they headed to St. Louis for an afternoon game against the Spirits. Once again, the Spirits were too much for the Colonels. The only bright spot was Issel's 25th point of the game that gave him 10,000 career regular season points in just four-and-a-half years. Issel and teammate Louie Dampier were two of the five ABA players to reach this milestone.

With a home win against Virginia, rare road wins at St. Louis and Salt Lake City, the Colonels once again regained first place in the Eastern Division.

After a 19-point loss to the Nuggets in Denver, where they had now won 23 straight games, the Colonels announced that a deal had been completed that would send Roche to the Utah Stars for cash and further considerations. The team traveled to Virginia, where the Colonels got back on the winning track. A win the next day in New York against the Nets would assure that first year coach Hubie Brown would be the coach for the East team in the ABA All-Star game. Before the game, it was announced that the Colonels Artis Gilmore, Louie Dampier and Dan Issel were named to the East All-Stars.

1974-75 ABA Champion
Kentucky Colonels

1974-75 EASTERN DIVISION CHAMPION   **1974-75 EASTERN DIVISION PLAYOFF CHAMPION**

Playing their sixth game in eight days, and five of them on the road, proved fatal to the weary Colonels as the Nets prevailed 108-93 behind 40 points by the Doctor. If New York beat Virginia later that week, Kevin Loughery would coach the East team, which they did.

After their loss to the Nets and the Doctor, Hubie told the team, "From now on, if Dr. J is going in for a wide open slam dunk, I want you to grab him around the waist. Don't tackle him, don't injure him, just stop him. If you don't, I am going to fine you $125. He turns the crowd against us, sometimes even at our home games!"

Kentucky would return home with outstanding wins against the ABA league leading Denver Nuggets, the floundering Memphis Sounds and the San Diego Q's. Against Denver, Dampier cut his hand in three places after colliding with a typewriter on press row while chasing down a loose ball. The cuts required 17 stitches. As we entered the locker room, Louie said, "Sew it up in a hurry, Doc (Ellis), so I can get back out there." I said, "I thought Wendell Ladner was the only person who was that crazy.

Kentucky would travel to Memphis for the last game before the All-Star game on January 28. Kentucky would defeat the Sounds and boast a 33-14 record going into the break.

At the league meeting, John Y. Brown was elected president of the ABA by the league's board of trustees.

In the Colonels home game against San Diego, Ron Thomas got his first start after learning that Artis had left his size 18 shoes back at the hotel. Because of this large size, the Q's didn't have a pair that would fit him, so he had to go back to the hotel and retrieve his shoes. Five minutes into the game, the Big A subbed for Thomas and Kentucky squeaked out a one-point win 115-114. Chit chat had been flying around that John Y. Brown, Jr., had been trying to trade Issel and Dampier during the All-Star meetings. John Y. flatly denied this rumor.

Later, the Spirits of St. Louis and their "bad boys" came to town with a chip on their shoulders. With about seven minutes to play in the first half, Maurice Lucas landed a knockout punch to Artis Gilmore's jaw. A video replay showed that Lucas had pushed Artis out of bounds into the basket support. On the return trip, Lucas broke away for a dunk. Then, on a Dampier shot that went in the basket, more contact was made between the two. Artis turned and started back down the floor when Lucas' left hand made contact with the back of Artis' head. The big fella turned and pointed his finger at Lucas' face. Lucas pushed Gilmore away. It was then that the Big A started after Lucas. Artis was slapping and whacking at Maurice. It was then that Maurice landed a haymaker on Artis' jaw. Referees Bob Serafin and Wally Rooney ejected both players from the game. Behind a stellar performance from Ron Thomas, Artis' replacement, and a total team effort, the Colonels lost the fight, but won the game 114-107. Thomas had 14 points and 13 rebounds.

Kentucky went on the road and lost two games by two points each at San Antonio and Denver. This was Kentucky's third two-point loss within a 48-hour period. It was also the Colonels fifth defeat in their last seven games. Kentucky now trailed the Nets by two-and-a-half games. Jim Bradley had cracked a bone in his foot while practicing in Denver.

We then returned home where we would win three games against the Sounds, the Pacers and the Nets. The win over the Nets pulled the Colonels into a first place tie with New York. The 95-84 win sent the crowd of 16,188 home smiling. Julius Erving had a season low 15 points. After the game, a writer asked Wil Jones how he stopped the Doctor and Jones quickly replied, "You're not going to get me to say I stopped the Doc. Are you crazy? Let's just say he had an off night. I had nothing to do with it." Both teams have identical records at 45-19. Artis suffered a bruise on the back of his hand.

Kentucky had now defeated the Virginia Squires for the ninth consecutive time. The 107-95 triumph was marred by a fight between McClain and former Colonel Cincy Powell. Powell threw an elbow at Ted, who threw one blow at Powell that sent him sprawling to the floor. Powell never returned to the game. Issel took the night off in an effort to rest his sore calf muscle.

In prior years, if your team needed a win, Memphis was the place to look. But not anymore. Former Colonels general manager Mike Storen and coach Joe Mullaney had put together a competitive team, as the Colonels were aware. For only the second time in the previous 33 meetings, the Sounds defeated Kentucky 103-100. In the loss to Memphis, Dan led the Colonels with 28 points followed by Gilmore's 24 points and 17 boards. The defensive minded McClain had a season high 18 points and 10 assists. The team still trailed New York by two games.

On Tuesday, March 18, 1975, we lost at Denver, and after the game were notified that Babe McCarthy lost his battle with cancer. He was 51.

The big question, everybody in the media from New York to Los Angeles was asking, is will the Kentucky Colonels fold once again? Could they handle the PRESSURE?

After the shoot-around, Hubie had a team meeting in the locker room. He had outlined on the board every possibility for us to win the Eastern Division.

1. We must beat New York both times we play them.
2. We cannot lose a game. We must go on an earth-shattering winning streak.
3. We must get some help.

He said, "We have to play every game like it is our last. We must take them one game at a time. I don't want to talk about conceding. There will be no quitting or relaxing."

It's crunch time, time for a gut check, live or die, turn it up a notch!

Game 1 – Freedom Hall – March 23 – Spirits of St. Louis

With Dan recovering from the flu plus a leg injury, Artis with a bruised hand, McClain nursing an ailing knee and Gene Littles with a sore back, the walking wounded Colonels began their final charge to catch the Nets with a 120-110 whipping on St. Louis. Issel threw in 20, Artis dropped in 29 plus 20 rebounds and Louie hit for 24. Add to that, 14 by McClain, 10 by Averitt and a season high 16 and nine rebounds by Ron "The Plumber." Meanwhile, the Nets lost at home to Denver 114-111

One down … eight to go … 4 games behind New York.

Game 2 – University of Kentucky Memorial Coliseum – March 24 – Utah Stars

With McClain fighting through picks, plucking three steals and pestering the hell out of the ABA's highest scoring guard, Ron Boone (25.1 ppg), the Colonels won their second game in a row. Boone finished with a season low 12 points. McClain also scored 14 points. Six players scored in double figures. Artis finished with 22 and 18 rebounds. Dan also had 22 along with nine boards. Wil Jones had 13, Averitt 12, and Louie 10. The Nets did not play this night. Utah's 20-year-old rookie, Moses Malone, had only 10 points. Malone averaged 19.0 ppg against the rest of the teams in the ABA, but only 11.1 against Kentucky.

Two down … seven to go … 3 ½ games behind the idle Nets.

Game 3 – Nassau Coliseum – March 26 – Uniondale, New York – New York Nets

With Jim Bradley still recovering from a cracked bone in his foot and Gene Littles in the hospital with pleurisy, we must face the Nets with only eight healthy players. To tell the truth, McClain stole the show. With 52 seconds remaining and Kentucky leading 101-100, McClain dove to the floor and tapped the ball away from Julius Erving. He shoved it to Artis who tossed it to Wil Jones for an uncontested dunk. Even Dr. J's 37 points and 14 rebounds and Billy "The Whopper" Paultz's 16 points and 20 rebounds weren't enough to stop Kentucky from winning. McClain, who caused numerous turnovers, finished with a season high 24 and eight rebounds. Issel and Jones each had 16. Kentucky wins 103-102.

Three down … six to go … 2 ½ games behind the Nets.

Game 4 – Norfolk Scope – March 28 – Norfolk, Virginia – Virginia Squires

It was a good thing that we had a day off after the big win in New York. There wasn't any time to celebrate. We couldn't let this team slip up on us. Kentucky has a 9-0 record against the Squires this year. We won 110-88.

Four down … five to go … 1½ games behind New York who lost 111-106 at Memphis.

Game 5 – Freedom Hall – March 29 – New York Nets

Issel threw two knock out punches to the New York Nets. With 10 minutes left in the game and Kentucky leading 98-78, ex-Colonel Wendell Ladner repeatedly leaned on Dan while waiting for the Colonels to throw the ball inbounds from under their basket. Issel shoved Ladner and followed with a right hook. Ladner retaliated and struck Dan on the cheek, cutting the skin, which required three stitches after the game. But Issel landed a much bigger blow to the Nets. He was scoring every way possible, jump shots, put backs, off the break, driving the baseline and 10-11 at the free throw line. What a night. He registered a season high 38 points (14/22), and 10 rebounds. But Dan wasn't the only player knocking the Nets to the canvas. Louie had 25 points and five assists. The Big A had 24 and 20 boards with support coming from

Wil's 12 points, and 10 points each by Bird and Ted. The Colonels out rebounded the Nets 61-33. It wasn't a close decision. Kentucky Colonels 126 – New York Nets 95.

The Colonels riding a five game winning streak and the Nets, who had lost five in a row, were now even in the loss column.

Five down … four to go … Kentucky now trailed by ½ game.

Game 6 – Mid South Coliseum – March 30 – Memphis, Tennessee – Sounds

Now came the real test. Playing our sixth game in eight days, we defeated the Memphis Sounds 113-109 in overtime, but it wasn't easy. Kentucky's Mr. Clutch, Louie Dampier, scored eight points in overtime finishing with 27. Once again the Big A was the game's leading scorer with 32 points and 19 boards.

Six down … three to go … the Colonels stayed ½ game behind the Nets, who defeated San Antonio.

Game 7 – University of Kentucky Memorial Coliseum – March 31 – San Antonio Spurs

It's down the stretch they come, and without warning, Dan woke up with an infection in his foot. Although he had numerous nagging ailments, aches and pains throughout the season, he had only missed two games. To top that off, Artis didn't arrive in Lexington until 25 minutes before tip-off. He had taken his two-year-old daughter, Shawna Danielle, to the hospital. When he found out her illness wasn't serious, he drove to Lexington. Dan could only play 15 minutes, so Ron Thomas replaced him at the power forward position. He finished with 10 points and a career high 16 rebounds and five assists. Kentucky cruised to a 103-88 win behind Gilmore's 36 points and 25 boards. In support, Dampier had 19, McClain 15, Marv Roberts and Wil Jones, nine each. Kentucky and New York were now tied for the Eastern Division crown with identical records of 56-26. Each team had two games remaining on the ABA 84 game slate.

Seven down … two to go … all square … New York beat Memphis 119-97.

Game 8 – Freedom Hall – April 2 – Virginia Squires

Rule #1 in sports: Beat the teams you are supposed to beat! The Virginia Squires came into Freedom Hall with an ABA leading 64 losses. Don't let this team spoil what you have accomplished in the last 11 days! Well, they didn't. Kentucky beat the Squires for the 11th time this season. With Littles and Bradley still unable to play, behind a balanced scoring attack, we beat Virginia 88-81. With less than a minute to go, the score was just one point shy of the ABA record for the fewest points by two teams in one game – 158.

Eight down … one to go … all even, New York crushed San Antonio 119-97.

Game 9 – Mid South Coliseum – April 3 – Memphis, Tennessee – Sounds

If there had ever been a must game for the Colonels, it was this game against the much improved Sounds. They had managed only two wins against us, and this was no time to make it three.

After leading early, then falling behind by three late in the second quarter, we rallied to lead 53-52 at halftime, but not before a colossal controversy between the scorekeeper, the Colonels coaches, and officials Wally Rooney and Ed Middleton over the number of fouls that were called on Tom Owens of the Sounds; nothing was changed. With all the hullabaloo surrounding the bookkeeping, the timer let the last two seconds run off the clock, so after halftime intermission, Kentucky got the ball out-of-bounds with two seconds remaining. We failed to score. With Kentucky leading 78-77, Owens in foul trouble and on the bench, we put the game out of reach.

With the Colonels out rebounding the Sounds 57-33, and ex-Memphis player Wil Jones scoring 16 of his 24 points in the second half, the Colonels accomplished what NOBODY thought we could, win nine games in a row and catch Dr. J and the New York Nets. Issel finished with 24/13, Gilmore 18/14, Dampier tossed in 19 points, Averitt 13, and McClain 10, and, oh yes, Jones had 13 rebounds. We won nine games in 12 days to close out regular season play.

The Nets rallied from a 16-point deficit in the final four minutes and 18 seconds to beat the Squires in overtime behind Dr. J's 38 points. The Squires finished with the worst record in ABA history.

Nine down … after the American Basketball Association's 84 game schedule is completed the Colonels and the Nets are deadlocked with identical records … 58-26.

There would be a one game playoff in Freedom Hall on April 5. Many believed that the game was played in Louisville because the Colonels had won the series 6-5, but in reality it was a coin toss.

Regular Season Standings

EASTERN DIVISION	W—L
Kentucky Colonels	58-26
New York Nets	58-26
Spirits of St. Louis	32-52
Memphis Tams	27-57
Virginia Squires	15-69

WESTERN DIVISION	W—L
Denver Nuggets	65-19
San Antonio Spurs	51-33
Indiana Pacers	45-39
Utah Stars	38-46
San Diego Conquistadors	31-53

IT'S TIME FOR THE SHOWDOWN; PUT UP OR SHUT-UP; IT'S FOR ALL THE MARBLES...WHICH TEAM WILL POP THE CORKS ON THE CHAMPAGNE BOTTLES?

It was the first ever one game playoff in ABA history. You may remember at the end of the 1967-68 season that the Colonels and the New Jersey Americans (Nets) were tied. The game was never played. The Americans had to forfeit after their floor was declared unplayable.

It was just two weeks earlier that the Nets beat the Colonels 115-101 in New York, and left us in second place and 4½ games behind with nine games remaining.

For the 13,672 fans, it was a game for the ages. Nobody asked for their money back. With Wil Jones and Ted McClain hitting from the outside and Dan and Artis controlling the inside, the Colonels shot a blistering 60% for the first 16 minutes of the game. The explosion put the Colonels ahead 47-29 with 8:07 left in the first half.

But Julius Erving, as he had done in the past, would have no part of the run-away. It only took him 29 seconds to cut the lead to 49-36. But John Williamson gave the Doc plenty of help as the Nets pulled to within three at 102-99 with 1:40 remaining in the game.

In came Marv Roberts. With Jones on the bench in foul trouble, Roberts did what he had done all year; he made big plays. He drove the lane for two shots that he missed, but were put back in by Issel and Gilmore. Marv also dished out three assists for clutch baskets.

Julius Erving was amazing, but not anymore than Artis, who finished with 28 points and 33, yes, 33 rebounds. Wil Jones, who had always had the task of trying to guard Erving, finished with 20/5. Issel and McClain had 17 each, while Averitt came off the bench to score 12.

In a big time, high intensity game the Kentucky Colonels won their 10th game in a row (108-99) and for the second time in franchise history are the Eastern Division champions.

What do you do after such a historical comeback? I'll tell you what. You pop the cork on the 24 bottles of New York State pink champagne that I had iced down before the game. You hug the beautiful owner, Ellie, and her female board of directors. You hug and kiss your wife, and for some, even kiss the cheerleaders.

But that's not all. While conducting an interview by the media, the team stormed the man who had given this team the confidence to come back when everyone else had given up. Fully clothed, and without much resistance, he was lugged off to the shower. Not far behind was majority owner Ellie Brown.

No, this was no time to relax. There was a bigger prize waiting if we could continue to play with the heart that we had shown for the previous two weeks. The biggest prize in all professional sports is the honor to earn and wear that championship ring. The money is great, but it will be gone in time. The ring will be there forever.

Before the playoffs started, Hubie met with the team and told them to vote on the distribution of the playoff money before the playoff started. Should we lose, he didn't want the players to have ill feelings about any individual that could cause future dissention on the team. All playoff money belonged to the players and NOT the franchise. The players on the active roster each had a vote, coaches and trainers were not

Ellie Brown taking a shower after win against the New York Nets to win the Eastern Division title 1975.

allowed in the meeting. The players could vote the coaches and the trainer a half share, full share, or nothing. They could also vote funds to players that were on the active roster at the beginning of the season, or those that had joined the team later in the year. We didn't have that problem. The money was awarded to the team that finished first in each division and progressed until the team was defeated or a championship was won. We were scheduled to practice at 12 noon at Crawford Gym on the University of Louisville campus. The players scheduled a meeting for 11 a.m. to discuss how the playoff money would be divided. After taping the players, I sat outside the locker room and waited for practice to begin. As the team exited the meeting, Ron Thomas gave me a thumbs-up meaning that I was voted a full share. Thomas had lied to me. After practice, Artis, Dan and Louie called another meeting.

1967-68, opening night team, front row, left to right: Dave Gaines, Darel Carrier, Bobby Rascoe, Head Coach Johnny Givens, Cotton Nash, Larry Conley and Bill Bradley. Back row: Jim "Goose" Ligon, Randy Mahaffey, Orb Bowling, Assistant Coach Buddy Cate, Kendall Rhine, Howard Bayne and Stew Johnson.

1968-69, front row: Jim "Goose" Ligon, Wayne Chapman, Darel Carrier, Louie Dampier, Bobby Rascoe and Reggie Lacefield. Back row: Head Coach Gene Rhodes, Randy Mahaffey, Sam Smith, Jim Caldwell, Harry Akin, Manny Leaks and Gene Moore.

1969-70, front row, left to right: George Tinsley, Darel Carrier, Louie Dampier, Tommy Kron, and Oliver Darden. Back row: Wayne Chapman, Bud Olsen, Gene Moore, Jim "Goose" Ligon and Sam Smith.

1970-71, front row, left to right: Darel Carrier, Louie Dampier, President-General Manager Mike Storen, Coach Frank Ramsey, Howard Wright, Mike Pratt. Back row: Trainer Lloyd Gardner, Cincy Powell, Jim "Goose" Ligon, Dan Issel, Dan Hester, Les Hunter, Walt Simon and Tommy Hagan.

1971-72, seated left to right: Mike Pratt, Jimmy O'Brien, Head Coach Joe Mullaney, General Manager Mike Storen, Louie Dampier and Darel Carrier. Standing: Pierre Russell, Walt Simon, Cincy Powell, Dan Issel, Artis Gilmore, Les Hunter, Mike Gale and Trainer Lloyd Gardner.

1972-73, seated left to right: Jimmy O'Brien, Rick Mount, General Manager Mike Storen, Head Coach Joe Mullaney, Mike Gale and Louie Dampier. Standing: Trainer Lloyd Gardner, Pierre Russell, Ron Thomas, Artis Gilmore, Dan Issel, Walt Simon, Wendell Ladner and Assistant Coach Bud Olsen.

1973-74, seated left to right: Joe Hamilton, John Roche, Head Coach Babe McGarthy, Chairman of the Board Ellie Brown, General Manager Gene Rhodes, Louie Dampier and Chuck Williams. Standing: Assistant Coach Bud Olsen, Walt Simon, Austin "Red" Robbins, Jim Bradley, Dan Issel, Artis Gilmore, Collis Jones, Ron Thomas and Trainer Lloyd Gardner.

1974-75, standing, left to right: Chairman of the board, Ellie Brown, Louie Dampier, Ted McClain, Wilbert Jones, Marvin Roberts, Artis Gilmore, Dan Issel, Jim Bradley, Ron Thomas, Gene Littles, Bird Averitt, General Manager Gene Rhodes. Kneeling: Trainer Lloyd Gardner, Coach Hubie Brown and Assistant Coach Stan Albeck.

1975 ABA World Champions. Front row: William Bird Averitt, Gene Littles, Assistant Coach Stan Albeck, Owner Ellie Brown, Head Coach Hubie Brown, Louie Dampier, Ted McClain. Back row: Assistant General Manager David Vance, Ron Thomas, Wil Jones, Jim Bradley, Artis Gilmore, Dan Issel, Marv Roberts, Trainer Lloyd Gardner, General Manager Gene Rhodes.

1975-76, standing, left to right: General Manager David Vance, Jimmie Backer, Jan van Breda Kolff, Maurice Lucas, Artis Gilmore, Jim McDaniels, Wilbert Jones, Ron Thomas, Trainer Lloyd Gardner and Vice President-Operations Gene Rhodes. Seated: Johnny Neumann, Jimmy Dan Conner, Bird Averitt, Assistant Coach Stan Albeck, Ellie Brown, Head Coach Hubie Brown, Louie Dampier, Kevin Joyce and Allen Murphy.

1971-72 ABA East All-Star Team, front row, left to right: Charlie Scott, Warren Jabali, George Thompson, Louie Dampier, Mack Calvin and Bill Melchionni. Back row: Coach Joe Mullaney, John Brisker, Jim McDaniels, Artis Gilmore, Dan Issel, Julius Erving, Rick Barry and trainer Lloyd Gardner.

ABA Commissioner Dave DeBusschere, 1975-76.

Left to right: Brenda Winders, Susan Mooser, Vickie Thomas, Karen Beil, Debbie Dahl, Geri Langley, Mary Lee Bryant, Sherry Creech, Donna Grubbs, Pam O'Banion, Melanie Hamilton and choreographer Barbara Korfhage.

Kneeling, left to right: Patty Graves, Debbie Johnson, Pam Zirnheld, Brenda Kent. Standing: Vickie Thomas, Peggy McGrath, Kathy Carter, choreographer Barbara Jenkins, Marylee Bryant, Donna Grubbs and Eddie Lueken. Not pictured: Karen Beil and Melanie Hamilton.

#44, worn by Cotton Nash/Dan Issel, 1967-38, 1968-69, and 1969-70.

#10, worn by Louie Dampier, 1970-71, 1971-72, 1972-73, and 1973-74.

#53, worn by Artis Gilmore, 1974-75 and 1975-76.

Louie Dampier's blue game uniform.

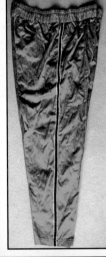

Above and right: #44 Dan Issel's shoes and socks.

Left: Two colors of the warm-up pants worn.

All photos on this and the facing page are courtesy of Nathan Gardner.

Blue and white practice jersey.

Red and blue practice jersey.

Kentucky Colonels Championship Ring. Courtesy of Kyle D. Eberle.

Kentucky Colonels Championship Trophy. Courtesy of Kyle D. Eberle.

1975 Kentucky Colonels Championship Medallion.

This collection and all photos on the facing page, except as noted, are courtesy of Nathan Gardner.

#42 Ron Thomas and Kim Hughes (New York Nets).

Jimmy Dan Conner

#6 Billy Shepherd (Memphis Sounds), Ted McClain (Kentucky Colonels), Wil Jones (Kentucky Colonels).

#53 Artis Gilmore and Indiana Pacers #30 George McGinnis, #20 Darnell Hillman, and Kevin Joyce, and referee John Vanak.

#53 Artis Gilmore and New York Nets: #40 Willie Sojourner, #35 Larry "Mr. K" Kenon, Brian Taylor, #12 Mike Gale.

1975-76 Playoffs against the Denver Nuggets ... is this coach Larry Brown?

Louie Dampier receives game ball after scoring 15,000 career points in ABA. General Manager Dave Vance.

Freedom Hall scoreboard at the end of the first quarter of the Championship game, May 22, 1975.

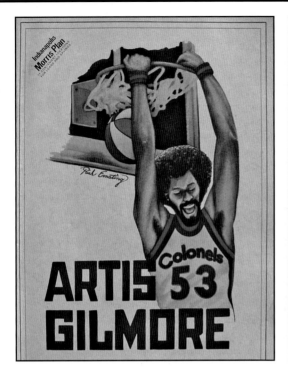

1975-76 Pacer Program

75-76 Marv Roberts' Program

MVP for the ABA, Julius Erving, star forward for the New York Nets, poses prior to the playoff game with the Virginia Squires. Erving was named the ABA's most valuable player this season. Erving, #24, led the ABA in scoring the previous two seasons.

#53 Artis Gilmore, #24 Ted McClain, #41 Len Elmore (Indiana Pacers) and #25 Billy Knight (behind Elmore).

#10 Louie Dampier, #53 Artis Gilmore and #30 George McGinnis (Indiana Pacers).

Van Vance, the voice of the Colonels on WHAS Radio and TV.

Left to right: Wilt "The Stilt" Chamberlain, Artis Gilmore All-Star MVP, Ray Scott and East Team Coach Babe McCarthy.

259

Artis relaxes on the hood of his new Rolls Royce.

#24 Ted McClain and #25 Bill Melchionni (New York Nets).

Artis Gilmore and #24 Ted McClain, #44 George "Iceman" Gervin, #31 Swen Nater, #33 Rich Jones (San Antonio Spurs).

Artis Gilmore and Pacers #30 George McGinnis.

#5 Jan van Breda Kolff

#25 Maurice Lucas

#45 Jim McDaniels and #1 Ron Boone (Spirits of St. Louis).

#43 Kevin Joyce, Dave Twardzik (Virginia Squires).

#31 Johnny Neumann

#10 Louie Dampier and Milwaukee player.

#14 William "Bird" Averitt

#53 Artis Gilmore and #32 Dr. J (Julius Erving) and Billy Paultz of the Nets.

#22 Wil Jones and #5 Billy "The Whopper" Paultz (New York Nets).

David Vance, Director of Publicity/Public Relations. 1975-76 General Manager.

INDIANA PACERS

AMERICAN
BASKETBALL
ASSOCIATION

BOB LEONARD
Coach

TOM BINFORD
President

DON BUSE

NATE BARNETT

LEN ELMORE

MIKE FLYNN

DARNELL HILLMAN

CHARLES JORDAN

BILLY KNIGHT

BILL KELLER

ED MANNING

DAN ROUNDFIELD

FOR BOX OFFICE USE ONLY
GAME #3
$5.00
WED. OCT. 15, 1975

AISLE ROW SEAT

INDIANA PACERS
VS.
NEW YORK KNICKS
MARKET SQUARE ARENA
ADMISSION
$5.00
SOUTH
CONCOURSE
No Refund or Exchange

OCT.
15
1975

SO. CONCOURSE

WED. OCT. 15, 1975 8:05 P. M.
AISLE ROW SEAT

AMERICAN BASKETBALL
ASSOCIATION

GEORGE McGINNIS

BOB NETOLICKY

MARK SIBLEY

WAYNE PACK

JOHN WEISSERT
Pres. & Gen Mgr.

DICK TINKHAM
Executive Vice President
ABA PRESIDENT

BOB LEONARD
COACH

JERRY OLIVER
ASST. COACH

AMERICAN BASKETBALL
ASSOCIATION

JOHN BAUM

DON BUSE

CHARLIE EDGE

LEN ELMORE

DARNELL HILLMAN

KEVIN JOYCE

BILL KELLER

BILLY KNIGHT

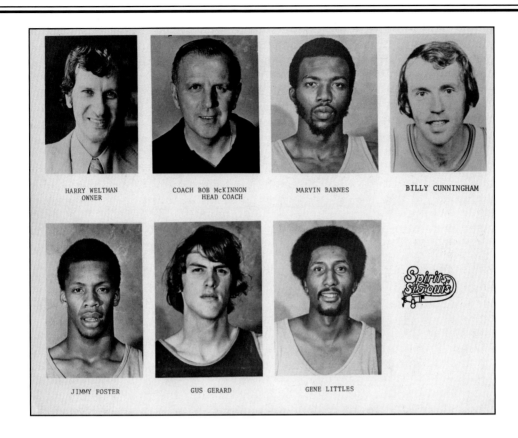

HARRY WELTMAN
OWNER

COACH BOB McKINNON
HEAD COACH

MARVIN BARNES

BILLY CUNNINGHAM

JIMMY FOSTER

GUS GERARD

GENE LITTLES

ED MANNING

RUDY MARTZKE

ALLIE McGUIRE

TOM OWENS

DOUG RICHARDS

FLY WILLIAMS

DENNIS WUYCIK

DENVER ROCKETS

AMERICAN
BASKETBALL
ASSOCIATION

BYRON BECK

DAVE BUSTION

FRANK CARD

WARREN JABALI

JULIUS KEYE

WILLIE LONG

MARV ROBERTS

DAVE ROBISCH

DENVER ROCKETS

AMERICAN
BASKETBALL
ASSOCIATION

RALPH SIMPSON

AL SMITH

CLAUDE TERRY

J.W."BILL"RINGSBY
Owner-Trustee

ALEX HANNUM President
General Manager Coach

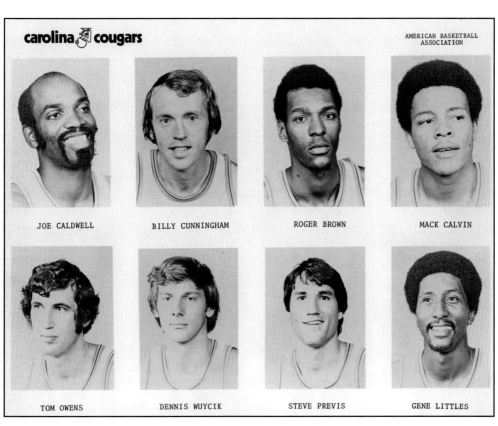

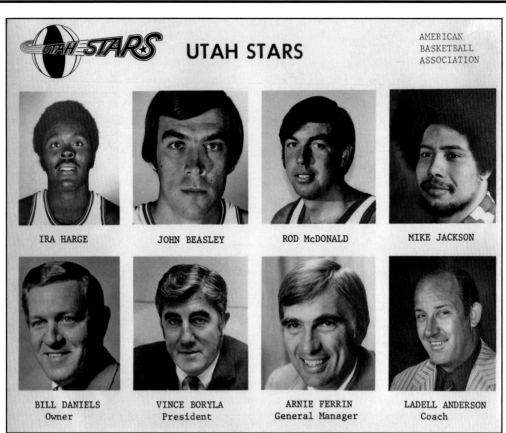

UTAH STARS

AMERICAN BASKETBALL ASSOCIATION

IRA HARGE   JOHN BEASLEY   ROD McDONALD   MIKE JACKSON

BILL DANIELS   VINCE BORYLA   ARNIE FERRIN   LADELL ANDERSON
Owner   President   General Manager   Coach

AMERICAN BASKETBALL ASSOCIATION

RONNIE ROBINSON   ROY EBRON   BRUCE SEALS   WIL ROBINSON

BILL DANIELS   VINCE BORYLA   ARNIE FERRIN   JOE MULLANEY
Owner   President   General Manager   Coach

UTAH STARS

AMERICAN
BASKETBALL
ASSOCIATION

ZELMO BEATY   WILLIE WISE   JAMES JONES   GLEN COMBS

RON BOONE   CINCY POWELL   LARRY JONES   GERALD GOVAN

AMERICAN BASKETBALL
ASSOCIATION

LIONEL BILLINGY   GLEN COMBS   DARRELL ELSTON   BILL HIGGINS

GEORGE IRVINE   MIKE JACKSON   JOHN NEUMANN   BARRY PARKHILL

271

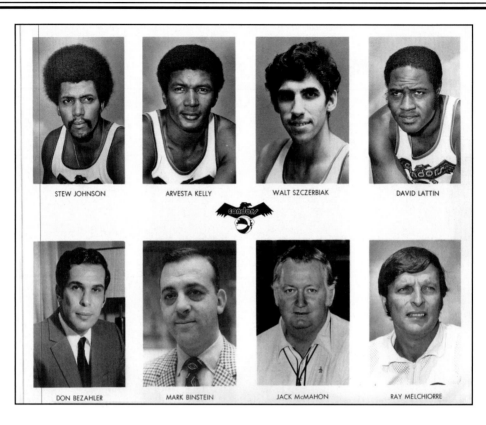

STEW JOHNSON · ARVESTA KELLY · WALT SZCZERBIAK · DAVID LATTIN

DON BEZAHLER · MARK BINSTEIN · JACK McMAHON · RAY MELCHIORRE

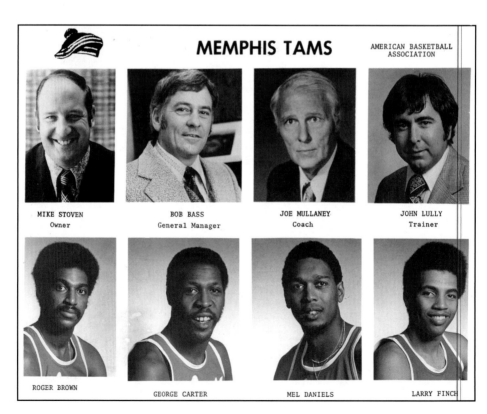

MEMPHIS TAMS

AMERICAN BASKETBALL ASSOCIATION

MIKE STOVEN
Owner

BOB BASS
General Manager

JOE MULLANEY
Coach

JOHN LULLY
Trainer

ROGER BROWN · GEORGE CARTER · MEL DANIELS · LARRY FINCH

They told the rest of the team that they weren't leaving until they voted Hubie, Stan, and me a full share.

Winning the division was huge. It meant that we would play the Memphis Sounds in the playoffs and not the Spirits of St. Louis in the first round. St. Louis was a team that had caused us problems all year. Although we were 7-2 against them, every game was a melee. The Nets were 11-0 against them.

Round One

Game 1 – Freedom Hall – April 6

It was just three days earlier that Kentucky had played the Sounds in Memphis. In front of the smallest crowd this season and the smallest in a playoff game in four years, former Colonels coach, and now Sounds coach, Joe Mullaney's strategy was to milk the 30-second clock and not get in a running game.

The Colonels led 52-48 at halftime. With all five starters in double figures, the Colonels won and take a 1-0 lead in this best of seven series. Although he was double and triple teamed at times, Artis led all scorers with 25 points and 20 rebounds. Issel had 23.

Game 2 – Freedom Hall – April 8

The Colonels performance this night against the Sounds wasn't as bad as game one. Actually it was just the opposite. Kentucky was clicking on all cylinders. With three players scoring 20-plus points, and three others in double figures, we took a two game lead over the Sounds. Louie hit 11 of 15 shots and was the game's leading scorer. The Sounds had seven players in double figures.

Game 3 – Mid South Coliseum – April 10

Dan had always been known for his outstanding offensive skills. That's what made him an All-Star. But tonight, Issel played defense for the Colonels like Dick Butkus did for the Chicago Bears. He was drawing charges, fighting through picks and rotating to the basket from the weak side. It had been a long time since Hubie praised his defense, but that was the story tonight. He was one of six players with double figure scoring, and he paced Kentucky with 21 points. Hubie was smiling after the Colonels took a 3-0 lead in the playoffs.

Hopefully they could close out the series tomorrow night and return to Louisville for a little rest and relaxation. After the 101-80 win they had now won a club record 13 games in a row.

Game 4 – Mid South Coliseum – April 11

It has often been said that all good things must come to an end. Well, tonight one good streak came to an end. With the Memphis win, the two teams would now return to Louisville to try and settle this playoff spot. Kentucky still lead the series 3-1.

Game 5 – Freedom Hall – April 13

With guards, Dampier (21 points) and McClain (20 points), combining for 41 points and 10 assists, Kentucky ended the best-of-seven series in five games. Mr. Defense, Wil Jones, was brilliant. His defense on Stew Johnson was a big key to our victory. In all, Jones had 13 points and a season high 18 rebounds, 15 in the first half. Artis, after two subpar games, came back with 31 points and a game high 20 boards. We won 111-99.

It was time to start the semifinal games … and you would never believe who we would be playing. St. Louis! They beat the Nets 4-1.

Semi-Finals

Game 1 – Freedom Hall – April 21

Ted McClain had been one of the big reasons Kentucky was playing in the semifinals. His play the previous four weeks had been spectacular. With 20 seconds remaining in the game and the Colonels trailing 109-108, Steve Jones was holding the ball over his head trying to make a pass. Ted whacked the ball loose and tapped it to Dampier. Little Louie, Mr. Clutch, lost his balance, and while falling to the floor, put a high arching shoot off the glass for two points, and Kentucky led 110-109. With 10 seconds left, St. Louis called timeout. Taking the ball out at midcourt, they inbounded the ball to Freddie Lewis, who already had 35 points. Lewis headed for the goal and shot an off balanced shot that missed. Marv Roberts snatched the rebound and was fouled. Because it was a backcourt foul, Roberts went to the line and made two free throws to seal the game 112-109.

The Kentucky Colonels led the best-of-seven series 1-0.

Game 2 – Freedom Hall – April 23

One thing that was certain … this best-of-seven series would be played above the rim.

Balance on a team is better than a bunch of individuals. That's why we came out on top once again, winning 108-103.

We led the series 2-0, and were headed to St. Louis for a game the next night where the Spirits had a 4-2 edge in the regular season.

Bob Costas, the rookie broadcaster for the Spirits, gave the account of the time Marvin Barnes, while reviewing his itinerary from Louisville back home to St. Louis, noticed that the plane was to leave Louisville at 8 a.m., and arrive in St. Louis at 7:59 a.m. and announced to the travel party that, "I ain't goin' on no time machine. I ain't takin' no flight that takes me back in time."

Game 3 – St. Louis Arena – April 25

We simply could not put the ball in the basket. But, behind the play of Marv Roberts (13 points), and a good shooting night by Issel (31 points), we cut the lead to two before Lewis and Lucas took over.

With Barnes contributing 27 points and 13 rebounds and Lucas with 18 points and a game high 20 boards, the Spirits sent their 10,142 rowdy fans home happy after a 103-97 victory.

Early in the game after protesting a foul, Hubie got his first technical foul. Late in the first half, Thomas was called for getting physical with Don Adams. Hubie protested, knocked assistant Stan Albeck over backwards in his chair, and the referee came out and charged me, the trainer, with a technical foul.

Why do I tell this story? For once I didn't earn the "T." Every time we played in St. Louis, Hubie, Stan and I would have dinner after the game with Stan "The Man" Musial in his restaurant, "Stan and Biggies." It was here that Albeck told Hubie that he had sent him tumbling, and that the referee called the "T" on me because he wasn't sure if it was me or Hubie that had yelled. If the referee had called it on Hubie, he would have been ejected and sent to the locker room.

So he called it on me. No, Hubie didn't pay my $50 fine. Why? Because they took it out of our paycheck.

Game 4 – St. Louis Arena – April 27

In the first three games, the Spirits led by the M & M boys, Marvin and Maurice, had out rebounded us by 18. Hubie could not, and would not, accept the pounding we were taking on the glass. They had been tougher, nastier and more aggressive than we had.

With 8:06 remaining in the third quarter and a 69-67 lead, the roof fell in on the Spirits.

Lewis turned his ankle. He had been the catalyst of St. Louis down the stretch. He had been the super glue that held the youngest front line in basketball (three rookies) together. He had more playoff experience than any guard in the ABA, and now he was injured.

Enter Steve Jones. Jones answered the call by scoring nine points in the quarter and extended the St. Louis lead to seven, 82-75. That's when the guillotine fell on the Spirits. The Plumber and The Hound gave a fierce defensive clinic that would lead to a 22-3 eruption. Coming off the bench, Thomas contributed six rebounds, four points and a jarring defensive effort on Barnes in just 17 minutes of play. McClain also cashed in 18 points, 11 assists and six boards.

Artis, after a dismal Game 3, caught fire. He was amazing at both ends of the floor. When it was all over, the stat sheet had him with 33 points, hitting 12 of 16 shots, 16 rebounds, two blocked shots and a steal. Dan, who guarded Barnes most of the game, gave a solid defensive effort in the clammy arena. His play was spectacular, although he just scored 10 points in 31 minutes. Wil Jones was solid with 18 points and eight rebounds and his partner at the small forward position, Marv Roberts once again was a factor off the bench. Bird Averitt, who missed Game 3 because of a hamstring injury, played 17 minutes and scored eight points and dished out four assists.

The Kentucky Colonels, by winning 117-108, were only one game away from opening the spirits.

Game 5 – Freedom Hall – April 28

Lewis stayed home. The Kentucky Colonels went high-octane – they outrebounded St. Louis for the first time in the series 64-45. Make no mistake about it, Lewis' absence was crucial, but the pounding of the boards was more crucial for Kentucky. The Colonels didn't play around. With Gilmore and Issel leading the way, and solid performances from seven other players, we would not be denied a chance to wear a Championship Ring. The Colonels were never behind on the scoreboard in this fifth and deciding game. Issel was amazing, with 28 points and nine rebounds, but Artis was unconscious. He hit 10-15 shots, scored 29 points, pulled down 20 rebounds, and blocked seven shots. The small forwards Wil Jones (10/9) and Marv Roberts (12/4) came through with 22 points and 13 boards. The always reliable Dampier finished with 17 points and 12 assists, while McClain once again played solid defense and handed out eight assists. The lightning quick Averitt, who was recovering from an injured hamstring, came off the bench to score 18.

And now the wait.

We had a long lay-off, 14 days to be exact. Kentucky eradicated the Spirits of St. Louis on April 28 by winning the best of seven series in five games. Meanwhile, it took the Indiana Pacers seven games to overpower the Denver Nuggets. Indiana defeated Denver 104-96 on May 3.

We took a few days off, but never two days in a row. We never took a day off on the floor. Hubie won't allow a let-up. Now that it was early May, Ted, Artis, Walt Simon and I usually played golf. Ted was close to a scratch golfer. Walt ... who knows, that's why we call him "Trick Man." You never knew what his real score would be. We were playing at Seneca Park one day and Walt sliced a ball on Hole #3 that went over I-64. When we got up in the fairway he said, "My ball must have hit a tree. It's right here." Do I need to say more? Artis and I both started playing golf for the first time when he signed with the Colonels. We were about equal, 95 to 110.

I am sure you can guess where Dan was in early May. Of course, Churchill Downs. During the playoffs, Dan was always looking at the schedule just to see if he was going to be able to go to the Derby. By dumping St. Louis in five games, he got to go to the Derby and Churchill Downs almost every day. I'll tell you this, he didn't bet on the Derby winner Foolish Pleasure. Louie, he worked in his yard.

Before the championship series started, there were several words everyone was tired of hearing, "fold," "choke," "pressure," and "wait-till-next-year." The Colonels and the Pacers had met in the playoffs three times. Indiana had won each. Four years earlier Artis signed with the Colonels and since he inked his contract we had the best won-lost record in the ABA, 235-101. The closest one to us was Utah, which was 25 games behind, and the Pacers with a 189-147 record were 36 games behind. The problem was, we have never won that "Big Ring."

The Colonels were 5-3 against the Pacers in the regular season this year.

The I-65 Series

Game 1 – Freedom Hall – May 13

John Y. Brown's friend, Jimmy "The Greek" Snyder, picked the Colonels to win Game 1 by a single point. He also said that if Kentucky wins, majority stockholder Ellie Brown, was ready to offer the NBA champion a $500,000 winner-take-all challenge.

I don't know how much more exciting it can get. The Pacers brought none other than Dancin' Harry with them. Dancin' Harry got into basketball by running out on the floor during timeouts and dazzling the crowds at the NBA New York Knicks and Baltimore Bullets games.

But hold your fried chicken. The Colonels director of promotions, Gordon Crawford, countered with Colonel Superfly, Michael Tolliver, an eighth-grader at Samuel V. Noe Middle School. David Vance, assistant general manager, named him Colonel Superfly after the song "Superfly" was chosen for Tolliver's theme song. In a *Sports Illustrated* article dated May 26, 1975, Barry McDermott described him this way, "Superfly was 13-year-old Michael J. Tolliver, who made the clothes-conscious Dancin' Harry seem shabby by comparison. He showed up in a gleaming white suit, hat, gloves, shoes and cape. Besides that, he had youth on his side, displaying footwork, tumbles and splits that his panting rival could not match. Humbled, Harry slunk around the sidelines and cast baleful gazes at the youngster, trying unsuccessfully to win back the crowd by spinning a basketball on his fingertips."

When teams come off of a long lay-off, everyone fears a let-down, but not tonight. Kentucky went after the Pacers like the Hatfields went after the McCoys. At one point in the game, Kentucky held a 15 point lead. But with 8½ minutes remaining, Indiana had cut it to five. But in a minute and a half the game was over. With three fast break baskets by Dampier, McClain and Thomas, combined with two free throws by Issel, the lead was 97-84. In the final seven minutes we scored 23 points and deep-fried the Pacers 120-94. There would be no choking tonight.

Dan Issel had 19 rebounds … yes, I said 19 rebounds. Artis Gilmore had 26 points and 16 boards while playing only 36 minutes and Louie was fantastic, finishing with 22 points.

After the game, majority owner Ellie Brown told the media that she and John Y. had met with Roone Arledge of ABC, and Bob Wussler of CBS, the heads of two major networks. They were houseguests during Derby week. They inquired about the possibility of one of them putting up $500,000 to produce a Super Hoop, best-of-three contest between the ABA champions and the NBA champions. Ellie's rationale, "If they back down, they don't deserve to be called the super league."

Game 2 – Freedom Hall – May 15

At a meeting in Louisville the 10-man board of trustees of the American Basketball Association named former New York Knick and NBA All-Star Dave DeBusschere the new commissioner. He is leaving the General Manager's position with the New York Nets to replace interim commissioner Tedd Munchak.

We played so poorly in game two, that I don't even want to waste the paper it is written on to tell you about the game, but ….

There might not be enough paper or ink to tell the drama that unfolded in the last 46 seconds of the game. Marv Roberts, as he had done throughout the playoffs, was incredible.

McGinnis tied the game with 46 seconds remaining after he stepped over Roberts, who had been shoved to the floor, and then he plowed over Ron Thomas for a lay-up.

We missed a shot with a little over 10 seconds remaining, and the Pacers had the ball. On the ensuing inbound pass, Marv dove for the ball and it ricocheted off McGinnis and out-of-bounds.

Hubie called timeout and set up a play for Mr. Clutch, Louie Dampier, but he was heavily guarded. The second option was to go to Issel, but McGinnis had him covered. Artis, who was MIA most of the night, was being played one-on-one by Hillman. The gigantic center received the pass, elevated high into the air, and shot down into the basket. There were two seconds left and Indiana was out of timeouts. Kentucky was leading 95-93.

That's when pandemonium broke out. Billy Keller took the inbound pass from Darnell Hillman, took two dribbles around Louie, who had fallen, and let a 46 footer fly. It went in, good for three points in the ABA! Veteran referee Ed Rush, who was waving his arms "no good, game over" before Keller released the ball, was surrounded by Pacers players and coaches.

After Rush ruled the shot no good, he quickly conferred at the scorer's table with his partner Norm Drucker and alternate official Eddie Middleton, who was seated behind the timekeeper, Donnie Beckhart. Several police officers tried to hold the Pacers back as they crowded up to the three officials. Slick Leonard, the Pacers coach, contended that, "we weren't going to hit anybody; we were just arguing."

As the police were escorting the three officials off the floor under the basket, fuzzy-faced Kevin Joyce lost his cool and went after Ed Rush. Joyce's actions could best be described as that of a ranting and raving madman. In the altercation, Joyce struck officer Joel Lampkin in the eye and busted his cap. That's when a quick case of amnesia set in; Joyce said he couldn't remember hitting the officer.

Sporting a raw eye, Lampkin then asked an off duty policeman, hired by the Colonels, to go get Joyce out of the locker room and arrest him.

That's when John Y. and Pacers' trustee Bill Bindly stepped in. They asked officer Warren

Strahl and Lampkin not to press charges. However, Lampkin had been embarrassed, and officer Strahl was going to back him.

Through the negotiations by John Y., an apology by Joyce and the agreement that the Pacers would pay Lampkin's doctor bills and buy him a new hat ($25), the arrest was averted.

The Pacers general manager, John Weissert, sent a formal protest to the league, along with the required $200 check, contending that Keller's shot should indeed count, giving Indiana a 96-95 victory. Former Colonels player and assistant coach Bud Olsen was the supervisor of ABA officials, and along with the new commissioner, Dave DeBusschere, were to view the tapes and make a final decision, hopefully the next day.

Kentucky headed off to Indy for games four and five leading the series 2-0.

Game 3 – Market Square Arena – May 15

It was decided that the new commissioner, Dave DeBusschere, would rule on the protest. Unfortunately, he was in Las Vegas playing in a celebrity tennis tournament prior to attending the Muhammad Ali-Ron Lyle fight.

Bud Olsen, director of officials, who was at the game, said that until somebody presented a copy of a tape or a picture showing both the clock and the ball leaving Keller's hands, they had no grounds for a hearing.

Olsen spent much of the day collecting reports from the game officials and watching film footage shot by WLKY-32's Vince DeSalvo. The footage showed everything from the time Gilmore's shot went in until the ball swished through the basket at the other end. There was one problem, it did not show the clock.

What did the films show when viewed one frame at a time? It concluded that it took 66 frames from the time Keller touched the ball on the inbound pass until it left his hands. There were 24 frames per second. That meant it took 2.75 seconds to get the shot off.

A decision would not be made until the new commissioner met with Olsen, and reviewed the film and interviews that had been gathered.

Before the game started, the Pacers rolled a huge Kentucky Fried Chicken Bucket out to center court. Dancin' Harry emerged and close behind was three-year old Mark Feske, dressed in a cape and putting the whammy on our Michael Tolliver. The house was rockin'!

An ABA record crowd of 17,388 witnessed Game 3 of the ABA playoffs in Market Square Arena, and did they ever get their money's worth.

As the old saying goes, when everything else fails, try something else, so Artis, who had been trying to play cautiously to stay out of foul trouble, tried something else, and did it work!

All the 7'2" center did was score 41 points equaling his career high. Oh, he also grabbed 28 rebounds to help rally the Colonels to a 109-101 victory. If the new commissioner upheld the 95-93 score, which the Pacers had protested, Kentucky would take a 3-0 lead in this best-of-seven series. A decision was not expected until late Monday afternoon, just before Game 4 was to be played.

It took 10 of Issel's 26 points and 11 of Gilmore's points in the last 10 minutes to overcome the Pacers lead. A driving lay-up by Louie and a foul on the play by Pacers' rookie Len Elmore allowed Louie's free throw to tie the game at 97-97, and we didn't look back.

With McClain proving that crime does indeed pay on the basketball floor by stealing the ball, and a tenacious team defensive effort, Kentucky was able to force the Pacers into taking tough shots, and when they missed, Issel and Gilmore would not allow Indiana to get a second shot.

As Issel remarked after the game, "This may not be the best game Artis has ever played in the last four years, but he hasn't played a bigger one."

Along with the gigantic game by Artis, combined with Issel's 26 points and 13 boards and a supporting cast led by the always consistent Dampier, McClain and super sub Roberts, the Colonels now led 3-0, at least until the protest hearing.

Next question please, Could the Kentucky Colonels sweep the Indiana Pacers in four games?

Game 4 – Market Square Arena – May 19

Dave DeBusschere flew into Indianapolis to make a ruling on Keller's last second desperation shot in Game 2 in Louisville four days earlier. He met with Indiana officials along with Ellie and her husband John Y., general manager Gene Rhodes, and assistant general manager Dave Vance. The meeting took place at 2 o'clock in a conference room at WTTV, an Indianapolis television station. In only his first week on the job, the contingent from Kentucky was already upset with DeBusschere because he didn't accept the recommendations made by his supervisor of officials, Bud Olsen.

Just minutes before the team checked out of the Stouffer's Inn to depart for Market Square Arena, we were notified by Vance that DeBusschere had ruled in favor of the Colonels. The bottom line he said was, "We have to rely on the referee's judgment."

After the verdict, Kentucky officially led the series 3-0.

How can a team play to perfection one night and stink up the gym two days later? Some say it is a mental breakdown having a 3-0 lead. No team in the eight year history of the ABA has ever won the championship series in the minimum four games.

How can you lose? You can lose by shooting 35%, have 23 turnovers and get out rebounded 63-53. In the first half alone, Kentucky shot 37%, had 17 turnovers. What was even more astonishing is the fact that Kentucky was leading by three at the half 44-41, and by two going into the final quarter. But after playing just as bad as the Colonels, the Pacers turned the game around with 7½ minutes to go when they outscored Kentucky 10-1 and led 79-72.

Then Keller decided to put on a shooting exhibition, and Indiana matched their biggest lead in the series, nine points. With the score 92-81 at that point, the Pacers coasted the rest of the way to finish off the Colonels 94-86. The last time the Pacers scored 94 points in the playoffs, they lost.

Both teams were awful and the fans should have asked for their money back. Unfortunately, somebody had to win and tonight the Pacers came out on top. The only bright spot was McGinnis' 22 points and 21 rebounds, and Billy Keller's 20.

Put the champagne back in the boxes. There would be no bubbly tonight.

Game 5 – Freedom Hall – May 22

The Indiana Pacers came into town with only one thing in mind, "Let's go back to Indiana for game six." We had another idea, "Let's win it for the hometown fans."

Tied at 29-29 at the end of the first quarter, one thing was for sure, Indiana wasn't going to surrender or die.

By halftime Kentucky had fought and scrapped its way to a six point lead, 54-48.

Because we had never won the big one, the fourth quarter seemed as though it took hours to play. Indiana still wouldn't go away. They wouldn't throw in the towel. It was evident that if we were going to win, we would have to dig-in, grind our teeth and keep on pounding.

Rookie sensation Billy Knight was on his game. He was almost a one man wrecking crew. After the Colonels got what they thought was a comfortable lead, Knight, once again with his brilliant play, cut the Kentucky lead to 100-97. Marv Roberts answered with a 12-foot jumper. Then McClain set an ABA record when he stole the ball from the Pacers for the 15th time in the series. It was his sixth of the game. It led to a short hook shot by Gilmore that bounced and bounced around the rim before falling through the net.

Finally, with 57 seconds remaining in the game, Kentucky took a nine point lead. Room to breathe … wrong!

With 25 seconds remaining and Kentucky leading 108-101, Louie penetrated to the free throw line and let it fly and missed. We had played impeccably until the last 22 seconds. We took a bad shot and then fouled in the backcourt, giving the Pacers two free throws. All we had to do was hold the ball and we would win by seven. Two free throws and a basket by Knight cut the lead to three points at 108-105 with only nine seconds left after Dampier's miss.

The Pacers fouled Artis. He stepped to the line and hit the two biggest free throws of his life. The Colonels led 110-105. He then hauled in his record breaking 31st rebound after the Pacers took their last shot. At last, the Kentucky Colonels were the kings!

Bye Bye Ziggy ... Hello Championship

The players jumped with jubilation, piling on each other, shaking hands, and kissing their wives, family and friends. It was then that many of the 16,662 fans crowded the floor.

By now the floor was packed with the Colonels family, which included the all-female board of directors and lots of loyal fans. Who will ever forget Ellis Thomas, Hardy Martin, Mac McKinney, Nell Fisher, Marie Breehl, Scott Regan, and Jackie Estes?

First up in the order of business was the presentation of the MVP Award to Artis. Along with the award came a brand new car presented by *Sporting News* Magazine. The much deserved Marv Roberts was second in the voting for the MVP Award.

Then ABA Commissioner Dave DeBusschere joined Kentucky Governor Julian Carroll at center court to present majority owner Ellie Brown, the 10-man squad, two coaches and the trainer the coveted sterling silver championship trophy.

Then Hubie took the arena microphone. He said, "First of all, I want to thank 13 dedicated people, the 10 players, a great assistant coach, Stan Albeck, and our trainer, Lloyd "Pink" Gardner. A lot of unselfishness, dedication and a helluva lot of camaraderie went into this championship.

"Second, I'd like to thank John Y. and Ellie, who have done so much for basketball and the ABA, and more for you people in Louisville.

"Third, we're proud of you, the fans who have given us so much support this year.

"And last, I'd like to thank my family. Without my wife, Claire, and my four kids, and the Guy Upstairs who watches over that Big Court in the Sky."

Subsequently, every light in Freedom Hall went out. A few security lights came on to illuminate the backboards as the Colonels were cutting down the nets. A thunderstorm outside had caused the darkness.

Then it was off to the locker room, the place where team chemistry is built, to pop the top on the bubbly and a few minutes of private celebration behind closed doors.

After the last regular season game in 1973-74, John Y. came into the locker room and told the players that if they won the ABA Championship he would send the entire team to Las Vegas. At the time he was a majority owner in Lums, a beer and hot dog specialty restaurant.

Lums was also a part owner of Caesars Palace in Las Vegas. Needless to say, we got beat in the second round 4-0 by Dr. J and the Nets. After the series, Babe was fired and Hubie was hired. As I was walking to the locker room with Dan after the championship game, Dan said, "Pink, ask John Y. when we are going to Vegas." We both knew that he wouldn't remember that his offer was last season and not this.

When the doors opened, the champagne corks flew everywhere; the fun had just begun. Ron Thomas plastered his sidekick Bird Averitt in the face with a meringue pie while Jim Bradley and board member Joni Coleman enjoyed a cigar. Finally, I got enough courage to approach John Y. about his offer. I walked up to him and said, "John, you said that you would send us to Vegas for a week if we won the championship, so when do I start planning for the trip?" He said, "Start planning it, and let me know."

Then it was time to do what champions do, throw the coach and the owner in the shower. In all, we went through 35 bottles of New York State pink champagne. We sprayed each other until our eyes burned so badly that you could hardly see.

Hubie had orchestrated a team led by a 7'2" center, a Horse moved from center to forward, a veteran guard who was going to be replaced for each the previous eight years, a thief, a Bird, a Plumber, a Shaft and a supersub. We had finally shut the mouths of all those who doubted it would ever happen.

Early in the season Jimmy O'Brien of the *New York Post* and *Basketball Times*, wrote an article criticizing Hubie's 10-player rotation system. Hubie was the first coach in professional basketball to initiate a rotation system so that every player on a 10-man roster would get playing time. The system was set-up with the players so that they could get off the bench and check themselves into the game. Roberts and Bradley would replace Issel and Jones as the forwards. Averitt and Littles would replace Dampier and McClain, and at the two minute mark of every quarter, except the third, Thomas would replace Gilmore. The rotations were set-up on different times so that two of the three, Issel, Gilmore or Dampier, were always on the floor together. Playing time could be altered if a player got into foul trouble, was out because of injury, or was having an exceptional game. Hubie was the master motivator. His philosophy was very clear to everyone, "No one is bigger than the team. You're going to be on time; you're going to play

---

FINAL PLAYOFF SERIES, 1975

Championship Game No. 1

May 13, at Freedom Hall, Louisville

INDIANA (94)

PLAYER	Pos.	Min.	2-Pt. FG-FGA	3-Pt. FG-FGA	FT-FTA	Rebounds O- D- T	A	E	PF	TP
Knight, Billy	F	45	7-18	0-0	4-4	2- 6- 8	3	2	2	18
McGinnis, George	F	41	12-21	1-4	8-12	5- 7-12	9	7	5	35
Hillman, Darnell	C	26	2-8	0-0	2-6	6- 5-11	0	1	5	6
Buse, Don	G	22	0-0	0-1	0-0	0- 2- 2	3	1	0	0
Joyce, Kevin	G	40	6-19	1-0	5-6	0- 3- 3	3	4	3	20
Keller, Billy	G	34	2-8	1-2	0-0	0- 1- 1	2	0	2	7
Edge, Charlie	F	3	1-2	0-0	0-0	1- 0- 1	0	2	2	2
Elmore, Len	C	29	1-6	0-0	4-4	1- 7- 8	0	3	3	6
TOTALS		240	31-81	3-8	23-32	15-31-46	20	20	22	94

KENTUCKY (120)

PLAYER	Pos.	Min.	2-Pt. FG-FGA	3-Pt. FG-FGA	FT-FTA	Rebounds O- D- T	A	E	PF	TP
Jones, Wilbert	F	21	3-4	0-0	0-0	1- 2- 3	6	0	5	6
Issel, Dan	F	44	6-18	0-0	6-6	7-12-19	4	3	2	18
Gilmore, Artis	C	36	11-19	0-0	4-7	3-10-13	0	4	6	26
Dampier, Louie	G	39	10-17	0-0	2-2	1- 1- 2	6	4	1	22
McClain, Ted	G	30	2-9	0-0	0-0	1- 3- 4	6	3	6	4
Averitt, Bird	G	24	6-16	1-1	0-0	0- 2- 2	1	0	4	15
Littles, Gene	G	3	0-2	0-0	0-0	1- 0- 1	0	0	0	0
Roberts, Marv	F	25	6-10	0-0	7-7	4- 3- 7	4	2	4	19
Thomas, Ron	F	18	3-6	0-0	4-5	5- 4- 9	3	0	2	10
TOTALS		240	47-101	1-1	23-27	23-37-60	29	13	30	120

Blocked shots—Hillman 2, Elmore 5, Jones, Gilmore, McClain 2, Dampier, Issel.

Steals—Knight, Joyce, Jones, Issel 2, Gilmore 2, Dampier, McClain, Thomas 2.

Indiana	21	24	28	21	— 94
Kentucky	27	29	27	37	—120

Referees—Madden and Vanak.

Attendance—14,368.

281

hard; you're going to know your job; and you're going to know when to pass and shoot. If you can't do those four things you're not getting time here and we don't care who you are."

After the game, O'Brien was interviewing Dan. Dressed in his New York lawyer three piece suit, O'Brien was in the hallway just outside the Colonels locker room. Issel, standing with a towel draped around his neck and one foot on a chair, shared his excitement with O'Brien. In came a woman with a briefcase. She walked down the hallway, "click," "click," she opened the attaché case and took out a banana cream pie, one that had been secured from the freezer early that morning. It was mushy, topped with whipped cream and bananas that had turned brown. The plan was working to perfection. She walked over, didn't say a word, and "Bam," right in O'Brien's face. Without a word she turned and left the facilities. As the pie dripped from O'Brien's face and mustache, he was blinded momentarily. He would later say, "I'll never forget that Issel offered me a towel and apologized for the incident."

It was several years later that O'Brien learned that it was Claire Brown, Hubie's wife. She had gotten her revenge for criticizing

FINAL PLAYOFF SERIES, 1975

Championship Game No. 2

May 15, at Freedom Hall, Louisville

INDIANA (93) PLAYER	Pos.	Min.	2-Pt. FG-FGA	3-Pt. FG-FGA	FT-FTA	Rebounds O-D-T	A	E	PF	TP
Knight, Billy	F	27	5-12	0-1	2-2	1- 2- 3	1	1	4	12
McGinnis, George	F	32	9-17	1-2	9-11	3-13-16	5	5	4	30
Hillman, Darnell	C	32	4-11	0-0	0-0	1- 7- 8	0	3	4	8
Buse, Don	G	39	3-4	0-1	1-2	0- 1- 1	2	0	2	7
Joyce, Kevin	G	41	7-12	0-0	2-2	0- 5- 5	7	0	2	7
Brown, Roger	F	18	5-7	0-0	2-2	0- 1- 1	2	4	4	16
Keller, Billy	G	16	1-2	0-3	0-0	1- 0- 1	2	0	1	2
Elmore, Len	C	25	2-7	0-0	2-2	1- 2- 3	0	1	1	6
TOTALS		240	36-72	1-7	18-21	7-34-41	19	15	21	93

KENTUCKY (95) PLAYER	Pos.	Min.	2-Pt. FG-FGA	3-Pt. FG-FGA	FT-FTA	Rebounds O-D-T	A	E	PF	TP
Jones, Wilbert	F	22	4-8	0-0	1-2	2- 2- 4	4	2	2	9
Issel, Dan	F	42	10-19	0-0	2-3	2- 6- 8	3	3	6	22
Gilmore, Artis	C	47	5-11	0-0	2-2	3-12-15	3	2	6	12
Dampier, Louie	G	43	4-14	0-0	7-9	0- 4- 4	4	1	1	15
McClain, Ted	G	37	4-7	0-0	2-2	0- 6- 6	3	3	4	10
Averitt, Bird	G	16	2-11	0-0	2-2	1- 3- 4	1	2	0	6
Roberts, Marv	F	24	6-10	0-0	4-4	2- 2- 4	4	0	4	16
Thomas, Ron	F	9	2-3	0-0	1-3	3- 1- 4	1	1	1	5
TOTALS		240	37-83	0-0	21-27	13-36-49	23	14	24	95

Blocked shots—Hillmas, Elmore, Jones.
Steals—Knight, McGinnis 3, Buse 3, Brown 2, McClain 2, Jones, Issel, Roberts.

Indiana	19	31	18	25	— 93
Kentucky	27	18	26	24	— 95

Referees—Drucker and Rush.
Attendance—13,212.

FINAL PLAYOFF SERIES, 1975

Championship Game No. 3

May 17, at Market Square, Indianapolis

KENTUCKY (109) PLAYER	Pos.	Min.	2-Pt. FG-FGA	3-Pt. FG-FGA	FT-FTA	Rebounds O-D-T	A	E	PF	TP
Jones, Wilbert	F	17	0-2	0-0	0-0	1- 1- 2	3	2	4	0
Issel, Dan	F	43	9-18	0-0	8-10	7- 5-12	4	0	5	26
Gilmore, Artis	C	47	17-28	0-0	7-8	11-17-28	1	6	4	41
Dampier, Louie	G	41	6-10	0-3	0-1	0- 1- 1	3	2	1	13
McClain, Ted	G	37	3-10	0-0	4-4	0- 4- 4	7	4	2	10
Averitt, Bird	G	18	3-11	0-1	0-0	0- 0- 0	4	2	1	6
Roberts, Marv	F	31	6-14	0-0	1-1	4- 2- 6	5	0	4	13
Thomas, Ron	C-F	6	0-0	0-0	0-0	0- 1- 1	0	1	1	0
TOTALS		240	44-93	0-4	21-24	23-31-54	27	17	22	109

INDIANA (101) PLAYER	Pos.	Min.	2-Pt. FG-FGA	3-Pt. FG-FGA	FT-FTA	Rebounds O-D-T	A	E	PF	TP
Knight, Billy	F	44	13-15	0-0	2-3	3- 9-12	5	3	2	28
McGinnis, George	F	26	7-11	0-5	5-7	4- 6-10	3	6	6	19
Hillman, Darnell	C	34	7-12	0-0	4-6	4- 4- 8	2	2	5	18
Buse, Don	G	37	3-10	1-1	0-0	2- 0- 2	5	1	1	9
Joyce, Kevin	G	35	5-9	0-0	2-2	0- 2- 2	2	1	4	12
Brown, Roger	F	9	0-2	0-0	2-2	1- 0- 1	2	1	3	2
Keller, Bill	G	24	2-6	0-5	0-0	0- 0- 0	1	3	0	4
Elmore, Len	G	31	4-9	0-0	1-1	1- 7- 8	4	2	4	9
TOTALS		240	41-71	1-11	16-21	15-28-43	26	18	25	101

Blocked shots—Gilmore, McGinnis, Hillman, Elmore, Joyce.
Steals—Jones, McClain 4, Issel, Dampier, Joyce, Hillman, Buse 2, Brown.

Kentucky	31	25	17	36	—109
Indiana	30	21	30	20	—101

Referees—John Vanak and Ed Middleton.
Technical foul—Kentucky, bench.
Attendance—17,388.

Championship Game No. 4

May 19, at Market Square, Indianapolis

KENTUCKY (86)

PLAYER	Pos.	Min.	2-Pt. FG-FGA	3-Pt. FG-FGA	FT-FTA	Rebounds O-D-T	A	E	PF	TP
Jones, Wilbert	F	23	2-5	0-1	0-0	2- 4- 6	2	2	5	4
Issel, Dan	F	41	10-22	0-0	6-7	3- 6- 9	1	4	5	26
Gilmore, Artis	C	46	4-15	0-0	10-13	4-14-18	2	4	2	18
Dampier, Louie	G	42	2-11	1-2	1-1	1- 3- 4	6	2	5	8
McClain, Ted	G	37	5-9	0-2	2-2	1- 4- 5	2	5	4	12
Averitt, Bird	G	17	1-5	0-0	2-2	1- 2- 3	2	1	2	4
Roberts, Marv	F	25	6-16	0-0	2-2	4- 2- 6	2	4	0	14
Thomas, Ron	F	9	0-0	0-0	0-0	0- 0- 0	1	1	0	0
TOTALS		240	30-83	1-5	23-27	16-35-51	18	23	23	86

INDIANA (94)

PLAYER	Pos.	Min.	2-Pt. FG-FGA	3-Pt. FG-FGA	FT-FTA	Rebounds O-D-T	A	E	PF	TP
Hillman, Darnell	F-C	28	6-14	0-0	2-2	4-14-18	0	1	5	14
Knight, Billy	F	45	5-14	0-0	6-6	3- 6- 9	4	3	3	16
Elmore, Len	C	29	5-8	0-0	0-0	0- 1- 1	0	2	3	10
Keller, Bill	G	40	7-17	1-3	3-3	1- 3- 4	2	4	1	20
Joyce, Kevin	G	32	3-8	0-1	4-4	0- 2- 2	2	5	2	10
Buse, Don	G	24	1-3	0-2	0-0	3- 2- 5	2	1	2	2
McGinnis, George	F	42	9-20	0-3	4-6	5-16-21	6	5	4	22
TOTALS		240	36-84	1-9	19-21	17-43-60	15	18	23	94

Blocked shots—McClain 2, Issel 2, Jones, Gilmore, Hillman 3, Elmore 3, McGinnis, Joyce 2.

Steals—Issel, Jones, McClain 2, Thomas, Dampier, Knight, Elmore 4, McGinnis 2, Buse 2, Joyce.

Kentucky	18	26	25	17 — 86
Indiana	19	22	26	27 — 94

Referees—Norm Drucker and Ed Rush.

Technical Fouls—Indiana, Leonard, Kentucky, Brown.

Attendance—14589.

Championship Game No. 5

May 22, at Freedom Hall, Louisville

INDIANA (105)

PLAYER	Pos.	Min.	2-Pt. FG-FGA	3-Pt. FG-FGA	FT-FTA	Rebounds O-D-T	A	E	PF	TP
Hillman, Darnell	F	33	0-4	0-0	2-3	0-10-10	1	2	3	2
McGinnis, George	F	43	7-15	3-5	8-11	1-10-11	9	6	5	31
Elmore, Len	C	44	4-13	0-0	2-3	5- 6-11	1	1	5	10
Knight, Billy	G	47	18-29	0-0	4-5	4- 4- 8	4	3	1	40
Joyce, Kevin	G	39	6-13	1-1	1-2	0- 0- 0	2	2	2	16
Brown, Roger	F	6	1-1	0-0	0-0	0- 0- 0	0	1	1	2
Buse, Don	G	9	0-0	0-0	0-0	1- 2- 3	0	0	0	0
Keller, Billy	G	17	0-2	0-4	4-4	0- 1- 1	2	2	2	4
Edge, Charlie	F	2	0-0	0-0	0-0	0- 0- 0	0	0	0	0
TOTALS		240	36-77	4-10	21-28	11-33-44	19	17	19	105

KENTUCKY (110)

PLAYER	Pos.	Min.	2-Pt. FG-FGA	3-Pt. FG-FGA	FT-FTA	Rebounds O-D-T	A	E	PF	TP
Jones, Wilbert	F	24	4-16	0-0	2-2	4- 2- 6	3	2	3	10
Issel, Dan	F	44	7-15	0-0	2-2	4- 8-12	2	2	4	16
Gilmore, Artis	C	47	11-20	0-0	6-8	8-23-31	5	1	5	28
Dampier, Louie	G	40	6-8	0-1	0-0	0- 1— 1	12	3	4	12
McClain, Ted	G	39	8-21	0-0	3-3	4- 2- 6	7	3	5	19
Averitt, Bird	G	17	5-12	0-0	1-2	2- 1- 3	2	0	2	11
Roberts, Marv	F	24	7-11	0-0	0-2	1- 1- 2	0	1	0	14
Thomas, Ron	F	5	0-1	0-0	0-0	0- 0- 0	0	0	2	0
TOTALS		240	48-104	0-1	14-19	23-38-61	31	12	25	110

Blocked shots—Elmore, Hillman 2, Joyce, Buse, Issel, Gilmore 3, Dampier.
Steals—McGinnis, Knight 2, Elmore, Issel, Gilmore, Dampier, McClain 6, Roberts, Jones.

Indiana	29	19	28	29 —105
Kentucky	29	25	26	30 —110

Referees—Madden and Vanak.

Attendance—16,622.

our coach in his national publication.

After we went through 35 bottles of champagne, we all proceeded to Harry Jones' house in Hurstbourne Estates. The party lasted until the wee hours of the morning. I had never been drunk, or even close to drunk in my life – well, I won the prize for being the drunkest. I was filling my glass ¾ with vodka and ¼ with orange juice, a potentiate screwdriver. As the party ended, I was lying on the floor with all the partier's kids yelling, "Pinky, get up."

My wife, Sandy, drove the Kentucky Colonels van home while I rode in the passenger seat with a five gallon bucket in my hand. I'm not proud of this, and I have never had a drop of vodka again to this day. I am thankful that I don't have a taste for alcohol or beer.

With everyone wanting to go back to their home towns after a long season, I started planning this the next day. The team and our wives, or significant other, left one week later for our trip to Las Vegas. John Y. told me to give every team member $200.

Upon arriving at the Vegas airport, we were met by Jimmy "The Greek." When we arrived at Caesars Palace, we were greeted by one of the hotel managers, Dan Chandler, the son of

1974-75

former Governor and Baseball Commissioner Happy Chandler, former heavy weight boxing champion Joe Louis, and former major league infielder and Cleveland Indians manager Ken Aspromonte. Before we checked into our rooms, we took a team picture in front of the hotel marquee which said, "Welcome to the 1975 ABA World Champion Kentucky Colonels."

The hotel had made reservations for all of us to see Tom Jones. Another highlight of the week was the marriage of Ron Thomas and Sharman Pride. Artis was Ron's best man. We all attended the wedding in a small chapel, so small that Artis' afro touched the rafters. After the ceremony, Joe Louis hosted a reception in the penthouse atop Caesars.

After a week of golf, gambling and several late night shows the team returned home. I stayed two extra days before I flew to Los Angeles for the National Athletic Trainers Association meeting. Jimmy "The Greek" offered to give me a car for my extended stay. I was sure he would let me have a Corvette or some awesome sports car. He told me that he would leave the keys at the front desk at Caesars Palace and that I could identify the car by the license plate "GREEK5." Well, I found the vehicle exactly where he said it would be. WOW!!! It was a 1966, dirty, beat-up Oldsmobile.

When we got our playoff checks from John Y., the $200 was deducted that he had given each of us for the Las Vegas trip.

In that very first year, the fine pool was $8,250. Jim Bradley alone paid $7,550.

After winning the championship, the players met and divided the money. They gave: $2,000 to the Crusade for Children, bought the three secretaries a pendant duplicating our championship ring, gave our two Olliebird pilots, Charlie Clay and Ron Gehring, and golf bags with sets of Titleist golf clubs. The rest of the money was spent on a team party for the players, coaches and trainer ONLY. The banquet was held at the Normandy Inn. Our favors were 19" color TVs and, remember, this was 1975. Oh, by the way, Bradley was a no show; he missed his own party.

American Basketball Association commissioner Dave DeBusschere issued a challenge to the National Basketball Association champion Golden State Warriors for a $1 million, winner take-all world championship series with the Kentucky Colonels. The telegram was sent to Warriors President Frank Mieuli, NBA Commissioner Walter Kennedy, and Commissioner-elect Larry O'Brien.

The telegram dated May 26, 1975 stated: "Congratulations to you and the NBA champion Golden State Warriors. On behalf of the ABA champion Kentucky Colonels and the ABA league we would like to challenge the Warriors to a $1 million, winner-take-all series for the world championship. The television networks would like to put on the world championship between the two leagues. A three-to-five game series would provide up to an additional $1 million in revenue for the teams, the league and the players. I'm sure you'll agree that this series will be good for the sport, the owners, the players, but more importantly, for the fans. Baseball has a World Series, and football has a Super Bowl between the leagues. Professional basketball should have some method to determine the true world champion. We stand ready to prove who has the best team in professional basketball."

It was issued by the American Basketball Association and signed by Commissioner Dave DeBusschere.

On May 27, 1975, the NBA rejected the ABA challenge in a response that was rather monotonous. Walter Kennedy, the outgoing commissioner of the National Basketball Association had this response to the telegram sent by DeBusschere. "The NBA, as usual with these annual challenges, rejects the 1975 proposal, period."

John Y. also let Kennedy know that if the Warriors didn't agree to a playoff game, the Colonels were going to put "World Champions" on their rings. That's exactly what we did.

The total playoff pool was $95,000 divided into 13 equal shares = $7,307.69 per share. $200 had been deducted for our per diem to Las Vegas.

Hubie, Stan and I met in a coffee shop at the Executive Inn and drew out on a napkin what we wanted put on our championship ring. David Vance and Ellie were very much involved, but not until after we had put our thoughts down on paper.

One side would be easy. The player's name at the top. The Colonels logo in the middle and the player's number at the bottom. If you were not a player, your title would be in place of a number (Trainer, GM, Coach, etc.)

The other side is what the three of us came up with. At the top is the scoreboard at Freedom Hall with the final score 110-105. Under that is a scrolling ribbon with: Season 59-26, Playoffs 12-3, Pressure 22-3 (Down the stretch every game a pressure game).

The top of the ring is in the shape of Freedom Hall. On the inside it reads WORLD CHAMPIONS. On the outer ring is, KENTUCKY COLONELS; on one side of the top it reads 19 and on the other side, 75.

Chapter Fifteen
A Rude Awakening

Jim McDaniels

Jim McDaniels was one of the biggest names the ABA had ever landed. His signing with the Carolina Cougars served notice to the NBA they couldn't get 'em all.

After three All-American seasons at Western Kentucky, a 1971 Final Four, and standing 7' tall with a deft scoring touch, and always underappreciated rebounding skills, whoever signed him would surely capture one of the big ones.

Almost instantly McDaniels was a star in the ABA, a force to be reckoned with. His average of 27 points and 14 rebounds for Carolina were stats that made everyone take notice, even the NBA.

He was named to the ABA East All-Stars his rookie year in a game that would be played back in his home state at Freedom Hall in Louisville.

He loved Freedom Hall. He had played there several times during his high school and college careers and couldn't wait to return.

"I can't tell you how much I enjoyed playing there," he said. "It was just a shooter's place. I've played in them all, the Forum, Madison Square Garden, you name it, but Freedom Hall is special. It was very friendly to my jump shot."

For McDaniels it was much more than just words; he had the walk and facts to prove it.

As a high schooler at Allen County in Scottsville, Kentucky, he first played in Freedom Hall during the Louisville Invitational Tournament, and then in the 1967 state tournament. His 42 points that summer in the Kentucky-Indiana All-Star game in Freedom Hall still stands as Kentucky's all-time record. McDaniels also played there in the Kentucky-Tennessee All-Star game, and his 27 points and 18 rebounds earned him MVP honors.

One of the greatest college games ever played in Freedom Hall was December 23, 1970, when Big Mac and his Hilltoppers took the court against Artis Gilmore and his Jacksonville Dolphins.

"I remember looking down at their end of the floor during warm-ups and thinking Artis looked like a Goliath out there," laughed McDaniels. "Here we were in Freedom Hall, two top-10 teams. They were national runner-ups the year before. It was unbelievable.

"I could have shot it from the Ohio River that night and it would have gone in," he continued. "I was in a zone. I loved playing in that place."

Big Mac had good reason to like playing there. He lit up Jacksonville for 46 points and 11 rebounds. He made 20 of 29 shots from all over the floor, inside and outside. They were falling as he recorded a game for the Freedom Hall ages.

And for the record, Gilmore didn't exactly have an off night, compiling 29 points and 18 rebounds.

That same season Western again defeated Jacksonville, this time in an NCAA first-round game, before the Hilltoppers advanced to the Final Four.

But it was the ABA All-Star game in Freedom Hall that McDaniels, playing for the Carolina Cougars, includes among his best ever games.

"I was on a team with Dr. J, Artis, Rick Barry, Dan Issel and Charlie Scott," he says. "I scored 24 points."

Lloyd Gardner remembers it well. "Mac put on a show in the fourth quarter," he says. "He scored 18 of his points in that period."

Although lots of time has passed since that game was played, McDaniels recalls a little controversy over the MVP record.

"I remember them voting three times on it before John Y. gave them the okay," he laughed. "Finally Dan (Issel) got it. There were some boos, not against Dan, but because there were a lot of fans there that thought I should have won it."

Not too many years ago, McDaniels was doing a sports show in Bowling Green and had Issel as his guest. Just before they signed off, Issel told McDaniels, "By the way, I have your trophy any time you want it." "That really felt good to me for him to say that," he added.

McDaniel's odyssey with the ABA had actually begun a couple of years earlier.

In the summer of 1970, between his junior and senior years at Western Kentucky University, McDaniels was selected to play on a college all-star team that traveled throughout Europe. When he returned, his life was about to take a turn that growing up in Scottsville had not prepared him for.

He was on everybody's pre-season All-American team, and his Western Kentucky team was considered one of the best. With his game at the level it was, he was in the perfect position to capitalize on the bidding war going on between the ABA and NBA. That is, if an ABA was still around by the time he finished playing in March of 1971.

Lots of players stood to lose millions if the merger happened. The winner would be the owners and fans.

McDaniels, by his own admission, was about as naïve as any poor black kid from Scottsville, Kentucky could be about the ways of the world. Oh sure, there were the hangers on. They had been there since high school. He had his pick of colleges, even to the pretty-much all-white University of Kentucky team. Instead, he decided to play at Western Kentucky, a school in Bowling Green only 23 miles from his home.

In college there were even more people willing to help Big Mac, most just being friendly, just letting him know how great a basketball player he was. Sure there were the occasional meals for him and his wife, and even a $5 or $10 bill every now and then, but nothing that hasn't happened at any school in America.

Everything seemed above board, even when another student, a young girl from New York, approached him on campus, complimenting him on his game. That was nothing new for McDaniels; he heard it everywhere he went.

But one day that same friendly girl walked up to him, and in an odd sort of way said to him "Oh, by the way, I have a friend back home who says if you ever need someone to represent you later on, he would like to do it."

She gave McDaniels a card with the name of the friend on it.

He thought little more about it until a couple of weeks later in late September when she sought out Jim and informed him that her friend was going to be in Bowling Green and would like to meet him.

Big Mac's life was about to change forever.

McDaniel's fellow-student's friend turned out to be Norman Blass, a New York sports agent, and good friend of Carl Scheer, general manager of the ABA's Carolina Cougars.

The Western Kentucky All-American was asked to bring four of his teammates to the young lady's off-campus apartment on State Street for a meeting with Blass.

"It was on an afternoon. I rode down there with a couple of the guys and we met the other two there," McDaniels said. "We all gathered in a small living room, and this guy said he wants to talk to us individually.

One by one we went into another room to talk to him," McDaniels said. "It was just one-on-one, and I was the first. I came out and waited for all of the others to have their turn. When we left, none of us said a word about what we had talked about. I'm not sure what they were told or did, but I have my thoughts and opinions.

McDaniels heard from Blass again in November, this time telling him he wanted to talk further, and that he would be bringing two others with him to Bowling Green. When he showed up at his small one bedroom shanty-style house near the south part of campus, in what was known as Vet Village, Blass had Carolina Cougar general manager Carl Scheer, and team owner Tedd Munchak with him.

What Norman Blass showed him and told him that day would be difficult for anyone, 22-year-old or not, to mentally sift through.

Making sure that McDaniels knew all of the talk of an ABA merger that would be happening any day, Blass spread out 15 ABA contracts that current college players, like him, had signed.

"I saw their names, everybody knew them," said McDaniels. "He said it plain and simple, if I didn't sign with him I'd be left out and all of the money would be gone."

McDaniel's mind was racing. After all, he was just a guy looking out for his best interest. It wasn't like he was actually signing with a team. This would just be security, in case the two leagues merged before he finished playing at Western Kentucky. What would be the harm, he thought. After all, this guy Blass would be dealing with the teams, not him.

His thoughts quickly flashed to his mother working two jobs, and his grandmother watching the kids in Scottsville. Even though there was always food on the table growing up, his refrigerator was often empty.

When I first started playing in high school, our family didn't even have a radio. So, when we played a game on the road, they didn't know if we'd won or lost until I came home," says McDaniels. "But at the home games, Coach (Jim) Bazzell made sure they got in the games."

He thought about his wife. The two had married during their sophomore year of college, and jumping on this ship before it sailed would surely give them financial security for life.

McDaniels wished he had someone he could talk to about this. But who would it be? Even though he had tried to quickly process it all, his mind was a blur. There was still enough of a grey area for him to think maybe, just maybe, this was not right, and that somehow there may be rules against this sort of thing.

He concluded that he couldn't talk to the two most trusted people in his life, his high school coach at Allen County, and his current coach at Western, John Oldham. They could not find out.

For an instant he started to leave the room where Blass stood. Perhaps the merger wouldn't happen. But that's when Blass played the trump card, and it was a winner.

"He pulled out a nice black leather brief case and put it on the table with a contract," recalled McDaniels. "He opened it and it was stuffed full of money. It was $5's, $10s and $20s. He said there was $25,000. I tried to count it, but it was so overwhelming I had to stop."

All Jim had to do was sign the contract on the table in front of him, and his life, and that of his family, would be financially secure for a very long time to come.

Keep in mind that in 1970, a nice home could be purchased for $23,000, and a new car for $3,900. The $25,000 was not chump change.

He signed the contract and closed the briefcase.

"I took the money and hid it under the bed," he remembers. "I got it out once and started to count it. I got through several thousand dollars and said, 'what the heck.' I trusted that the $25,000 was there like he said. I still couldn't believe it. I had never seen that much money. Whenever I needed cash, I'd just pull the briefcase out and stuff a few bills in my pocket."

According to McDaniels, he never splurged or went wild with any of the money he received over his professional career. And even though the All-American basketball player, at that time, had never come close to being around, much less having, that kind of money, he carefully guarded it.

No one at Western needed to know about the money. He and his wife never told anyone else. It was their secret.

"The only thing I bought was a car. I went down to talk to Norman Burks at his Pontiac dealership," says McDaniels. "I could have paid cash, but instead I signed papers that I would pay them at the end of the season when I signed a pro contract. He knew I was good for it. I had been poor, and I didn't want to throw any of my money away. Besides that, I didn't want it to look like I had money."

McDaniels had arrived in a white 1966 Caprice and departed in a new brown 1971 Pontiac Gran Prix with a black top.

Years later, McDaniels says he sold his soul to the devil, but didn't realize it then.

When news reached McDaniels about the potential of an NCAA investigation, at first he didn't give it much thought.

"I had so much going on in my life that I didn't think much about it," he recalls. "The reality and implications of it all, I just didn't understand at the time."

But it all became real when the NCAA forced Western to vacate its third-place finish and return its share of the 1971 NCAA gate.

Two years later when Western's basketball team was put on probation, it had nothing to do with Jim McDaniels, as some thought. Instead, it was for violations after McDaniels had graduated and nothing to do with his signing a professional contract early. Back then, the assistant director of the NCAA, Warren Brown, said "it had nothing to do with McDaniels."

"I never intended to ever, and I mean ever, do anything that would harm or embarrass Western," said an emotional McDaniels. "I brought my A-game every night in representing my university."

That was his first experience with a sports agent and McDaniels says that guys back then were nothing more than predators.

As predicted, Big Mac had a fabulous senior year. Leading his team past Jacksonville, Kentucky, and Ohio State, and before you could say Western Kentucky Hilltoppers, they had won the Mideast Regionals and were headed to Houston for the school's first and only men's Final Four.

A double overtime loss to Villanova and a consolation win over Kansas earned Western the third place trophy, a reported $66,000, and a place in basketball record books for all time.

That was about to change, too.

At the ABA all-star game in Greensboro, North Carolina, in January of 1971, the league's commissioner Jack Dolph, for whatever reason, left his briefcase in a room in the Coliseum. It was a room media types were in and out of, and one of the reporters found signed ABA contracts with the names of two of the NCAA's biggest stars, McDaniels and Howard Porter. Opinions differed as to whether Dolph wanted them found or not. Some said the briefcase was open, while others said it was pried open.

Big Mac's contract with the Cougars was negotiated by Norman Blass, and it was a six-year agreement for $1.4 million, payable over 25 years.

"I was the one who wanted the longer terms," he said. "I came from being poor and I wanted the security of never being poor again."

But as McDaniel's ABA stock was rising, so was interest from the NBA.

Soon after the All-Star game at Freedom Hall he received a call from Al Ross, a Los Angeles attorney with close ties to the Seattle Supersonics. Ross wanted to meet with McDaniels. He even put the current Seattle player Spencer Haywood on the phone in an attempt to convince McDaniels that Ross was okay.

It worked. Soon after, Ross flew to Greensboro, North Carolina to meet the Carolina star.

"I picked him up at the airport. We got something to eat and went to my house," recalls McDaniels. "I let him look over my contract and of course he found things, things he said I should have gotten.

"He said I should have gotten another $500,000 and my contract was stretched out way to long. He really got into my head. I know I was young, but he really got me confused.

"People get in your lives that shouldn't be there," he continued. "When I was at Western, I was around good people. They were people that cared about me. I found out real quick that in the real world it wasn't like that."

On February 29, 1972, a little more than two weeks after the ABA All-Star game, McDaniels was a Seattle Supersonic. He had played 58 games with the Carolina Cougars.

AMERICAN BASKETBALL ASSOCIATION
UNIFORM PLAYER CONTRACT

AGREEMENT made this __16__ day of ___December___ 19__70__

AMERICAN BASKETBALL ASSOCIATION

between _____
called the "CLUB"), _____

_____ and ___HOWARD PORTER___ of the City of _____
(hereinafter called the "PLAYER").

IT IS AGREED AS FOLLOWS:

1. Employment and Term Thereof. The CLUB hereby employs the PLAYER as a skilled Basketball Player for the term of _____ years from the first (1st) day of October, 19_____, subject, however, to termination, renewal or renewal as specified herein. The PLAYER'S employment shall include attendance at training camp.

Howard Porter's Name Appears on Copy of ABA Contract

EXAMINE THIS CONTRACT CAREFULLY BEFORE SIGNING IT.

IN WITNESS WHEREOF the PLAYER has hereunto set his hand and the CLUB has caused this contract to be executed by its duly authorized officer.

WITNESSES:

AMERICAN BASKETBALL ASSOCIATION
CLUB

By _____ Commissioner

___HOWARD PORTER___ Player

Player's Address ___1500 29th Street___

___Sarasota Florida___

Signature of Porter and other participants affixed to contract

I hereby acknowledge that the payment of the bonus of $15,000.00 provided for pursuant to the contract between me and the American Basketball Association dated December 1, 1970, has been paid to me by the American Basketball Associ...

___HOWARD PORTER___

Witness:

Copy of acknowledgment by Porter that he received bonus

Ross had put together a deal for McDaniels that was for six years and worth $2 million.

Looking back on it, he says he should have stayed with the Cougars at least to the end of the year.

"I was treated well there," he offers. "But no one knows the pressure those agents put on you back then. It was bad. I know I did it and blame myself, but what was going on with players and agents was a shame.

"I went from bad to worse with agents," said McDaniels. "Ross was representing Haywood, Elmore Smith and John Brisker when I first went to Seattle. He was supposed to be taking care of my money I was making, all of this money, taking just $500 a week for pocket money. I was investing my money and putting it away, at least I thought. He was supposed to be paying all my bills, and I was supposed to be playing basketball."

McDaniels thought that he owned a shopping center in Killeen, Texas, and a Holiday Inn, but he soon found out he didn't, or at least any that were making money. A law suit several years later allowed him to recoup $35,000 of a $140,000 deal Ross had put together.

"All we heard about was the great tax write-offs we got, but that was all," he says. "And then we found out Ross had frozen our investments. We sued. I didn't have any cash. He had it all, using our money to get rich. You know it's hard to eat a tax write-off."

But still Ross, who had been given the nickname "The Pirate" from other agents, remained the agent of record for McDaniels.

"I felt trapped by him; I was so confused I didn't know where to turn," he said. "There were bad people all around me. I was not focused on basketball at all. He was taking away from what I should be doing."

Decades later McDaniels has had time to look back and think long and hard about how his game went down the tubes in such a short time.

"I was a hell of a player. I could do it all," he says. "I really felt like I was on track to be one of the best players ever, even in the NBA. But my game went south."

When McDaniels arrived in Seattle, Lenny Wilkens was the coach for his last 12 games of the season. McDaniels liked Wilkins and had high hopes of elevating the gaudy scoring and rebounding numbers he had brought with him from Carolina.

He hoped the next year would be a fresh start for him.

The following year Bill Russell was named coach of the Supersonics. Anyone who can spell basketball knows that Russell is often mentioned as one of the five best players to ever play the game. He had seen and done it all on the hardwood. He knew the game from every angle, as player, coach, and even as a broadcaster. Plus, he was a big man, had been an inside player, and McDaniels could only guess how much he was going to develop under a man like Russell.

From the beginning with Russell, McDaniels felt like he never had a chance. All of the off-court financial problems with his agent, and now here was one of the greatest names in basketball, who McDaniels says was an idiot as a coach.

"He completely demoralized me," he says. "He took any confidence I ever had away and totally destroyed my game.

"I know everything they said about Russell, but in my opinion he was not a very nice person. I know he was a great player, but I think it should be more than that," he stated. "I remember after one of our games, a little boy came up to him in a wheelchair. He was a paraplegic and had to talk through one of those tubes. He asked Russell for his autograph and none of us could believe it when he told the little boy he didn't sign autographs, and quickly turned his back on him. This is the kind of man Bill Russell was."

Perhaps McDaniels should have known about Russell. Years before, while just an eighth grader in Scottsville, he had his first encounter with the basketball legend.

"The Boston Celtics were playing the Atlanta Hawks in an exhibition game in Diddle Arena," he says. "A bunch of us piled in a car and went. After the game, I couldn't wait to get his autograph. I went up to him and asked him for it and he said, 'no,' and turned and walked away. I was devastated. Then I saw him do it again in Seattle."

There was a short period of time that Big Mac thought he had his game back. But only for a short time.

"We were playing the Bucks," he said. "I go out there and had a 29 point, 18 rebound game against Jabbar. I felt I was back. The next night Russell didn't even start me. It was Jim Fox instead. Russell was playing mind games with me."

What did McDaniel say to Russell about it all?

"I didn't say anything," he recalled. "No one could talk to him; he was so arrogant. In any normal situation Fox would have been my back-up, but there was nothing normal about Russell. I was the kind of guy who needed to be in the starting five in order to be the player I know I was."

Through it all McDaniels continued to struggle emotionally, he says, not knowing who his friends were.

McDaniel's stint with Seattle also included another off-court situation that involved some of his teammates experimenting with the black Muslim sect.

"I roomed for a while with Walt Hazzard who went through it," McDaniels says. "He changed his name to Mahdi Abdul-Rahman, but later changed it back to his given name. John Brisker, Bud Stalworth, and Spencer Haywood experimented a little with it. It was just another distraction I had to put up with, and mentally I was a mess, there's no better way to describe it."

McDaniels says Ross was still pulling his chain.

"He convinced me to sign off on a no-guarantee contract with Seattle, and two weeks later they cut me."

It was the fall of 1974, and even though the Supersonics paid him $100,000 in January, he was for all practical purposes out of basketball. He had averaged 5.5 points a game at Seattle.

Ross wanted McDaniels to go to Italy to play, but instead he headed down to Louisville and met with John Y. and Ellie Brown, owners of the ABA Kentucky Colonels.

"We met at the Executive Inn," he said. "Ross was on the phone and all of us talked. Seattle still owed me a lot of money and we were trying to get it worked out as to who was going to actually pay me. We just couldn't get it done. I remember Ellie crying."

McDaniels spent a year playing in Italy, getting most of his money up front. By this time his mother had moved from Scottsville to Indianapolis to be closer to her sister. He bought her a home there.

McDaniels says he could not believe he was still dealing with his agent, Al Ross.

"I gave him $40,000 to make sure my mother's house was paid off and that she had some money," he says. "I was in Italy, where I had been one of the top players in the league. It was like a fresh start for me. Then I find out that he had not paid my mother's house off. When I got back to the states I met with him. I backed him in the corner, ready to bust his ass. It finally took this with my mother to get rid of Ross. I don't know what I was thinking. I went from being one of the top players in basketball to the bottom."

McDaniels returned to Los Angeles and soon talked to Laker coach Bill Sharman.

"I tried out and made the team" he said. "They cut Happy Harriston and kept me to be Kareem's back-up. It was going good and then I got sick and missed practice without calling the coach, and they cut me. I should have called, but didn't have the number. I actually read about it in next morning's paper before practice that I had been cut."

McDaniels says that he did a good job through it all of hiding his emotions to everyone else. Everyone except his mother.

"My mother knew my pain; she was the only one who could tell," he said. "She called me Jimmy and would say, 'Jimmy I know something's wrong. What is it?'"

"I had no one else to turn to but Christ," he said with tears in his eyes. I was at my end and I came to Christ the hard way."

With that said, he quotes a biblical verse: "What does it profit a man to gain the whole world yet lose his soul?"

"I did it," he added.

Meanwhile the Colonels were in a drive to make the playoffs, keeping their hopes alive to repeat the ABA title they had won the year before.

A phone call from the Colonels general manager, Dave Vance, to McDaniels convinced him he needed to give the ABA another shot.

"They only had a few games left," he says, "and thought I could really help in the playoffs. I still had money coming from Seattle, so playing in Louisville now wasn't about the money."

It was sort of like old home week for the former Western Kentucky star.

"I enjoyed playing with Big A, (Artis Gilmore) he smiled. "It was pure relief to be back around people you liked. I wish it could have worked out a few years before where I could have been a Colonel. And I loved Hubie Brown. What a great coach; I enjoyed playing for him. He really encouraged me."

Judy Gaw was an avid Colonels fan, working for several years as a volunteer with the team's booster club. She will never forget a trip she and her husband took during that final season to Denver for the playoffs.

"We flew with the team for my birthday on April 15," she recalled. "I'll never forget it. We were on the elevator at the hotel and Jim McDaniels was on it, too. My husband had gone on the trip, but was not a big fan at all. When Jim said he was looking for a ticket for his girlfriend, my husband gave his to him. Jim sang Happy Birthday to me on the elevator. It was awesome. We all went to the game, and my husband went to the bar."

Big Mac played 28 games for the Colonels that year, averaging six points and four rebounds in 12 minutes a game. They weren't numbers he thought he would be posting at this point in his career, but by his own admission he was not the same player he had been a short time before.

"I was old emotionally, even though I was a young man in years," he said.

McDaniels' Colonels career came to end along with the rest of his teammates when the team folded at the end of the 1975-76 season. His career, however, took one last breath when he signed on and played a year for the Buffalo Braves, the team that John Y. bought with his Colonels money.

Decades later McDaniels says he's had lots of time to think about the twists and turns and the highs and lows of his life. He is a proud man. Proud of many of his accomplishments, and not so proud of a few other. Several years ago he quit beating himself up, but there's one thing that still lingers in the back of his mind.

"You know, I've often wondered about the girl at Western that put me in contact with Norman Blass," he says. "I've concluded that she might have been a plant, there for one semester or maybe not even a student, with a purpose to put me in contact with this guy. That's how serious it was between the ABA and the NBA back then."

Today, McDaniels' number 44 jersey hangs from the rafters in Diddle Arena signifying just how great a college basketball player he really was.

NINTH SEASON
1975-76
by Lloyd Gardner

In the early seventies the Temptations performed a song, *Ball of Confusion* that hit the nation right smack in the eye. That song describes exactly the state of our nation and the title also portrays the 1975-76 season in the ABA. This time it was the "Red, White and Blue Ball of Confusion."

There are sad days in sports when you lose, but time takes away the pain. But there are heartbreaking times in your life that take eternities to heal the grief in your heart. Such was that day, Tuesday, June 25, 1975, when a wind sheer hit Eastern Airlines flight #66 and took the life of Wendell Ladner. Wendell, the fierce competitor, the ladies' man, the teammate, the friend that finally met his match. He had been home visiting his family in Necaise Crossing, Mississippi. He boarded the plane in New Orleans and was headed to Kennedy Airport in New York City.

In the inspection of the crash site, police found a body with Ladner's championship ring on it, and nearby was a Nets' travel bag with the #4 on it, Wendell's jersey number. I remember Fritz Massmann, the Nets' trainer, telling me that he had been called to the county morgue to identify his body.

I will never forget that day, I will never forget the flight number, and I will never forget Wennie. There have been a lot of stories told about him, probably more than any other player, but every one of those legendary tales are told out of respect ... not to make him look bad, but to show just how much everyone respected him and enjoyed being around him. Wendell was Wendell, absolutely, unequivocally, nothing counterfeit about him.

Although, he played with reckless abandon like nobody else, he was just a big fun-loving kid outside the arena. I cannot use the terms "on the court" or "inside the arena" because he spent a lot of time outside the lines, and when Wendell walked in the door for a game, he had his game face on. One time he was playing in Pittsburgh and when he passed the Condors locker room he yelled, "Hey Brisker, we gonna fight tonight."

Ball of Confusion, First Verse
People moving out,
People moving in,
Why, because of the color of their skin,
Run, run, run, but you just can't hide.

I had to leave the day after the crash for El Paso, Texas, and wasn't able to go to the funeral. The pallbearers were Dave Vance and Jay Bauer of the Colonels, and Julius Erving, Bill Melchionni, trainer Fritz Massman, and coach Kevin Loughery of the Nets.

On July 17, 1975, at a party for season ticket holders, it was announced that the Kentucky Colonels signed their top two draft choices Jimmy Baker out of Hawaii and the University of

Louisville's Allen Murphy. In a surprise move, they also signed Jimmy Dan Conner. We gave the Virginia Squires a high 1976 draft choice and future consideration for his rights. His name recognition in the state is big.

It was also announced that Kentucky would play 18 home games in the new Riverfront Coliseum in Cincinnati.

It was early August and rumors were already flying that John Y. Brown Jr. was going to trade either Dan or Artis in an effort to recover some of the team's financial losses. One thing for certain, the championship team was going to be destroyed if he did.

School had now started in Louisville, and the federal courts ordered the school system to end segregation. It was not a pretty picture; it was one this city would like to forget forever. Let me just say that the demonstrations and violence were so out-of-hand that it was the lead story on the national news networks for countless days.

> Segregation, demonstration, integration, determination,
> Aggravation, humiliation,
> Obligation to our nation.
>
> Ball of confusion,
> That's what the world is today, hey, hey.

On September 9, 1975, I did not go to work. I stayed home with my family because of threats. If you didn't have a "STOP FORCED BUSING" sign on your picture window, chances are a brick would end-up in your living room.

Just one week later John Y. was trying to make a deal that would send Artis to Denver or San Diego but Artis had a no trade clause in his contract. Thursday, September 18, I was told in a meeting today that Ellie threw a glass at John Y. and hit him in the ear. I don't think she wants to bust up her team.

I went to Freedom Hall and picked up Dan's blue road uniform. An Army helicopter picked us up in the parking lot at the fairgrounds and flew us to Fort Knox, where Dan taped a public service announcement on the prevention of alcoholism.

The next morning I learned that John Y. was going to trade both Dan and Artis. Herb Rudoy, Artis' agent, was in town and put an end to that talk.

Hubie, Stan and I were in the Colonels office at the Executive Inn when the phone rang. It was September 19, and David Vance was calling from the Brown's residence. He told Hubie that John Y. had traded Dan Issel to the Baltimore Claws. The phones were already ringing off the hook in response to the possibility that Gilmore might be traded. The three of us went to the Red Garter Lounge there in the hotel and "cried in our beer."

John Y. concluded that it was either make a trade or move the team out of Louisville. It stated in the September 21, 1975 edition of the *Courier-Journal* and *Times* Sunday that Issel and his attorney, J. Bruce Miller, flew to Washington yesterday to confer with officials of the Baltimore Claws. Following their return last night, Miller issued this statement:

"At 9:30 p.m., Sept 20, 1975, the following telegram was sent by me on behalf of Dan Issel to John Young Brown Jr., owner of the Kentucky Colonels, and Mr. Lee Silverman and David Cohan, who are principal owners of the Baltimore Claws, and Thurlo McCrady of the American Basketball Association league office. The telegram reads:

Gentlemen:

"Paragraph 5b1 of addendum three of Dan Issel's contract with the Kentucky Colonels reads as follows:

"There are no restrictions upon club's right to trade or sell player except that no such trade or sale shall be binding on player without his prior written consent, which consent shall not be unreasonably withheld.

"You should be advised that as of 9:30 p.m., Sept 20, my client, Dan Issel, has not given his prior written consent to this trade to Baltimore and furthermore, until such prior written consent is given, the trade is not binding upon him. (signed) J. Bruce Miller, attorney at law, Louisville."

Also in that same article, Ellie Brown made this statement, "On a number of occasions last year, his agent asked that Issel be traded. He said Dan was unhappy here, that he was not getting enough playing time and was not getting to play his natural position." His agent wrote a long letter to Hubie Brown saying how Hubie was ruining his (Issel's) career. Now he doesn't want to be traded.

John Y. was trying to get Tom Owens, but he was in Houston trying to join an NBA team. He was part of the Issel trade along with $600,000 to $700,000.

David Vance asked me to call Jim Richards, the coach at Western Kentucky, and see if I could get Jim McDaniels' phone number. All Richards knew was that he was somewhere in California.

Artis and I played golf the next day and he told me, "I would like to make Louisville my home for the rest of my life." David and Hubie called and told me to forget Jim McDaniels.

Monday, September 22, the team had a welcome aboard party at Louisville Downs, a local trotting track. They paged David Vance. John Y. told David that Dan was going to try to block the trade.

Now the phones are ringing to cancel season tickets. We have traded one of the greatest white players to ever put on a uniform in the state of Kentucky at the height of demonstrations over integration. No wonder the fans and community are angry.

It's Press Day, September 23, 9 a.m., the first day of practice. The team met with Hubie at 2 p.m. and briefly discussed the Issel trade. Dan was to meet with the Baltimore Claws today. There is a verbal battle going on in the local newspapers between the Browns and Dan.

Dan has announced that he will go to Baltimore. He has three years left on his contract and they have agreed to pay all of his living expenses.

September 25 the news broke that Denver president Carl Sheer and the Nets' owner Roy Boe had applied for admission to the National Basketball Association. The two had been working together for over a month on this application. They contended that they would go in as expansion teams. NBA commissioner Larry O'Brien stated that they would give these applications serious consideration. John Y. Brown Jr. said that if they did, the ABA would file suits against them. Sources in both leagues said that they invited the ABA champion Kentucky Colonels to join them. Brown confirmed that and said he and his wife Ellie, who owned the club, declined the offer. Before this could ever happen there were numerous legal matters regarding other NBA teams, their draft choices and territorial rights that would need to be worked out.

Dan called and told me that he was going to sell his house. He also invited Sandy, my wife at the time, and me to a farewell party for all his ex-teammates. We practiced twice today and were not able to get to Dan and Cheri's until 11p.m. We didn't get home until 3 a.m. Thank goodness we had only one practice today.

The Kentucky Colonels two-a-day practices at Bellarmine College have been quite an experience. Working out might not be the right word to use; how about boot camp. Over twenty-five college coaches have made the trip to Louisville to watch Hubie direct the troops in hopes that they can take a few tidbits home that will improve their team performances.

Some of the college understudies were Chuck Daly (University of Pennsylvania), Frank Layden (Niagara), and Norm Sloan (North Carolina State), just to name a few. Every day was a clinic. Hubie's intensity could be compared to that of Jack Nicholson as Col. Nathan R. Jessep in "A Few Good Men." But Hubie was a remarkable coach. He knows the professional game and the players. He treats his players as men, but knows how to push each of them to their limits.

October 1 we started the exhibition season in the new Cincinnati Riverfront Coliseum. Dave Vance, John Y. and Ellie didn't show-up; something must be going on behind closed doors.

We defeated the Chicago Bulls 95-86. Bird Averitt and Jimmy Baker did not dress.

Now I know why they didn't show-up for the game. When I got to practice the next morning at Bellarmine, Travis Grant was waiting for me in the locker room. We purchased him from the San Diego Sails for an amazingly low price of $30,000 and a third round draft choice. It's evident that the Sails are already in financial trouble. It was a good thing I always took extra practice equipment with me.

We flew to Landover, Maryland, to play the New York Knicks in a double-header. Hubie and Stan met us there. Jay Bauer, my locker room attendant, met us in Landover. He had driven Issel's car to Baltimore. The Washington Bullets were playing Dr. J and the New York Nets. With 1:26 left in the game Jake O' Donnell, the NBA referee, told Jimmy Dan Conner, "You are in a high school league." I remarked, "You ref like a high school ref." He called one technical foul on me and ordered me to the locker room. The Knicks beat us 107-102.

We were finally back home to face the Buffalo Braves. Hey folks, Artis is back, and his back is much better. Tonight he scored 36 points in 36 minutes, 17 in the last quarter and 10 in the final 2:48 to revive the Colonels in time to win the game 120-116. Jim McMillian led the Braves with 32.

John Y. told me after the game that we were going to join the NBA.

Last season George McGinnis shared the ABA Most Valuable Player Award with Julius Erving. He was tremendous against the Colonels in the playoffs, but when money talks, players walk … when they can. McGinnis walked all the way from Indianapolis to Philadelphia, where he found a $3 million contract waiting after playing out his ABA option. He now plays for the NBA 76ers.

Big George had a big night, but Artis matched him with 25 points. It took a stellar defensive effort by Jones against McGinnis and a clutch shooting performance to pull out the victory 112-110.

The next day we only practiced once, so I got to play golf with Artis, Ron Thomas, and Ted McClain. It's been a long hard stretch. We have one more exhibition game with the Washington Bullets before the regular season starts.

John Y. told me today that we could trade Ted and Marv to San Antonio for Larry Keenon and Mike Gale. Jimmy Dan and I played golf after practice … boy is he good, a scratch golfer. I'm no threat to him!

Kevin Grevey and Jimmy Dan Conner, who led Kentucky to the final game of the NCAA championship, were reunited on their old stomping grounds at the University of Kentucky's Memorial Coliseum. It was also the site where Clem Haskins ended his college career when Western Kentucky lost to Dayton in double overtime. Haskin's had broken his wrist and Dayton went on to the championship game of the NCAA tournament against Lew Alcindor and the UCLA Bruins. You know who won that game. Our game was a total team effort, but after outscoring the Bullets 40-27 in the fourth quarter, we won 121-111. Artis played 36 minutes and scored 23 points, pulled down 15 rebounds, had four blocked shots and one assist. Dampier finished with 20 points. For the Bullets, Campbellsville native Clem Haskins came off the bench in a reserve role and contributed 16 points. Wes Unseld, after banging with Artis, got in early foul trouble and played only 20 minutes. He finished with 12 points.

We have played nine games in 19 days, with only three of them played in Freedom Hall. In all, the ABA won 31 games and lost 17 against NBA teams in exhibitions. The average margin of victory in those games was 1.5 points.

Over the last five years that the two rival leagues have faced each other, the ABA holds a slim 79-76 margin. But over the last three years, the ABA leads 62-34.

There are times in your life that you will never forget. That same day, October 20, the team met at John Y. Brown's house for a party and, most importantly, we received our championship rings. Each person was to say a few words. I said, "Thank you, I accept." As great as it was, one thing was missing, Dan and Cheri Issel.

It was opening night, October 24, 1975. In a pre-game ceremony before the game, Commissioner Dave DeBusschere presented us with our championship rings. Actually, we had taken our designer boxes that our rings came in to the game, and he handed us an empty box.

With six players scoring in double figures, led by Gilmore's 25 points and Dampier's 15 assists, the Colonels come out victorious 100-94 over the Spurs.

There is one thing that avid sports fans all possess … a good memory. ABA commissioner Dave DeBusschere was loudly booed by Pacers' fans when he was introduced at Indiana's home opener. He jokingly said, "I have reversed my decision, and this is really game #6 of the championship series." The game with the Pacers, paced by Billy Knight's 40 points, was a game that was never as close as the score would lead you to believe. Indiana sent Kentucky south with a 103-100 whipping.

Kentucky's record improved to 2-1 as Artis scored 27 points and grabbed 15 rebounds and Wil Jones had 24 to lead the Kentucky offense to an inspiring 130-112 rout of the Virginia Squires. All of the other nine players scored, and five of them finished with 10 or more points.

Fatty Taylor talked to some of our players about the predicaments the Squires face every day: late pay checks, low team morale, management, and the shooting of rookie David Vaughn after a high-speed chase. It also looks like coach Al Bianchi is on the way out. Fatty told the guys, "I'm not very happy, but it's better than being unemployed."

After 35 days practicing, playing and traveling, we finally got one day off. Hubie met with Jimmy Baker, Ron Thomas went to Churchill Downs, and I worked on house plans for a new house on the property where I grew up in Fairdale. We have five days without a game. Everybody on the team put up $100, and we had a bowling tournament. Ron Thomas won $1000 and Bird $500.

It was a playoff atmosphere when Dan and Denver came to town for the first time since he was sold, with lead changes, coaches getting technical fouls, two great teams, and controversial calls by the referees, Norm Drucker and Jess Kersey, in the closing minutes. It was Brown vs. Brown, Hubie vs. Larry, Artis vs. Dan, and Colonels vs. Nuggets.

In the end, Dan's "homecoming" ended with a loss 106-103, but only after outscoring Denver by 10 points and a heroic effort by Ted McClain in the fourth quarter. Issel, #25, finished with 18 points and 14 rebounds, but his teammate Ralph Simpson, who was wearing #44, had a team high 26. Gilmore finished with 29/16 and Dan's best friend Louie Dampier tallied 18 points.

After the game, Issel commented, "I didn't have anything to prove to the people in here. It certainly wasn't a grudge match to make the Browns sorry they traded me. I just wanted to beat the Colonels."

After playing only 11 games under the new ownership, Frank Goldberg, the San Diego Sails' owner, dropped the anchor. It only took a one paragraph statement by the ABA to tell of the Sails' demise. It read, "San Diego confirmed today they were ceasing business operations effective immediately. In accordance with league by-laws, this action automatically terminates the membership of the franchise in the league."

Now that San Diego has folded, another draft will be held to place the players. The Colonels will be the last team to make a pick.

It was also reported that for the fourth time since 1974 the sale of Bill Daniels' Utah Stars was off. The team is reportedly delinquent on numerous bills. Nobody really knows what's going to happen.

With this said, we are now in first place in the Eastern Division with a 7-1 record after our first road win 98-91 over St. Louis.

Instead of having a draft for the San Diego players, the ABA owners decided to have an auction. Caldwell Jones, the brother of the Colonels' Wil Jones, and Kevin Joyce were held out of the auction in an effort to sell them to an NBA team. The 6'11" Caldwell has already signed a five year, $2 million contract with the Philadelphia 76ers that goes into effect in the 1977-78 season. Kevin Joyce was drafted by the Los Angeles Lakers and, at one time, they were interested in buying him. Kentucky did not bid on any players.

We play in Denver tonight, November 14. Just as we were leaving the hotel for a shoot-around, Hubie got a message to call Dave Vance in the office. Hubie called, and David put Ellie on the phone. She told him "We just bought Caldwell Jones. He will be able to play small forward." The price tag was $100,000.

Commissioner DeBusschere met for 1½ hours with 76ers' general manager Pat Williams in an effort to sell Jones to the NBA team. Williams refused to engage in any bidding war for a player. Williams called this situation one of the sloppiest and sleaziest he'd seen in sports. John Y. Brown Jr., president of the ABA, responded "That's the pot calling the kettle black. He's the biggest pirate in pro basketball. He stole George McGinnis, and he's trying to steal Jones."

John Y. accused Larry Fleischer, the attorney for the NBA Players Association, of blocking the merger. After meeting with almost half of the NBA owners, he expressed that they did not feel they could starve the ABA out.

We lost to Denver 117-111. Hubie was very upset with Artis although he had 27/17. Averitt matched the Big A with 27 points. Rookie David Thompson had a career high 34 points and Issel chipped in 18.

We practiced in Denver before flying home. Ted and I got into an argument over his shoulder injury. When I ask him if he can play, all I get is a "whatever." Personally, I think he is trying to keep from getting traded. No team will take a player if he is injured.

Now the rumors are really flying: C J to Denver for Issel's return; C J to St. Louis for Maurice Lucas; C J to San Antonio for Mark Olberding.

I have never seen so much drama and we have played only nine games.

Louie was having chest pains and had an EKG. Everything was negative. McClain is still sidelined with his shoulder injury.

We flew to Terre Haute and got killed by the Pacers 106-92. There was an article in the Terre Haute paper that quoted John Y. Brown Jr. as saying we could beat anybody playing four against five with Artis, C J, Louie and Travis Grant.

Bill Musselman became the fourth coach this year for the Virginia Squires. A group of black businessmen came to the rescue of the Virginia Squires at the 11th hour, saving the team from collapse.

If you go to an NBA game today, you will find every possible gimmick to entertain the fans. The ABA was doing this back in the 70s. We were playing the Pacers in Freedom Hall and Hardy Martin experimented with a "laughing scoreboard." The scoreboard was the brainchild of Hardy. He created a tableful of electronic devices that produced an assortment of sounds such as bombs falling when Artis scored, or somebody chuckling when Louie scored. But referees Jess Kersey and Norm Drucker were not laughing. Actually, they thought things got out-of-hand when it gave out a Mortimer Snerd laugh when the Pacers missed a free throw. Jess Kersey demanded that we put a halt to the laughing scoreboard. Then, when I laughed out loud at a Kersey foul, Norm Drucker hit me with a technical foul. After three straight losses, this was a great night. The Jones brothers combined for 33 points and 20 boards. Caldwell finished with 14/12 and brother Wil contributed 19/8. Gilmore came alive after being inconsistent in the early season. Artis had the last laugh by scoring 31 points and corralling 22 rebounds to lead the Colonels to a 108-91 triumph.

With only 1,307 fans in the 18,000 seat St. Louis Arena, the Spirits fell to Kentucky 93-85. The front line of Gilmore and the Jones brothers combined for 59 points and 39 rebounds.

TV stations in Salt Lake City are reporting that the financially troubled Utah Stars and the Spirits of St. Louis are negotiating a merger of the two teams.

It's now December and the league trustees are meeting in Chicago to discuss the fate of the ABA. Once again, the future of the Utah Stars is the hot topic in the locker rooms, in the media and in all of professional basketball. It's just December 1, and Stars' owner Bill Daniels reported, after failing to make payroll, that the club's chances of surviving the week are very slim. The merger with St. Louis is in a stalemate. Will the players go up for auction like they did in Baltimore and San Diego? At this point nobody knows.

In an effort to force the NBA Players Association to allow the ABA Players Association a voice in merger talks, Prentiss Yancey Jr., the legal council for the ABA Players Association, filed a motion to intervene in a suit to block a merger of the ABA with the NBA.

It took just six hours to reach a deal with ABA trustees that would cease the operation of the Stars franchise. After Utah's four top players, Moses Malone, Ron Boone, Steve Green and Randy Denton, were sold for cash to the Spirits of St. Louis, the ABA officially folded Utah. There are only seven teams in the ABA and all those remaining teams make-up one division. By combining the two divisions we went from second place in the Eastern Division to fourth place with the single division alignment. For the third time this season, the schedule must be revised.

It was also announced that the All-Star game would be played in Denver this year with last year's champion Kentucky Colonels, playing a squad of the best players in the league.

After playing only seven of 21 games this season in Freedom Hall there is no place like home as we beat the Virginia Squires 112-98. Four days later, December 11, Virginia's players voted to take less per diem. They also agreed to travel in coach class instead of first class on road trips.

On December 10, 1976, the Colonels pulled out of Cincinnati for good. Brian Heekin, president of Riverfront Coliseum, still owns 40% of the Colonels stock and threatened to take John Y. and Ellie to court if they didn't honor their 10 year contract in Cincy.

Last year we were the best defensive team in the ABA. This year, with our lack of speed, we can't stop anybody.

On December 16, 1975, the Kentucky Colonels traded C. J. Jones to the Spirits of St. Louis for Maurice Lucas … what a mistake this was. We had traded a great player as well as a great person for an egotistical, selfish, spoiled, arrogant, and rude Maurice "Luke" Lucas. He was a bully. As a matter of fact, when he was with St. Louis, he once blindsided Artis, knocking him to the floor. He was always trying to bully his own teammates in practice. As many confrontations as he got into, I never saw him hit anyone face to face. In all my years with the Colonels, he was the only player that I, along with many of his teammates and coaches, really didn't like.

Tom Owens and Caldwell Jones were both great people. They always gave 100%, but they were centers, and they were much better playing with their backs to the basket. I think Caldwell would have worked out fine in time, but it's December and our backs are to the wall.

From day one Hubie and Luke had their conflicts. As everyone knows, Hubie was always prepared, and always very intense. After several minutes in practice, everyone except Luke was practicing at full speed. Hubie said, "Luke … pick it up. I don't know what you are used to but we practice hard here." Lucas replied. "I'm not a practice player, I'm a game player." Hubie answered back, "You will practice hard here or go home to the tune of $250 (as stated in the Club Regulations and Fines in the players' playbook). That same day after practice I was sitting in the locker room and he said, "Hey trainer, get off your fat ass and get me some shampoo and toothpaste." I pointed to Artis and Louie and said, "I don't get it for them, why would I have to get it for you?" The rest of the team looked at him as if to say "where is he coming from?" He had set the tone for the entire season on the very first day.

After Maurice was on the team a few days, I called the St. Louis trainer, Mike Kostich, and asked him if he had a lot of problems with Luke. He said, "I had very little trouble with him. "I replied, "I guess with Marvin Barnes and Fly Williams on your team, you didn't have much time to worry about Maurice."

The smallest crowd in Kentucky Colonels history, 2,761, showed up to see the San Antonio Spurs hand us our fourth straight loss 115-102.

The team went to Norton Children's Hospital today and staged a Christmas party for patients that are suffering from terminal illnesses.

The four game losing streak finally came to an end. Hubie called the performance tonight the best game so far this season. With Gilmore playing with much more gusto than he has for much of the season thus far, Kentucky managed to beat the Pacers 131-116. Artis, who finished with 24/19, got a lot of support from Marv Roberts (21/6), Wil Jones (19/7), Averitt (21 and 6 assists), Dampier (12 and 10 assists), and Lucas came off the bench and scored 20 points and grabbed 11 rebounds.

One reason Ron Thomas is on this team is because he is a total team player. M.L. Carr was trying to rough-up Louie. Thomas called a timeout near the sidelines and, as he ran to the bench, he yelled at Hubie, "Run B out-of-bounds (our side out-of-bounds plays were letters A, B, and C) I'm gonna set a pick on Carr." The play called for Louie to run to the ball as Ron set a pick on his man Carr. Ron set the pick and lifted M. L. about three feet off the ground … roughhouse is over.

The New York Nets are the only team in the ABA that hasn't picked up anyone from the three franchises which folded. Kentucky, on the other hand, has made seven roster changes and Christmas is just two days away. The Nets are playing like a well-oiled machine; the Colonels still have a long way to go. Behind Dr. J's 31 points, New York beat Kentucky 107-102 for the fourth time in five meetings.

Van Vance interviewed most of the players before the game and asked us what we would like to tell our families back home. I told my six and a half year old son, "Chad, if you are not good while I'm gone, I'm going to call Santa Claus and tell him to come get your toys." We finished 1975 with a 16-14 record. Our record in December was 5-9.

Happy New Year! Everyone knew that Bird could score, but few thought that he would be the team's second leading scorer at this stage of the season. He is averaging 20.2 ppg, and tonight he had 26. Artis added 25 points and had 20 rebounds as we beat Virginia 116-104.

The wheels keep turning. We inked Kevin Joyce to a contract. We need a vaccine instead of a playbook to teach the new bodies our system. It was just last May in the playoff when Kevin got into an altercation with a local police officer. To make room for him, we placed rookie forward Jimmy Baker, who injured his knee on December 16, on the 15 day injured reserve list.

Whenever you need a win, bring in the Virginia Squires, a team that has not beaten us this season. We returned to Louisville Convention Center to face the 6-29 Virginia Squires. The game was not played in Freedom Hall because it was already booked when the Colonels pulled out of Cincinnati. The results were the same, Kentucky wins 129-110.

Maurice Lucas missed the flight to St. Louis for the game against the Spirits. That cost him $250, plus the cost of his airfare. Once he got there, he scored 26 points and 14 rebounds. Artis continues to play consistently as he tallied 32/19. Bird finished with 20. Former Colonel Caldwell Jones had 16/18 and Bad News Barnes finished with 26/12 as the Spirits squeaked out a 113-111 victory.

We traded Travis Grant to the Indiana Pacers for cash and a future consideration. Travis had trouble executing Hubie's complex offensive system. He fit better in a run-and-gun offense.

It was announced that Artis and Dr. J were unanimous selections for the 9th annual ABA All-Star team, which will face the league leading Denver Nuggets on January 27 in Denver. Maurice Lucas was also named to the team.

With the new alignment and just seven teams, the blanks in the schedule left by the defunct teams might have you playing the same team either back-to-back or twice in the same week. Just four days after losing to the Spirits in St. Louis, we returned to the Arena and won our second road trip in a row by downing the Spirits 123-115. We dressed only nine players and seven of them reached the double digit mark. Maurice Lucas, starting in place of the injured Wil Jones, scored 28 points and collected 12 rebounds.

One reason we have won two games in a row on the road is the fact that this is the longest we've had the same guys together for any amount of time. Are more trades in the works to screw things up again?

Rumors are flying high again that we are going to trade Marv Roberts. They simply will not leave this team alone. Hubie is beside himself about how to deal with all these rumors and changes. It's January 17, 1976, and we are playing Denver, the league leader, with a 30-9 record in Denver.

Roberts tied his career scoring high with 30 points, but he had no reason to celebrate. After the game of his life, coach Hubie Brown pulled him aside as the team was leaving the floor and told him that he had been traded to the lowly Virginia Squires for Johnny Neumann and Jan van Breda Kolff. In all the years I have been in professional basketball, I have NEVER seen a locker room in a more emotional state than it was on that Saturday. Some say men are not supposed to cry, but plenty of tears and hugs were shared in that locker room on that day. Who said our team didn't have cohesiveness? I was not with Dan the day he was traded, and it still hurt. But after all we have been through and all that Marv has done for this team for two years, the Championship and all, this was absolutely devastating. This might have been the toughest to swallow of all. The pain of losing Marvin was much worse than the 137-113 pounding that the team took.

Neumann was one of those ABA characters. In 1971, at the age of 19 and only a sophomore, he left Ole Miss with two games remaining in the season to sign a five year, $2 million contract with Memphis. At Ole Miss he led the nation in scoring at just over 40 points per game. He had played for four ABA teams before coming to the Colonels, but in spite of being described as cocky, abrasive, and a braggart, Hubie liked him. Hubie said that Neumann understood the game.

Neumann and van Breda Kolff were the ninth and tenth players to show up on the Colonels roster this year. Many believe that Marv was traded in an effort to put more white players on a franchise that has seen its attendance drop drastically. We have now added three new players, all white, including Joyce. At recent home games, the fans have been distributing handbills calling for a boycott of Colonels and University of Louisville games until more whites are on the team. Surely they are aware of the busing controversy in our city. General Manager David Vance adamantly denied that the player's race had anything to do with the recent trades.

This game is crazy! Last night we lost by 24 points in Denver, and tonight we beat them at Freedom Hall 119-117. History will show that the Denver teams that traveled to Louisville since the ABA opened the doors in 1967 have managed to win only two games. Bird Averitt was sensational. He came off the bench and scored 29 points in just 19 minutes. He was forced to leave the game with 9:34 remaining with a minor knee injury. Wil Jones returned to the starting lineup after being hampered with a dislocated finger and scored 24 points and grabbed 10 rebounds. Artis also had his usual double-double with 25 points and 17 boards.

With the latest shake-up of the roster, the unquestionably-talented Colonels still have a lot of unanswered questions. Who will back-up Jones? Will Neumann and van Breda Kolff play guard or small forward? Where will Allen Murphy and Jimmy Dan get their minutes? With five games in the next six days, there is not a lot of time to practice, and the key veterans need rest.

Hubie gave six of the 12 players a day off.

Early this morning, before the shoot-around in preparation for tonight's game with the Spirits, I went to observe Dr. Rudy Ellis and Dr. Walter Badenhausen operate on Jimmy Baker's knee. He is expected to miss the rest of the season.

The ax fell once again as Virginia Squires coach Bill Musselman was fired. Musselman had drawn much criticism from his players on the grueling and crazy drills he ran in practice. Several players walked out in protest. Former Colonels business manager, and now general manager of the Squires, Jack Ankerson, will co-coach with veteran player Willie Wise until a successor is found. It wasn't long before Zelmo Beaty became the sixth coach of the Virginia Squires this season.

The 1976 ABA All-Star Game was played on January 27, 1976, at McNichols Arena in Denver. The Nuggets earned the honor to play the All-Stars, chosen from the other six teams by being in first place on Sunday January 25.

Denver President and General Manager Carl Sheer put together a spectacular weekend leading up to, and including, the All-Star game. He arranged a tennis-basketball doubleheader on January 23. The tennis match featured Arthur Ashe, the No. 1 player in the world, against Tony Roche, followed by a game between the Nuggets and the Spurs.

The All-Star game was preceded by a concert featuring Glenn Campbell and Charlie Rich.

The All-Stars led 57-55 at halftime. It was at halftime of that game that the ABA showcased an event that would mark a place in history forever. The ABA was out to make a big impression on the basketball world, and it certainly succeeded on that night. Professional basketball introduced the world to "The First Slam Dunk Contest." The contestants were Artis Gilmore, Larry Kenon, George Gervin, David Thompson and the Doctor. Of course the partisan crowd was pulling for Thompson, but everyone knew that the Doctor would be tough to beat.

David Thompson was amazing, but it was Dr. J who stunned the 17,798 fans that night. There were three required dunks. One was a dunk from under the basket. Doc dunked two basketballs at once. But it was his second dunk that would go down in history as the greatest dunk of all times. The rules stated that the dunk must be made from behind a hash mark three feet inside the free throw line. Julius started at the free throw line and took long strides to mark off his steps. As he crossed the half court line, the players seated on the bench and the sell out crowd rose to their feet in anticipation. Some of the players moved to the playing floor, and several were seated in the center jump circle so they could view the Doc as he passed by. What he did was tell the NBA, 'you need to take notice.' The crowd was in a frenzy. He took off running, with every step his stride got wider, and when he reached the free throw line he went airborne as if he was being carried by the wind. With his enormous afro being controlled by the jet stream, Dr. J defied gravity, took off from the free throw line, glided above the lane and slammed the red, white and blue ball through that 18 inch rim. The Doctor made an electrifying house call. Mission accomplished!

I don't think anybody remembers his third dunk, nor does it really matter.

The Nuggets came back in the second half by scoring an All-Star record 52 points in the fourth quarter to win the game 144-138. The Nuggets' David Thompson was named MVP after scoring 29 points, 14 in the fourth quarter. It just proves that a TEAM with cohesiveness will prevail over pure talent.

John Y. and Ellie Brown have made it clear that this will be their last season in Louisville unless new investors are found, or the NBA and the ABA can work out a merger.

It's February, and considering our physical condition, we had an outstanding effort against the league leading Denver Nuggets in the Mile High City, but we lost 116-114. Artis and Luke combined for 64 points. Artis contributed 37 points along with 16 rebounds and Lucas pitched in 27 points. We have now lost 21 games on the road...12 of those by four points or less.

In the first quarter of that game, Louie became the first player in ABA history to reach the 30,000 minute plateau.

The revolving door, however, just won't stop turning. This time McClain, our defensive ace, got caught in it! He was traded to the Nets, our opponent tomorrow night. General Manager Dave Vance announced just before midnight that the Kentucky Colonels had signed Jim "Big Mac" McDaniels. He had been waived by the NBA's Los Angeles Lakers on February 3.

It's February 18 and the NBA owners passed a resolution saying that they were not interested in a merger. They said the vote was unanimous. Privately, they admitted what they oppose is a merger with all seven teams in the ABA. Carl Sheer, principal owner of the Denver Nuggets, believes that five teams would be accepted.

Today wasn't a good day for the Bird. To start the day, he missed the team's flight to Norfolk (that's a $250 fine), then he had to pay his own way on a puddle-jumper that stopped more often than a Greyhound bus. Things didn't get any better once he arrived. He scored only one point, and the guy he was guarding, well chasing, Mack Calvin, scored 33 points. We have now lost to Virginia three out of the last four times we played them. Our 82 points was the lowest point total since the 1972-73 season.

The Colonels are trying to break out of a slump that has seen them lose six of their last eight games, and they are going up against the hottest team in the league since the All-Star break, the San Antonio Spurs. They are 10-3 since the short vacation. The game was a match-up of Bird Averitt and James Silas. It was a shootout as both guards poured in 34 points. The Colonels won the game 116-112 in overtime.

It's back to the city with the Arch for the fifth time this season. It will be the 11th time we have squared off so far. The Spirits of St. Louis are about as unpredictable as the Colonels. They are absolutely loaded with talent: Moses Malone, Ron Boone, Marvin Barnes, Caldwell Jones, Freddie Lewis, Mike D'Antoni and M.L. Carr.

Kentucky overcame a 49 point, 17 rebound performance by Marvin Barnes to defeat the Spirits 121-119 in overtime. Louie led the Colonels with 25 points and six assists followed by 23 points from Lucas and Averitt, 18 from Artis, who had a chest cold, and 10 each from Wil Jones and Jan van Breda Kolff. This is only the second time in our 59 games that Artis didn't lead the Colonels in either scoring or rebounding.

Last year we lost three games in Freedom Hall. This year we still have 23 games to play and we have already lost six games at home. We had beaten the Spirits eight out of ten times this season, but tonight St. Louis gave Kentucky the worst whipping since the Pittsburgh Condors came to Louisville and the Colonels bowed 149-131. We lost 116-102. Gilmore and Barnes had a dead heat in the scoring column with 33 points each.

Dr. You-Know-Who did it to us again. Julius Erving & Co. beat Kentucky 113-101. With 2:22 remaining in the game, Erving drove for the basket and collided with Artis. The Nets were leading 104-98. Artis was called for blocking and Hubie went berserk. Referee Norm Drucker assessed a technical foul on Hubie, and when Hubie followed Drunker onto the floor, he called two more. The technicals resulted in automatic ejection. After the game, the two of them became involved in a shoving match outside the referees' dressing room and had to be pulled apart by a policeman.

If the Colonels are going to finish third or fourth in the race for a playoff spot, they must beat the teams that are in pursuit of them, Indiana and St. Louis.

It is not in Hubie Brown's DNA to use the words concede, quit, throw-in-the-towel or any other words that are negative that resemble losing.

1975-76

I was an eye witness in Freedom Hall to one of the most bloodcurdling incidents that I have ever seen. During a timeout with 6:57 remaining in the first quarter and the Colonels leading 16-8, I saw what I thought was a mannequin falling from the ceiling near the end of the court near our bench. I quickly realized that it was a young boy, and he was trying to reach for the American flag that was hanging from the ceiling in Freedom Hall. In seconds, people were gasping in disbelief at what they had witnessed and police were coming from every direction. A 14-year-old boy, Marty Smith, had fallen 65 feet to the concrete floor on the walkway between the end zone bleachers. He and two friends had crawled into the catwalk above the ceiling tiles, and he slipped and fell through an opening. It was a very emotional scene, and I think it took its toll on our players. Somebody bigger than you and I was watching over Marty on that night, because he survived the accident. He had a broken arm, a shattered wrist, fractured pelvis, a torn liver, and his spleen had ruptured and had to be removed. He was in the hospital for nine weeks. We lost the game 118-105.

The last time we played the Squires in Virginia, Bird missed the plane and his shooting was horrendous, as he was one for nine. The tide has turned, as the Bird was flying high after scoring a game high 36 points in 40 minutes of play. He got plenty of help from the center position as the Big A (27) and Big Mac (21) combined for 48 points as the Colonels came out on top 130-115. With Denver's win over Indiana, they have mathematically eliminated Kentucky from any chance of winning first place in the regular season.

Preceding the game with the Nets, Louie Dampier was honored for having become the first American Basketball Association player to score 15,000 career points. Louie actually reached the milestone in a game against Virginia earlier in the week, but was honored in front of the home crowd.

Tonight, a rare occurrence took place against the Nets … the Doctor, Julius Erving, had an unusually bad game compared to his usual standards. He scored only nine points, 21 below his average and matching his worst night since joining the Nets. He missed his first nine shots. Much of this mystifying performance must be linked to the physical beating he took in St. Louis and Denver the last two nights. Add that to the strenuous travel schedule, I guess the Doc deserves a rest. Kentucky didn't play great, but they squeaked out a 104-97 win.

In a game on March 20, Maurice Lucas turned an ankle. It was not severe, but it did hamper him enough that Ron Thomas started two games and Maurice came off the bench. It was a team rule that if you were injured, you had to report to practice one hour before practice to get treatment and have your ankles taped. If you didn't show up, it was a $50 fine for the first offense and $100 the second. One day before practice, Luke didn't show up to get in the whirlpool. He got his ankles taped and went to practice. About midway through practice, he walked off the floor and went to the locker room and got in the whirlpool. Hubie said, "Tell Luke to get back out on the floor and get in the whirlpool after practice." I went to the locker room, and that's when things got scary. I told him what Hubie had said, and with that, he got out of the whirlpool … and lifted all 210 pounds of me off the floor and held me against the wall. I had read in the newspaper the day before about him paying a rather large paternity suit in Milwaukee, so the first thing that came to my mind was, "Let me down, or you will be working for me." With that statement, he let me down. He said, "Let me in my locker. I'll take care of you" (I kept the keys to the player's lockers in a safe in the locker room). I opened the safe … he got his key … I thought he might have a gun in his locker so I walked as fast as I could, without running, down the hallway. There was only one way out. I can remember it like it was yesterday; I said to myself, "Lord, if he shoots me in the back let me get out into Freedom Hall where somebody can find me." To this day I don't know whether he had a gun or not, but I wasn't waiting around to see.

That afternoon I met with Hubie, Stan Albeck, and David Vance to discuss the situation. They agreed that if I wanted him off the team, he would be suspended immediately. At the time, we were fighting for a playoff birth and we needed every able body. After having 24 hours to think about it, I decided that as long as they told him where he stood, that his conduct would not be tolerated and that he would be traded at the end of the season (unfortunately the ABA folded), I could live with that. I am sure Hubie would not have kept him another season had Kentucky gone on to the NBA.

It was the second game in a row that went into overtime. First it was the last place Virginia Squires; tonight it was the first place Denver Nuggets. With 11 seconds remaining in the overtime period and the score tied at 117, Artis took a desperation inbound pass near the three point line. He didn't want to shoot and we didn't want him to shoot either. He took a couple of dribbles and tried to find a teammate open. He leaped in the air to pass or shoot, nobody knows, but Chuck Williams grabbed his arm and the referee called a shooting foul and the Big A went to the line and hit the first free throw but missed the second. With two seconds left, Allen Murphy forced a turnover and the Colonels won their ninth game out of the last 12, 118-117. Can they keep it going? Little Louie had one three pointer intermingled in his 14 points, and that was enough to reward him with his ABA record 900th basket from behind the line.

I am sure that referees need to be mentally ready just like players and coaches do. Last night Eddie Middleton and Jess Kersey called technical fouls on Hubie after he protested a charging call on Lucas. It was Hubie's third early trip to the dressing room. To top that off, Mel Bennett went to the line and missed both free throws, but Middleton called a lane violation on us. Bennett once again shot and missed, and Middleton once again blew his whistle and called another lane violation. Bird protested vehemently and pow, pow, pow ... three technical fouls and a trip to an early shower. Hubie now has some company in the locker room ... they can each have a beer. Murphy's Law was in full gear tonight as we went down 128-122.

We have five games remaining in the regular season, three at home and two on the road at New York and St. Louis.

Lucas broke Issel's 1970-71 record for most points in a quarter. Issel's record was 19 and Maurice had 21 in the first quarter in the Colonels 111-103 victory over the visiting Squires. Gilmore was feeding him the ball as he hit 10 of 13 shots in his big quarter.

Vice–president of sports for NBC-TV announced that the network will televise ABA playoff games starting April 11 in the Nets/Spurs seven game series.

From what Hubie shares with me and what I hear behind closed doors, the Atlanta Hawks are trying to convince Hubie to jump ship and come to Atlanta, one of the NBA's weakest franchises. Hubie is on the "hot list" of prospective coaches. The Washington Bullets and Milwaukee Bucks have already made a pitch to secure his coaching tactics and enthusiasm.

It's April and we are headed north to Uniondale, New York where our record is 0-7. In the season series, the Nets hold a 9-5 advantage.

The Nets' 111-87 galling victory over the Colonels, combined with the San Antonio Spurs' win over the Pacers, eliminated us from contention for third place. On one occasion this year we had nine players score in double figures; tonight we had two, Artis and Maurice. As a team we shot 38 percent.

With fourth place locked up we returned home to beat the Spirits 106-102.

I am almost certain John Y. and Ellie Brown are bailing out. J. Bruce Miller has agreed to form a syndicate to purchase the Kentucky Colonels.

Tomorrow is also the 84th game of the ABA regular season, and Kentucky is hosting Issel, Thompson and the Denver Nuggets.

If Denver plays every night the way they did tonight, you can ship the ABA Championship trophy to the Rocky Mountains tomorrow. The Colonels played like Barbie Dolls and the Nuggets like Androids as the 27 point loss matches the Colonels worst defeat ever in Louisville. On November 23, 1967, when the ABA was still in diapers, Babe McCarthy brought the New Orleans Buccaneers to the Derby City and embarrassed Ziggy & Co. 129-99. The Nuggets took the Colonels, dressed in their all white suits, behind the wood shed and gave us a good whipping 130-103. Larry Brown, the Nuggets coach, was a starting guard on that New Orleans team.

1975-76 Regular Season Final Standings

Denver Nuggets	50-24
New York Nets	55-29
San Antonio Spurs	50-34
Kentucky Colonels	46-38
Indiana Pacers	39-45
Spirits of St. Louis	35-49
Virginia Squires	15-68
San Diego Sails*	3-8
Utah Stars*	4-12

*San Diego folded November 12; Utah folded on December 2

1976 ABA PLAYOFFS

Hubie has always advocated that there are three seasons in professional sports: exhibition, regular season, and playoffs, and in each one you must raise your game. After last night's lackadaisical performance, we must put it in high gear or we will be packing our bags very soon.

Our regular season record against the Indiana Pacers was 6-6 but we have managed to win the last three.

Wow, what a difference a day makes! Last night we were apathetic; tonight we were dynamite as we won game one of the best of three series 120-109. Artis' production was dynamic as he had five blocked shots, 25 points and 17 rebounds in just 35 minutes, but he wasn't alone. Wil Jones climbed the boards and brought down 10 missed shots along with 24 points. Maurice Lucas had 20 points, Dampier and Averitt each dished out 10 assists and had 18 and 16 points respectively. Billy Knight led all scorers with 43. We now have won the first game of the three game series, and we head up I-65 for game two in Indianapolis.

Game two was much like game one, where one team played good and one played bad. Tonight the tables turned; the Colonels played bad and the Pacers played good, so they won the game 109-95.

Tonight's winner of game three will advance to the best-of-seven series against talent-laden Denver. We are facing a do or die game and reports are coming out of Wisconsin that Hubie will replace his friend Larry Costello as the head coach of the Milwaukee Bucks.

For nine years people have counted Louie out … out of basketball. On the other hand, Little Louie is a winner, and that's why the Colonels have won more games than any other franchise. Kentucky came out smoking and held the Pacers to an American Basketball Association playoff record tying 11 points in the first quarter. The Pacers' record broke a tie held by Kentucky against the Pacers when they scored only 11 points in the third quarter of the seventh game of the championship series in 1973. However, the Pacers have a lot of tradition, and they weren't about to give up. They scratched and clawed their way back. The game was a knockdown, drag-out affair which featured a fight between Bird and Indiana's Mike Flynn. This game was going down to the wire. Nobody is throwing in the towel.

With five seconds on the clock and the Pacers leading 99-98, Hubie called a timeout and set up a play designed to go inside to Artis. They were guarding Artis like the guards at the Gold Vault in Fort Knox. After the first two options broke down, the ball went in to Louie. As the clock ticked away Louie worked his way open, then at the last second, Don Buse, the All-ABA defensive guard, came out of nowhere and challenged Louie's desperation shot. He has never taken a more important shot in his illustrious career. He was off balance, had an odd angle, and had Buse's hand in his face. With one second remaining, the shot went in and the Colonels will live another day. The 100-99 victory gave us a spot in the ABA semifinals against the Nuggets. Hubie has always said, "If the game is on the line and I have one shot remaining, I want the ball in Louie's hands … he is clutch … a pro's pro."

Hubie made a statement to the press today regarding the Milwaukee coaching job. Brown said, "The only way I'm going back to Milwaukee is if Larry moves on to another coaching job or decides he's had enough of pro basketball. I'm NOT going to be the guy who's going to get him fired. I wish they'd let Larry coach his team right now and let me coach mine."

It seems like every time a close game ends, the words protest, controversy, clock, no good, counts, doesn't count, and referees creep into the conversation. Game one ended that way against Denver. The scoreboard in the new arena "blew up" about five o'clock yesterday. When the company hired to maintain the scoreboard turned it on to test it, the computerized monster self-destructed. Could Mission Impossible have been there to sabotage us? Therefore it was necessary for the timer to use a stopwatch, and the public address announcer called out the time. The horn was also malfunctioning, so hand signals were used to send substitutes into the game, and the first three quarters ended on the announcer's say-so.

With 1:48 left in the game and Denver leading 109-100, it appeared that the Nuggets were headed to a victory in game one. But Maurice Lucas hit two jump shots and Jan van Breda Kolff stole the ball and drove in for a layup and was fouled. When play came to a standstill there should have been five seconds remaining.

At that point, the timekeeper proceeded to put five seconds on the shot clocks to minimize the possibility of a dispute of when time would officially expire … but the stop watch showed 4½ seconds and shot clocks don't operate on half-seconds.

After Jan's free throw, Denver called a timeout. Kentucky went into a full court, man-to-man denial press. Bobby Jones tried to inbound the pass, but he couldn't find an open man, so he called another timeout. Hubie protested (there's that word again), claiming that five seconds had expired and we should be rewarded with the ball on the violation. Referee Norm Drucker claimed that he had only reached three in his count.

Denver lined up and threw the ball in to Chuck Williams and Louie fouled him immediately. The announcer said three seconds were remaining, but this time the time was not displayed on the shot clock … hmmm.

Williams missed the shot, and Bobby Jones whacked it to half court where Kevin Joyce smacked it to Louie, who drained a three-point shot from 26 feet. While all of this was going on, the announcer was saying, "Three-two-one-that's it." A canister horn was sounded and Drucker and partner John Vanak waved Louie's shot no good. The third official, who is seated at the scorer's table and is used in the playoffs to insure that the time is properly kept was Joe Belmont, a former Denver head coach. He wouldn't change the call.

In the hallway outside the Colonels locker room after the game, Hubie confronted Norm Drucker and demanded to know why the shot clock wasn't used to time the final three seconds. The shot clock had a horn that was working.

In a nutshell Hubie summarized the situation by saying, "We all agreed before the game that we'd play under these primitive conditions."

The outcome of this game was devastating. Although we lost the game 110-107 there was some encouraging performances by our front line.

Game two was one for the little guys, the guards Louie, Bird, K. J. and Neumann. They almost caused the scoreboard to explode trying to tally-up their points. Louie, after missing his first two shots, found the range and hit 11 in a row and finished the night with a game-high 26 points. Johnny added 22, Bird had 20 and nine assists, and Joyce scored six along with four assists. An exploding offensive performance led to a 138-110 victory.

In Game three, the Colonels soared to a 126-114 win as the Bird was flying high … and so was Artis … and Louie. Averitt didn't get off to a good start. As a matter of fact, he was playing so out of control in the first quarter that Hubie replaced him with Joyce. From the start of the second quarter, it became obvious that Denver was going to be in a fight for their life. Bird scored 10 points in the second period and eight more in the third. Then he went to work. He was more irritating than a gnat in the summer, weaving, bobbing, shuffling his feet faster than a hummingbird flaps its wings, a driving layup here, a jumper there, an assist here and there. He was all over the place making eight of nine shots in the final stanza. In the end, it was a game most kids dream of having. He had 40 points. He made 17 of 28 shots and served up seven assists.

It wouldn't be fair to let the performance by Artis go unnoticed. He had a Zombie performance, a game of a lifetime. Although Gilmore averaged 25 points and 16 rebounds, there were many nights when people were saying, "*Where have you gone, Artis Gilmore; can you tell me where he's gone?*" Not tonight. Artis hit 15 0f 20 shots, scored 36 points, grabbed 16 rebounds and blocked four shots.

And let's not forget Louie, the nine-year veteran who hit the last 11 shots that he took in Denver. His string was broken when he missed the first shot of the game, a three-point attempt. Then the eagle-eyed Dampier finished by banging home eight of 14 shots for 20 points. When the final ticks clicked off the Freedom Hall scoreboard, the Colonels had a 2-1 lead in the best- of-seven series by shooting a remarkable 56.4 percent for the game.

The performance by the trio of Colonels overshadowed Thompson's 29 points, Simpson's 28 and Issel's 20.

The ABA has submitted an offer to the NBA in an effort to merge the two leagues. The offer included these proposals:

1. Six of the seven teams would be admitted.
2. The ABA would pay $19.5 million over several years.
3. The ABA would not share in the television revenue for three years.

In every game thus far in the playoffs against the Pacers and the Nuggets, the margin has been either 10 points or more, or four points or less, no in between. Game four against the Nuggets ended with Denver winning by two points, 108-106. It's amazing how things can change in two days. That's why they play a seven-game series to determine the winner.

Has anyone realized that the Kentucky Colonels have a former player on every team in the ABA: Denver–Dan Issel and Chuck Williams; Indiana–Travis Grant; New York–Ted McClain; St. Louis–Tom Owens and Caldwell Jones; San Antonio–Mike Gale; Virginia–Marv Roberts.

Entering game four, the Nuggets have lost three games in a row only once this season. If Artis was extraordinary last night, he was shades below that tonight, and Bird, who had a fever of 102 degrees before the game, was flying high, playing as if his wings had been clipped.

Averitt hit a 17-foot jumper with less than two minutes to play giving the Colonels a four point lead, 102-98. Denver's Chuck Williams countered with a 17-foot jump shot. Bird took the inbounds pass and streaked up the floor, stopped at the free throw line, and forced up a shot that rimmed out. There was 1:22 to go and the score was tied 102-102.

Artis and Bobby Jones each hit two free throws to tie the game at 104 with 51 seconds to play. We had the ball … Hubie called a play designed for the big man to get the ball in close. He couldn't make a move to the basket, so he tossed it back out to Bird. He put up a 19-foot shot that resulted in an air ball. Denver got the rebound, and seconds later Byron Beck scored on a lay-up. Timeout Kentucky, six seconds remaining. Hubie diagramed a play that resulted in an uncontested lay-up by Jan van Breda Kolff, that tied the game at 106 with four seconds remaining.

Denver called a timeout and Larry Brown, the Nuggets coach, sent David Thompson into the game. He had been on the bench when Kentucky had the ball because he had six fouls (you could play with six fouls, but if you committed another foul, the team you fouled gets two free throws and the ball back). We were concerned about Thompson. Hubie, noticing Maurice Lucas was guarding the much quicker Chuck Williams, quickly sent Bird back in the game to guard him. All the time, Hubie was yelling, "Get Williams." After two quick passes, Williams got the ball just inside the arc. Where was Bird? Williams' shot hit the bottom of the net just as the horn sounded. Game over … Denver wins 108-106. There is no joy in Freedom Hall tonight!

It's back to Denver for game five. With just a little bit of luck and an operating scoreboard we might be playing for the ABA Championship once again.

There are not enough adjectives to describe Bird Averitt's love of the game, his willingness to help his team win or his determination to not quit. And there are not enough words to describe how much we need him and how much his tonsillitis and high fever have impinged on his play. In Game Five, he was only able to play 26 minutes, all in four to six minute stretches. He hasn't been able to eat for two days. Our other point guard, Kevin Joyce, suffered a ruptured ligament in his thumb and played only 13 minutes before being injured.

1975-76

Artis wasn't at his best, although the box score showed him with 26 points and 14 rebounds, 10 of those points were scored after Denver had pulled away in the third quarter. Meanwhile, David Thompson played like he was possessed. He finished with a game high 34 points to lead the Nuggets to a 127-117 victory and a 3-2 lead in this hotly contested showdown.

When a reporter asked Hubie about a negative remark Larry Brown had made about the Colonels play, Hubie told the reporter, "Go tell Larry to coach his own team and quit worrying about us."

Although the Colonels had a 14 point lead in game six, at one point the game was nip-and-tuck for the most part. Once again Larry Brown moaned and groaned about the officials. He must have forgotten that in game five played in Denver just three days ago, the Nuggets shot 31 free throws and Kentucky shot 24. His crybaby antics to the media must have worked back home.

The game was marred by a fight between Jim McDaniels and Denver's 7'0" Marvin Webster. The fist-a-cuffs were like rapid fire. McDaniels landed a punch on Marvin's head; Ron Thomas clobbered Webster; McDaniels managed a left hook on Issel; and Maurice Lucas tagged Webster as both benches emptied. While all of this was going on, Hubie and Larry were making verbal exchanges at each other.

Would you believe Larry Brown bitched about that too? He thought we were trying to hurt his 270- pound center, Webster.

Bird's play was far from his 40-point exhibition in game three. At one point, he was shooting a miserable 1-11, but with 2½ minutes left in regulation, he rose to the occasion. He scored three baskets that kept us breathing. His two field goals in overtime resurrected us from elimination, and his three baskets in the early minutes of the second overtime gave the Colonels a six point cushion allowing us to hold on and force a game seven with a 119-115 double-overtime win. That's the good news, now the bad news. Our flyweight basketball hero pulled his Achilles tendon when Ralph Simpson stepped on his heel in the second overtime. It's unthinkable that Artis would go 0-7 in the second half, but he snapped out of his slump in the overtimes and scored six points. In all, Bird and Artis combined for 18 of the 22 points in the extra periods. Averitt finished with 34 points and seven assists and his pal Artis had 21 points and won the battle of the boards with 26. Neumann came off the bench and tallied 16 points. Lucas, still fired-up after the fight, had 16 points and 17 boards. Scoring honors went to the Nuggets' Ralph Simpson, who was playing relentless basketball and had 35. Issel, in a losing cause, had 22 points and 18 rebounds.

There is one game left in the series. The winner moves on to face the New York Nets, who defeated the San Antonio Spurs in their series, and the losers hang up their sneakers and wait to see what happens to the ABA.

Game seven will be played on April 28, 1976, in McNichols Arena in Denver. Will Dan Issel be facing Dr. J and the Nets, or will he be in his box seat at Churchill Downs watching the Kentucky Derby on May 7?

With two days off between games, Bird has received treatment for his Achilles tendon injury, and he will play. I will tape Kevin Joyce's thumb, and he should be available for duty despite the ruptured ligament.

An American Basketball Association standing-room only record crowd of 18,821 fans piled into McNichols Arena to witness the final game of the knock 'em-down, drag 'em-out series.

For five years Artis Gilmore has been the cornerstone for the Kentucky Colonels. Who will ever forget last year's championship game when he scored 28 points and pulled down 33 rebounds?

Tonight just wasn't his night. For some reason, the planets didn't line up. Tonight the giant was David Thompson. The extraordinary 6'4" rookie hit 13 of 20 shots and scored 40 points to lead the Nuggets to an overwhelming pounding of the Kentucky Colonels 133-110. With the win, Denver earned the right to play the New York Nets for what might be the last American Basketball Association Championship.

Artis was intimidated and tormented all night by Issel and Webster as they continually pushed him off the low post area. Because of this, Artis managed only 10 shots, 11 rebounds and 17 points … not nearly enough for us to make the championship round. At one point during a timeout, Hubie was doing everything he could to fire the big fella up. That's when our know-it-all forward Maurice Lucas stepped in and told Hubie, "Stop yelling at him." From that point on things got worse. Hubie benched Lucas for his outburst, and things went downhill from there.

The statistics don't lie. Denver shot 52.4 percent, Kentucky 45.7; Denver out-rebounded us 58-47, blocked 10 shots, and handed out a team playoff record 36 assists.

In all, I would say Hubie's passion for winning is voracious, and that's why we were so successful. Louie was always consistent, the pro's pro. Wil Jones was tenacious defensively and often unheralded. Bird was faster than a speeding bullet. And Artis was one of the greatest centers to ever play the game.

Last season we surrounded our team with good people. We had a nucleus of a team, and management let Hubie take control. Early on, there were highs and lows, peaks and valleys, but I will never forget what Phil Johnson, the coach of the NBA's Kansas City-Omaha Kings, told us after our very first exhibition game in 1974, "When you guys learn to react to your system instead of thinking about what you need to do, you are going to be great."

It became very evident that the NBA would accept only four ABA teams, not five. At the time, the New

GAME SEVEN OF SEMI-FINAL PLAYOFFS — OFFICIAL ABA BOX SCORE — FINAL
DATE 4-28-76 SITE DENVER, COLO. OFFICIALS RUSH, VANAK, KERSEY ATT 18,821

No.	VISITING TEAM: KENTUCKY	Pos.	Min.	2-Point Field Goals M	A	3-Point Field Goals M	A	Free Throws M	A	Rebounds Off.	Def.	Total	Assists	Errors	Fouls	Total Points
22	JONES, WILBERT	F	28	2	6	0	0	4	4	2	2	4	2	3	6	8
25	LUCAS, MAURICE	F	36	10	20	0	0	3	5	5	10	15	0	3	3	23
53	GILMORE, ARTIS	C	43	7	10	0	0	3	3	3	8	11	1	1	5	17
10	DAMPIER, LOUIE	G	38	4	11	3	4	0	0	0	1	1	11	1	1	17
14	AVERITT, BIRD	G	33	8	21	0	0	5	5	0	1	1	7	2	4	21
5	VAN BREDA KOLFF, JAN	F	20	4	6	0	0	3	3	3	4	7	1	2	2	11
31	NEUMANN, JOHNNY	G	16	3	7	1	3	0	0	0	0	0	1	1	2	9
42	THOMAS, RON	F	12	0	0	0	0	0	0	0	0	0	1	0	2	0
43	JOYCE, KEVIN	G	9	0	4	0	0	2	2	0	1	1	4	0	0	2
45	McDANIELS, JIM	C	5	1	2	0	0	0	0	1	1	2	0	0	1	2
20	MURPHY, ALLEN							D	N	P						
21	CONNOR, JIMMY DAN															
	TOTALS		240	39	87	4	7	20	22	19	28	42	28	23	26	110

Percentages	Combined F.G. Pct. 45.7	44.8	57.1	90.9	Team Rebs. 5	Dead Balls 1

No.	HOME TEAM: DENVER	Pos.	Min.	2-Point Field Goals M	A	3-Point Field Goals M	A	Free Throws M	A	Rebounds Off.	Def.	Total	Assists	Errors	Fouls	Total Points
24	JONES, BOBBY	F	34	8	10	0	0	0	0	3	5	8	6	1	4	16
33	THOMPSON, DAVID	F	42	13	20	0	0	14	16	4	6	10	5	3	4	40
25	ISSEL, DAN	C	40	12	23	0	0	0	3	7	5	12	5	2	4	24
11	WILLIAMS, CHUCK	G	28	7	13	1	1	2	3	0	6	6	3	1	4	19
44	SIMPSON, RALPH	G	45	6	21	0	0	3	4	4	4	8	14	5	1	15
10	WEBSTER, MARVIN	C	16	4	6	0	0	1	4	0	6	6	1	0	2	9
15	FOSTER, JIMMY	G	2	2	2	0	0	0	0	3	0	0	0	0	0	6
21	TERRY, CLAUDE	G	19	0	4					2	0	1	1	1	0	2
22	GERARD, GUS	F	5	1	1	0	0	0	0	1	1	0	2	1	2	
40	BECK, BYRON	F	9	0	2	0	0	0	0	1	1	1	0	5	0	
	TOTALS		240	53	102	1	1	24	35	18	35	53	36	14	26	133

Percentages	Combined F.G. Pct. 52.4	52.0	100	68.6	Team Rebs. 5	Dead Balls 7

VIS. (6) BLOCKED SHOTS (10) HOME		VIS. (8) STEALS (6) HOME	
GILMORE	4 WILLIAMS 2	LUCAS 3 THOMPSON 2
DAMPIER	1 GERARD 1	AVERITT 1 SIMPSON 1
THOMAS	1 JONES, B. 5	DAMPIER 2 JONES, B. 1
	WEBSTER 2	NEUMANN 1 ISSEL 1
		JOYCE 1 FOSTER 1
		WEBSTER 1

TECHNICAL FOULS NOTES: LARGEST WIN MARGIN IN PLAY-OFF BY DEN, TIES RECORD. MOST ASS'T IN PLAYOFF GAME BY SIMPSON-14, DEN TEAM RECORD

Remarks: NEW ABA ATTENDANCE RECORD DEN WINS SERIES 4-3

Score By Quarters	1	2	3	4	OT	OT	F
KENTUCKY	26	30	26	28			110
DENVER	27	30	37	39			133

```
                            INCENTIVES

James Bradley
        $10,000 - for first time elected to First Team All ABA
        $ 5,000 - for any previous selection to First Team All ABA


Jimmy Dan Conner
        $ 2,500 - ABA All Rookie First Team
        $ 5,000 - ABA Rookie of the Year
        $ 5,000 - ABA All ABA Team (first or second team)
        $ 5,000 - ABA All Defensive Team (first team)
        $ 1,500 - ABA All Defensive Team (second team)


Louie Dampier
        $ 5,000 - ABA Championship win


Ted McClain
        $ 5,000 - Avg. 30 min in regular season
        $ 5,000 - Avg. 15 points regular season
        $5,000  - 6 assists regular season
        $ 5,000 - Association playoffs              10% to SHAPIRO
        $ 5,000 - Division Champions
        $ 5,000 - League Champions


Allen Murphy
        $ 2,500 - ABA All Rookie First Team
        $ 5,000 - ABA Rookie of the Year 1975-76
        $ 5,000 - All ABA Team (first or second)
        $ 5,000 - ABA All Defensive Team (first)
        $ 1,500 - ABA All Defensive Team (second)
```

York Nets and the Denver Nuggets were obviously the strongest teams. Kentucky was not far behind.

On June 16, 1976, I went to the closing on the house I had built on the property where I had grown-up. It was a beautiful setting on three acres in Fairdale. Now I own two houses, one that I was trying to sell in Okolona, a hotbed area against forced busing. Families were moving out of Jefferson County, not buying homes.

The next day on June 17, John Y. Brown Jr. threw in the towel and took his ABA red, white, and blue ball and $3 million dollars after reaching a financial agreement with the remaining ABA teams. He also sold Artis Gilmore's contract to the Chicago Bulls for $1.1 million.

The Colonels players, according to the ABA-NBA merger agreement, were placed in a dispersal draft. Before releasing our players, John Y. signed several of them to personal service contracts. This was done in an effort to make money by selling the contract to a team for more than he had invested in it. Some players were under contract for 15 years or more. It was a great deal if the players made an NBA team, but a losing proposition if they were released before his money was recouped.

Hubie was now coaching the Atlanta Hawks in the NBA, and we talked quite often. When I told him I still had two houses and two house payments, he told me, "Don't miss a house payment. If I need to help you, I will." Two weeks later I sold the house in Okolona. What a relief!

On the morning John Y. called it quits, I headed to our offices in the Executive West Hotel, not expecting what was coming. About 9:30 a.m., general manager David Vance came out into the outer office and said, "Everyone come into my office for a short meeting." Our Business Manager, Alice Miller; Secretary, Pam Schaftlein Thomas; Director of Publicity, John Y. Hamilton; Director of Sales, Gordon Crawford; Director of Promotions, Bob Bedell and I strolled into David's office. He said, "Folks, get your coats, hats and personal belongings and go home, the ABA folded 15 minutes ago. Pink, you go see John Y. Brown tomorrow."

John Y. had always told me that he wanted me to work for him if I ever decided to get out of basketball. I worked for the rest of the summer closing out the Colonels office, and was the Captain of his 65' boat that was docked on Harrods Creek, a tributary of the Ohio River.

Red Forgey, who was in charge of the facilities at Freedom Hall, called me and said I needed to get all the Colonels equipment and souvenirs out of the locker room and storage rooms or they were going to throw them in the garbage. For some reason, I was smart enough to empty the rooms and take it to my dad's barn and store it for some 22 years before I realized most of it had become collectors' Items.

Several teams inquired about my services as a trainer. The Washington Bullets and the Detroit Pistons showed some interest, but I had a young family and a new home, and I didn't want to raise a family in those cities. Hubie got me an interview with the Milwaukee Bucks. I was the trainer with the Kentucky Bourbons Professional Softball Team, and we were playing in Menomonee Falls, Wisconsin. I met with head coach Don Nelson and John Steinmiller at the Menomonee Falls Holiday Inn. I interviewed, but was not chosen for the position. Later that summer, Stan Albeck, an assistant coach for the San Antonio Spurs, recommended me for the Spurs opening, but I was content to stay home.

John Y. has always been very good to me. After working for six months and having nothing definite in my future, I decided to return to Fairdale High School as a teacher and a basketball coach.

I will believe until the day that I die that if we had not sold Dan Issel, we could have won another ABA Championship and we would have been accepted into the NBA.

CHAPTER SIXTEEN
WHEN THE CROWD STOPPED CHEERING

JAY BAUER

Jay Bauer was the locker room attendant. At least that was his title in 1975, and at the age of 23 he had been involved with the Colonels for all nine of their ABA seasons. He started as a ball boy during that first year in 1967.

Bauer, like everyone else in the Colonels organization, had many more "jobs" than what his title stated. One of those extra duties began in 1972, when the Colonels traded Goose Ligon to Pittsburgh for guard Jim O'Brien. O'Brien flew Bauer to Pittsburgh to drive his car back to Louisville. And then in 1974, after O'Brien had been traded to San Diego for Red Robbins, Bauer drove his car to San Diego and returned in Robbins' car to Louisville.

Then Bauer's "on the road again" treks really began to pick up. He drove Mike Gale's car to Uniondale, New York and flew home, immediately hopped into Wendell Ladner's car and drove back to New York. A later trip had Bauer driving Bird Averitt's car from Louisville to Los Angeles. Averitt was playing in a summer pro league and didn't have time to drive. Of course when that league finished, Bauer returned to L.A. by air and drove Averitt's car back to Kentucky.

Then the pace really picked up. In late September 1975, Issel was traded to the Baltimore Claws from the Colonels. Bauer drove his car to Baltimore, and then six days later Issel was traded again, this time to Denver.

But you haven't heard anything yet.

In mid-October 1975, Bauer drove Chuck Williams' car from Denver to Baltimore when Williams' former team, the Memphis Sounds, was moved to Baltimore. Williams had been busy in Colorado, his home state, for the summer. But while Bauer was heading for Baltimore, the franchise was dissolved. So it was back to Louisville in Williams' car. Williams was picked up then by the Virginia Squires, and as Bauer prepared to set sail for Norfolk, he learned that Denver had traded Fatty Taylor to the Squires for Williams. That afternoon he headed out in Williams' car for Denver. On return, he drove Taylor's van from Denver to Virginia.

Bauer actually turned the driving thing into a full time job.

He even said it would take 10 full-time employees to keep up with the "You-trade-em, we drive-em," business that had sprouted up on the fringe of the American Basketball Association. He offered that drivers could be on the road 24 hours a day, 365 days a year in order to keep up with the trades of pro basketball players in the ABA and NBA.

But when the ABA folded it took lots of people and business with it, and Jay Bauer was one of them in the cruelest of ways.

It was 2:37 a.m. Saturday, December 10, 1983. A phone call to Louisville police claiming that intruders with intent to commit robbery had apparently broken into a house at 2609 Fordyce Lane in eastern Louisville. The caller told police that a glass had been knocked out of the back door in order to gain entry. The caller went on to say that both of his parents were dead.

The caller was 29-year-old Albert Joseph "Jay" Bauer, Jr.

Immediately upon arriving police found a horrific scene with both his father, Albert Joseph Bauer, and mother, Mabel, dead. Mrs. Bauer was found lying in the kitchen and had been stabbed repeatedly in the neck and throat with a kitchen utensil. Albert Bauer was lying in the front hall of the red brick, one-story home near Atherton High School where Jay had graduated in 1973. He was initially thought to have been shot, but closer examination revealed he had been strangled.

The Bauers' were both 63-years-old, and Albert was a Jefferson County Deputy Sheriff whose main duties included checking titles of out-of-state automobiles that were registered in Jefferson County to make sure they were not stolen. Before that, he had been in the restaurant and bar business in Louisville.

Earlier that evening the Bauers had attended the annual Sheriff's Fraternal Order of Police Christmas party at the Loyal Order of the Moose Lodge on Fegenbush Lane. A few minutes after 11 p.m. they left, heading to their home in Dundee Estates.

Detective Dene Ashcraft, at the time, said that Jay Bauer's jogging suit he was wearing was soaked in blood. He went on to tell police that he had fought off two intruders who had killed his parents during a burglary, even showing cuts he had on both hands.

As Bauer continued to talk, his story became even more bizarre.

Evidence of a burglary didn't support Bauer's story. Police believed whoever entered the home had keys. The broken glass in the kitchen door, where he said the attackers came through, did not mesh with what detective Ashcraft felt like it should look.

Most of the broken glass was scattered in a way as to indicate that the door was wide open at the time the pane was broken, and not shut tight and locked as Bauer reported to police. And, to even further cause police to doubt the younger Bauer's story, was the fact that some of the glass fragments were in a pool of Mrs. Bauer's blood. However, none of the tops of the fragments had blood on them.

Ashcraft's conclusion was that the glass landed on the floor after the blood was there. Police continued their questioning of Bauer. He had been that night, he said, at Rick's, a nightspot on Poplar Level Road during the time his parents were killed.

Rick's was owned by former University of Louisville basketball star Rick Wilson, who had been a classmate of his at Atherton High School, and they even roomed together for part of a semester at U of L. Occasionally Bauer worked as a bartender there. Bauer told police the jogging suit he was wearing when they arrived was what he had worn earlier in the evening to Rick's. But friends of his told a different story. They told police Bauer was dressed in a two-piece suit, white shirt and suede Hushpuppy shoes.

From the beginning, it was a "fishy" story. The crime scene certainly didn't fit the story Bauer was telling, and within a few minutes, Jay was most certainly viewed as a person of interest. A search of the house that early morning found Quaaludes, a prescription sedative that belonged to Bauer, who had moved back home with his parents some six months earlier.

That Saturday afternoon around 5 p.m., Bauer was arrested. The charge: possession of Quaaludes. Police requested a high bond for their double homicide suspect. But, as sometimes happens in the judicial system, laws and technicalities will override common sense.

Jefferson County District Judge John K. Carter set Bauer's bond at $1,000 cash. He said in an interview that a higher bond would have been appropriate, "only if Bauer had been charged with the crime for which it was requested."

He had only been charged with possession. Five and a half hours after being brought to the Hall of Justice, he was free to go. The $1,000 had been paid by family attorney Mike Greene and, with his assistance, Bauer had checked into a room at the Galt House for the night. He could not go home. After all, it was a crime scene.

As unimaginable as this story became in such a short time span, it was about to take its final twist.

Sometime in the early hours of Monday morning on December 12, Jay Bauer made sure the door to his 20th floor Galt House room was securely locked, even latching the extra chain on the door. After moving a small stool that would normally serve as a foot rest to one of the chairs in the room close to the window, he made his final decision in life, jumping through the center portion of the room's large plate-glass window that faced toward west Louisville.

—⌇—

It was a rainy, misty night in Louisville and a leak had been reported by a night security guard in the roof and ceiling of the Archibald Cochran Ballroom, one of the Galt Houses' premier locations that would host many of the city's festive Christmas holiday events. It was very important that any maintenance problems pertaining to the ballroom were immediately addressed. The security guard directed his flashlight toward the ceiling and spotted much more than water coming through the roof.

Sometime around 4:30 a.m. Monday morning, hotel employees discovered what looked like a human body protruding from the roof and ceiling of the third-floor ballroom.

Tom O'Hearn's phone rang at his home a few minutes later. At the time, he was general manager of the Galt House, so he dressed quickly and headed to the hotel. He had been told something over the phone, but he wouldn't know the full gravity of the tragedy until he arrived there. Firefighters were called in to help remove Bauer's body from the ceiling, and then O'Hearn and several others were on their way to the 20th floor.

After forcing their way in with police investigators, he would never forget the strange feeling he had upon entering the room from which Bauer had leaped to his death.

"There wasn't a note," O'Hearn said. "It was just eerie going in there and seeing the stool next to the window and all of the broken glass. I was with Detective Richard King and to both of us it looked like he had used the stool as a springboard to jump through the window. There was also a candy wrapper lying on the floor."

For those who knew Bauer, none of it made any sense. Sure there was talk, talk that started soon after the Kentucky Colonels professional basketball folded up in Louisville following the 1975-76 season. According to those around him, the basketball team was the real positive element in his life, both professionally and emotionally. It was something he could talk about, all of those big time professional basketball players, not only the ones who played for the Colonels, but opposing players as well. He knew them and they knew him.

Although Jay was a good size young man, standing 6-feet-2 inches, he was never able to play basketball with any degree of success. That, however, did not deter him from being around the game. While still in high school, he began working as a locker room attendant and ball boy for the Colonels, and when the team was in town, Bauer figured out a way to be involved.

Lloyd Gardner said Bauer would even be at team practices.

"All of the players and coaches really liked Jay," Gardner recalled. "He loved the Colonels and everything that went with being a part of them."

Jim Ellis, son of the Colonels team doctor, Rudy Ellis, and a friend of Bauer's from their days at Atherton, recalled that he just never seemed to find what he was searching for. Shortly after the Bauer family deaths, Ellis told a reporter from the *Louisville Times* that he believed Bauer started taking drugs "sometime after the Colonels left."

"One by one, he saw the players who had been such a part of his life leave the city," Ellis offered.

Bauer had worked at odd jobs along the way with the steadiest being as a bartender for over two years at the Toy Tiger, a Bardstown Road nightclub.

Working as a bartender allowed Bauer to tell his Kentucky Colonels stories, even to the point of name-dropping some of the biggest stars in the game. In a certain way, it was a way for him to stay connected.

But then Bauer felt like it was time to get back to his schooling, enrolling as a full-time student at Sullivan Business College. However, in sort of a typical Jay Bauer move, he dropped out after five days.

For the most part, the facts of the murder of Albert Bauer and his wife Mabel were all on the table. There wasn't any burglary. There was no coming home and finding them dead. There was no fighting off intruders. Any fighting that happened early that morning came from Jay's mother, Mabel, resulting in the cuts on both of his hands.

Everything was there but the motive. That, however, would soon become evident.

Jay's parents had become very concerned about their son's behavior and lifestyle, even phoning his friends asking if they knew of any drug use by him. Some speculated that the Bauers had told him that fateful night they had had enough with the drinking and suspected drug use, and they were preparing to cut their son off financially. Thus the motive.

Bauer snapped, and in a drug-alcohol self-induced rage, he killed his parents.

On January 25, 1984, 46 days after the double homicide, a Jefferson County coroner's jury ruled.

They had heard 3½ hours of testimony from homicide detectives; Mike Greene, the Bauer family lawyer; and a relative of the murdered couple. Even though they never visited the house at 2609 Fordyce Lane, they watched an hour-long video of the crime scene.

When the 4½ hour inquest was concluded, the jury needed only 15 minutes to reach their conclusion.

It was first degree manslaughter that Jay Bauer had been charged with posthumously. His death was ruled a suicide.

The announcement of all of the findings was made by Jefferson County Coroner Richard Greathouse, the same Richard Greathouse who had been the first Colonels team doctor back in 1967 when Joe and Mamie Gregory started the team.

Greathouse told the media the jury unanimously agreed that the killings were manslaughter, and not murder.

"They believed that Jay had come home, had a violent confrontation with his parents, blew his cool and totally wiped them out," Greathouse said.

It was pointed out that "under Kentucky law, a person who causes the death of another person cannot be convicted of murder if he acts under the influence of extreme emotional disturbance."

Call it what you will, manslaughter or anything else, the fact was and still is, unfortunately Jay Bauer murdered his parents.

Of course, even in a stretch, the demise of the Kentucky Colonels cannot be blamed in this horrible tragedy. On the surface, Jay Bauer seemed like a typical 20-something, single young man who enjoyed sports. But beneath it all, there were the demons.

The Colonels had been his security blanket, offering everything he wanted in life: rubbing elbows with superstar basketball players, hobnobbing to a certain degree with Louisville shakers, considering himself an insider of a professional basketball team, feeling good about his contributions that helped make the team successful, and enjoying all of the notoriety that came with it. Suddenly, when that blanket was pulled away, with it came all of those demons.

CHAPTER SEVENTEEN
NEVER, NEVER GIVE UP

J. BRUCE MILLER

A book cannot be written about professional sports in Louisville, particularly basketball, without talking about attorney J. Bruce Miller.

It has been Miller's lot in life, at least it seemed, to be a vocal leader in Louisville and throughout the state in trying to bring an NBA basketball team to the commonwealth.

In the beginning, it was about keeping what was already here, the Kentucky Colonels. But once that opportunity was gone, he turned to courting existing NBA franchises who had let it be known they were looking to re-locate. Miller's efforts, concentrated on bringing public government dollars, combined with private investors to help propel Louisville along side cities like Indianapolis, Cincinnati, Memphis, and Orlando.

Miller's bottom line observation has been that the lack of a professional sports franchise in Louisville has held the city back in its efforts to increase economic development, quality in life, and perhaps the most important, a spot along side some of the great cities in America.

In 2004, Miller documented it all, including his anger and frustration, with the publishing of "Air Ball." The book chronicles efforts made to bring pro basketball to Louisville without success.

"It's hard to believe so few people were able to deny what would have been good for Louisville and the entire state." Miller said several years after the book's publication.

Growing up in Louisville and graduating from Atherton High School, Miller had his sites set on being a golf pro. Florida State had offered him the opportunity to play golf at the collegiate level, but Bruce's dad, J.R., had other ideas. There was no discussing it. His son would go to Vanderbilt University. Any golf to be played would come after law school.

Even though criminal law was his focus in the beginning, sports, at least the contract side of the business, was always there.

The Kentucky Colonels were there to help him get his feet wet.

Tommy Kron, through his dad Max Kron, was a distant family relative to the Millers, and when the former UK star began to explore leaving the NBA Seattle Supersonics, he turned to Miller for advice in 1968.

"Tommy was the first player I represented," Miller recalled. "He jumped from Seattle to the Kentucky Colonels, and when word got out that I was charging by the hour and not a percentage, my phone started ringing all over the place."

Miller soon had more than 200 athletes he was representing, including Kenny Anderson and Anthony Munoz of the Cincinnati Bengals football team, basketball player Butch Beard, and a host of others.

Eventually Miller made a business connection with Dan Issel and Mike Pratt, who had previously signed with the Colonels. It was with Issel, in particular, that Miller developed a relationship that moved beyond a client attorney relationship.

Times were good for Miller and the Kentucky Colonels. In fact, Miller laughed in recalling the time in the early '70s when he, Issel, Pratt and Dampier were playing a round of golf at Big Springs Country Club.

"It was No. 16, a par-5," Miller says. "Big Dan hit his driver and it must have gone 300 yards straight up into the parking lot. He was really worried about whose car he had hit and the damage he had done. When we got up there, we discovered he had hit his own car. We all got a big laugh out of it."

It seemed that professional basketball anywhere in America couldn't get any better when the Colonels won the ABA title in 1975. Averaging close to 9,000 fans a game at Freedom Hall, the team that John Y. and wife Ellie had put together for Coach Hubie Brown, was on top of the basketball world, at least in the ABA.

But not so fast. The totally unexpected was about to happen. In a million years with a million guesses, no one would have guessed that the Colonels were about to sell Dan Issel.

It was the summer of 1975 and several ABA players that included Louie Dampier, Artis Gilmore and Issel were in Japan teaming up with several NBA players putting on exhibition games. Years later Dampier recalls Issel receiving a phone call in Japan from John Y., after which he told his buddy Louie that the Colonels were probably going to trade or sell Gilmore.

"Dan loved everything about being in Kentucky," says Dampier. "He certainly didn't want to leave the team or the state, and I remember him saying "better Artis than me.""

It wasn't long after they returned to Louisville that the situation with Issel was not what he had thought.

Some of the Colonels players and their wives were at the Louisville Downs enjoying the horses. It was a Friday night, September 19, 1975. Dan and his wife Cheri really enjoyed horses, and in fact, next to basketball, that's what the Issels liked most about living in Kentucky.

Halfway through the evening, a page came over the track's loud speaker informing Issel that he had a phone call. Who would be calling him now? "It must be important for someone to have him paged," Dampier remembers thinking.

When Issel returned to his family and teammates, he dropped a bombshell. "He said the call was from Ellie Brown," remembers Dampier. "She told him he had been traded."

Dampier still has trouble understanding the Browns' decision to send Issel packing. "Why would we trade the best player on the team just after we won the championship?" ask Dampier. "He couldn't be, and wasn't, replaced the next year. He was my best buddy."

Miller, 35 years later, has very little trouble remembering the phone call he received from Louisville Downs that night. He answered the phone and it was Issel on the other end.

"He said Ellie had called him," Miller said in remembering the conversation. "I told him he needed to get over to my house with Cheri and his daughter, Sheridan."

Issel and his family had just built a custom home on Wolf Pen Trace in Louisville. They had planned on staying there for a very long time, as the house was laid out to accommodate Dan's 6'9" frame, including higher than normal ceilings and doorways that assured him of being able to walk through without having to lower his head.

And on top of that, Miller was proud of the fact that Issel, at the time he signed his contract with the Colonels, had the largest committed personally guaranteed contract in all of professional sports.

But right then on this particular evening, his new home was not really on his mind. Where he would be playing basketball was.

While Miller was on the phone with Issel, he glanced at his TV and could not believe his eyes.

"Scrolling across the bottom of the screen was news that Dan Issel had been sold to the Baltimore Claws," recalls Miller. "I told Dan for sure not to go to his house, and to get over here. As soon as they got here I headed out to a 7-11 store to get some beer for Dan, tobacco for my pipe and a pacifier for Sheridan. The guy at 7-11 said, "I'm not sure what kind of party you're going to have, but it sure does look interesting.""

To completely avoid the media, the Issels stayed that night with Bruce and Norma Miller. Needless to say, word of the Issel's deal spread across Louisville like wildfire. No one was happy about it, and furthermore, no one seemed to really know what was going on. Neither Issel nor Miller even knew who the Baltimore Claws were.

Confusion was rampant. Issel had revealed to Miller that Ellie Brown had, indeed made the initial call to him at the racetrack, but when in stunned disbelief he told her of his contract and the inclusion of requiring Issel's prior written consent for a trade or sale to be valid, she handed the phone to John Y.

"Dan's contract was breached," said Miller. "It had a no-trade clause that had been personally guaranteed by the previous owner group, of which John Y. was a part of. It was a mess. His contract included several Ollie's Trolley eatery franchises in New Orleans, Miami, Nashville and Southern Indiana."

Miller began immediately to gather information about the team in Baltimore. He learned quickly they were the old ABA Memphis Tams, recently purchased by a Baltimore group headed by a local rock concert promoter.

According to Miller, Issel flew to Baltimore to meet with their lawyers and for a press conference at Pimlico Race Track. "They wanted to impress Dan with horses," Miller laughed years later.

John Y. had not been paid his money from the Baltimore group headed by David Cohan, and although it had been reported for years that the Issel deal was for $500,000, Miller says it was initially for $700,000 and later reduced to $550,000 when the Baltimore soap opera began to fall apart and the Denver Nuggets emerged.

By now it had been almost two weeks since the city of Louisville and the Kentucky Colonels basketball fans everywhere had been smacked in the face with the news of Issel's departure. Some insiders felt that John Y. and Ellie had a chance to save face, perhaps even undo the deal and bring Issel back. After all, there was a public outcry, and Miller had even made plans for a law suit and injunction against the Browns. He said he was within hours of filing it. But the Browns stood pat.

Along the way, Miller, with Issel's knowledge, had spoken with New York Knicks' associate, Sonny Werblin. "They wanted Dan," Miller says. "But he wanted to stay in Louisville. Because of the contract breach, we only talked to New York to get some leverage. And then we found out there was interest from Cincinnati, but he definitely didn't want to go there."

With the obvious instability of the Baltimore Claws, for good reason, someone, either John Y. or Miller, contacted Carl Scheer, general manager of the Denver Nuggets in early October. As good as the Colonels were the year before in winning the ABA championship, Denver was not far behind, at least on paper.

Issel and Miller met with Denver and struck a deal. Issel officially became a Nugget and the footprint he left was wide, long, and deep enough that at the conclusion of a 15 year career, he was inducted into the Naismith Basketball Hall of Fame. It should be pointed out that, as great as several Colonels were in their careers, only Issel and Gilmore at this point are in The Hall. His 416 games as a Colonel and 1,100 more as a Nugget would reveal he scored 27,482 career points. At the time of his retirement in 1985, these numbers ranked eighth of all-time in professional basketball.

One who questioned the trade and wasn't bashful about saying so was columnist Jim O'Brien of the *Sporting News*. He told Miller the Issel deal was the third dumbest sale in the history of American sports. The first, he said, was Babe Ruth from the Red Sox to the Yankees. O'Brien couldn't think what the second was, but surely there was one dumber, he said.

In light of Issel's career numbers it might be difficult to argue against O'Brien's assessment.

The last time Louisville and Colonels fans saw Dan Issel play in Freedom Hall was not what they wanted to see — Dan Issel wearing #44, trotting to mid-court in a Denver Nugget uniform after being introduced by PA man John Tong. For Tong, now deceased, it must have been awkward, too.

That sixth game of the playoffs was something. It was a jam-packed Freedom Hall, and although the Colonels had averaged only 6,935 in attendance, down from 8,727 the previous championship season, electricity filled the air. Everyone loved the Colonels, but they equally loved Dan Issel.

Denver, too, had lots on the line. A loss to the Colonels would create doubt about the future of the Nuggets and their coach, Larry Brown. After all, with a cast of talent to rival anything in the NBA, or maybe even the Kentucky Colonels the previous year, the only difference seemed to be one player, #44, Dan Issel.

Kentucky won the game 119-115. It's all documented in basketball history. But what's not there for anyone to read in a record book was what happened on the opening tip.

With everyone in Freedom Hall on their feet, it was a given that the 7'2" Gilmore would easily control the tip over the 6'9" Issel. They had probably jumped against each other hundreds of times in practice and several times back in their collegiate days when Gilmore was at Jacksonville and Dan was at Kentucky. If Issel had ever controlled a tip, no one could remember it.

Miller remembers this jump. "Either Artis didn't jump or Dan jumped the highest in his life," he said.

Miller, without saying it and probably without really knowing, thinks the classy Gilmore even with a championship on the line, yielded to his friend Issel on this one center jump.

"He gave me kind of a wink years later," and said, 'Bruce, who said slow white guys can't jump,'" Miller recalled.

J. Bruce Miller, by the mid-1980s, had grown tired of representing athletes as a profession. He had been elected Jefferson County Attorney in Louisville, and what had once been enjoyable encounters with sports figures was turning into something other than just signing contracts between teams and players.

But, there are the memories. Memories of friends and businesses, who stepped up to support his efforts. There are also the memories of those whom Miller identifies in "Air Ball" who blocked any chances for Louisville to have NBA basketball, among them former Louisville mayor Dave Armstrong, former University of Louisville President John Shumaker, current U of L Director of Athletics Tom Jurich, and basketball coach Rick Pitino.

It is, Miller wrote, those few turf protectors who have denied the city, county and state the opportunity to grow economically.

In an oddity of sorts that has perhaps been lost in history, Dick Fenlon wrote in the November 1975 edition of the *Louisville Times* that John Y. Brown and Denny Crum had actually had conversations concerning a new University of Louisville on-campus 20,000-seat arena to be shared by the Cardinals and Colonels.

Ellie Brown was quoted by Fenlon. "We've talked to U of L about a new championship arena. U of L would like to have us play there, which is something we'd certainly be interested in," she said.

Fenlon's column continued:

"We've been exploring the possibilities of a new arena ever since I've been here," said Crum. "And we've talked to John Y. Brown about them using it."

In the article, Crum was asked by Fenlon if he shouldn't be opposed to such an arrangement.

"Definitely not," he said. "I'm 100 percent in favor of it. I can't imagine anything nicer than a professional organization like the Colonels coming in to share it with us. I'm in favor of anything that's in the best interest of basketball, and anything that keeps the Colonels here and keeps John Y. Brown in the game is in the best interest of basketball."

Crum said he was not worried about a battle for the spectator. "We have our fans, they have theirs, and we share some. I don't see any problem over dates either. That can all be worked out."

Miller today is still at a loss. He points out that the four ABA teams taken by the NBA, San Antonio, Denver, New York and Indianapolis, are all worth over $1 billion according to *Forbes Magazine*.

A *Street and Smith Sports Business Journal* article is mentioned in his book. It emphasized that Louisville is one of America's largest metropolitan areas without major league professional team sports.

"At the time, Larry O'Brien was NBA Commissioner, and he was very upbeat about the NBA in Louisville, so much so that he told the media that, "not having the NBA in Kentucky was like having a fine dinner without wine – it doesn't make any sense."

But Miller also half-heartedly points a finger at John Y. Brown, and not just about the sale of Dan Issel. According to Miller, Brown had said he would move his NBA Buffalo Braves team to Louisville if 20 individuals were willing to invest $100,000 each. In return, they would receive 49% of the team's stock. Only 16 stepped up, and even though some in the group offered to make up the $400,000 shortfall, Brown stood by his original requirement of wanting 20 individuals involved. Had Brown accepted the 16 investors, Miller's thinking was that Louisville would have had an NBA team that was competitive from the start.

(Miller reported that the substantial commitments came from Al Schneider, Wendell Cherry, Ellie Brown, who by now is divorced from John Y., and John Y. Brown, Sr., Frank L. Jones, Jr., Jack Gruneisen, auto dealer Ed Coyle, coal entrepreneur Martin Twist, restaurateur Ed Hasenour, CPA Louie Roth, developer Frank Metz, and lawyer Frank Haddad. John Y. pulled together several Lexington investors, and even though John Hubbuch, restaurateur Fred Kunz, Jerry Abramson and John Anson were willing to put together four groups of $100,000 each, Brown insisted on 20 individuals at $100,000 each. Sixteen individuals wouldn't cut it with John Y.)

In 1978, years before he wrote "Air Ball," Miller suggested that someone should write a book about Louisville's failure to put together enough financial backing to land an NBA team. He even had a suggestion for the book's title: "While Louisville Slept."

Years later, even after "Air Ball," Miller reflects on it all, recalling a visit in 2000 to the NBA executive offices in New York. There, in one of the hallways, were framed action shots of Artis Gilmore, Dan Issel and Dr. J. Pretty impressive: Old ABA photos, two of which had been Kentucky Colonels, in the NBA offices.

"We talk a big game here in Louisville," says Miller, his voice and eyes revealing the total frustration of it all. "We have the PGA at Valhalla, Breeders Cup, and of course the Derby, but we're not competing with Nashville, Indianapolis, Charlotte or even Memphis anymore. We're now competing with Lexington."

Miller has decided to give it one more shot at the NBA. With the Louisville Metro Council's blessings, plus financial support for his expenses and effort, he is aggressively going after a team. By his own admission, over the years he has spent $1.5 million of his own money in doing so, and what does he have to show for it? Nothing, at least for now.

BOB TIELL

There would never be enough room to list all of those individuals and their efforts to keep the Kentucky Colonels playing basketball. And then most of those same people, as volunteers, worked tirelessly to entice an NBA team to Louisville after the Colonels were gone

"We had heard all the rumors," recalls Bob Tiell, one of those "booster club" volunteers who supported efforts to have a professional team in Louisville. "But our focus was to make sure the Colonels would survive and be positioned to go into the NBA."

However, when John Y. and Ellie Brown decided they had had enough and shut down the team, although disappointed, the worker-bee group set about to re-focus their efforts.

"Bruce Miller was a big part in helping keep the dream alive of getting an NBA team here," says Tiell. "And we were a lot closer than most realized."

Those 15 to 20 individuals actively involved in the Kentucky Booster Club pulled out all stops in helping the city put its best foot forward in its efforts to attract a team. They arranged for a series of NBA exhibition games, referred to as the "NBA 6-Pak," to be played at Freedom Hall over the course of the 1977-78 season. At one of those games, the halftime entertainment included a performance by the Louisville Ballet.

"It may well be the only time in pro basketball history where a ballet company performed," offered Tiell. "The mix of jocks and highbrow was something to behold."

And then there was a night in January 1978. Tiell headed to the Louisville Airport in the midst of one of the worst snow blizzards in some 50 years. His mission was to pick up Atlanta Hawk owner Ted Turner, in town to see his Hawks play at Freedom Hall.

"It was amazing they were even letting planes land," says Tiell. "When we got to the game, there were 8,000 fans there. Turner was incredibly impressed, couldn't believe it. If he moved his Hawks, which he was seriously considering, he said it would be to Louisville or Charlotte."

For more than two years, the boosters operated out of office space donated by Al Schneider at the Executive Inn West Hotel. There were others who helped out with time and money, one being Coyle Chevrolet in New Albany, who made cars available when needed.

Len Hayes, Judy Gaw, Bob O'Leary and Bob Bedell, who had actually played in the ABA in 1967 for Dallas and later worked in the Colonels organization, all were active in the "6-Pak" project.

Chapter Eighteen
Memories That Never Fade Away

The Reunion

Steve Higdon was 12-years-old when he attended his first Colonels game with his dad. That was in 1975. That was also the championship year.

The impression the Colonels made on Higdon was unlike anything he had ever experienced. He thought about the Colonels. In fact he couldn't think about basketball without thinking about that championship year, not necessarily that they won a professional basketball title, but the fact that they received so little fanfare.

How could it have been that right here in Louisville so little attention was given to this elite basketball team, a team that had brought so much to the city through sports and community good will?

Over the years, it nagged at Higdon. And as he moved along in a professional career that included being president of Greater Louisville, Inc., he was finally in the position to right some wrongs he felt were long overdue.

"That championship team never even had a parade." Higdon says. "Can you believe it? They never really had anything done to recognize their accomplishment."

He set about to help make it right. Time was of essence.

Higdon hooked up with Lloyd Gardner, and the two of them put a plan in motion to bring the entire 1974-75 championship team back to Louisville for a reunion.

Almost anything about the Kentucky Colonels now-a-days usually begins with Gardner. His reputation in regard to the ABA and the glory years of the Colonels in Louisville is well-known, so it was easy to see why Higdon would contact him first. Over the years, Gardner had kept in touch with many of the Colonels, to the point of it being almost like a family. But it had been such a long time. Players, coaches, management, and owners had dispersed much like seeds in the wind.

Higdon was not to be denied as he committed himself to make the gathering of all these former Kentucky Colonels stars a reality. He started planning early, even flying to Jacksonville and meeting for a couple of hours in the airport with Artis Gilmore. "I can't begin to tell you what it was like sitting there talking with Artis about all of this, getting the team together, the parade, the recognition they deserved," he recalled.

Calculating was this fellow Higdon. So much, in fact, that the reunion was timed to be the week of all the Kentucky Derby goings on.

For 49 years the Pegasus Parade had been one of the major highlights of anything that happened outside of Churchill Downs. But for the 50th Parade, Higdon made something happen that was really special.

The 1974-75 Kentucky Colonels Team and organization was named honorary grand marshals in 2005. "They got their parade 30 years later." Higdon said.

Perhaps it worked out for the best, you know, with the parade happening all these years later. More times than not the successes of our youth is not really appreciated until the passing of time. Had those ten players, in the prime of their athletic lives, been able to comprehend, and not taken for granted a parade in downtown Louisville, who knows how many people would or wouldn't have shown up? It could have been a few hundred or a few thousands. We'll never know, because it didn't happen.

But what we do know is on May 5, 2005, some 400,000 people, lining the streets for blocks and blocks, screamed, yelled and waved as those World Champion Kentucky Colonels, sitting in and on the back seats of brightly colored convertibles, soaking up every bit of the adulation that came their way. Most in the crowd probably never saw them play. That wasn't important. What was important, however, was that they knew who they were. They had read about the team, even heard some of the stories from their fathers or grandfathers, and just seeing them pass in front of them was the next best thing.

But Higdon didn't just stop with the parade. There were private parties for those who helped Higdon with sponsorships that brought the Colonels back to town. And then there was the public reception for the real fans. These are the ones who would have stood on the sidewalk back in April 1975, perhaps in a chilly drizzle, to watch their heroes ride by. For sure those were the ones who would have been at the parade that never happened.

There was more. A banner was finally hung in Freedom Hall recognizing those championship achievements. And then the following September, the entire team was inducted into the Kentucky Athletic Hall of Fame. This is a shrine that usually takes in only individuals, but to further applaud the rarity of it all, the entire team and its coaches were inducted.

When the team folded many of the players went on to be gobbled up by the NBA. But only one ever won a championship again. Ted McClain, a guard on the Colonels title team had been traded to the New York Nets, and they won it all the last year of the ABA.

The reunion, parade, induction, and all the fanfare that came with it, brought back so many good memories. They were often shared with a family member or friends, and whether the stories has been embellished over the years mattered little.

Doug Gibson

It was the summer of 1964, and Doug Gibson was getting ready for his senior year at Elizabethtown High School, expecting big things for himself and his team. Several local high school and college players would gather each night on the outdoor courts just behind the school. The play was often rough in the no-harm-no-foul rule games, and for high schoolers, the competition against the collegians was often memorable.

"A couple of big guys showed up one night and played," remembers Gibson. "They were living in a basement apartment on Perry Avenue near the high school and said they were here working the summer to build the Bluegrass Parkway. Their college coach at the University of Miami in Florida had gotten them the jobs, they told us."

The two returned each night, along with another college player in town for the summer, Butch Hill from Murray State. Hill had been an all-state player at Beaver Dam and could play.

But it was one of the big guys in particular that stood out, not just for his two-on-two or three-on-three games, but for his work ethic.

"This guy would play for a couple of hours, then go over to the track and run lap after lap in the grueling heat and then came back and practice free throws, underhanded," Gibson said. "We all knew he was good, but didn't realize we had spent the summer playing with the leading college scorer in the nation until *Street and Smith's* magazine came out and he was on the cover. What a surprise! It was Rick Barry, all-world."

A few years later, Barry returned to Kentucky while playing for the ABA Oakland Oaks and now coached by his old Miami coach, Bruce Hale. By now Barry had even married his coach's daughter. The game against the Kentucky Colonels would give Gibson a chance to see and perhaps even talk to the guy who was considered one of the best of all-time, and in a competitive sort of way had gotten to know him a few summers ago.

"I told my friend Kenny Tabb that I knew Barry and we would go to the game and I would introduce him," Gibson says. "As Barry was leaving the floor for the locker-room just before the game, Tabb and I positioned ourselves so we could say something to him as he ran off the floor. I tried to get his attention, but he just looked at me without any kind of acknowledgment and kept running. I was disappointed, but looking back, Barry was all business, and we should have waited until after the game and he probably would have been more approachable. My friend has never let me forget the night I introduced him to Rick Barry."

GIL LAWSON

Gil Lawson grew up in Louisville, and although still in elementary school, he was a big Colonels fan. In fact, his entire family was, and going to the Colonels games together was a big event.

"We went quite often," recalls Lawson. "And even when they traveled, I remember listening to Van Vance broadcast games while juggling homework."

Like many people in Louisville in 1973, Lawson was upset when he got word that the team might be sold and move out of town.

"My childhood friend, Bill Deatrick, and I hatched a plan to start a petition to keep the team in Louisville," says Lawson. "We both spent several days going door to door in our neighborhood. While doing it, we learned that Jimmy O'Brien, a guard on the Colonels, was holding a clinic at Assumption High School, which was just a few blocks from where we lived."

The two youngsters were not going to be denied in their efforts to keep their Colonels in Louisville, so off to the basketball clinic they went in hopes of turning over their labor of love petition to O'Brien.

"He was very cordial and friendly," Lawson said. "I forgot exactly what I said, but after delivering the petition, both Bill and I were confident that it would get to the right person and convince Mr. (John Y.) Brown the team needed to stay in Louisville."

Lawson, like so many Colonels fans back then, also had his Wendell Ladner memories.

"We usually got to the games early," he said. "I closely watched him in warm-ups. He seemed to know everyone and he always had young ladies approaching him for autographs. I was impressed. His play was even more impressive. If there was a loose ball anywhere on the court, Ladner would be there — usually flat on the floor. He was an inspiration for kids like me — with average basketball ability and less than fast."

KENTUCKY COLONELS FANS MEMORIES

The memories of the Kentucky Colonels run deep. They were here for such a short time and, in the early days, if not downright laughed at, at least drew snickers. Perhaps they were taken for granted to the point of being under appreciated. But in spite of it all, there were those who just couldn't get enough. Those fans didn't laugh; they cheered and cherished those wonderful memories of Louie, Dan, Darel, and Goose in the beginning, and Big A and Wendell soon-after.

There's even an internet site tagged "Kentucky Colonels Fan Memories." Decades after that last game, there are still those who take the time to share their emotions and memories about this team.

One wrote: "I remember as the teams were coming out for their warm-ups before the second half of a game against the Virginia Squires, my best friend and I ran up to courtside to get a closer look at our heroes. The arena security guards let us go right up to Charlie Scott and Dan Issel and "give them five." Could you imagine any NBA arena allowing that?"

Another said: "Carrier was the only player that I can remember who would actually jump when he shot free throws. I remember my dad commenting that the Colonels offense back then consisted mainly of Dampier and Carrier dribbling down court and shooting."

Said another: "I was a big Colonels fan when I was growing up in Louisville in the 1970s. As a matter of fact, when I turned 15-years-old, I got a job with Brantley Ushering Service just so I could watch the Colonels at every home game. Consequently, I was the envy of all my friends."

Another wrote: "One of my favorite Colonels memories was riding a Greyhound bus to Indianapolis to watch game four of the '75 Finals at Market Square Arena. It was the only loss of the series for the Colonels."

One more wrote: "Growing up in Eastern Queens, New York, I was a huge Nets fan from 1969 onward. I attended most Nets home games from 1972 until the end. In following the ABA, I would listen as often as I could to Van Vance doing Colonels games on WHAS. I picked up the broadcasts pretty easily at night. By the way, I was able to meet Van at Nets games. In fact, one time he put me on the "Star of the Game Show," after he talked with Dr. J. Van would do that type of thing with fans around the country from time to time."

Jim Pickins, Jr., today a sportswriter in Owensboro, recalls a trip to Louisville with his dad to see the Colonels play the Virginia Squires.

"I think I was 11-years-old," he says. "Bobby Rascoe had invited us up and after the game we met Larry Brown, one of their players at the time and a friend of Bobby's.

"I'll never forget that one of Virginia's players, Neil Johnson, got a technical that game and challenged the crowd to a fight. He even took off his jersey and motioned for them to "come on.""

ABA YEAR-TO-YEAR STANDINGS

1967-68 FINAL STANDINGS

Eastern Division				Western Division			
Pittsburgh Pipers	54	24	.692	New Orleans Buccaneers	48	30	.615
Minnesota Muskies	50	28	.641	Dallas Chaparrals	46	32	.590
Indiana Pacers	38	40	.487	Denver Rockets	45	33	.577
Kentucky Colonels	36	42	.462	Houston Mavericks	29	49	.372
New Jersey Americans	36	42	.462	Anaheim Amigos	25	53	.321
				Oakland Oaks	22	56	.282

ABA FINALS: Pittsburgh 4, New Orleans 3

1968-69 FINAL STANDINGS

Eastern Division				Western Division			
Indiana Pacers	44	34	.564	Oakland Oaks	60	18	.769
Miami Floridians	43	35	.551	New Orleans Buccaneers	46	32	.590
Kentucky Colonels	42	36	.538	Denver Rockets	44	34	.564
Minnesota Pipers	36	42	.462	Dallas Chaparrals	41	37	.526
New York Nets	17	61	.218	Los Angeles Stars	33	45	.423
				Houston Mavericks	23	55	.295

ABA FINALS: Oakland 4, Indiana 1

1969-70 FINAL STANDINGS

Eastern Division				Western Division			
Indiana Pacers	59	25	.702	Denver Rockets	51	33	.607
Kentucky Colonels	45	39	.536	Dallas Chaparrals	45	39	.536
Carolina Cougars	42	42	.500	Washington Capitols	44	40	.524
New York Nets	39	45	.464	Los Angeles Stars	43	41	.512
Pittsburgh Pipers	29	55	.345	New Orleans Buccaneers	42	42	.500
Miami Floridians	23	61	.274				

ABA FINALS: Indiana 4, Los Angeles 2

1970-71 FINAL STANDINGS

Eastern Division				Western Division			
Virginia Squires	55	29	.655	Indiana Pacers	58	26	.690
Kentucky Colonels	44	40	.524	Utah Stars	57	27	.679
New York Nets	40	44	.476	Memphis Pros	41	43	.488
Floridians	37	47	.440	Texas Chaparrals	30	54	.357
Pittsburgh Condors	36	48	.429	Denver Rockets	30	54	.357
Carolina Cougars	34	50	.405				

ABA FINALS: Utah 4, Kentucky 3

1971-72 FINAL STANDINGS

Eastern Division				Western Division			
Kentucky Colonels	68	16	.810	Utah Stars	60	24	.714
Virginia Squires	45	39	.536	Indiana Pacers	47	37	.560
New York Nets	44	40	.524	Dallas Chaparrals	42	42	.500
Floridians	36	48	.429	Denver Rockets	34	50	.405
Carolina Cougars	35	49	.417	Memphis Pros	26	58	.310
Pittsburgh Condors	25	59	.298				

ABA FINALS: Indiana 4, New York 2

1972-73 FINAL STANDINGS

Eastern Division				Western Division			
Carolina Cougars	57	27	.679	Utah Stars	55	29	.655
Kentucky Colonels	56	28	.667	Indiana Pacers	51	33	.607
Virginia Squires	42	42	.500	Denver Rockets	47	37	.560
New York Nets	30	54	.357	San Diego Conquistadors	30	54	.357
Memphis Tams	24	60	.286	Dallas Chaparrals	28	56	.333

ABA FINALS: Indiana 4, Kentucky 3

1973-74 FINAL STANDINGS

Eastern Division				Western Division			
New York Nets	55	29	.655	Utah Stars	51	33	.607
Kentucky Colonels	53	31	.631	Indiana Pacers	46	38	.548
Carolina Cougars	47	37	.560	San Antonio Spurs	45	39	.536
Virginia Squires	28	56	.333	San Diego Conquistadors	37	47	.440
Memphis Tams	21	63	.250	Denver Rockets	37	47	.440

ABA FINALS: New York 4, Utah 1

1974-75 FINAL STANDINGS

Eastern Division				Western Division			
Kentucky Colonels	58	26	.690	Denver Nuggets	65	19	.774
New York Nets	58	26	.690	San Antonio Spurs	51	33	.607
Spirits of St. Louis	32	52	.381	Indiana Pacers	45	39	.536
Memphis Sounds	27	57	.321	Utah Stars	38	46	.452
Virginia Squires	15	69	.179	San Diego Conquistadors	31	53	.369

ABA FINALS: Kentucky 4, Indiana 1

1975-76 FINAL STANDINGS

Denver Nuggets	60	24	.714
New York Nets	55	29	.655
San Antonio Spurs	50	34	.595
Kentucky Colonels	46	38	.548
Indiana Pacers	39	45	.464
Spirits of St. Louis	35	49	.417
San Diego Sails*	3	8	.273
Utah Stars*	4	12	.250
Virginia Squires	15	68	.181

*Disbanded and did not finish season

ABA FINALS: New York 4, Denver 2

My dad asked Brown about the guy standing next to his locker, 'Now what's his name again?' Brown replied that it was Julius Irving. 'You'll be hearing a lot about him, he told us."

HARLEY "SKEETER" SWIFT

Harley "Skeeter" Swift had a five year career in the ABA after the New Orleans Buccaneers made him their number two pick in 1969. And, he too has his memories.

Swift had been a high scoring guard out of East Tennessee State, and was good enough to be named Co-Player of the Year in the Ohio Valley Conference along with Western Kentucky's Wayne Chapman in 1968.

"I was making my official visit to New Orleans after they drafted me and had just arrived at the airport," says Swift. "The buses were supposed to pick me up, but after waiting and waiting, I couldn't believe it when I saw the Kentucky Colonels basketball team. Their head coach asked me if I wanted a ride with them to their hotel. Wow! Here I was riding with Darel Carrier, Bobby Rascoe and Louie Dampier ... the Kentucky Colonels. I remember asking the coach why he didn't draft me."

But why didn't the Bucs pick him up at the airport?

"They said they forgot about me coming in," laughed Swift. "I wonder what would have happened if I'd been their number one draft pick?"

Almost anyone who ever played in the ABA has stories to tell, and they must be true, as it would almost be too much to make up.

Swift has one that involved a game between the Bucs and the Carolina Cougars in New Orleans. The Cougars were coached by Bones McKinney, and the legendary coach was having some problems with the Bucs' crowd seated behind his bench.

"I look up and here comes the Cougar trainer, Buddy Taylor, running past our bench heading toward the concession stand," says Swift. "Little did I know that he purchased a cup of Jax Beer. It was a local and nasty beer. He headed back to his bench and gave the cup to Bones, who set it on the floor beside him.

"Now here's a Baptist deacon coaching a game and he sends his trainer for a beer during the game. But then a call was made on the floor that Bones didn't like. He grabbed the cup of Jax Beer and hurled it back over his shoulder into the crowd. Immediately he grabbed a towel and went into the stands wiping off those fans who had been riding him."

Swift had some fond memories of Babe McCarthy, his coach at New Orleans.

"I actually met Babe when I was playing at East Tennessee and he was coaching at George Washington University in D.C.," Swift said. "He tried to get me to transfer to his school since my home town was nearby Alexandria, Virginia."

But Swift stayed put. However it seemed that everywhere he went he heard the Babe stories, and then when he arrived in the ABA and was coached by him, he soon found most of the stories to be true.

"He was considered to be one of the great ambassadors for the game of basketball," Swift says. "But, I will tell you this about Babe. He flew B-52's in World War II, he loved the young ladies, and he enjoyed hard liquor, straight."

GAME-CALLERS

Today in the NBA, sportscasters might interview a player before the game via a pre-game recording. A coach, perhaps at halftime, might be interviewed, and a live interview with one of the players might happen after the game, but never like in the old days.

In ABA days, it was predominately radio, but those radio guys got it done.

It was common to see one of the game-callers walk to the edge of the court during pre-game or halftime warm-ups and yell out and motion to one of the players to come over for an interview. Most of the time the player would oblige the broadcaster, but when they didn't want to, they simply ignored the request, pretending not to hear or moving over to the other side.

It was memories like these that made the ABA special.

BALL GIVEAWAYS

Everyone who ever saw an ABA game remembers it forever. Some of those memories were not necessarily on the court.

In the beginning, the league was all about promotion, always keeping in mind that if you attract the kids, the parents will follow.

Frequently the league promoted giveaways that included the popular red, white and blue basketball. On several occasions, the balls were given out fully inflated to kids as they entered the arena. Can you imagine what it was like at halftime, the fiasco when hundreds of kids swarmed the court to shoot their new balls. Second halves were delayed while ushers and security had to literally herd the youngsters off the floor.

It finally dawned on league and team officials that in the future such promotions would involve giving away deflated balls.

DANCIN' HARRY

Marvin Cooper, as the old saying goes, had more moves than a checkerboard. The former sausage salesman from Baltimore, better known as Dancin' Harry, became a fixture in the early 1970s, first with the Baltimore Bullets and then the New York Knicks.

But then after being pushed aside and underappreciated by the higher-ups at Madison Square Garden, Dancin' Harry took out his voodoo-like hex on opposing teams to the ABA, where in 1974 he would cast a whammy on anyone who played the Nets in New York.

At 6'2" Dancin' Harry would suddenly rise from his seat during a timeout and begin to shimmy, shake, twirl around and extend his outstretched arms toward the opposing team. With one arm holding his black cape, the other arm would point to whoever the Nets were playing. Twitching fingers were a sure sign that a spell was in the process of being cast on the visiting team.

Every eye in the arena watched Harry, flash bulbs popped, cameras rolled, and even the opposing team's players often paid more attention to the flamboyant Harry with his floppy cap than they did to what their coaches were saying.

Dancin' Harry first showed up at a Baltimore Bullet game, it was said mainly to support Earl "The Pearl" Monroe, and then when he was traded to the Knicks, Harry followed him to New York.

As popular as he was with the players and fans, it was not the same with Madison Square Garden management. Wearing platform shoes and a flowing cape, he would work the home crowd into a frenzy. Everybody seemed to want a piece of him. He had endorsements, and nightclub and restaurant appearances. Through it all, he never received as much as a free ticket from the Knicks. Finally, when he showed up for a Knicks game in 1973, he found out he had been banned from the Garden by owner, Ned Irish. That's when he hooked up with the ABA Nets.

Dancin' Harry speaks for himself. The Knicks won while he was on their side. When he left, they went into a downhill spiral and his new team, the Nets, won the ABA title in 1974.

Mid-America came calling in the form of the Indiana Pacers in 1975 and he moved to Indianapolis, where he was welcomed with open arms and even paid for his finger-pointing whammys on the opposition, who often were the Colonels.

CONCLUSION

By some accounts, today's professional basketball players are the most recognizable, if not the best athletes in the world. On the global scene their size, speed, power, agility, quickness, and skills make for a gifted lot.

From the late '60s to the mid-70s, by all accounts the Kentucky Colonels and the other American Basketball Association teams had their fair share of these marvelous athletes who have left their mark on the evolution of the game as it is now played.

By mid-June of 1976, all anyone was talking about in Louisville was the Colonels and their apparent demise. The print media and radio airwaves had plenty to say. However, it left far more unanswered questions than answers.

But soon after the 1975-76 season ended, the Browns, John Y. and Ellie, let it be known they would not be held hostage to what they considered insane financial requirements to join the NBA. Brown had at one time agreed to fork over $2 million, but never the reported $8 million needed. He always felt the ABA, talent-wise, was better than the NBA, and his $2 million was contingent on a merger, not a takeover.

When Louisville Mayor Harvey Sloane sent out a letter to 50 influential in the city telling them the team should become a community project, it was thought there could still be a chance for pro basketball. But the meeting was cancelled because none of the 50 could be there.

"There's not a heartbeat in the city, there's just a faint murmur," said J. Bruce Miller at the time. With tongues wagging, it seemed like everyone was in favor of the Colonels continuing in Louisville.

But not so fast. *Louisville Times* columnist Mike Barry was not one of them.

Barry wrote that for the most part Louisville will survive without professional basketball, and that the 50 no-show businessmen to Mayor Sloan's meeting showed their good business judgment. For sure Barry had his day, and leaving little doubt to where he stood on the issue, he finished off his column and, for that matter the Colonels, with this dagger: "Pro basketball, I say it's garbage, and I say the hell with it."

The reaction to Barry's words brought the predictable deluge of letters to the Courier-Journal/Louisville Times building. One wonders where this passion had been hiding.

For the American Basketball Association it had been a tough nine-year adventure, with a shot clock, 3-point play, and a red, white and blue colored basketball. In the summer of 1976 it all came to an end — except for four teams.

Nine years, 28 different teams, and some $50 million in losses had been a burden for many of the owners who came and went like the often described game of musical chairs. Suddenly the music stopped and there were only four chairs left and San Antonio, Denver, Indiana and New York took them.

The Kentucky Colonels were the odd team out with no place to sit. For Louisville, not only had the music stopped, but the lights had been turned out on big time professional sports in Kentucky.

The only thing that remained was what Pink Gardner had stored in his daddy's barn out in Fairdale. And, oh yes, the thousands of memories he had locked away in his mind ... until now.

ALL-TIME ROSTER

#	Player	67-68	68-69	69-70	70-71	71-72	72-73	73-74	74-75	75-76
2	Walt "Trick Man" Simon				X	X	X	X		
3	Penny Ann Early		X							
3	Howard Wright				X	X				
3	Jimmy O'Brien (14)					X				
3	Joe Hamilton (12)							X		
4	Dennia Hamilton				X					
4	Les "Big Game" Hunter				X	X				
4	Wendell "Wenny" Ladner						X	X		
5	Sam Smith (50)				X					
5	Travis "The Machine" Grant									X
5	Jan van Breda Kolff									X
8	Dan Hester				X					
8	Ron "Plumber" Thomas (42)						X	X		
9	Cincy Powell				X	X				
9	Austin "Red" Robbins						X			
10	Louie "Little Louie" Dampier	X	X	X	X	X	X	X	X	X
11	John Roche							X	X	
12	Joe "Joe Ham" Hamilton							X	X	
14	Kendall Rhine (41)	X								
14	Johnny Jones		X							

#	Player	67-68	68-69	69-70	70-71	71-72	72-73	73-74	74-75	75-76
14	Gene Williams			X						
14	Jimmy O'Brien						X			
14	William "Bird" Averitt								X	X
15	Pierre Russell					X	X			
15	Chuck Williams						X			
20	Allen Murphy									X
21	Jimmy Dan Conner									X
22	Jim "Goose" Ligon	X	X	X	X	X				
22	Collis Jones							X		
22	Wil "Shaft" Jones								X	X
23	Gene Littles								X	
24	Stew "Stu" Johnson	X								
24	Jim Caldwell	X	X							
24	Bud Olsen			X						
24	Claude Virden					X	X			
24	Ted "The Hound" McClain								X	X
25	Elton McGriff	X	X							
25	Randy Mahaffey	X	X							
25	Dan Anderson		X							
25	Keith Swaggerty			X						
25	Gene Williams			X						
25	John Fairchild			X						
25	Bobby Croft				X					
25	Jim Bradley							X	X	
25	Maurice "Luke" Lucas									X
30	Rick "Rocket" Mount						X	X		

#	Player	67-68	68-69	69-70	70-71	71-72	72-73	73-74	74-75	75-76
31	Marvin "Marv" Roberts								X	X
31	Johnny Neumann									X
32	David Gaines	X								
32	Rubin Russell	X								
32	Wayne Champman (40)			X						
32	Tommy Hagan				X					
32	Mike "Philly Dog" Gale						X	X	X	
32	Jimmy Baker									X
33	Mike Pratt					X	X			
33	Billy James							X		
34	Bill Bradley	X								
34	Paul Long		X							
34	George Tinsley			X						
34	Bobby Washington			X						
35	Darel Carrier	X	X	X	X	X				
35	Ron King						X			
40	Larry Conley	X								
40	Wayne Champman (32)		X							
40	Sammy Little			X						
40	Tommy Kron			X						
42	Joe Roberts	X								
42	Manny Leaks		X							
42	Oliver Darden			X						
42	Willie Murrell			X						
42	Al Williams				X					
42	Ron "Plumber" Thomas								X	X
43	Kevin Joyce									X

#	Player	67-68	68-69	69-70	70-71	71-72	72-73	73-74	74-75	75-76
44	Cotton Nash	X								
44	Reggie Lacefield		X							
44	Tom Thacker			X						
44	Steve Chubin			X						
44	Dan Issel				X	X	X	X	X	
45	Bobby Rascoe	X	X	X						
45	Jim "Big Mac" McDaniels									X
50	Howard Bayne	X								
50	Henry Aiken		X							
52	Orb Bowling	X								
52	Sam Smith (5)		X	X						
53	Artis "Big A" Gilmore					X	X	X	X	X
54	Tommy Woods	X								
54	George Sutor	X								
54	Gene Moore		X	X						

Kentucky Colonels (1967-76)
(Player Statistics of Top 20 Scorers)

Compiled by Robert Bradley and used with permission

#	Name	GP	Min	FGM	FGA	FG%	3PM	3PA	3P%
10	Louie Dampier	728	27770	5290	12047	.439	794	2217	.358
44	Dan Issel	416	16586	4255	8781	.485	9	53	.170
53	Artis Gilmore	420	17449	3671	6588	.557	2	7	.286
35	Darel Carrier	334	12148	2422	5707	.417	393	1043	.377
22	Goose Ligon	337	12431	1792	3688	.486	3	19	.158
2	Walt Simon	314	6089	1182	2431	.486	7	51	.137
8	Cincy Powell	146	5221	1008	2080	.485	8	29	.276
54	Gene Moore	159	4639	1047	2310	.453	2	6	.333
14	Bird Averitt	162	4503	968	2288	.423	47	175	.376
22	Wilbert Jones	167	5324	941	1963	.479	3	11	.273
32	Mike Gale	207	5146	619	1364	.454	3	20	.150
52	Sam Smith	168	4085	513	1234	.416	2	16	.125
25	Randy Mahaffey	106	3084	475	1126	.422	0	3	.000
45	Bobby Roscoe	159	2887	450	1061	.424	3	21	.143
4	Les Hunter	145	2383	457	989	.462	15	65	.231
42	Ron Thomas	264	3292	439	938	.468	3	14	.214
30	Rick Mount	78	2056	424	955	.444	11	43	.256
31	Marv Roberts	123	2373	371	852	.437	0	1	.000
24	Ted McClain	115	3202	395	910	.434	2	10	.200
3	Jimmy O'Brien	180	3199	304	955	.402	6	42	.143

#	Name	FTM	FTA	FT%	OReb	TReb	AST	PF	Dq
10	Louie Dampier	2352	2849	.826	-	2282	4044	1633	3
44	Dan Issel	2374	3038	.781	1707	4503	902	1216	14
53	Artis Gilmore	2018	3022	.688	2177	7169	1273	1543	-
35	Darel Carrier	1699	1998	.850	-	1173	886	1051	16
22	Goose Ligon	1263	1974	.640	-	3941	753	1354	25
2	Walt Simon	409	571	.716	-	1152	746	814	-

#	Name	FTM	FTA	FT%	OReb	TReb	AST	PF	Dq
8	Cincy Powell	487	654	.745	-	1390	492	542	-
54	Gene Moore	413	601	.687	663	1819	278	693	43
14	Bird Averitt	515	666	.773	106	398	616	420	-
22	Wilbert Jones	297	393	.756	441	1232	465	679	-
32	Mike Gale	271	387	.700	-	728	648	571	-
52	Sam Smith	299	456	.656	-	1177	189	379	4
25	Randy Mahaffey	349	512	.682	-	868	193	371	9
45	Bobby Roscoe	325	423	.768	-	438	208	292	3
4	Les Hunter	256	359	.713	-	697	186	396	-
42	Ron Thomas	170	317	.536	437	1075	198	230	2
30	Rick Mount	178	223	.798	57	198	223	209	0
31	Marv Roberts	215	277	.776	165	405	281	296	-
24	Ted McClain	158	207	.763	90	403	472	396	-
3	Jimmy O'Brien	167	209	.799	261	351	612	302	-

#	Name	Stl	Trn	Blk	Pnts	PPG	Hi	Years
10	Louie Dampier	-	-	-	13726	18.9	55	67-76
44	Dan Issel	-	1009	-	10893	26.2	51	70-75
53	Artis Gilmore	-	1579	1431	9362	22.3	-	71-76
35	Darel Carrier	-	-	-	6936	20.8	53	67-72
22	Goose Ligon	-	-	-	4850	14.4	-	67-72
2	Walt Simon	38	-	10	2780	8.9	-	70-74
8	Cincy Powell	-	-	-	2511	17.2	-	70-72
54	Gene Moore	-	464	-	2509	15.8	-	68-70
14	Bird Averitt	193	453	35	2498	15.4	-	74-76
22	Wilbert Jones	192	399	124	2182	13.1	-	74-76
32	Mike Gale	-	346	-	1512	7.3	21	71-74
52	Sam Smith	-	-	-	1327	7.9	-	68-71
25	Randy Mahaffey	-	318	-	1299	12.3	-	67-69
45	Bobby Roscoe	-	193	-	1228	7.7	-	67-70
4	Les Hunter	-	-	-	1185	8.2	-	70-72
42	Ron Thomas	-	234	-	1051	4.0	-	72-76
30	Rick Mount	-	140	-	1037	13.3	-	72-74
31	Marv Roberts	48	168	10	957	7.8	-	74-76
24	Ted McClain	211	276	28	950	8.3	-	74-76
3	Jimmy O'Brien	-	261	-	941	5.2	-	71+74

COACH AND OWNERSHIP HISTORY

Courtesy of Robert Bradley.

Coaches

1967-68: John Givens & Gene Rhodes
1968-69 through 1969-70: Gene Rhodes
1970-71: Gene Rhodes, Alex Groza & Frank Ramsey
1971-72 through 1972-73: Joe Mullaney
1973-74: Babe McCarthy
1974-75 through 1975-76: Hubie Brown

Ownership History

March 6, 1967	An ABA franchise is awarded to Don Regan for $30,000.
1967	The franchise is purchased by Joseph E. Gregory, Mamie Gregory and William C. Boone.
1969	The franchise is purchased by a group Headed by H. Wendell Cherry and including Bill DeWitt, Stuart Jay, David Jones, John Y. Brown and Mike Storen.
July 31, 1973	The franchise is purchased by a group headed by John Y. Brown and Ellie Brown.
June 17, 1976	Brown reaches a financial agreement with the remaining teams in the ABA, folding his team for $3 million as part of the ABA/NBA merger agreement.

Kentucky Colonels Roster

Henry Akin, 1968-69

Dan Anderson, 1968-69

Bird Averitt, 1974-76

Jimmie Baker, 1975-76

Howard Bayne, 1967-68

Orb Bowling, 1967-68

Bill Bradley, 1967-68

Jim Bradley, 1973-75

Jim Caldwell, 1967-69

Darel Carrier, 1967-72

Bill Chamberlain, 1972-73

Wayne Chapman, 1968-70

Steve Chubin, 1969-70

Larry Conley, 1967-68

Jimmy Dan Conner, 1975-76

Bobby Croft, 1970-71

Louie Dampier, 1967-76

Ollie Darden, 1968-70

Penny Ann Early, 1968-69

John Fairchild, 1969-70

David Gaines, 1967-68

Mike Gale, 1971-74

Artis Gilmore, 1971-76

Travis Grant, 1975-76

Tom Hagan, 1970-71

Dennis Hamilton, 1970-71

Joe Hamilton, 1973-75

Dan Hester, 1970-71

Les Hunter, 1970-72

Dan Issel, 1970-75

Billy James, 1973-74

Stew Johnson, 1967-68

Caldwell Jones, 1975-76

Collis Jones, 1973-74

Johnny Jones, 1968-69

Wil Jones, 1974-76

Kevin Joyce, 1975-76

Ron King, 1973-74

Tommy Kron, 1969-70

Reggie Lacefield, 1968-69

Wendell Ladner, 1972-74

Manny Leaks, 1968-69

Goose Ligon, 1967-72

Sam Little, 1969-70

Gene Littles, 1974-75

Paul Long, 1968-69

Maurice Lucas, 1975-76

Randy Mahaffey, 1967-69

Ted McClain, 1974-76

Jim McDaniels, 1975-76

Eldon McGriff, 1968-69

Gene Moore, 1968-70

Rick Mount, 1972-74

Allen Murphy, 1975-76

Willie Murrell, 1969-70

Cotton Nash, 1967-68

Johnny Neumann, 1975-76

Jimmy O'Brien, 1971-73

Bud Olsen, 1969-70

Tom Owens, 1975-76

Cincy Powell, 1970-72

Mike Pratt, 1970-72

Bobby Rascoe, 1967-70

Kendall Rhine, 1967-68

Red Robbins, 1973-75

Joe Roberts, 1967-68

Marv Roberts, 1974-75

Johnny Roche, 1973-75

Pierre Russell, 1971-73

Rubin Russell, 1967-68

Walt Simon, 1970-74

Sam Smith, 1968-71

George Sutor, 1967-68

Keith Swagerty, 1969-70

Ron Thomas, 1972-76

George Tinsley, 1969-70

Jan van Breda Kolff, 1975-76

Claude Virden, 1972-73

Bobby Washington, 1969-70

Al Williams, 1970-71

Chuck Williams, 1973-74

Gene Williams, 1969-70

Tommy Woods, 1967-68

Howie Wright, 1970-72

ABOUT THE AUTHORS

Gary P. West

Gary P. West has simple criteria when it comes to writing books.

"I only take on a project that I will enjoy writing about and I only write about something I think people will enjoy reading," he says.

West grew up in Elizabethtown, Kentucky and attended Western Kentucky University before graduating from the University of Kentucky in 1967 with a journalism degree. At U.K. he was a daily sports editor for the Kentucky Kernel.

Later he served as editor for the nation's largest civilian enterprise military newspaper at Fort Bragg, North Carolina. From there he was employed in the corporate advertising office of one of the country's largest insurance companies, State Farm Insurance in Bloomington, Illinois, where he was a copywriter.

He returned to Kentucky in 1972 where he began an advertising and publishing business.

Along the way, for twelve years, he was the executive director of the Hilltopper Athletic Foundation at Western Kentucky University, and provided color commentary for Wes Strader on the Hilltopper Basketball Network.

In 1993, he became the executive director of the Bowling Green Area Convention and Visitors Bureau. He retired from there in 2006 to devote more time to his writing.

He is a freelance writer for several magazines in addition to writing a syndicated newspaper travel column, *Out & About ... Kentucky Style*, for several papers across the state.

Gary is in demand as a speaker and for book signings throughout Kentucky.

This is his sixth book. Previous books are *King Kelley Coleman – Kentucky's Greatest Basketball Legend (2005), Eating Your Way Across Kentucky (2006), Eating Your Way Across Kentucky – The Recipes (2007), Shopping Your Way Across Kentucky (2009), and 101 Must Places to Visit in Kentucky Before You Die (2009)*.

Gary and his wife, Deborah, live in Bowling Green, Kentucky.

Lloyd "Pink" Gardner

Lloyd "Pink" Gardner was born in Louisville, Kentucky and raised in nearby Fairdale. To say he has roots in this small rural community outside the river city is an understatement. Fairdale High School, where he graduated in 1962, was built on his grandfather's farm. Little did he know that his life would be changed forever when Coach Forest "Frosty" Able cut him from the basketball team in 1958. From there it was off to Western Kentucky University where he was a manager and trainer for Hall of Fame coaches Ed Diddle and Johnny Oldham. After graduation in 1967, he volunteered part-time for the Kentucky Colonels and was a teacher for Jefferson County Public Schools. During the 1970-71 season he returned to the Colonels full-time. When the ABA took down the nets and closed the doors,

Gardner returned to Fairdale High School where he served as a teacher, athletic trainer and assistant basketball coach.

During his career Gardner has accumulated five championship rings: 1975 Kentucky Colonels, 1983 Kentucky Bourbons Professional Softball, two as an assistant coach on Fairdale's 1990 and 1991 back-to-back state champion basketball teams and in 1994, as the head coach, he guided Fairdale to their third state title in five years.

After 19 years as an assistant coach and 14 years (1991-2005) as Fairdale's head basketball coach, Gardner hung up his whistle. He is the tournament director for the prestigious King of the Bluegrass Holiday Classic that began in 1981.

Lloyd and his wife, Janet, live in Louisville, Kentucky.

351

352